Russia's New Authoritarianism

For Olivia

Russia's New Authoritarianism

Putin and the Politics of Order

DAVID G. LEWIS

EDINBURGH
University Press

Edinburgh University Press is one of the leading university presses in the UK. We publish academic books and journals in our selected subject areas across the humanities and social sciences, combining cutting-edge scholarship with high editorial and production values to produce academic works of lasting importance. For more information visit our website: edinburghuniversitypress.com

© David G. Lewis, 2020, 2021

Edinburgh University Press Ltd
The Tun – Holyrood Road, 12(2f) Jackson's Entry, Edinburgh EH8 8PJ

First published in hardback by Edinburgh University Press 2020

Typeset in 10/13 Giovanni by
IDSUK (DataConnection) Ltd

A CIP record for this book is available from the British Library

ISBN 978 1 4744 5476 6 (hardback)
ISBN 978 1 4744 5477 3 (paperback)
ISBN 978 1 4744 5478 0 (webready PDF)
ISBN 978 1 4744 5479 7 (epub)

The right of David G. Lewis to be identified as the author of this work has been asserted in accordance with the Copyright, Designs and Patents Act 1988, and the Copyright and Related Rights Regulations 2003 (SI No. 2498).

CONTENTS

Preface / vii
Acknowledgements / xiv
Note on Transliteration and Translation / xv

ONE / Authoritarianism, Ideology and Order / 1

Understanding Russian Authoritarianism / 1
Order, *Smuta* and the Russian State / 6
Russia as Weimar / 12
Carl Schmitt and Authoritarian Order / 17

TWO / Carl Schmitt and Russian Conservatism / 24

Carl Schmitt in Moscow / 29
Normalising Schmitt / 45

THREE / Sovereignty and the Exception / 49

The Centrality of Sovereignty / 49
Sovereignty in International Affairs / 52
Domestic Sovereignty: Deciding on the Exception / 61
The Dual State / 77

FOUR / Democracy and the People / 81

Putinism and Democracy / 81
The Decline of Parliamentarianism / 86
Constructing a Majority / 88

FIVE / Defining the Enemy / 100

Russia and Its Enemies / 102
The End of Consensus / 114

SIX / Dualism, Exceptionality and the Rule of Law / 117

Law in Russia / 119
Conceptualising Dualism / 123
Politicised Justice / 126
Mechanisms of Exception / 130
The Exception Becomes the Norm / 137

SEVEN / The Crimean Exception / 139

Crimea: The Sovereign Decision / 140
Legality as Imperialism / 144
Order and Orientation / 151

EIGHT / *Großraum* Thinking in Russian Foreign Policy / 161

A World of Great Spaces / 161
Russia's Spatial Crisis / 165
The New Schmittians / 190

NINE / Apocalypse Delayed: Katechontic Thinking in Late Putinist Russia / 193

Russian Messianism / 197
Russia as Contemporary *Katechon* / 200
Katechontic Thinking and the Syrian Intervention / 206

CONCLUSION / 215

Bibliography / 223
Index / 268

PREFACE

Post-Soviet Russia is the most significant case study of the struggle between democracy and authoritarianism in the post-Cold War world. The regime headed by Vladimir Putin after 2000 has often been studied as an isolated case – explained by Russia's troubled political history, its limited experience of democracy, the kleptocracy of its business elites, or the legacy of seventy years of Soviet rule. Yet twenty-first-century Russia also developed a new version of authoritarian politics with much wider international resonance. In many countries around the world – from Budapest to Beijing – many familiar elements of 'Putinist' politics could be identified in the first two decades of the twenty-first century. Understanding the nature of 'Putinism' became critical for understanding wider trends in global politics, and the rise of a new wave of authoritarian and illiberal regimes.

The rise of illiberal politics simultaneously in many parts of the world in the 2010s suggests that Russia's political development under Putin should be understood as part of a broader global backlash against liberal ideas and liberal order. This reaction took multiple forms, ranging from radical Islamist movements in the Middle East to left-wing populist movements in Europe. But the most significant trend has been towards forms of radical conservatism, which have produced right-wing populist movements in parts of the West, and authoritarian regimes in many countries in Eastern Europe, Africa and Asia. Disparate in form, in leadership and in vision, these political trends nevertheless had much in common in their worldviews and ideological frames. They shared, above all, a profound rejection of a form of liberal internationalism that had come to dominate global discourse and global institutions in the post-Cold War world.

These political movements were not only ranged against modern liberalism and its proxies, but they also began to coalesce around emergent alternative visions of both domestic and international order. They rejected the claim that the international system was a benign form of liberal international order, a rules-based system that ultimately benefited all. Illiberal movements and authoritarian political leaders rejected universal values, such as human rights, and instead advocated essentialised national or religious cultures and principles. Against a cosmopolitan vision that argued for diminished state sovereignty and porous borders, they instead promoted hard boundaries and frontiers, carving out national and civilisational spaces. At the centre of political life, once again, was the state, as a reassertion of centralised political power against global institutions, international civil society and multinational corporations. Within society, they advocated fixed definitions of gender and sexual identity against notions of equality, LGBT rights and 'gender fluidity'. Instead of liquidity and movement, in personal life as in the international order, they advocated fixity, hierarchy and order.

Russia played a central role in this emerging trend of anti-liberal politics. In Russia, perhaps more than anywhere else, the post-Cold War liberal order appeared to represent an existential threat both to political order within the state and to Russia's place in the international system. After 1991 Russia adopted all the institutions of liberal democracy, and permitted unprecedented international influence within its domestic politics, from monitoring elections to shaping economic reforms. The result under President Boris Yeltsin was a regime beset by economic decline and internal factionalism, which had capitulated in the face of the Chechen insurgency, and which had been unceremoniously demoted from the role of superpower to a weak, troubled, regional player in a US-led global order. A reaction to Russia's crisis of the 1990s was inevitable, and it was never likely to be in the direction of greater liberalisation, as advocated by many Western critics. Russia instead became a political laboratory for the construction of new forms of authoritarian political order, which sought to consolidate decision-making power in the hands of a political leader, while remaining engaged with a global, neo-liberal economic system.

Political scientists struggled to conceptualise this new type of authoritarianism. The dominance of theories of democratisation skewed political science towards a misleading frame of analysis that focused primarily on the movement of countries on a path between dictatorship and democracy. In Chapter 1 I argue that an alternative binary – that between chaos and order – has been more influential in Russian thinking about politics, and is more helpful in understanding the politics of Russia over the past two decades. Other values – democracy, justice, equality – were always secondary to a particular understanding of political and social order. The form of political order pursued by the Russian political elite was shaped by many influences, and was often contested within the system by different ideological and political forces. But while 'Putinism' never cohered into a clear belief system, there was sufficient agreement across parts of the elite to talk about shared elements of a worldview, a collective agreement on the meanings of concepts, a paradigm that imposed meaning on the world and structured Russia's potential responses.

To understand the emergence of this anti-liberal political order in Russia, I turn to the most influential anti-liberal thinker of the twentieth century, Carl Schmitt, the German jurist and political theorist who for a short time in the 1930s was described as the 'crown jurist of the Third Reich'. Writing in 2000, Gopal Balakrishnan could still comment that Carl Schmitt's writings 'form what is arguably the most disconcerting, original and yet still unfamiliar body of twentieth-century political thought' (Balakrishnan 2000: 2). No longer. His work remains frequently 'disconcerting' – not only because of his disastrous association with the Nazis, and his virulent anti-Semitism, but also because of the implications of his arguments for contemporary politics. His work is often still strikingly original, but it is no longer unfamiliar – in the past two decades his work has prompted a vast array of commentary and interpretation. Schmitt's status as the 'twentieth century's foremost critic of liberalism' (McCormick 1998: 830) proved irresistible both for intellectuals in the European New Right and many on the post-Marxist left (Müller 2003).

By the late 1990s William Scheuerman could write that the 'ghost of Carl Schmitt haunts political and legal debates not only in Europe, but also in the contemporary United States' (Scheuerman 1999: 1). Two decades later, the spectre of Schmitt haunts liberal politics across the Western world, inspiring illiberal opponents in a powerful transnational 'alt-right' movement in America and Europe and informing the rise of a wave of authoritarian regimes around the world (Lewis 2016b). '[Schmitt's] political views are thoroughly discredited', writes his most recent biographer, Reinhard Mehring (2014: xvi), but in authoritarian states, such as Russia, his renaissance has been welcomed as 'evidence of a crisis in contemporary liberal theory' (Mikhailovsky 2008a) and as an inspiration for new forms of authoritarian politics and law (Bowring 2013; Lewis 2017b). Schmitt's influence has spread rapidly in China too, both as a critique of liberal thinking and – paradoxically – as an inspiration 'for those who aim to move from an authoritarian state to a democratic state' (Zheng 2012: 52).[1]

In Chapter 2 I trace the remarkable impact of Schmitt on conservative political thinking in post-Soviet Russia. After a short dalliance with liberal ideas in the late 1980s and early 1990s, political debate in Russia took place primarily between more mainstream and more radical strands of conservative thought. Schmitt was an important intellectual source for radical conservative thinking; his apocalyptic style and binary approach to politics seemed ideally suited to the existential crisis that Russia seemed to face in the late 1990s. Yet Schmittian thinking went far beyond a small circle of right-wing disciples, and informed a worldview that became influential across much of the Russian political class. This is not a claim for any direct ideological influences. Attempts to identify 'Putin's philosopher' by citing selective quotations from thinkers such as Ivan Ilyin are usually misleading (Laruelle 2017b; Snyder 2018). Rather the book outlines a Schmittian conservative paradigm, a way of thinking that defines certain concepts in particular ways, with profound implications for political developments in contemporary Russia.

All paradigms prioritise some elements of political thinking over others. For Schmitt, it is the concept of sovereignty, understood not in legalistic terms, but as the capacity to take decisions free from the constraint of liberal ideas of rule of law or international norms and agreements. In Chapter 3 I explore how this notion of 'sovereignty as freedom' – the freedom to declare an exception – became the driving force of Russian domestic and foreign policy under Putin. From the beginning of his presidency, Putin prioritised the return of sovereign decision-making to the Kremlin as the basis for reasserting political order, taking power back from the regions, from political parties and civil society, from oligarchs and from international actors. Yet the rule through the exception – the willingness to break the rules – challenged the very order that the authorities sought to achieve.

These contradictions of Russian conservatism were equally evident in the approach to democracy. On the one hand, Putin viewed himself as a democrat, who had come to power through the ballot box; he repeatedly stated that there was no alternative in the twenty-first century to some form of democratic legitimacy. On the other hand, there was a widespread consensus both in the elite and in much of society that political pluralism had undermined the state in the 1990s, and must be carefully managed and controlled. Schmitt's experience of the Weimar republic also prompted him to struggle to reconcile the challenges of twentieth-century mass democracy with the need to ensure political order: his solution was to force apart the two concepts of 'liberalism' and 'democracy', and instead propose forms of authoritarian democracy, a forerunner of Russia's own initiatives of 'managed democracy' or 'Sovereign Democracy'. In Chapter 4 I explore this version of illiberal democracy that emerged in Russia under Putin, and in Chapter 5 I explain how it came to rely on a friend/enemy distinction, in which the majority of the population was defined in opposition to critics and minorities, who became labelled as 'fifth columnists', working for foreign powers and alien influences.

Schmitt's emphasis on the exception as a mode of governance for truly sovereign rulers struck an instant chord in post-Soviet Russia. From the beginning of his presidency, Putin asserted his willingness to break the rules to impose order, whether through arrests of oligarchs on flimsy charges or a violent counterinsurgency in Chechnya. Putin came to power with a popular mandate to reimpose order, at almost any cost, and he had no compunction about violating legal norms along the way. In Chapter 6 I examine the workings of exceptionalism in the Russian justice system, where a dualism emerged between mundane, everyday law, which is often enacted quite adequately, and a much smaller set of 'prosecutions-to-order', often in highly politicised cases, which are directed according to the interests of political and business elites. Russia's dysfunctional justice system also acts as a warning of the profound problems created through the culture of exceptionality. Exceptionality as a mode of governance can hardly be confined; it spreads throughout the system, until the distinction between the norm and the exception becomes irretrievably blurred.

In the second part of the book I examine Schmitt's thinking on international order and its relevance to the evolution of Russian foreign policy. Western interventions in Yugoslavia and Iraq only intensified the sense of Russian exclusion from the post-Cold War settlement, while the upheavals of 'colour revolutions' in Ukraine, Georgia and Kyrgyzstan, and subsequently the Arab Spring, all contributed to a perception that Western advocacy of humanitarianism and democracy disguised a policy of both deliberate and unintended destabilisation. Schmitt has long been used as an intellectual weapon by leftist critics of US foreign policy, particularly his insistence that the promotion of universal liberal norms, such as human rights, was nothing more than a cynical cover for American attempts to dominate the world. After 2005 Russian foreign policy pursued the idea of Russian sovereignty in the face of what was perceived as a US-led unipolar system, in which Russia was deliberately marginalised. This interpretation of international relations led to two important outcomes: first, Russia extended its exceptionalism to the international arena. As a sovereign power, Russia would be willing to violate the rules of the system, just as the US and its allies had done in Yugoslavia and Iraq. The result – discussed in Chapter 7 – was the annexation of Crimea, an assertion of sovereignty through exceptionality that defined the Putin presidency.

Second, Russian foreign policy became a struggle against a liberal vision of globalisation that proclaimed that the 'World is Flat', as Thomas Friedman put it, a homogeneous order constructed according to the rules and norms of the West. In Chapter 8, I explore how Russia asserted an alternative topography, articulated in a series of spatial projects – the 'Russian World', 'Eurasian integration', 'Greater Eurasia' – which aimed to carve out a space in opposition to the 'spacelessness' of Western-dominated global order. Influential Russian foreign policy thinkers viewed the emerging twenty-first-century international order as being constituted not by institutions of global governance, but by a few major political-economic regions, dominated by major powers, a return to the sphere-of-influence politics of the past. It was Russia's goal to assert its own central role as a great power, in just such a 'Great Space', that of Eurasia. These ideas of regional hegemony and spatial division echoed many of Schmitt's own conceptualisations of international order, based on a world divided into 'Great Spaces', or *Großräume*.

Finally, I discuss Russia's sense of its own moral mission, a long-standing component of Russian political thought, dating back to the proclamation of Moscow as the 'Third Rome' after the fall of Constantinople. Schmitt's eschatological understanding of politics provides important insights into the perception among Russia's elites of Russia's role in the world. In particular, I explore the idea of Russia as a bulwark against chaos and disorder, a messianic role that had long been central to Orthodox conceptualisations of history, in which Russia is portrayed as the *katechon*, the biblical figure said to restrain the Antichrist. A secularised version of the figure of the *katechon* became central to Schmitt's later thinking about international relations, embodying resistance to his own personal dystopia, a totalising global liberal order that would finally elide any sense of the political on a global scale. This idea of Russia as a moral, tragic bulwark against the chaos and destabilisation wrought by the West has become central to official thinking on Russia's role in the Middle East. Russia's mission in Syria has been imbued with a moral certitude that echoes Schmitt's *katechontic* thinking, and portrays Russia's mission as a triumph of civilisation over barbarism.

This sense of historical mission became increasingly pronounced in Russian official discourse. President Obama berated Russia for being 'on the wrong side of history' (Wall Street Journal 2014), but global trends under his successor in the White House appeared to be going Moscow's way. As Beate Jahn has argued, the many failures of the post-Cold War liberal project raised serious 'doubts concerning liberalism's alignment with the forces of history' (Jahn 2012: 151). Triumphant Russian intellectuals agreed, and saw Russia – unlike the USSR – as standing 'on the right side of history', aligned with 'a powerful conservative reaction against the grip of postmodernism, ultraliberalism and globalisation in the West itself and in the whole world' (Karaganov 2017a). Russian conservatives saw Russia as the vanguard of a new political trend, evident in everything from 'America First' to Brexit, from the rise of Hindutva in India to the emergence of Xi Jinping Thought in China. Vladislav Surkov, the Kremlin's most articulate ideologue, called it the 'ideology of the future' (Surkov 2019). But its ideological origins were in the twentieth century, and no thinker was more central to this conservative turn in global politics than Carl Schmitt.

Russia was a leader of reaction against liberalism, and led the search for new, illiberal forms of political order in response to the rise of post-Cold War liberalism. Yet it was in Russia, too, that the stark limitations and contradictions of Schmittian, anti-liberal politics also became increasingly clear. The search for sovereignty and the willingness to embrace the exception undermined state institutions and the rule of law. Russia's political order became marked by increasing repression and rising discontent, and the economy was stymied by endemic corruption and inefficiency. A Russian foreign policy characterised by the identification of geopolitical enemies and the pursuit of spatial hegemony become fixated on confrontation with the West and enmired in conflicts with its neighbours. Putin's Russia demonstrated both the allure and the failure of authoritarian political thought in its attempt to bypass liberal constraints on power to produce short-term political order. The long-term consequences of a Schmittian anti-liberal political paradigm in Russia were ultimately self-destructive, undermining the very political order that conservative thinkers so craved. This book is an attempt to understand the failure of Putinism, but also to explain why illiberal ideas and philosophies had such resonance with many communities in the first two decades of the twenty-first century, not only in Putin's Russia, but across the globe.

Note

1. On the remarkable reception of Schmitt in China, see Marchal and Shaw (2017) and Zheng (2012, 2015).

ACKNOWLEDGEMENTS

This book developed from a short conference paper presented at the International Studies Association Convention in Baltimore in February 2017. I would like to thank the fellow-panellists and audience for their comments on that occasion. I am also grateful for the invitation to present part of the argument at the conference '1917 in 2017: Russia's Unfinished Revolution?' at King's College London in November 2017. I would also like to thank participants at the International Studies Association Convention in San Francisco in 2018, for feedback on a second conference paper, 'Großraum Thinking in Russian Foreign Policy', which served as the basis for Chapter 7. I am indebted to fellow-panellists and discussants for comments on a similar paper at the EISA conference in Prague in September 2018. Thanks are also due to two anonymous reviewers for their comments and suggestions, and to the editorial staff at Edinburgh University Press for all their work in producing this book. I would particularly like to thank my colleagues at the University of Exeter for producing such a supportive and intellectually stimulating environment, and for providing a period of research leave that enabled me to complete the writing of this book.

NOTE ON TRANSLITERATION AND TRANSLATION

Transliteration is based on the conventional British system, with exceptions for names that are widely used in English. All translations from Russian-language texts are mine, unless otherwise indicated.

ONE

Authoritarianism, Ideology and Order

'Our land is rich, but there is no order in it', they used to say in Russia. Nobody will say such things about us anymore.

President Vladimir Putin (2000c)

Understanding Russian Authoritarianism

In the first two decades of the twenty-first century, Russia's political leaders constructed a new type of authoritarian political system. Many elements of the system were recognisable from the history of Russian autocracy or the experience of twentieth-century authoritarian states – the persecution of dissidents, the banning of demonstrations, attempts to censor the media, or the violation of laws by an untouchable political and security elite. But there were also innovative aspects of this political order, which reflected a very specific historical moment. The post-Soviet Russian political system emerged alongside, and in reaction to, a triumphant liberal international order, characterised by the march of liberal ideas and the rise of new technology. The system of power that developed in Russia under Vladimir Putin was always penetrated by and interwoven with a globalised economy and a set of liberal norms and ideas, creating a state marked by variegation, exception and hybridity. These contradictions in the Russian state were not a temporary aberration, but constituted innovative elements in a new type of post-liberal political system.

This complex and contradictory set of political dynamics encouraged scholars to conclude that Russia enjoyed a 'peculiar combination of authoritarian and democratic elements', and that Russia was best characterised as a 'hybrid regime' (Petrov et al. 2014: 2; Hale 2010; Robertson 2010; Treisman 2011). Yet hybridity was an unsatisfactory description of a political system that also corresponded clearly to traditional definitions of an authoritarian regime in terms of the classic question of political science: 'who rules?' Guillermo O'Donnell wrote that 'all forms of authoritarian rule . . . have somebody (a king, a junta, a party committee, a theocracy, or what not) that is sovereign in the classic sense: if and when they deem it necessary, they can decide without legal constraint' (O'Donnell 1998: 21, n 56). Russia under Putin corresponded to just such an understanding of authoritarianism, as a political regime above the law, a political system in which a single centre of power was able to make sovereign decisions without legal limitations. However, simply identifying Russia's political regime as 'authoritarian' told us little about how the system worked, and even less about why its leaders had built such a regime after a decade of free-wheeling semi-pluralist politics in the 1990s.

Attempts to answer these questions were often constrained by the different theoretical frames through which analysts view Russia. Democratisation theory interpreted Russia solely in terms of regime type, measuring Russia on a binary scale between democracy and dictatorship. It told a simple story of democratic backsliding, in which a flawed – but real – democracy under Boris Yeltsin was subverted by the rise to power of Vladimir Putin, a former KGB officer, who ended Russia's democratic experiment and introduced an authoritarian regime (Fish 2005; McFaul and Stoner-Weiss 2008). Putin's return to the presidency in 2012 only intensified the shift to a fully authoritarian state, which was now also accompanied by an increasingly assertive foreign policy, including military interventions in Ukraine (2014) and Syria (2015). Its political status at any time in this journey could be measured through indicators such as Freedom House's rankings, in which Russia's democratic status declined sharply between 2003 and 2018 from the category of 'partly free' to 'not free', and from a rating of 4.96 to 6.5 (on a scale where 7 represented the most consolidated form of authoritarianism).

While containing many truths, the democratisation framework produced only a partial picture of Russia's complex realities. It provided only limited information on how the system worked in practice (Dawisha 2015). It highlighted some political forces in the system – the opposition and civil society, for example – and certain events – anti-government protests, or discriminatory legislation – at the expense of others (Monaghan 2016: 15). This made it difficult to explain countervailing trends, such as the popularity of Vladimir Putin, and it tended to produce a 'crisis reading' of the system: by focusing on protests and opposition, the regime always seemed to be in trouble. As Oleg Kashin writes: 'The collapse of the regime was inevitable ten, 15 and 18 years ago, countless points of no return were passed, but the system, just as it emerged in 2000, still carries on to this day' (Kashin 2018). In short, the democratisation paradigm severely underestimated the resilience of the Putinist political system.

A second analytical frame presented Russian politics as a form of utility maximisation, in which elites were motivated only by a striving for power and wealth. In Vladimir Gelman's study of Russian authoritarianism, every politician is a 'rational power maximiser', whose ultimate goal 'is to impose his own dictatorship in a given polity' (Gelman 2015: 24). In pursuing this goal, according to Gelman, Russian politicians acted like 'textbook examples of the Homo economicus', acting according to 'effective calculations of their costs and benefits' (Gelman 2015: 36). This theoretical framework builds on an extensive literature on comparative authoritarianism that uses a rational choice approach to model 'the endless power struggle at play between elites and dictators' (Frantz and Ezrow 2011: 7), but tends to produced highly abstracted and parsimonious accounts of political realities and human motivations.

A sub-set of this literature focused on the role of formal institutions in mediating relations between dictators and elites. Instead of a more traditional focus on institutions of repression, such as the secret police, this 'new institutionalist' (Schedler 2009) approach analysed formal institutions in authoritarian regimes that had previously been dismissed as window-dressing, such as multiparty elections, ruling parties and parliaments (Brownlee 2007; Gandhi 2010). In the Russian context, however, this literature offered few insights: it typically ignored informal institutions, which were critical to understanding the workings of Russian autocracy, and it failed to overcome the objection that formal institutions in authoritarian states are always likely to be epiphenomenal – what really matters are the underlying political realities that produce a particular party system, not the system itself (Pepinsky 2014).

Studies of Russian political economy did provide detailed accounts of informal institutions and practices, but struggled to conceptualise these as a system. In a ground-breaking study of high-level corruption, Karen Dawisha argued that Russia was a 'kleptocracy', in which elites constructed an autocracy in order to maximise personal financial gain (Dawisha 2015). Certainly, despite Putin's promise of a campaign against oligarchs, wealth inequality in Russia continued to expand under Putin to become among the highest in the world, with the top 1 per cent of society owning more than one-third of all assets (Meduza 2019). Ideological posturing by senior Russian officials about 'traditional values' often sat uneasily with the well-publicised reality of their endemic corruption, international property portfolios and offshore bank accounts. Yet the idea of Putinism as driven simply by personal greed was too one-dimensional to explain the many political decisions that undermined elite wealth rather than maximised it (Sakwa 2015b).

Above all, these theories of authoritarianism left little room for the role of ideas or beliefs. Investigation of the ideological building blocks of contemporary authoritarianism remains quite rare in comparative literature.

Ideational or other non-material factors were deemed irrelevant in economic theories of authoritarianism (Acemoglu and Robinson 2006: 20) and in rational choice accounts. Indeed, for Gelman, a politician with ideas is a theoretical (and political) liability: 'If an authoritarian ruler is guided by his ideas – a set of values, beliefs and faiths – . . . then he might behave not as a well-informed power maximiser but rather as an explorer travelling with an inaccurate or outdated map' (Gelman 2015: 32).

In this book I argue that all politicians work with an 'inaccurate map' of the world, a set of concepts that interprets reality in particular ways and conditions potential policy responses. These cognitive maps emerge through a complex interaction of direct and indirect ideological influences, constant daily encounters with social and political reality, long-standing historical and cultural tropes, and the impact of individual personalities and experiences. Political theory helps us to understand how maps are put together, and why some dominate elite thinking, while others lose all relevance as a guide to political developments. Different maps offered alternative destinations, and different paths for getting there. On the Russian cognitive map, the destinations of 'democracy' and 'dictatorship', which dominated Western conceptual frameworks, were often faded, sometimes invisible. A completely different set of destinations, labelled 'chaos' and 'order', were marked out in bold, and constituted a completely different conceptual binary that helped to interpret reality and guide policy choices.

These conceptual maps shape how we understand political threats and appropriate responses. Dan Slater's study of south-east Asian authoritarianism concludes that scholarship 'has overemphasised the importance of economic benefits and has underappreciated the significance of shared perceptions of endemic threat in holding authoritarian coalitions together' (Slater 2010: 34). Slater argues that resilient authoritarian regimes in southeast Asia can be traced back to post-colonial counter-revolutionary 'protection pacts', in which elites banded together in authoritarian institutions to counter outbreaks of popular unrest. These collective memories of unrest continue to motivate and justify authoritarian regimes in the present day, reproduced by an 'attitudinal mechanism of reproduction', which 'entails elite perceptions of earlier historical episodes of contentious politics', as well as views on how likely it might be for mass unrest to re-emerge under a more liberal system (Slater 2010: 20). Slater does not fully follow through on this process of threat construction, but constructing real and imaginary threats through hegemonic discourses and interpretive frameworks is the everyday work of any authoritarian regime, whether based on historical experience or not (Lewis 2016a). Memories of past unrest and potential future revolt are constructed and shaped by discourse, by ideology, and in the domain of ideas. 'The riot', as one of Jane Austen's waspish characters once remarked, 'is only in your own brain'.

Slater's argument that authoritarian regimes are driven by shared threat perceptions suggests that we need to understand the realm of ideas, the shared worldviews, 'frames' and 'discourses' that interpret and impose order on reality and determine which political responses are considered legitimate. There has been a growing research agenda on the evolution of political thought in Russia in recent years (Laruelle 2008, 2016b; Clover 2016; Blühm and Varga 2019), yet there was still a tendency among many scholars to dismiss the role of ideas in contemporary Russian politics, instead arguing that the Russian regime was non-ideological, driven by rational calculation, simple pragmatism or a basic desire for self-enrichment (Krastev 2011; Dawisha 2015; Hale 2015; Galeotti 2019). Krastev, for example, argues that the rapid shift in government slogans in Russia – for example, from 'Sovereign Democracy' to 'modernisation' – 'exemplifies the post-ideological character of the current regime' and demonstrates that elites consider it 'as a variant of, and not as an alternative to, Western democracy' (Krastev 2011: 8). In this mode of thinking, Putin himself remains the ultimate pragmatist, able to step outside any ideological straitjacket to unsettle his opponents with unexpected moves. As Evgeny Minchenko, a well-known political consultant, phrases it, 'Putin is a judoist, so he really does have no ideology at all' (Biznes-online 2019).

The antipathy towards thinking about ideas in post-Soviet politics was partly a reflection of the end of the Soviet ideological project, which appeared to bury not only Marxism-Leninism, but any kind of ideology. In a newspaper article at the end of 1999, effectively his first election manifesto, Putin himself argued against 'the restoration in Russia of a state, official ideology in any form'. Yet he then went on to call for a social consensus about the types of values and goals that would be acceptable to the majority of Russians (Putin 1999), listing 'patriotism', 'great-powerness', 'statehood' and 'social solidarity' as central ideas that should be shared by right-thinking Russians. Such a worldview was not an explicit ideology in the Soviet sense, but it corresponds closely to how Michael Freeden defines ideologies – not as explicit belief systems, but as 'distinctive configurations of political concepts', which 'create specific conceptual patterns from a pool of indeterminate and unlimited combinations' (Freeden 1996: 4). An ideology in this sense is a kind of mental map that interprets the reality around us in accordance with our pre-existing understanding of contested political concepts.

This meaning of ideology can be confusing, however, since there is no explicit codification of these ideas into a coherent system. True, the main intellectual architect of early Putinism, Vladislav Surkov, has begun to call

Putinism an ideology; indeed, he declares it the 'ideology of the future' (Surkov 2019). But it is more comprehensible to refer to a paradigm, in the Kuhnian sense, as a 'framework of concepts, results, and procedures', which is neither rigid nor mechanical in its application (Blackburn 2008). In this sense, we are investigating the different elements of a holistic worldview, or *Weltanschauung*. It is constituted by a set of linguistic tropes and discursive frames that amount to a 'hegemonic discourse' (Prozorov 2005), or what Blühm – following Snow and Benford – calls a 'meta-frame', a menu of meanings and interpretations for events in everyday life designed to simplify the world and offer both analytical tools and imperatives for action (Snow and Benford 1992; Blühm 2016).

To talk about the ideational aspects of 'Putinism' is therefore to identify not a clearly articulated belief system, but a set of shared understandings of contested concepts among a group of political actors (Freeden 1996; Guzikova 2015). In this understanding, ideas are not considered as one independent variable among many, forming part of a simplistic causal chain leading from ideas to action. 'Ideas' do not exist prior to a 'policy decision' in some simple cognitive pipeline. Nor are they merely a cynical ideological smokescreen constructed *post factum* for public consumption to justify policies driven by very different motivations. In this kind of interpretive approach to understanding politics, 'to understand actions, practices, and institutions, we need to grasp the beliefs – the intentional meanings – of the people involved' (Bevir and Rhodes 2015: 11).

I use as far as possible the language and discourse of Russian political elites and intellectuals themselves in attempting to understand this conceptual paradigm, with the obvious caveat that official discourse is not always designed to make clear political beliefs and motivations. Yet, official speeches, articles and doctrines can nevertheless be highly revealing as the shared interpretation of external reality and as a collective narrative that – whatever its desired political effects – also always reflects the essential conceptual framework within which leaders function.

Order, *Smuta* and the Russian State

Democratisation theory assumed that the main fulcrum of all political debate was the binary relationship between democracy and dictatorship. In post-Soviet Russia, however, both elite and popular political discourses often highlighted a completely different binary, ranged between the two fundamental concepts of 'chaos' and 'order'. In an earlier period of the Cold War, scholars such as Carl Friedrich had argued that order was just one value among many in society, and that some disorder was a price worth paying to allow democracy, justice and other values to flourish. In a pluralistic society, where different groups pursue different goals, 'the political community, by organizing itself into a political order, is required to allow for a measure of disorder' (Friedrich 1968: 346). By contrast, at almost the same time, Samuel Huntington famously argued that 'the differences between democracy and dictatorship' were much less important than the difference between those states which could maintain order and those which could not (Huntington 1968: 1). When apparently orderly Soviet regimes collapsed one after another in the late 1980s, Huntington's thesis appeared discredited, and Friedrich's emphasis on the valorisation of democracy over order was vindicated.

Friedrich's prioritisation of democracy over order dominated political debates in the West – and in Eastern Europe – in the immediate post-Cold War period. From his first months in power as prime minister in 1999, Vladimir Putin challenged this prioritisation, and turned the equation on its head. After a decade of chaotic democracy in Russia, he insisted instead that political order must come first. During his first presidential election campaign in February 2000, he said:

> I know there are many now that are afraid of order. But order is nothing more than rules. And let those who are currently engaged in substituting concepts for one another, trying to pass off the absence of order for genuine democracy – let them, I say, stop looking for hidden dirty tricks and trying to scare us with the past. 'Our land is rich, but there is no order in it', they used to say in Russia. Nobody will say such things about us any more. (Putin 2000c)

This statement encapsulates much of the political philosophy of early Putinism, a philosophy that has remained remarkably consistent through his two decades in power. In this vision, the political order embodied in a strong, centralised state represents not a threat to freedom, but the precondition for freedom, and for any functioning democratic system. The strong state was prior to, and not dependent on, rule of law, democracy or federalism; order was the foundational value for Russian society, ahead of any other. In a much-quoted speech from December 1999, for example, Putin said:

> The key to Russia's recovery and growth today lies in the state-political sphere. Russia needs strong state power [*vlast'*] and must have it. I am not calling for totalitarianism . . . Only democratic systems are lasting . . . Strong state power in Russia is a democratic, law-based, workable federal state. (Putin 1999)

Putin's most important point is that without a strong state, democracy will not be possible. Liberal thought had often viewed the state as primarily a repressive force, to be balanced by a strong civil society, a powerful legislature and independent media. Putin took a different position: 'A strong state for Russia is not an anomaly, not something to fight against, but on the contrary is the source and guarantor of order, the initiator and driving force of any change' (Putin 1999).

In constructing his political campaign around the binary of order–chaos, Putin was following a long-standing Russian philosophical position. Russian conservative historians viewed history not as a process of progressive advance over centuries, culminating in a liberal 'End of History', but as a constant oscillation between periods of chaos and periods of authoritarian consolidation (Yanov 1978; Solovei 2004; Buldakov 2005; Buldakov et al. 2010; Marchenya 2010; Petersson 2013; Mjør 2016). In this philosophy of history, order is understood as the alternative to 'lengthy states of disorder and times of trouble' (Petersson 2013: 310).

Aleksander Akhiezer – writing in samizdat in the 1970s, but subsequently widely read in the post-Soviet period – identified a series of historical cycles, characterised by schisms (*raskoly*) in society and consequent social 'catastrophes'. His historical cycles began with the collapse of the Kievan state, followed by the chaotic interregnum between the Rurik and Romanov dynasties in 1598–1613, later dubbed the *smuta*, or *smutnoe vremya* (Time of Troubles), and culminating in the twentieth century in the demise of the Tsarist empire in 1905–17. The collapse of the USSR in the late 1980s was later added as the most recent historical *smuta* (Mjør 2016). This periodisation has become commonplace, with these cataclysmic events viewed as analogous to each other, characterised by certain defining features: a breakdown in relations between 'the people' and 'power' (*vlast'*); the influence of liberal or reformist ideas; the weakness of the state and empire; and malign influence or intervention by foreign powers.

Dissident historian Alexander Yanov was a rare voice in identifying these periods in Russian history as opportunities for liberal ideas to disseminate and for the exploration of 'alternatives to despotic government, of seeking limitation of power, and of reconstituting the political opposition' (Yanov 1978: 3). For most Russian historians, on the contrary, periods of disorder were considered profoundly damaging periods of chaos and state breakdown, and moments of existential threat to the very existence of the Russian state. '[I]n the past century . . . Russia twice appeared on the edge of a complete loss of its civilisational identity', writes historian Pavel Marchenya (2010), referring to 1917 and 1991. At each point of crisis in the cycle, moreover, there is a risk that the Russian state will not regroup, but will collapse. Solovei argues that although the *smuta* acts as Russia's own unique 'locomotive of history', the scale and intensity of the *smuta* is so great that there may not be a 'reassembly' of Russian society: 'From the Russian Chaos, there may not arise a new Russian Cosmos. And therefore the *smuta* has a binary meaning: Russia after it will either be preserved, or it will not' (Solovei 2004).

This existential mode of thinking became commonplace in official discourse. In 2000 Putin told television viewers: 'The state is not only . . . a geographical territory marked out by frontiers, it is above all the law, it is constitutional order and discipline. If these instruments are weak, then the state is weak. Or it simply ceases to exist' (Putin 2000b). In 2003 he told the Federal Assembly that 'during all of the periods when the country has been weakened, whether politically or economically, Russia has always inevitably faced the threat of the country's collapse' (Putin 2003). This sense of impending crisis continued to inform Putin's discourse, even after more than a decade in power. In 2012 in an address to the Federal Assembly, he said:

> In the 20th century alone Russia went through two world wars and a civil war, through revolutions, and twice it experienced the collapse of a unified state. In our country the whole way of life changed radically several times. As a result, at the beginning of the 21st century, we were faced with a real demographic and moral catastrophe. If the nation is unable to preserve and reproduce itself, if it loses orientations and ideals, it does not need an external enemy because it will fall apart on its own. (Putin 2012a)

Zygmunt Bauman reminds us that 'without the negativity of chaos, there is no positivity of order; without chaos, no order' (Bauman 1991: 165). For Putin and his cohort of Soviet-era security officials, the entire period from 1985 to 2002 – a periodisation used by Buldakov – was a time of systemic crisis (Buldakov 2005). The portrayal of the Gorbachev and Yeltsin periods as a modern-day *smuta* pervaded Russian thought in the 2000s (Petersson 2013). At times, this version of events was deliberately exaggerated, but the 'chaotic 1990s' was not simply a cynical narrative to justify an authoritarian turn. At the time, the potential 'disintegration' or 'collapse' of Russia was also widely discussed in Western commentary, with analysts pointing to a Russia 'in turmoil', a 'failed' or 'failing state', even 'another Somalia', which threatened to 'go the way of the Soviet Union' (Matlock 1996; Hoffman 1999; Jenson 1999; for discussion, see Evangelista 2004; Willerton et al. 2005).

The reality of Russia in the 1990s for many Russian citizens was a country that faced 'general chaos in administration in every sphere of political life' and 'the near-total absence of effective state control over Russian territory' (Hanson and Kopstein 1997: 275). Clashes over political sovereignty between the presidency and parliament led to armed conflict in central Moscow in 1993, in which over 170 people died. Military and security institutions effectively became actors in their own right on questions of sovereign power (Taylor 2011: 80–1). The presidency was no longer an effective sovereign decision-maker, but just one power centre among many. Chechnya became a de facto separate state, after a disastrous military campaign collapsed in 1996. Other regions ignored Moscow and were increasingly autonomous in both political and economic affairs. Law and order had broken down in parts of the state, and by 1993 Russia boasted one of the highest murder rates in the world. The demand from Russian society in response to these problems was never likely to be for more liberalisation and democratisation, as advocated by Western analysts (Fish 2005; McFaul and Stoner-Weiss 2008).

These national-level challenges obscure the individual experience of disorder. Collective memories were augmented by personal traumas – think of the famous story of Vladimir Putin, a young KGB officer, stranded in Dresden in 1989, as a crowd of protesters gathered outside. Having called a nearby Soviet base for back-up, and been told that 'Moscow is silent', Putin went out to meet an angry crowd of protesters alone, breaking the rules of engagement and threatening his career (Hill and Gaddy 2015: 181–2). Putin later said: 'I got the feeling then that the country no longer existed. That it had disappeared. It was clear that the Union was ailing. And it had a terminal disease without a cure – a paralysis of power' (Putin 2000a: 79). The state receded, no longer sovereign, and Vladimir Putin, a mid-ranking KGB officer in the German provinces, was forced to step outside the rules to make a decision.

Critics of Putin often downplay this portrait of the 1990s as a period of disorder, echoing Friedrich's point that a certain measure of chaos was a necessary precondition to achieve gains in freedom, justice and democracy. It was undoubtedly true that post-Soviet understandings of order were skewed by the Soviet experience: many normal activities, such as trade and private business, were initially labelled as types of 'disorder', reflecting the norms of the Soviet era (Humphrey 2002: 93–4). Institutional legacies – particularly among the intelligence and security services – the so-called *siloviki* – also played a role in reproducing a particular binary understanding of order and disorder that reflected Soviet-era institutional biases. Sociologist Olga Kryshtanovskaya explains:

What is disorder in the eyes of a man in uniform? It is the absence of control. If there is no control, it means there is an opportunity for independent influence. *Siloviki* see the existence of alternative centres of power in the country as a threat to the integrity of the state. The Duma is not subordinate to the presidential administration? Disorder. Vyakhirev – not the Kremlin – is running Gazprom? Disorder. Some parties want something, or some media outlets have been talking about something? This is all disorder, which needs to be liquidated. And they liquidated it. (Kryshtanovskaya 2007)

Yet the fear of chaos and the pursuit of order was not merely a KGB pathology, but reflected a wider consensus about order in Russian society. The traditional Russian understanding of order went beyond a generic definition of order as 'legible, predictable behaviour in accord with recognised norms' (Lebow 2018: 20), and reflected what Hedley Bull (1977: 4) called an 'Augustinian' approach, in which 'the concept is held to have an intrinsic moral content' (Macfarlane 2003: 176, n 4). A Russian dictionary defines order as 'a regulated well-organised, and correct (right) situation' (Macfarlane 2003: 176, n 4). Order has a moral quality of its own, irrespective of other values, and is therefore worth pursuing in its own right.

This understanding of order had popular support in Russia beyond the *siloviki*. The Levada Centre, a polling organisation, has asked the same question of Russians since the late 1990s: 'What is more important for Russia, democracy or order?' In April 2000 the proportion of the population preferring order ('even if it means the limitation of some democratic principles and individual rights', as the pollster framed the question) rose to 81 per cent, an all-time high.[1] Putin and his advisers seized on this popular mood and presented the pursuit of order as the government's response to a democratic demand. It was millions of ordinary people, claimed Putin in a 2000 television address, who suffered from a weak state: 'the cost of the state's disorderliness [*razboltannost'*] is personal security, the immunity of individual property . . . our own well-being, and the future of our children' (Putin 2000b). When Putin told the Federal Assembly in 2002 that 'we have a duty to introduce order' into local government, it was 'that order, the deficit of which citizens of the country are speaking and writing about' (Putin 2002).

Richard Pipes interpreted such mass public attitudes towards order as reflecting a historical antipathy among Russians towards freedom and democracy (Pipes 2004). In reality, more proximate causes played the most important role. On the basis of extensive interviews with Russian citizens at the turn of the century, Ellen Carnaghan argues that it was personal experiences of disorder and logical reactions to the 'dislocations of transition and its attendant bouts of hyperinflation and financial collapse' and 'not the experiences of their forebears centuries ago' that explained this preference for order (Carnaghan 2010: 6). In assessing long-term historical change, it is easy to forget how the individual experiences of the Soviet collapse shaped political perceptions and how much chaotic, dangerous and unpredictable social environments can prepare the ground for political philosophies that always prioritise order over other values.

Russia as Weimar

This breakdown in order in the 1990s invited comparison not only with other historical periods in Russian history, but also, almost inevitably, with the historical experience of Weimar Germany, another weak democracy that emerged after the collapse of empire (Yanov 1995; Hanson and Kopstein 1997; Kailitz and Umland 2016). Andrew Monaghan rightly warns against facile historical comparisons, arguing that they 'abridge . . . complex developments into simple, unambiguous and politically charged symbols' (Monaghan 2016: 48).[2] But the importance of the Weimar analogy is that it became a central trope in the intellectual discourse of post-Soviet Russia, and encouraged comparisons between the two situations in ways that shaped intellectual responses inside Russia to the post-Soviet crisis, including an interest in the work of Carl Schmitt, the most powerful theoretical critic of Weimar democracy. Portraying the 1990s in Russia as a period of 'dysfunctionality of central power', argues Ostromensky, ensures that the period is often viewed among Russian conservatives as an inevitable precursor to a subsequent assertion of Schmittian sovereignty (Ostromensky 2016: 88).

For many nationalist and conservative intellectuals in both Weimar Germany and post-1991 Russia, political instability was compounded by an assault on identity, both personal and national, in a cognitive world turned upside down. The process of reconstructing and reasserting identity in Russia became highly contested and confrontational, resulting in 'an explosive cocktail of resentment, conspirology, and palingenetic daydreaming' (Kailitz and Umland 2016: 11). Almost every Russian intellectual agreed with Vladimir Putin that 'the question of finding and strengthening national identity is of a fundamental nature for Russia' (Putin 2013a). The collapse of the USSR 'activated an elite search for a new identity and system of values aiming at preservation of Russia's international and regional influence' (Tsygankov 2016: 148). Russia's identity crisis emerged most obviously in its geopolitical visions about Russia as a great power, and its spatial imaginaries – from 'Greater Europe' to 'Greater Eurasia' (Lewis 2018a). These identity concerns were also evident in a new form of politics, in which identity could also be constructed through a vertical connection with a charismatic leader, a president who represented the identity aspirations of different groups in the nation; and through a search for political unity, mobilised above all by the apparent threat from an external enemy.

These uncertainties around identity were not only the result of a weak democratic system that was unable to contain social and political polarisation, but were also perceived as the consequence of an aggressive, triumphant liberal international order which appeared at times to relish the Soviet collapse, not as a shared defeat of totalitarianism, but as the defeat of the Russian state in a struggle against the West. In Germany, the Weimar republic was fatally damaged by allegations that Germany lost the war as a result of a 'stab in the back' by unpatriotic domestic democrats, and similar conspiracy theories about the role of the West in the Soviet collapse also became widespread in Russia. Such myths reappeared regularly in subsequent events, for example during the Ukrainian conflict in 2013–14, when claims that Ukraine was 'traitorous' to the wider Slavic family resonated with 'echoes of Weimar resentment and the theory of the *Dolchstoss*, the Jewish "stab in the back"' (Medvedev 2014).

Sergei Medvedev characterised the 2000s in Russia as a decade during which '*ressentiment* was transformed into state policy', through the propagation of a 'myth of geopolitical defeat, humiliation and pillaging of Russia by world liberalism and its henchmen Yeltsin, Gaidar and Chubais' (Medvedev 2014). Medvedev, along with other liberals, views this as a profound misreading of the actual reality of the 1990s, but acknowledges the power of resentment (or the subtly deeper meaning of the French and Russian term, *ressentiment*) both among elites and the wider population. Most significantly, argues Mikhail Yampolsky, *ressentiment* unites elites and the wider population:

> All of Russian society, from Putin to the last pointsman [*strelochnik*] are all equally the bearers of *ressentiment*. For Putin the source is the non-recognition of himself and of Russia as equal and respected players on the world stage; for the pointsman – his helplessness in the face of the police, officials, courts and bandits . . . The *ressentiment* fantasies of the authorities at a certain moment entered into a strange resonance with the *ressentiment* fantasies of ordinary people. (Yampolsky 2014)

This strangely democratic experience of *ressentiment* rested on a powerful bond between a disaffected population and an elite that itself felt marginalised by Western-centric global elites. Vladimir Putin was uniquely able to channel this resentment, as an individual who presented himself also as an outsider (Hill and Gaddy 2015), from a poor social background, from the second city Leningrad, not the capital, Moscow, and from the KGB, not from Soviet-era Communist Party and Komsomol circles. Gleb Pavlovsky – Russia's original 'political technologist' – argues that from his very first election campaign, Putin presented himself as on the side of those who felt marginalised by the Soviet collapse and the 1990s. Pavlovsky sought to build a 'Putin majority', based on a 'coalition of revanche', comprising all the social groups who had lost out in the 1990s. This coalition of marginalised groups included frustrated remnants of the Soviet intelligentsia, 'vegetating in penniless sectoral institutes', doctors, teachers, workers in the military-industrial complex, low- and mid-ranking military officers:

> By the end of the campaign, from being the protégé of the 'Family', the candidate had turned into the banner of revanche for all the social losers of Russia. The defender of the elderly and of pensioners, the head of an impoverished army, the idol of the educators [*obrazovantsy*] and of housewives, the leader of the growing majority. (Pavlovsky 2018)

This coalition of those who fail to thrive in periods of social and economic turbulence has become a more widely recognised social phenomenon with important political consequences. Collective resentment produces an important bond between counter-elites, who perceive themselves as marginalised by dominant 'liberal' elites, and a part of the population that is genuinely excluded from wealth and power. Resentment at perceived social and cultural marginalisation has resulted in important political outcomes: as Blühm and Varga observe, 'political knowledge . . . often emerges from concrete and often *resented* collective experiences' (Blühm and Varga 2019: 13). In this resentment at global order and 'liberal elites', Russian conservatism overlaps with its counterparts in the European New Right, in the American alt-right movement, and in the anti-liberal ideologies of Steve Bannon, Trumpism and 'America First'. This array of movements is united in its resentment at the imposition of a technocratic, neo-liberal mode of global governance, which asserts its own liberal values while being both highly disciplining and disruptive of the sovereignty and autonomy of illiberal subjects and contrary ideological positions (Drolet and Williams 2018).

Politicised forms of resentment in Russia were often articulated in terms of Russia's relations with the West. Sergei Karaganov, an influential foreign policy analyst, argued that after the Cold War 'the West saw itself as a victor and started to pursue what could be called a "Weimar policy in velvet gloves", pushing Russia off the political, security and economic stage'

(Karaganov 2016). Elsewhere Karaganov writes that 'Russia was treated like a defeated power, though we did not see ourselves as defeated', but 'Russia was told in no uncertain terms that it would play a modest role in the world'. As a result, Karaganov explains, Russia experienced 'a form of Weimar syndrome' that it has struggled to overcome (Karaganov 2014). The presentation of the end of the Cold War as a 'defeat' for the USSR and a 'victory' for the West was disturbing for many Russians. For Putin, there often seems also to have been a personal dimension, a sense of profound regret over what he views as his failed attempts to reach out to the West in his first presidential term. Nearly two decades later, Putin would claim – with some pathos – that 'our most serious mistake in relations with the West is that we trusted you too much' (Putin 2017a).

Critics often dismiss these grievance narratives as *post-factum* legitimations of an aggressive foreign policy, without any basis in history (Shevtsova 2015), but whether such perceptions of the actions of the West in the post-Cold War era are warranted by the historical record is rather beside the point. Grievance narratives became a central discursive framework for all conservative thinking in post-Soviet Russia. Indeed, anti-Western discourses of resentment circulated among Russian conservative thinkers long before they became central tropes in official discourse. In the introduction to *Russkaya doktrina: novoe oruzhie soznaniya* (Russian Doctrine: A New Weapon of Consciousness), one of the most important Orthodox conservative programmatic texts, launched in 2005, the writers ask rhetorically:

> Is it possible to satisfy [the West]? Is it possible to ever be recognized as equals? Today only complete idiots, whom it is easy to instil with a feeling of guilt or an inferiority complex, or total haters of their own country (of which there were always plenty in Russia) do not understand that the West has double standards. It is not that they are good and we are bad. In all cases when we behave like they do they react with universal outrage: How do they dare? Who do they think they are? Who gave them the right? And so we wait quietly for them to let us become like they are, to let us into the club of equals. But the answer is: Never. (Kobyakov and Aver'yanov 2005: part 3)

Resentment at the West among Putin's entourage was compounded by Western criticism of many of Putin's early initiatives – the war in Chechnya, the campaign against the oligarchs, or the reassertion of control over the regions. This fuelled a suspicion in Moscow that the construction of political order in Russia – and in the international system – would be achieved only in opposition to, rather than in cooperation with, the liberal West. As the invasion of Iraq evolved into civil war, US foreign policy was increasingly interpreted in Russia as promoting chaos, not order. In his famous Munich speech in 2007, Putin criticised 'an almost uncontained hyper use of force ... in international relations', which was 'plunging the world into an abyss of permanent conflicts'. The American-led unipolar order was 'extremely dangerous', creating a disorderly world in which 'nobody feels safe' (Putin 2007a). Russian political discourse came to characterise US foreign policy as a strategy of 'managed chaos' (*upravlyaemyi khaos*), marked by 'colour revolutions', military interventions and covert support for anti-government rebellions (Manoilo 2014).

This concern about disorder in the international system was always closely interrelated with the search for internal order inside Russia. Neil Macfarlane argued that the centrality of order in Russian political thought stemmed partially from the country's complex geography and the difficulty of achieving state consolidation in the face of shifting state boundaries and constant external threats. In response to these existential threats to statehood, Russian political leaders 'insist[ed] on the primacy of order over justice domestically' (Macfarlane 2003: 206). This relationship between order and geographical space ensures that internal order is always intertwined with Russia's sovereignty and international status. Domestic order was 'a precondition for reaching and upholding great power status' (Petersson 2013: 310).

The link between international and domestic order became increasingly explicit after the 'colour revolutions' in Georgia and Ukraine in 2003–4. New documentary films and school textbooks were imbued with a counter-revolutionary spirit. By associating revolutionary activity with foreign plots against the Russian state, they sought to discredit not only the 1917 revolution but also events such as the 1825 Decembrist revolt (Kurilla 2010). In a symbolic shift, in 2005 the traditional public holiday at the beginning of November in Russia, once associated with the celebration of the 1917 October Revolution, was renamed. Henceforth it would be the 'Day of National Unity', a commemoration of the famous uprising by Kuzma Minin and Dmitry Pozharsky against Polish forces – 'foreign interventionists' – which ended the original *smuta* of the early seventeenth century. Putin's speech in 2006 to mark the day outlined the ways in which order, political unity and sovereignty were now discursively interlinked:

> Almost four centuries ago, in the most difficult times of division and civil conflict, the multinational people of our country united to preserve the independence and statehood of Russia. Her great citizens Kuzma Minin and Dmitry Pozharsky headed a people's militia, which ended the Smuta and returned law and order to our land. (Putin 2006)

The official reworking of the story of Minin and Pozharsky served not only to emphasise the contrast of 'law and order' and 'civil conflict', but also to make an explicit link between internal disorder and external threat. In this way, in the first years of Putin's presidency the conceptual outlines of a new political paradigm had already been drawn. Over the next decade the connections between internal political order and foreign policy would become increasingly explicit, while political unity within the state would be constructed through the identification of both external and internal enemies.

Carl Schmitt and Authoritarian Order

The prioritisation of political order over other values – such as individual freedom or democracy – had long antecedents in Russian political thought. Yet the idea of an authoritarian, centralising polity constructing order in the face of a destabilising external liberal order also had clear resonance with anti-liberal political thinkers in a wider European tradition. The history of European counter-revolutionary thought is a history of responses to the chaos believed to be engendered by liberalism, and thus forms a 'politico-theological view based on the notion of order' (Camus and Lebourg 2017: 3). Among European anti-liberal thinkers in the modern period, the most influential theoretician of order was Carl Schmitt, the jurist and political theorist whose foundational works were written in Germany in the 1920s and 1930s. Reading Schmitt provides numerous insights into why Russia's search for political order in the 2000s followed a particular path, but also why it ultimately failed to achieve the sustainable forms of order that the Russian population imagined during the early years of Vladimir Putin's rule.

Carl Schmitt came of age during the collapse of an empire and a ruling regime; his most important ideas about social and political order emerged in the context of the dysfunctional pluralism of the Weimar republic in the 1920s. Born in 1888, Schmitt's early professional career as a jurist was accompanied by the travails of German defeat in war and the fall of the German Empire. His conservative political views were honed in the political and intellectual struggles of the Weimar Republic, but his reputation was forever tainted by his decision to join the Nazi Party in 1933. He was not merely a passive member of the party, but a leading defender of the regime, his articles and speeches marked by a crude anti-Semitism. He soon fell from favour with the Nazi regime, but never fully repudiated his affiliation with the Third Reich. In his post-war writings, he continued to advocate forms of authoritarian political order and he remained a consistent critic of liberal ideas and parliamentary institutions.[3]

Schmitt's most original works all emerged in the context of the fragile democracy of the Weimer Republic, in the aftermath of the humiliation of Versailles, with which he was profoundly out of sympathy, and in opposition to what he viewed as an American-led liberal order that was intent on global domination. Much of Schmitt's early writing can be understood as an attempt to reconstruct a conservative, European order in the face of the challenge of popular sovereignty, mass politics and the Bolshevik regime in Russia. Schmitt argued that the liberal attempt to 'neutralise' conflicts by channelling all disputes through constitutional and legal processes 'left the state powerless in the face of the menacing spectres of social revolution' (Balakrishnan 2000: 49).

Instead Schmitt argues for the 'reestablishment and supremacy of the state' (Kervégen 1999: 57), and many of Schmitt's early writings in the context of Weimar explore different ways in which this goal might be achieved. His first major work, *On Dictatorship* (1921), already reveals his concern with how states maintain political order in the face of existential danger (Schmitt 2014a). In *Political Theology* (1922), Schmitt briefly contemplated the possibility of ultra-conservative counter-revolution, as represented in the ideas of Donoso Cortés, the nineteenth-century Spanish aristocrat who argued that Europe faced a direct choice between 'dictatorship from below' and 'dictatorship from above', between 'the dictatorship of the dagger and that of the sabre' (Balakrishnan 2000: 49). However, in 1923, in *The Crisis of Parliamentary Democracy*, Schmitt explored the contradictions between liberalism and democracy, and laid the groundwork for the possibility of an anti-liberal but nevertheless 'democratic' political order (Schmitt 1985b), an idea reflected in the 'illiberal democracies' of the twenty-first century. Schmitt began to develop political ideas that did not seek to suppress popular sovereignty but rather to capture its potential, to channel 'the plebiscitary integration of the masses into a "homogeneous" national democracy' (Balakrishnan 2000: 41).

With the publication of *The Concept of the Political* (published as an article in 1927, and expanded as a book in 1932), and *Constitutional Theory* (1928), the fundamentals of Schmitt's thinking on politics and the state were largely complete. His famous ideas on sovereignty and the exception were already present in *Political Theology*, and in the *Concept of the Political* he develops his core propositions, including the centrality of 'the political', defined as a clear distinction between 'friends' and 'enemies', a binary view of human social life that is fundamental to Schmittian thought. His postwar work focused on international relations, notably *The Nomos of the Earth* (1950) and *The Theory of the Partisan* (1963), but they also had their intellectual origins in Schmitt's early work during the 1920s and 1930s.

The link between Schmitt's political ideas and his notorious participation as a leading defender of the legality of Hitler's regime remains disputed (Balakrishnan 2000: 182; Mehring 2014: 295–6). He engaged in virulent attacks on Jews, particularly in the legal system and the universities, and provided legal justification for growing political repression (Holmes 1996: 38–9). Contrary to the views of earlier critics, the publication of Schmitt's post-war private notes (the *Glossarium*) demonstrated that his anti-Semitism was far from simply a careerist ruse. But Schmitt was not the theoretician of the Nazi political system. As Rabinbach writes: 'Heidegger and Schmitt . . . held out the hope that *Vulgärnationalsozialismus* would be sooner or later replaced by a purer and more sublime *essence*, namely their own ideas' (Rabinbach 2013: 397). In 1936 Schmitt fell out of official favour with the regime, and critics attacked Schmitt as 'a reactionary preoccupied with the concept of the state . . . [who] had not taken the racial question seriously' (Bendersky 1983: 231). He retained his post as Professor of Law at the University of Berlin until May 1945, after which – having escaped prosecution at Nuremburg – he was barred from teaching at German universities, but continued to produce a prolific stream of work until his death in April 1985.

The concept of order – social, political, international – acts as a *leitmotif* throughout Schmitt's remarkably varied portfolio of work (Meierhenrich and Simons 2016). Schmitt's contributions to jurisprudence, political theory and international relations all return time and time again to the central question of political order – what it is and how to achieve it. Hooker (2009: 13) argues that '"Order" has a particular resonance for Schmitt', and Minca and Rowan concur that Schmitt was 'above all a thinker of order', arguing that '[h]is fundamental concern was how political and legal authority could be legitimated and maintained in an age of mass politics lacking theological foundations' (Minca and Rowan 2015b: 272). Schmitt's work can be read as a radical, revisionist intervention in a long-standing German historical debate about order and the state, addressing a 'theoretical preoccupation with the locus of the state's order-generating and order-maintaining capacity' in the face of rapidly changing political and social conditions (Bhuta 2015: 11).

Schmitt's conceptualisation of political order is grounded in a recognition of difference and antagonism, and a rejection of liberal attempts to disguise these divides through liberal conceits such as international cooperation or attempts to outlaw war. Schmitt makes a critical distinction between 'politics' and 'the political' that underpins his argument. By 'the political' Schmitt means something much more fundamental than the processes of everyday politics – the elections and parliamentary processes that Schmitt views as secondary, superficial and often downright deceitful. The political represents the drawing of a line between 'them' and 'us', between 'friend' and 'enemy', in a way that asserts the boundaries of a political community. In Chantal Mouffe's reworking of the concept, it is 'the dimension of antagonism which [is] constitutive of human societies' (Mouffe 2005a: 9). The political is therefore prior to the state, not derivative of it. In Schmitt's famous formulation: 'The concept of the state presupposes the concept of the political' (Schmitt 2007a: 19). Schmitt later claimed that in this one sentence, 'I can narrate the entire story of my constitutional-juristic life' (Schmitt 2018: 201).

Schmitt's conceptualisation of order is always reliant on this understanding of the political: 'stable order is characterised by the security of the concept of the political' (Hooker 2009: 13). Schmitt complains that liberals typically attempt to annihilate 'the political' as a domain, instead proposing a post-political technocracy dominated by questions about economics and ethics, which ignores underlying political differences. But such attempts to overcome the political, by pretending that differences do not exist, are futile and dangerous, argues Schmitt. Any attempt to suppress the political through liberal myths of cooperation will lead to 'the age of neutralizations and depoliticizations', as Schmitt wrote in 1929 (Schmitt 2007b), in which European thinkers 'sought a neutral domain in which there would be no conflict and they could reach common agreement through the debates and exchanges of opinion' (Schmitt 2007b: 89). But this is an illusory politics, which will ultimately pose a threat to the very existence of a political community. However much liberals may wish these conflicts away, argues Schmitt, 'state and politics cannot be exterminated' (Schmitt 2007a: 78).

This concern that liberal politics may gloss over fundamental differences between communities, and instead promote technocratic, elitist political solutions, has an obvious resonance in contemporary global politics. For its critics, projects such as the European Union represent just such a blurring of national divisions and a diminution of sovereignty, while reducing politics to questions of economic policy and ethical behaviour. For Schmitt, such efforts are destabilising in two ways. First, they deny the fundamental difference between communities, the friend/enemy relationship which defines the boundaries of a community, and which therefore defines who we are as humans. Second, liberal politics permits a weakening of the state through the development of democratic, pluralist politics. Influenced by his experience of the unstable Weimar republic, Schmitt identifies political pluralism as the most significant threat to domestic political order. Schmitt argues that liberalism made a fatal error that weakened the modern state: it 'misplaced pluralism' by locating it within rather than between states (Minca and Rowan 2015b: 110):

the concept of the political yields pluralist consequences, but not in the sense that, within one and the same political entity, instead of the decisive friend-and-enemy grouping, a pluralism could take its place without destroying the entity and the political itself. (Schmitt 2007a: 45)

In Schmitt's view, liberal democracy is an oxymoronic concept, producing 'a self-contradictory and self-undermining project' (Bielefeldt 1998: 27). Pluralist systems are dangerous because they can be hijacked by illiberal forces aiming to undermine the state. In such cases, 'the institutions and concepts of liberalism, on which the positivist law state rested, became weapons and power positions in the hands of the most illiberal forces'; in this way, 'party pluralism has perpetuated the destruction of the state by using methods inherent in the liberal law state'. In Schmitt's characteristic phrase, 'the organizations of individual freedom were used like knives by anti-individualistic forces to cut up the leviathan and divide his flesh among themselves' (Schmitt 2008b: 74).

In this reading, a weak, pluralistic state becomes vulnerable to manipulation of its liberal principles and institutions by unconstitutional actors. The state does not stand above society as the ultimate arbiter, but becomes just one political actor among many: 'The state simply transforms itself into an association which competes with other associations; it becomes a society among some other societies which exist within or outside the state' (Schmitt 2007a: 44). In such a situation, not only is state unity threatened, but so is individual freedom, which becomes oppressed by other, non-state actors. Schmitt argues that

> When social pluralism is opposed to state unity, it means nothing other than abandoning the conflict of social duties to the decision of social groups. And that means the sovereignty of social groups, but not the freedom and autonomy of the single individual. (Schmitt 1999: 201)

As the state becomes just one social actor among many, it loses its ability to protect the people, and citizens turn to other 'organised parties' for defence: 'If within the state there are organized parties capable of according their members more protection than the state, then the latter becomes at best an annex of such parties, and the individual citizen knows whom he has to obey' (Schmitt 2007a: 52). As Rasch paraphrases Schmitt's conclusion: 'the pluralist relativization of the legitimacy and sovereignty of the state ... leaves us all dangerously exposed. The group cannot defend us, Schmitt insists, only the state can' (Rasch 2000: 3).

Schmitt's account of how state authority becomes dispersed by a fissiparous multiparty system and by multiple interest groups was only too familiar to citizens of post-Soviet Russia. Parliament became a domain, first, of illiberal communist and nationalist forces that threatened the constitutional order of the state, and subsequently the playground for corporate and business interests masquerading as political parties. Sovereignty in the country was dispersed among an array of actors, including 'violent entrepreneurs' (Volkov 2002), new business groups and networks (Humphrey 2002), street gangs and criminal groups (Stephenson 2011), fragmented political parties, politicised state agencies, separatist rebels and semi-autonomous regional leaders. These diverse forces threatened the monopoly of the state over decision-making, and instead produced multiple sovereignties across Russia's territories, and thus the prospect of variegated loyalties for its citizens.

Svetlana Stephenson's work on organised crime in Kazan demonstrates, for example, how 'grass-root gangs may mobilise to "solve" the problem of order' (Stephenson 2011: 342). Across Russia in the 1990s, 'gangs were perceived not merely as a source of violence and danger . . . but also as a "necessary evil", an agent of social regulation in a situation when the state was weak, inefficient and corrupt' (Stephenson 2011: 328). In the absence of an effective state, street gangs produced order, both creating and implementing local norms and rules, and thus creating what Robert Latham has termed 'social sovereignty' (Latham 2000), in just the way that Schmitt predicted. Instead of a single sovereign power, society faced what Clifford Shearing termed 'a mosaic of contradictory controls that simultaneously bear on the individual' (cited in Stephenson 2011: 331).

Schmitt's response to what he views as the threat of state dissolution in the face of social upheavals and a hijacked parliamentary system is twofold. On the one hand, he argues that a political community must rediscover the capacity to make existential decisions when faced with a threat to its identity and way of life, through the reassertion of sovereignty, most commonly embodied in a single political leader. Sovereignty is defined as the capacity to take decisions to preserve the state unconstrained by domestic or international law, in other words, the capacity to declare an exceptional case (Schmitt 1985a). The sovereign's ability to decide on the exceptional case provides a mechanism to ensure order and to preserve the state, but the mechanism for doing so lies outside the normal political and juridical order. It is this paradox – the use of the exception to construct order – which lies at the heart of the internal contradictions of Russian authoritarianism.

Second, the nature of the political community becomes a question of politics, not of legal definition. The political community is not defined by passports or formal registration or even the accidental geography of birth, but by the articulation of a defining boundary around a political community based on clear lines of distinction between two peoples. Order requires boundaries, frontiers and walls, and these are defined not primarily through legal agreement, but by the limits of the political, a division of the world along lines of amity and enmity, friend and enemy, 'us' and 'them'. For post-Soviet Russia, where identity has often been contested through spatial projects that question territorial boundaries (the 'Russian World', 'Eurasia') (Clowes 2011; Shevel 2011; Lewis 2018a), a Schmittian definition of political community constructed around a common enemy had intuitive attractions. It is on these two interlinked principles – sovereignty defined as the capacity for exceptional decision-making, and the defining of a political community through a friend/enemy distinction – that Schmitt constructs an entire theory of illiberal political order that demonstrates remarkable affinities with the political system that has come to be known as 'Putinism'.

Notes

1. The number of Russians preferring 'order' to 'democracy' has gradually declined, to 61 per cent in 2015 (Levada 2011a, 2015).
2. These historical analogies also tend to produce an automatic moral response that is misleading. In the most facile examples, 'Crimea' became 'Sudetenland', Putin was compared with Hitler, the World Cup in Russia was labelled the new 'Munich Olympics', and any sign of compromise with Russia was portrayed as 'Munich' and 'appeasement' (BBC 2014; Business Insider 2014; Wintour 2018).
3. The standard, most comprehensive biography is Mehring (2014). Other useful accounts are the very readable, but now dated, work by Bendersky (1983) and Balakrishnan (2000).

TWO

Carl Schmitt and Russian Conservatism

> We are undoubtedly conservatives, we just don't yet know what that means.
> Vladislav Surkov (Remizov 2006)

Any understanding of the dominant worldview among Russian decision-makers in the Putinist period requires an understanding of the evolution of Russian conservative thought since the 1990s. By the early 2000s, liberalism as an ideology was effectively moribund in Russia, clearly demonstrated by the complete collapse of liberal parties at the December 2003 parliamentary elections and the domination of the new parliament by a new conservative ruling party, Edinaya Rossiya (United Russia). Subsequently, all meaningful political debates in Russia took place within a 'hegemonic discourse' of conservative ideas and worldviews (Prozorov 2005; Blühm 2016). There were still groups and individuals who were termed 'systemic liberals' in the Russian establishment, but their liberalism was primarily that of corporate neo-liberalism, not of political democratisation or civil rights. Figures such as Alexei Kudrin or Anatoly Chubais retained a role primarily as the (often unsuccessful) advocates of Russian private business or the prioritisation of economic over geopolitical goals. Liberal ideas were still articulated, but, as Elena Chebankova argues, liberalism 'functions merely as a discursive alternative, not as a meaningful option seriously considered by the majority of the population' (Chebankova 2017: 3).

Russia has a long tradition of conservative thought, albeit one repressed in the Soviet period. The principles of nineteenth-century Russian conservatism, articulated by figures such as Sergei Uvarov, Mikhail Katkov and Konstantin Pobedonostsev, centred on opposition to any constitutional limitations on autocracy and the centrality of Orthodoxy to Russia's political and geopolitical identity (Pipes 2005). It reached its heyday as a reactionary force in the 1880s under Alexander III, yet it was ultimately a fragmented and failed movement, unable to forge a common political programme to respond to the challenge of rapid modernisation (Khristoforov 2009). A more 'liberal' conservative trend, led by Sergei Witte and Petr Stolypin, aimed to reconcile economic modernisation with political conservatism, but failed to forestall revolution. After 1917 Russian conservative thought developed in exile, including in Eurasianist circles in Prague in the 1920s, and through the work of the philosopher Ivan Ilyin. These thinkers were rediscovered in the post-Soviet period, but their influence on official thinking remained marginal until the 2000s.

Some of the ideas of pre-revolutionary 'liberal conservatism' were reappropriated during Putin's first term in office by groups such as the Seraphim Club. Putin himself was labelled a 'liberal conservative', combining a neo-liberal economic policy with the pursuit of enhanced sovereignty and a strong state (Polyakov 2000; Prozorov 2005; Blühm 2016). Among the most significant dividing lines among conservatives was their attitude to the Soviet regime, and to its collapse in 1991. Liberal conservatives did not reject the achievements of the Soviet period, but they did seek to find a balance between 'admitting to the wrongs of the Soviet period and acknowledging its rights' (Chebankova 2017: 8). In any case, their main credo – at least initially – was economic progress, not historical revisionism or questions of cultural and civilisational identity. However, in foreign policy they also promoted a revival of the Russian state and a reassertion of Russian 'subjectivity' in international relations (Verkhovskii 2004).

A version of liberal conservatism became effectively official policy in the 2000s, with 'conservative modernisation' appearing as a centrepiece in the United Russia manifesto at the 2008 elections. Polyakov and others maintain that Putin has retained his liberal conservative position (Polyakov 2015). In 2013 Putin called himself 'a pragmatist with a conservative bent'. For Putin, '[c]onservatism certainly does not mean stagnation', it means 'reliance on traditional values but with a necessary additional element aimed at development' (Putin 2013d). Yet, as we explore in later chapters, the dominant paradigm of Russian elite decision-making also shows the imprint of a wider array of Conservative thought from beyond liberal conservatism, including elements of Schmittian thinking, which had become central to the intellectual development of an array of more radical conservative thinkers.

The most dynamic intellectual debates in Russian conservatism took place among a spectrum of radical conservative groups. Neo-Eurasianists, National Bolsheviks, Orthodox conservatives, 'Young' or 'Left' Conservatives and other groups were often deeply divided among themselves, but were united in their rejection of the basic tenets of liberal conservatism. While liberal conservatives had come to terms with the dissolution of the Soviet state, radical conservatives rejected the idea that the 'August revolution' of 1991 was a founding moment of the modern Russian state, seeing it instead as an 'axial black hole', a moment of fundamental crisis (Remizov 2002: 31). The collapse of the USSR was the centrepiece of the *smuta*, which had begun under Gorbachev, and continued in the 1990s under Yeltsin, promoted and exacerbated by the West. Instead of seeking ways to ensure Russia's successful engagement with the liberal international order, radical conservatives were united in their anti-liberalism, which, to a greater or lesser extent, translated into a geopolitical anti-Westernism (Prozorov 2005; Remizov 2002, 2006; Blühm 2016). Whatever their ideological divisions, they were united in their discontent with Russia's post-Soviet direction and by a desire to see a transformation in both domestic and international policies towards a more radical anti-liberal and anti-Western trajectory.

The debate between and within these two conservatisms – and the struggles of both schools of thought with domestic and international liberalism – took place among a bewildering array of think tanks, newspapers and online journals, semi-independent foundations and different factions of the Russian Orthodox Church, with overlapping and interlocking membership (Blühm 2016; Laruelle 2016b). Evidence of these debates occasionally emerged in official public politics – in the Kremlin's funding of certain think tanks or conservative groups – or in the citations of conservative political thinkers, such as Lev Gumilev or Ivan Ilyin, which sometimes punctuated Putin's official speeches. But assessing the influence of specific intellectuals and their ideas on Russian politics has always been difficult (Laruelle 2016a).

Some scholars viewed conservatism as purely a cynical ploy by the Kremlin, which used conservative thought in an instrumental manner to bolster regime legitimacy. Certainly, aspects of moral conservatism were sometimes more or less emphasised by political technologists to gain popular support. Overt commitments to ideological thinking were often treated with some suspicion in the Russian elite.[1] However, this view of 'ideology' as an explicit, codified set of beliefs that could be promoted instrumentally by an elite which is somehow devoid of any beliefs and worldviews of its own is misleading. Many of the ideas that conservative intellectuals espoused indirectly permeated and shaped the worldviews of many in the political elite and set the parameters and direction of political debate. In part, this reflected a deliberate policy on the part of conservative circles in Russia, who did not seek to seize political power directly or even to have direct influence on policy, but – in a conscious evocation of Antonio Gramsci – sought to fight a 'war of position' to achieve 'cultural hegemony' (Engström 2016: 329–30; Laruelle 2009: 63, 2016b: 629). Conservatives sought to influence public debates, shift public and elite opinion and challenge the language and discourse of liberalism. Dugin reportedly said in 2001 that 'our aim is not to reach power and not to fight for power; our aim is to fight for influence over the regime' (Clover 2016: 259).

One strand within this radical conservative camp sought intellectual inspiration primarily from a Russian conservative tradition. Natalya Narochnitskaya, for example, a former Soviet diplomat, denounced the liberalisation of the late Soviet period as 'Sakharov–Gorbachevian infantilism', and became an eloquent spokesperson for an ultra-conservative Russian Orthodox worldview (Horvath 2016: 871). She argued that the Renaissance and the Enlightenment had undermined traditional Christian beliefs, and viewed Protestantism in particular as causing a fundamental rift between 'Anglo-Saxons' and Orthodox Russia. Narochnitskaya described contemporary Europe as a 'post-Christian society', which had become 'the kingdom of the Beast, the anti-Christ' (Narochnitskaya 2003: 421). These anti-Enlightenment views were inextricably intertwined with a now familiar schema of Russian nationalist geopolitics, in which disputes over values – and in the contemporary period issues such as human rights – are tools used by Western states to pose an existential threat to Russian civilisation and statehood. 'It was precisely under the ideological flag of West European liberalism and human rights', she argues, 'that the conscious destruction of Russia took place' (Horvath 2016: 875; Narochnitskaya 2003: 518).

Narochnitskaya makes a conscious effort to work within a Russian and Orthodox conservative tradition, and criticises neo-Eurasianism – such as the work of Alexander Dugin – calling it an intellectual 'chimera' without respect for Russia's own history and culture (Horvath 2016: 875). She played an important role in the rise of Russian Orthodox political conservatism, but Narochnitskaya and other Orthodox thinkers faced the challenge both of the relative weakness of Russian religious conservative thought, particularly in the nineteenth century (Byrnes 1969: 67), and of the fundamental intellectual rupture in political and philosophical thought that occurred inside Russia during the Soviet period (Scanlon 1994).

The major Russian conservative thinkers in the first half of the twentieth century – Ivan Ilyin, Nikolai Berdyaev and the Eurasianist groups in Prague – all lived a large part of their lives in exile, and their thinking was intertwined with European conservatism in the inter-war period. Ivan Ilyin, for example, although now presented as a major figure in Russian philosophical thought, had been expelled with Berdyaev from the Soviet Union in 1922 on one of Lenin's famous 'philosophers' ships'. Settling in Berlin, Ilyin quickly became familiar with ultra-conservative and fascist thought in Europe, one of many Russian intellectuals who, as Timothy Snyder puts it, 'confronted Russian problems with German thinkers' (Snyder 2018b). He initially praised the rise of Mussolini in Italy, and following the appointment of Hitler as chancellor in 1933, he welcomed the 'spirit of National Socialism' (Ilyin 1933). But his subsequent disaffection with the Nazi regime forced him to flee Germany in 1938 to Switzerland, where he died in 1958. His remains were reinterred in Moscow in 2005, and his works have often been quoted by officials, including by Putin (Robinson 2012).

Snyder argues that Ilyin's work is a 'metaphysical and moral justification for political totalitarianism' (Snyder 2018b), but the reality is more complex: Ilyin repeatedly condemned the totalitarian state and emphasised the need to develop a form of *pravosoznanie* ('legal consciousness') among the population. As A. G. Sytin argues, Ilyin's call for a strong state and a unity of the people does not necessarily imply support for a totalitarian state; on the contrary, he notes that Ilyin argues that the state 'must know its limits' (Sytin 2014: 104). Nevertheless, it is difficult to agree with Paul Robinson's characterisation of Ivan Ilyin as a 'liberal conservative' (Robinson 2012). Ilyin viewed early fascism as a 'concentration of state-guarding forces [*gosudarstvenno-okhranitelnykh sil*] from the right', which was a necessary response to the threat of Bolshevism and 'leftist totalitarianism'. This kind of dictatorship, he argued, was needed to guard against enemies, because 'in the hour of national danger healthy forces will always concentrate in the direction of a preservative dictatorship' (Ilyin 1948a). Ilyin's admiration for early fascism, his arguments for a strong state, organically connected to the people, and his assertion that 'at the head of the state there must be a single will' have inevitably produced comparisons with his German counterpart Carl Schmitt (Sytin 2014). Grier rejects any apparent influence, arguing that much of Ilyin's thought had already been formed before his exile in 1922, but the affinities in their thinking are still notable (Grier 1994: 177).

If Ilyin represented a kind of 'half-way house' for Russian intellectuals en route to the conservative revolutionaries and fascists of inter-war Europe, many conservative thinkers in post-Soviet Russia went directly to the canon of the German Conservative Revolutionaries of the 1920s and 1930s, and to the texts of its modern incarnation, the various strands of the European New Right (ENR). The ENR is a loose designation for an array of far-right groups and journals in Europe, of which the French Nouvelle Droite (ND) has been arguably the most influential. The ND emerged initially in France as the GRECE movement, founded in 1968 by its most prominent leader, Alain de Benoist, in response to leftist student unrest (Bar-On 2016).

The ENR claimed an eclectic range of intellectual sources, including neo-pagan and traditionalist thinkers. Its critics characterised it as 'extreme right' or even 'fascist', although its agenda was often ambiguous and eclectic, drawing at times also from the New Left (Griffin 2000). Its supporters were united by a critique of globalisation, liberal democracy and multiculturalism. The ENR was strongly opposed to universal values, which were viewed as part of a homogenising liberal ideology that sought to efface difference and undermine traditional identities (national, sexual, religious, etc.). Some of its most important influences were thinkers of the inter-war Conservative Revolution, including Ernst Jünger and Arthur Moeller van den Bruck, particularly relevant for German variants of the New Right (Müller 2003: 211–14). Carl Schmitt – whose relationship to the Conservative Revolutionaries is disputed – was perhaps the most significant ideological influence.[2] In Sunic and de Benoist's outline of ENR thinking, they devote separate chapters to historian Oswald Spengler and the economist Vilfredo Pareto, but allot Carl Schmitt the role of primary political theorist of the thinking of the New Right (Sunic and de Benoist 2011: 85). De Benoist's own work is also heavily influenced by Schmitt.

The ENR was probably the most important intellectual influence on the strands of European right-wing populism and the American 'alt-right' that emerged in the 2010s (Camus and Lebourg 2017; Drolet and Williams 2018), but its thinking was also extremely influential in Russia in the post-Soviet era (Parland 2005; Peunova 2008; Bassin 2015; Shekhovtsov 2017). Affinities between Russian radical conservatives and the ENR had already emerged in the Soviet period, despite the barriers of the Cold War; Mark Bassin demonstrated overlaps between the ideas of Lev Gumilev and the ENR, even though Gumilev never met any of the key figures in the ENR movement nor read their work (Bassin 2015). Underground discussion groups in the late Soviet period, such as the dissident Yuzhinskii circle, admired many of the core texts of the ENR canon, such as the work of Italian fascist Julius Evola (Umland 2010: 145–7; Laruelle 2015b). As the Soviet Union opened up in the late 1980s, Russian intellectuals began to meet directly with members of the ENR in different countries. Several of de Benoist's works were later translated into Russian (de Benoist 2013, 2014), but de Benoist himself disengaged from Russian intellectual circles after 1992. During his visits to Moscow, he later explained, he had been 'disturbed by the crude imperialism and Jacobinism of the vast majority of the so-called [Russian] "patriots"' (Shekhovtsov 2017: 45).

Carl Schmitt in Moscow

Whether through the conduit of the ENR or through scholarly translations and exegesis of his texts by Russian scholars, Carl Schmitt's influence became one of the most important influences in Russian conservatism in the 2000s. By 2009 Oleg Kildyushov of Moscow's Higher School of

Economics could talk of a 'Schmittian renaissance' in Russia, noting that 'today his books are actively published, his works are cited (by intellectuals of very different persuasions), and his serious academic reception is even accompanied by a certain intellectual fashion for his work in semi-intellectual circles' (Kildyushov 2009).

There are many reasons why Schmitt became the theorist of choice for many conservatives in Russia in the early twenty-first century. His style – apocalyptic, polemical and conflictual – seemed natural for the intense public intellectual debates of Russia in the 2000s (Senderov 2014: 171). Schmitt's constant sense of danger, of a coming apocalypse, also seemed strangely suited to the world of Russian conservatism, which often echoed this sense of existentialist angst. Senderov writes:

> Hardly a meeting of the neo-totalitarians passes without such incantations: we are on the edge of disaster! The World War has already begun! . . . Everybody understands: we are not talking about a possible fact. Or a concrete prognosis, which might or might not happen. We are talking about a permanent spiritual condition. About the condition that Ernst Jünger at the beginning of the last century called 'total mobilisation'. (Senderov 2014: 172)

Liberalism, by contrast, was seen to be 'deformed, empty, devoid of sacrifice and heroism, and . . . a triumph of businessmen and the common herd' (Engström 2016: 334). The reduction of politics to minor dissensions over economic policy or parliamentary procedure seemed inappropriate in a Russia that faced existential crises on an almost daily basis. By contrast, Schmitt offered an alternative philosophical framework that appeared to understand the scale of Russia's deep-seated political dilemmas. The recognition that post-Soviet Russia had some evident similarities with Schmitt's experience of Weimar certainly played a role in Schmitt's popularity (Kildyushov 2010), but that was merely a starting point. The clash between universal values and national culture; the apparent distinction between majoritarian democracy and liberal values; the challenge of creating decisive political leadership in a disorderly, pluralist state: all these challenges that Schmitt had considered so deeply also resonated with a new generation of post-Soviet Russian intellectuals.

Schmitt in the Academy

Scholarly work on Schmitt in Russia has been dominated by Alexander Filippov, a prolific translator, publisher and commentator on all things Schmittian. Filippov first published a Russian translation of Schmitt's

Concept of the Political in 1992, and has since presided over a small industry of Schmittiana in Russia, overseeing the translation of Schmitt's major works and providing his own regular analyses and commentaries (Akhutin and Filippov 2013; Filippov 2000, 2006, 2008a, 2008b, 2009a, 2009b, 2015, 2016a, 2016b; Shmitt 1992, 1996).[3] Filippov is head of the Centre for Fundamental Sociology at the Higher School of Economics in Moscow, and editor-in-chief of the journal *Sotsiologicheskoe obozrenie* (published in English as *Russian Sociological Review*), which has been one of the main platforms for publishing translations of Schmitt and commentaries by Russian and foreign scholars.[4]

Filippov dates his interest in Schmitt back to 1983, long before Schmitt had been 'rediscovered' by most Western academics. He began writing about Schmitt in the late 1980s, but only in the 2000s does he appear to have been able to find the resources to oversee translation and publication of many of Schmitt's major works. Filippov's work on Schmitt, developed through commentaries on his own or others' translations of Schmitt's work into Russian, are scholarly exegeses and interpretations of the texts, not politicised polemics, but they also 'hint that a modern sociologist or political philosopher can hope to find in the German author the key to understanding the tendencies of the contemporary Russian state' (Mikhailovsky 2008a).

Filippov writes that one of his early stimuli for studying Schmitt was to point to the dangers of a post-Soviet shift to the right by explaining the similarities between Soviet and Nazi totalitarianism though access to primary sources. Filippov has moved on from what he now terms a 'naive' position, to argue that Schmitt is open to multiple interpretations – including from the left – and is a philosopher who offers insights into many of the quandaries faced by Russia today. But his opponents categorise him, together with Alexander Mikhailovsky, as an 'academic rightist' (Smirnov 2009), although his work is often opaque in its conclusions and nuanced in its argumentation.

In one polemic with his opponents, Filippov points to five reasons why Schmitt is important for Russia, each of which emphasises Schmitt's willingness to illuminate a sometimes uncomfortable reality, against the formalist and technocratic hopes of his opponents (Filippov 2009c). First, Schmitt raises profound questions about the power of law, and the weakness of a legal order that is based solely on norms. Second, Schmitt poses fundamental questions about the relationship between liberalism and democracy, including the critical point that democracy is always also an exclusionary practice. Filippov hardly develops this point, and leaves hanging the possible implications for Russia. Third, Schmitt points out clearly that 'trust in formal procedures' can sometimes be misplaced, that there are times when the 'formal order is emasculated' and a different reality intrudes. Fourth, Filippov points to Schmitt's argument that war represents the 'highest existential tension' of a human, that the foundation of any 'solidarity of a people . . . is opposition to other peoples'. Filippov comments: 'We might find this terrible and curse [the idea], but who can doubt that this description is not without persuasiveness as a description?' Finally, Filippov notes how Schmitt argues that the formal and the rational cannot serve as the basis for political solidarity in place of powerful myths; his opponents may wish away political myths in favour of a more rational politics, but myths are powerful and will not disappear, whatever liberals might say.

Filippov uses Schmitt to inform discussions about conceptual aspects of Russian politics (2006, 2008b), and points to 'affinities' between Schmittian thought and the contemporary Russian state (2008a), but he does not follow his argumentation through to a polemical conclusion. In a chapter on sovereignty, for example, he uses Schmitt to explain the history of conceptualisations of sovereignty, with the clear intent of informing the highly politicised debate on sovereignty in Russia, but refrains from taking a stance on what exactly sovereignty should mean in Putin's Russia (Filippov 2006; see also Bowring 2013).

Filippov does not excuse the most disreputable moments in Schmitt's biography. He also does not gloss over Schmitt's most infamous articles of 1934–6, or suggest, as some have done, that there is a clear theoretical break in his work in 1933. Schmitt's most notorious article from 1934 – 'Der Führer schützt das Recht' (The Führer protects the law) – gave a quasi-legal justification of the extrajudicial executions during the Röhm Purge in July 1934, by arguing that the Führer 'immediately creates law by force of his character' (Mehring 2014: 322).

Filippov argues that this – and similar pieces – were not primarily an expression of loyalty by an unprincipled careerist, but reproduced an argument that was in essence true to Schmitt's own theoretical position. Since the sovereign is he who can declare the state of exception, as Schmitt had maintained since the early Weimar period, then Hitler, as sovereign leader, can also create 'a new kingdom of norms', thus effectively legitimating the extra-legal actions of his henchmen (Filippov 2016: 548). Despite identifying Schmitt's consistent theoretical position in this and other articles, such as the 1936 short article, 'Politik', Filippov argues that the trajectory of Schmitt's convergence with the Nazi regime was not an inevitable outcome of his theoretical position. What seems to be an apparently seamless theoretical process, from the 'formation of national unity' and the 'expulsion of alien elements', to the 'suppression of traitors' and an aggressive foreign policy, is actually a series of choices, argues Filippov, beginning with 'a mistaken, disreputable choice that narrowed the possibility of subsequent theoretical choices' (Filippov 2016: 551).

This argument provides an intellectual loophole for students of Schmitt, since Schmitt's experience provides sufficient warning of the possible consequences of making the wrong choices. Filippov suggests that anybody who wishes to follow 'even a short stretch of his theoretical path' must learn from Schmitt's personal 'experiment', which resulted in 'catastrophe', for Schmitt personally, but more importantly for the whole of Europe. But this does not delegitimise Schmittian theory as a body of work to understand contemporary politics. On the contrary: 'the theoretical relevance of Schmitt for our times means also that he has a political relevance', argues Filippov, before concluding rather obliquely that the 'meaning, uniqueness and the reproducibility of that politics' requires further thought (Filippov 2016: 551).

Filippov's colleague at the Higher School of Economics, Alexander Mikhailovsky, has also explored the work of German conservative philosophers of the 1930s, including Schmitt and Martin Heidegger, and is Russia's leading expert on Ernst Jünger. Mikhailovsky is an active public intellectual, who does not hide his sympathy for new conservative movements in Europe, criticising in 2016 German conservatives for their fear of 'political correctness', claiming that they are 'afraid to express their ideological position publicly for fear of "soft" repressions' (Mikhailovsky 2016). Mikhailovsky had long studied Schmitt, and recognised already in the 2000s the relevance of Schmitt's ideas for 'real politics', both in Europe and in Russia. In 2008 he wrote that Schmitt's ideas were becoming almost 'mainstream' in Russia, citing Surkov's idea of Sovereign Democracy as an example (Mikhailovsky 2008b).

In an article reviewing different views of Schmitt, published in *Voprosy filosofii* in 2008, Mikhailovsky argues that Schmitt's 'ideas have not only not lost their relevance but on the contrary command increasing interest among those who attempt to make sense of the contemporary political situation' (Mikhailovsky 2008a). He explores how both leftists and rightists 'skilfully use Schmitt as a sharp theoretical sword, cutting the gordian knots of the post-political tendencies of the modern world' (Mikhailovsky 2008a: 5). The turn to Schmitt on both right and left is a reminder of 'the danger of triumph of liberalism' and helps to 'uncover the dead-ends into which post-political tendencies lead'. Although divided in many of their goals, argues Mikhailovsky, both left and right Schmittians are united in opposing their common enemy – 'the new global imperialism' (Mikhailovsky 2008a: 7). Mikhailovsky offers sympathetic portraits of Schmitt's supporter, the New Right fellow-traveller

Günter Maschke, and de Benoist (Mikhailovsky 2008a: 7). Elsewhere, in a chapter published by the Moscow Spiritual Academy, Mikhailovsky outlines Schmitt's 'political theology', which he portrays as seeking to defend both the religious and the political from the implications of modernity and liberalism (Mikhailovsky 2015).

Filippov has dominated the recent study of Schmitt in the academy, but many other academics have read, translated and interpreted his work in relation to contemporary Russian realities. Zhikharev et al. argue that 'it is difficult to exaggerate the relevance' of Schmitt's work 'at the beginning of the 21st century', and note its growing importance for Russia, in particular (Zhikharev et al. 2015: 41). The question of whether Schmitt offers particular insights into contemporary Russia – beyond the more general application of his theory – preoccupies Kurennoi's use of his 'conceptual apparatus' to analyse Putin's Russia. Initially, Kurennoi – echoing Giorgio Agamben – argues that Russia is not substantively different from Western states, which are all also in a permanent state of emergency; Russia is simply more 'vulgar' in its exercise of political power. Writing in 2007, he argued that while Putin's Russia had become a 'presidential dictatorship', it was one still oscillating between a Schmittian commissarial dictator, limited in time and scope – and with some similarity to powerful executives in Western democracies – and a more revolutionary sovereign dictator, intent on introducing a new constitutional order (Kurennoi 2007). Yet this argument for a theoretical overlap between Russia and Western democracies is undermined by his insistence that Western and Russian conceptual languages have diverged starkly, as Russia introduced a new conceptual dictionary to define its public political language.

The centrality of conceptual language is also a preoccupation for Kildyushov, who compares Russia's discursive dilemma to that of Weimar: in both cases 'institutions and discourses', borrowed from the West, did not help to resolve their problems. Kildyushov argues that the crisis lies precisely in the disconnect between the 'essential semantic resources' of society and contemporary political realities: Carl Schmitt, argues Kildyushov, saw this problem more clearly than anybody else, but 'by his actions' demonstrated that he did not know how to resolve it (Kildyushov 2009). This discursive and conceptual task of self-definition is of critical importance; otherwise, others will define us, even to the point of 'unrecognizability' (Kildyushov 2009). Kildyushov argues that – paradoxically – it is the German thinker Schmitt who may be able to assist Russian intellectuals in rethinking their own conceptual frameworks.

This fixation on the problems of language emerged most strongly after 2006, in the official and semi-official debates over contested concepts such as 'sovereignty' and 'democracy'. As part of Russia's 'Schmittian renaissance', Kildyushov identifies a strong interest in Schmitt from thinkers within the system, including political technologists such as Gleb Pavlovsky and Vladislav Surkov. Schmittian conceptualisations of 'sovereignty' – further explored in Chapter 3 – have provided fertile ground for a wide range of debates in Russian academia (Makarychev 2005; Garadzha 2006; Polyakov 2007; Matveichev 2014; Guzikova 2015). The concept of the political as defined by the distinction between 'friend' and 'enemy' also has a particular resonance in Russian commentary (Moshchelnikov and Boitsovaya 2014), as does Schmitt's work on the partisan, which was translated into Russian in 2007 (Shmitt 2007; for reviews, see Artamoshin 2009; Ostromensky 2016; Aleinikova et al. 2017).

The often sympathetic use of Schmittian theory by conservative scholars to illuminate contemporary Russian realities has prompted bitter exchanges with liberal thinkers in Russia. Debates on the pages of *Russkii zhurnal* were vituperative, full of phrases such as 'intellectual fraud' and 'malicious slander'.[5] In a review of Mikhailovsky's translation of work by Ernst Jünger, in which Mikhailovsky calls for Jünger's anti-Semitic comments not to be taken out of context, Valery Anashvili comments: 'What if contextualisation helps to make racism, antisemitism, stylistically-glamorous fascism [*stil'no-glamurnyi fashizm*] and militarism perfectly acceptable ideas and practices, which can be found in normal homes and worthy discussions?' (Anashvili 2009). In a follow-up article, Artem Smirnov accused Mikhailovsky and Filippov of engaging in 'intellectual fraud', claiming that Schmitt's disreputable biography made him an unsuitable political theorist for modern Russia. 'Professor Filippov . . . is now enthusiastically wasting his academic reputation, speaking *ex cathedra* about the significance of the Nazi jurist, he ignores any kind of scientific ethics, at the same time demonstrating a striking moral flexibility' (Smirnov 2009). Filippov rejected all these arguments, asserting his right as a scholar to pursue research that interested him. It was interesting, he argued, because 'it helps to understand, what was, what is, and what will be' (Filippov 2009c).

Dugin, Schmitt and Neo-Eurasianist Thought

Smirnov's final accusation in his broadside against Filippov is that he is likely to end up in a disreputable list that ends with Alexander Dugin (Smirnov 2009). If Filippov's position on Schmitt's politics was often nuanced and ambivalent, there was no question about Dugin's views: Schmitt was his main intellectual inspiration for a programme of authoritarian rule at home and neo-imperial policy abroad. Dugin recognises Filippov's role in introducing Schmitt to many Russians (Dugin 2010), but Dugin has been arguably more influential in extending familiarity with Schmitt outside academic circles.

Alexander Dugin is much better known in the West than any other contemporary political thinker in Russia, but Dugin is often dismissed by Russian commentators as a marginal figure, whose influence is over-rated. Andrei Kolesnikov, for example, argues that 'his influence was of limited scope and duration', and that 'he is too esoteric, unintelligible, and, frankly, overrated' (Kolesnikov 2018). Rather than being 'Putin's brain' (Barbashin and Thoburn 2014), as one Western headline misleadingly dubbed him, Dugin's direct influence on decision-makers has been very limited, but he nevertheless articulates a set of radical conservative views, some of which have left a permanent imprint on Russia's intellectual *zeitgeist*.

Although Dugin held a post at Moscow State University until he was dismissed in 2015, his biography is not that of an academic, but a polemicist and far-right activist (Dunlop 2001; Ingram 2001; Laruelle 2006; Umland 2009; Clover 2016). His intellectual origins lie with the 'Yuzhinskii circle' network of Soviet-era dissidents, who rejected the traditional political positions of anti-Soviet dissidence to explore mysticism and esoteric philosophical doctrines, such as the work of René Guénon, alongside inter-war conservative writers, particularly Julius Evola, and German Conservative Revolutionaries, such as the novelist Ernst Jünger (Shenfield 2001; Umland 2009; Laruelle 2015b; Clover 2016). Alongside his political activism (Dugin joined the neo-fascist Pamyat' movement in 1987), he became a prolific author and publicist in his own right, writing books on Evola and other 'traditionalist' far-right thinkers, and commenting regularly in the nationalist newspaper *Den'* and in his own journal *Elementy: Evraziiskoe obozrenie* (Elements: Eurasian Review, 1992–8).[6]

Dugin appears to have been introduced to Schmitt's work by Alain de Benoist, probably during a trip to Paris in 1990 (Clover 2016: 180). Much of Dugin's thinking during the early 1990s stems from his acquaintance with de Benoist and other leaders of the ENR, such as the Italian far-right intellectual, Claudio Mutti (Laruelle 2006; Clover 2016: 203–5; Shekhovtsov 2017: 44–5). Schmitt's influence on Dugin's early intellectual evolution has been widely noted, although the extent of his intellectual debt to Schmitt has not been extensively researched (Dugin 1994; Ingram 2001; Laruelle 2006; Luks 2009; Shekhovtsov and Umland 2009; Clover 2016). Schmitt's ideas appear in Dugin's work from the early 1990s onwards, although they are not always clearly attributed to him.[7] One of Dugin's first articles to gain wide circulation, 'Velikaya voina kontinentov' (The great war of continents), published in the nationalist newspaper *Den'* in February 1992, outlines the essential geopolitical framework that pits the land powers of Eurasia (the 'tellurocratic powers') against the sea powers of Atlanticism ('thalassocracies') in a constant 'great war of continents' (Dugin 1992). Dugin at the time cited Halford Mackinder and Karl Haushofer as his main influences, although he was probably also aware of Schmitt's work on the subject.[8]

Dugin's first substantive engagement with Schmitt's wider work came in an article in *Nash Sovremennik* in 1992, entitled 'Karl Shmitt: 5 urokov dlya Rossii' (Carl Schmitt: 5 lessons for Russia), and subsequently repeatedly republished, for example, in *Konservativnaya revolutsiya* (Conservative Revolution) (Dugin 1994), but also in his recent *Russkaya voina* (Russian War) (Dugin 2015). This short piece played an important role in disseminating Schmitt's ideas to a wider audience in the political class, and perhaps contributed to Dugin's reported claim that Schmitt was the most widely read philosopher among members of the State Duma (Millerman 2014). The article provided a succinct summary of Schmitt's essential ideas, and also demonstrated how his thinking could contribute to a programme of Russian political resistance to the political and geopolitical power of the West.

In his 'first lesson' from Schmitt, under the heading 'Politics, politics above all', Dugin argues that Schmitt's understanding of politics was completely opposed to the artificial 'universal models' of society promoted by Marxism and liberalism, but instead was concerned with the will of the people of a concrete, unified nation in history. Just such an understanding was

> necessary for Russia and the Russian people to adequately order its fate and not once again – like seven decades ago – become hostage to an antinational, reductionist ideology, which ignores the will of the people, its qualitative unity and the spiritual meaning of its historical path.

Second, Dugin cites Schmitt's friend–enemy distinction and argues that Russia urgently needs to define its enemies and its friends, a theme that Dugin repeatedly returns to in his work. 'The "enemy-friend" pairing is both an external and internal political necessity for the existence of a politically developed [*pol'notsennoe*] society', argues Dugin. Third, Dugin highlights 'one of the most brilliant aspects of Carl Schmitt's thinking', the idea of the 'decision' in 'exceptional circumstances'. Dugin argues that Russia faces an existential choice: either the Russian people and the Russian state will make this decision themselves, which will ensure that 'our future will be Russian', or it will be decided by others, 'primarily supporters of "universalism" and "egalitarianism"'. In that case, 'then not only will our future be "non-Russian", "universal", that is "non-existent" [*nikakoe*] . . . but our past will lose any meaning'.

Dugin's fourth lesson for Russia relies on Schmitt's geopolitical theory of Great Spaces, or *Großräume*, and Schmitt's division of earthly powers into those of the sea and those of the land. Although Dugin bemoans the collapse of the 'Great Space, once known as the USSR' as an event that contradicts the 'continental logic of Eurasia', he believes that the end of Soviet ideology will nevertheless allow 'the spontaneous and passionate, strong recreation of an Eastern Eurasian bloc, since such a recreation serves the interests of all the organic, autochthonous ethnoses of Russian imperial spaces'. Moreover, the 'continental thinking of the brilliant German jurist allows us to outline the circle of "ours" and "not ours" on a global scale'. In this way, we can have a clear understanding of the enemy, which 'on a strategic, geopolitical, economic and strategic level for Europe, Russia and Asia is the United States of America and its telluric, island ally England'.

Schmitt's final lesson for Russia, according to Dugin, is derived from Schmitt's theorisation of the 'partisan', a figure resisting a totalising universal world order, defending a traditional understanding of the land, the nation and the community through any means available. This partisan figure, argues Dugin, is one very familiar in Russian history: 'Partisans in Russia won wars lost by the government, overthrew economic orders that did not fit Russian traditions, corrected the geopolitical mistakes of their leaders.' In this sense, he argues, Russia is 'a giant Empire of Partisans, acting outside the law, but ordered by some great intuition of the Land, the Continent, that "Great, Very Great Space", which is the historical territory of our people.' It is the Russian partisan, argues Dugin, who will save Russia from its new post-Soviet governments, who are under the sway of Western universalism.[9]

Dugin's *Five Lessons* summarises the different ways in which he would deploy Schmittian thought over the next two decades, but initially his primary focus was on Schmitt's theories of geopolitics. In the 1990s Dugin gave lectures in the Military Academy of the General Staff, where he further disseminated his geopolitical views among Russia's military officers. Dugin's *Osnovy geopolitiki* (The Fundamentals of Geopolitics), a book based on his lectures at the academy, was published in 1997 and became a bestseller. It was reportedly widely discussed in military and government circles (Shenfield 2001: 199). Chapter 8 of *Osnovy* is devoted to Schmitt's geopolitics, notably Schmitt's reworking of the idea of competition between 'Land' and 'Sea', and the political consequences of this struggle, and also Schmitt's concept of *Großraum* (Dugin 1997b: 45–6).

Dugin's interpretation of Schmitt's geopolitics has had a considerable influence on the 'geopolitical turn' in Russian foreign policy thinking, evident in a spate of university textbooks on geopolitics, such as a textbook for the Diplomatic Academy of the Russian Foreign Ministry, in which

Schmitt and other German geopoliticians are treated uncritically alongside other geopolitical thinkers (Isaev 2016; Smirnov et al. 2016). Despite Dugin's claims to be a Eurasianist, his geopolitical thinking owes more to Schmitt and Haushofer than it does to the original founders of Eurasianist thought, such as Prince Nikolai Trubetskoi, Petr Savitsky and other Russian emigrés in the 1920s (Laruelle 2006). Wiederkehr has argued that Dugin demonstrated limited familiarity with classical Eurasianism in the early 1990s, constructing Eurasia as a geopolitical anti-American bloc, including Europe, rather than as a geographical-cultural space between Europe and Asia (Wiederkehr 2010). Dugin does not disguise this reliance on German theorists, arguing that 'the texts of Schmitt and other conservative revolutionaries represent an inalienable part of the heritage of neo-Eurasian theory and help to understand better the meaning of neo-Eurasianism' (Dugin 2009: 214). In this context, it is worth noting recent research pointing to similarities between Eurasianist and German conservative thought, and some (unsuccessful) attempts by Eurasianists to make contact with leading German conservatives in the early 1930s (Baisswenger 2004).

Schmitt's influence is even more explicit in some of Dugin's later works. In *Chetvertaya politicheskaya teoriya* (Fourth Political Theory) (2009), Dugin outlines a radical programme of anti-liberalism, which he claims is a 'Fourth Political Theory' after the 'failure' of liberalism, communism and fascism. Echoing Schmitt's critique of global liberalism, Dugin calls for dissent against 'a global world . . . ruled by the laws of economics and the universal morality of "human rights" [in which] all political decisions are replaced by technical ones' (Dugin 2012: 20–1). He calls for a struggle 'against globalisation, against postmodernity, against the "end of history", against the status quo' (Dugin 2012: 20) by an alliance of 'Muslims and Christians, Russians and Chinese, both Leftists and Rightists, the Hindus and the Jews who challenge the present state of affairs, globalisation and American imperialism' (Dugin 2012: 194).

Dugin devotes a chapter to 'Carl Schmitt's Principle of "Empire" and the Fourth Political Theory', where he argues that Schmitt's theory of *Großraum* represents 'the fundamentals of the conception underpinning the neo-Eurasian project in Russia at the beginning of the 21st century' (Dugin 2009: 199). Dugin argues that

> the significance [of Schmitt's theory] far surpasses its [original] historical, political and geographical context, laying the foundation for a particular political-juridical way of thinking, which most probably is destined to come into being only in the 21st century and which has a fundamental significance for Russia. (Dugin 2009: 199)

For Dugin, Schmitt is a kind of intellectual godfather to his Fourth Political Theory: 'If one looks carefully at the ideas of Schmitt . . . we will easily discover that we are talking about the Fourth Political Theory (alongside Liberalism, Communism, and Fascism), which had been hidden behind the Third [theory] (Nazi and Fascist)'. According to Dugin, 'the tragedy of this idea is that the Fourth theory was historically obscured by the Third', i.e. by fascism, and conservative revolutionary ideas were distorted by 'vulgar Nazism' (Dugin 2009: 209). The problem with fascism was its 'unacceptable elements', according to Dugin, its 'racism, xenophobia, and chauvinism' (Dugin 2012: 195), with the implication that there was much to be salvaged from the rest of fascist theory. This attempt to rescue elements of fascism from its Nazi past is reflected in Dugin's frequent attempts to distinguish Schmitt from Nazi philosophy; he underlines, for example, Schmitt's emphasis on the continued existence of different peoples living within the *Großraum*, rather than German supremacist racism (Dugin 2009: 208; see also Ingram 2001; and Chapter 8 below). Dugin's ideology is above all an extreme extrapolation of Schmittian thinking, another version of the search for a 'non-fascistic fascism' (Remizov 2008) that became widespread among elements of the New Right in Russia and Europe.

The influence of Dugin and other far-right figures on mainstream politics in Russia is a matter of ongoing debate (Ingram 2001; Shlapentokh 2007; Laruelle 2015c). In the 1990s Dugin was a marginal figure, part of an ever-changing kaleidoscope of minor far-right figures, at the periphery of the ENR and with little influence on mainstream Russian politics (Umland 2007: 110–11). The nationalist right was deeply divided and had no coherent ideological stance or political programme. Andreas Umland tracked Dugin's subsequent trajectory 'from a lunatic fringe figure into a mainstream political publicist', as he phrased it, reflecting a significant shift in Dugin's access to media, to officials and to funding between 2000 and 2008 (Umland 2010). By 2004 Prozorov could note that 'the presently relatively low influence of Dugin *personally* should not be confused with his achievement in widening the space of legitimate political discourse to embrace formerly "extremist" stands' (Prozorov 2004: 63, n 202).

Dugin was boosted as a media performer by his connection with Mikhail Leontyev, the host of prime-time TV show *Odnako*. Leontyev became a supporter of Dugin's ideas, and promoted him on his geopolitically inspired talk show that aired hardline nationalist and anti-liberal sentiments (Umland 2007: 111; Clover 2016: 270–1). Dugin gained a high media profile during 2014, as the war in Ukraine accelerated, but his crude nationalism was too much for the Russian authorities, and his public profile declined sharply. Dugin himself argues that his influence is 'undeniable' but indirect, claiming that 'my ideas are being re-written by the Kremlin's political strategists and start living on their own' (cited in Engström 2014: 360). He asserts that his ideas filter up to the government, sometimes as a 'watered-down version', but that 'this version reaches the government, which incorporates it as if it were something obvious'. Admitting his lack of direct access to the government, Dugin nevertheless claims that 'my thought prevails, my discourse reigns' (Clover 2016: 296).

Remizov and the New Conservatives

Dugin's work was often crude and highly polemical, and his tendency for self-publicity – and his consequent international fame – often set him apart from a wider community of conservative writers and advocates. A more thoughtful group of conservative thinkers – variously identified as 'Young Conservatives', 'New Conservatives' or 'Left Conservatives' – emerged as an important intellectual current in 2002–3, and gradually grew in influence in public debates and in impact on official policy. The New Conservatives emerged in a loose grouping under the 'Conservative Press Club' of 2003–4, writing in a succession of print journals and websites, such as *Strategicheskii zhurnal* (Strategic Journal), the newspaper *Konservator* (in 2003), the online journal *Russkii zhurnal*, and the site *Agenstvo politicheskikh novostei*, among other outlets (Remizov 2006; Senderov 2007: 63). Senderov dubs them 'conservative revolutionaries', in conscious echo of the inspiration they derived from German conservatives of the inter-war period. There is certainly a self-conscious genealogical line drawn by Russia's New Conservatives from German conservative thought to the ENR. They distinguish themselves from other radical conservative movements, such as an Orthodox conservatism, on the one hand, which relies strongly on Russian political and religious thought, and 'liberal conservatism', or the 'liberal-national synthesis', on the other (Remizov 2006).

One of the most prolific of these new conservative thinkers was Mikhail Remizov, a graduate of Moscow State University's philosophy faculty, whose early work advocating a conservative renaissance was heavily influenced by Carl Schmitt. Remizov typed the word Schmitt so often that he took to complaining publicly about his spellchecker's tendency to autocorrect the word incorrectly to 'Shmit' (Remizov 2009). Only Lenin and Schmitt understood politics in the twentieth century, according to Remizov (2002: 33); Schmitt's works are classics, an 'unfading legacy', and the relevance of Schmitt will live on, as long as there is something called a modern state, perhaps even beyond it (Remizov 2009). Aged only twenty-four, in 2002 Remizov published *Opyt' konservativnoi kritiki* (Experience of Conservative Criticism), in which Schmitt's influence is evident, particularly his argument that liberalism represents a spacelessness that challenges spatially grounded political orders. According to Senderov's reading, in this work Schmitt emerges as 'the only genuine conservative' (Senderov 2014: 169).

Remizov seems to have taken a spatial turn from Schmitt, arguing for a conservatism of place and location, inspired by Schmitt's emphasis on 'Ordnung/Ortung' (order/orientation) (see below, Chapter 7). This conservative logic demands that every 'spiritual content – and to a certain extent, therefore, every person – remains *in place* – in that place, from which it emerged, socially, genetically and geopolitically' (Remizov 2002: 12). This 'located' conservatism argues that liberalism's universal Enlightenment principles – of free reason and rationality, which know no boundaries – are the opposite of the logic of conservatism. This produces radical conclusions, such as Remizov's claim that 'it would be stupid to try to disguise that the logic of conservative thinking is the logic of serfdom [*krepostnoe pravo*] in thought' (Remizov 2002: 12).

Remizov turns to Schmitt's thoughts on utopia in his post-war *Glossarium* to further his argument. Utopia, argues Schmitt, is 'an abstraction from ... the connectivity of place and order [*Ortung und Ordnung*]. Every order is a concrete, located legal order'. Schmitt writes that utopia is not a fantasy or an idealised system, but 'a specific system of thought, created on the basis of the erasure of space and the loss of location, the no-longer-connectedness of the social life of the person with space'.[10] This system of 'utopian thinking', remarks Remizov, is almost completely dominant in contemporary political culture: 'political space' has become 'subject to the deformational effects of "extra-spatial" thinking' (Remizov 2002: 13). For Remizov, both geopolitics and the civilisational approach stand in opposition to this spaceless 'utopianism': both are 'strategies of cultivating the spatial identity of communities' (Remizov 2006). Thus the correct conservative reaction to liberal utopian dreams of universal norms is not a 'defensive, apologetic' realism, but conservative 'radicalism' and 'fundamentalism'. Radicalism, explains Remizov, is 'an attempt to change the situation "epistemologically", on the level of its codes' (Remizov 2002: 14). It is 'a pathetic fate', he goes on, 'to be a centrist in a situation of pathological imbalance' (Remizov 2002: 19).

Schmitt is important to Remizov because he asserts the validity of a radical understanding of conservatism. Remizov rejects a 'status quo' conservatism, something akin to the 'situational' conservatism of Samuel Huntington, which is against radicalism, but has no wider worldview. Remizov identifies this form of conservatism as the official ideology of early Putinism, with its willingness to defend the first decade of post-Soviet achievements and accept the broad tenets of neo-liberal economic order. But Remizov advocates a second view of conservatism, as an ideology that challenges 'the whole family of ideologies, based on Enlightenment principles' (Remizov 2006). This is 'integral' or 'ideological conservatism'; in other words, 'conservatism as an independent ideology in opposition to both liberalism and socialism' (Remizov 2006).

Remizov is steeped in the work of the German Conservative Revolution, which he considers an attempt to return to a 'pure' ideological form of conservatism, unsullied by the experience of the French Revolution, the Enlightenment, or indeed the whole history of 'Western metaphysics' (Remizov 2006). What he terms the 'non-fascistic fascism' of the Conservative Revolution recurs in his work with some regularity. In 2008 Remizov writes that 'if we have in mind classical, Italian fascism, and not the "racial experiment" of Hitler, then in large part it represents nothing more than the combination of conservative thought with futurist aesthetics and the methods of street terror' (Remizov 2008). In the contemporary period, argues Remizov, the reconstruction of this 'style of thinking' belongs to the GRECE movement of the French Nouvelle Droit.

Remizov points to Dugin as responsible for the 'active import' of the New Right's ideas to Russia in the 1990s, but also notes the importance of academic work by Alexander Filippov and Aleksei Rutkevich – and their translations of original texts, which allowed Russian intellectuals access to the works of inter-war German writers: 'The basic pillars of the conservative-revolutionary enlightenment in Russia in the 1990s, under the cover of discussions about "Weimar Russia", were Schmitt, Heidegger, Junger in person' (Remizov 2006). Remizov views the Russian tradition of conservative thought as playing 'second fiddle' in Russia's conservative revival, although he recognises that the work of the nineteenth-century conservative philosopher Konstantin Leontyev (1831–91), the Eurasianists of the 1920s and 1930s, and the 'state-legal thought' of Lev Tikhomirov (1852–1923) or Ivan Ilyin also had 'an important formative impact on new generations of conservative intelligentsia' (Remizov 2006).

Schmitt's understanding of politics as the sovereign capacity to take a decision in an exceptional and even existential moment is particularly attractive for Remizov and other conservative thinkers. For Remizov, politics is not about everyday, mundane processes of government. Rather, 'politics lives in the cracks, the breaks, the intervals of the institutional routineness of management' (Remizov 2002: 21). Politics is really about 'how quickly an everyday situation becomes an exceptional one' (Remizov 2002: 22), and how quickly a decision can be made to resolve a 'limit situation'. The problem with liberals is their inability to take a decision, without getting enmired in process and endless debate. Remizov recites Carl Schmitt's favourite joke, first told by Donoso Cortés, who quips that liberals would respond to the question 'Christ or Barabbas?' with a proposal to appoint a commission of investigation.

Remizov offers a stark thought experiment to illustrate the decision to declare the exception, which must have seemed quite realistic in the context of post-Soviet Russia. What if an electricity company cuts off electricity to a nuclear weapons station, asks Remizov. Should a colonel complain to the courts, or put in a written appeal, like any normal official? Surely not – the people would simply demand that the colonel seize the electricity station and hold it as long as he deems necessary. 'The colonel will order – undoubtedly, by himself, personally – that the regimental special forces do exactly that' (Remizov 2002: 23). 'In this way', concludes Remizov, 'the colonel acts politically.' Remizov argues that 'the situation had gone beyond the limits of the institutional, of normative regulation . . . i.e. it had stopped being normal'. Instead, it required a 'meta-legal' decision; it required the colonel 'to take a risk, to make the political choice: the choice in favour of politics' (Remizov 2002: 23).

Remizov's example is telling about attitudes to politics in Russia in the early 2000s. What is required is not the normal public politics of parties, elections and parliament, but a response to Russia's exceptional circumstances:

> not only is our historical situation as a whole liminal [*pogranichno*], it is formed from multiple local sources of exceptionalism, it is teeming with, and ripened by extraordinary situations, which promise to an ever greater degree to determine the appearance of the future. And this means: *politics*, politics – running superior to the everyday meaning of management – is in equal measure an historico-philosophical and a tactical necessity. (Remizov 2002: 24)

Operationally, 'the extraordinariness of our situations indicate the necessity of strong, creative, risky, contested, value-based and meta-legal decisions' (Remizov 2002: 24). This need for a Schmittian sense of the political goes beyond an operational or even historical necessity. Like Schmitt, Remizov sees the political as responding to some basic human need. Politics in this sense is about something existential, which opens up the experience of limit situations – war, death and terror. 'This experience of stepping over the limits of the everyday . . . is in equal measure necessary for the people and for the individual'; it is a way of escaping the tedium of the everyday, of the mundane, of the normal.

In an article entitled 'Day of National Boredom', Remizov criticised the inoffensive holiday ('Day of Accord and Reconciliation') that replaced the Soviet-era October Revolution Day in 1996. He suggested that the ideological emptiness of this official holiday exactly symbolised the disappearance of the political in post-Soviet Russia. Remizov argued for a return to the political in the way it was understood by Schmitt, as a conflictual process, which could respond to the exceptional case. Politics should reflect an elemental, existential moment, asserting an 'authenticity of existence', an 'experience of stepping over the limits of the everyday', and an affirmation of the humanity of those who otherwise would be 'lost in the emptiness of the weekday and forgotten in the emptiness of state holidays' (Remizov 2002: 24–5). People may react in opposition to this state-instituted mundanity, concludes Remizov with hope; indeed, 'politics might even begin with boredom' (Remizov 2002: 25).

Normalising Schmitt

The presidency of Dmitry Medvedev appeared to offer a temporary revival of liberal conservatism as a guiding ideology, but the problems of the Medvedev presidency also discredited its moderate, pragmatic conservative leanings. Consequently, the divergence between liberal and radical conservatism became particularly significant in the early years of Putin's third term, and was reflected in competing institutions and publications, particularly between the more radical Izborsky Club and the officially oriented Institute for Socio-Economic and Political Research (Foundation ISEPR) (Laruelle 2016b; Blühm and Varga 2019). Although ISEPR continued a tradition of 'official conservatism' from the early 2000s, in reality its publications and affiliations demonstrated a rightwards shift. Its series of essays entitled *Tetradi konservatizma* (Essays on Conservatism) featured many of the ideas espoused by the former 'New Conservatives'.

The Izborsky Club was led by Aleksandr Prokhanov, a long-time intellectual leader of the Russian right. It attracted support from then deputy prime minister Dmitry Rogozin, presidential aide Sergei Glazyev,[11] minister of culture Vladimir Medinsky and other regime conservatives (Blühm 2016; Laruelle 2016b). While the Izborsky Club claimed to represent a platform for different views from Russian intellectuals ('from socialists and Soviet patriots to monarchists and Orthodox conservatives' [Izborsky Club 2019]), most of its publicists in one way or another represented a reworking of many of the familiar themes of the ENR, and, inevitably, many of the key tenets of Schmittian thought. By 2014 Valery Senderov could write that 'at meetings of the influential Izborsky Club, Schmittian concepts circulate without any direct citation' (Senderov 2014: 169).[12]

By the 2010s Schmittian views had become an integral part of the wider hegemonic discourse of conservatism in Russia. Russia's radical conservatives, apparently hopelessly divided and marginalised in the 1990s, had been remarkably successful in their mission to influence Russia's political culture, to transform the basic tenets of political 'common sense', understood in the Gramscian meaning of widely used and unchallenged ideas in political discourse (Buttegieg 2011: 56). Schmitt's ideas played an outsize role in the evolution of radical conservative thought, both directly through his own translated works, and through the works of his main interpreters in Russia, publicists such as Alexander Dugin and Mikhail Remizov. Although there were more and less radical versions of anti-liberal conservatism – institutionalised at one point between the Izborsky Club and the ISEPR – much of the political discourse in Russia had shifted to the right by Putin's third term. The dominant paradigm of political thought among elites increasingly reflected many of Schmitt's ideas, such as the centrality of sovereignty, the defining moment of the exception, illiberal forms of democracy, the identification of enemies, and a highly spatialised theory of geopolitics (Makarychev 2005; Garadzha 2006; Polyakov 2007; Matveichev 2014; Guzikova 2015).

Many of the principles of a Schmittian philosophical paradigm became normalised in the conservative worldviews of Russian elites. A few read Schmitt directly; many more were influenced by public intellectuals who based their work on Schmitt. For still others, the tenets of Schmittian thought overlapped with ideas that emerged from very different ideological sources, or simply made sense when considering the political logic of Russia's position in the world. As Filippov argues:

> the point, of course, is not who has read Schmitt, for what purpose and to what extent. The point is that between the arguments of Schmitt and the tendencies of our state there exists some sort of selective affinity, and one helps to understand the other. (Filippov 2008a: 51)

In the next chapters I unpack this 'affinity' of Schmitt's thought with the contemporary Russian political order, through his key concepts of sovereignty and exception, and democracy and the people. In an age when the state faced unprecedented demands from modernity and from mass politics, Schmitt's work explored 'possible – and impossible – solutions to the problem of social order' (Meierhenrich and Simons 2016: 6). Faced with an equally complex mix of technological and political change, Russia's conservative intellectuals once again turned to many of Schmitt's prescripts for national survival in the face of a global liberal challenge.

Notes

1. Mark Galeotti writes: 'Those who do appear to be genuinely motivated by Putin's rhetoric of mission (such as former Crimean prosecutor and now member of the State Duma Natalia Poklonskaya) are regarded by their own peers as naïve outsiders at best, and as dangerous fanatics at worse' (Galeotti 2018).
2. As Joseph Bendersky has argued, it is probably misleading to include Carl Schmitt as a member of the conservative revolutionary movement (Bendersky 1987). His antipathy towards many of its advocates became clear after the publication of his post-war notes in his *Glossarium*. See Jokubaitis (2013).
3. A full bibliography of Filippov's work is available on his website, <https://www.hse.ru/staff/afilippov#sci>. Many of his most important works on Schmitt are collected in Filippov (2015).
4. For example, translations of Schmitt's *Glossarium* (Schmitt et al. 2012); discussion of biographical accounts of Schmitt (Mikhailovsky 2009); and commentaries by foreign authors, such as work by Fredric Jameson (2009).
5. See the exchange in *Russkii zhurnal* in May–June 2009 among Alexander Filippov (2009a, 2009c), Artem Smirnov (2009) and Valery Anashvili (2009).
6. *Elementy* was modelled on the Nouvelle Droit journal *Eléments*. Alain de Benoist rejected any connection with the journal, apparently concerned by Dugin's imperialist views (Bar-On 2011: 210).
7. For example, in *Osnovy geopolitiki* Dugin attributes the theory of 'grand spaces' – the central argument of the book – to Alain de Benoist, despite the fact that these ideas are clearly borrowed directly from Schmitt. De Benoist has also rejected the attribution. See Clover (2016: 178).
8. On Mackinder's influence in Russia, see Bassin and Aksenov (2006).
9. It is worth comparing Dugin's 1991 interpretation of the partisan with Vladislav Surkov's text on Putinism as an ideology, in which the people also fufil a similar role. See Surkov (2019). Surkov describes the role of the people as a kind of political sediment, which constrains the leader and brings political elites down to earth. Political leaders may try to ignore the people, for example when 'they begin some galloping reforms without a glance at the people, but they quickly butted their head against them' (Surkov 2019). In other words, the people act as an inchoate veto-wielder over elite initiatives; the people 'constrains the fantasies of theoreticians, and forces practitioners to take concrete steps' (Surkov 2019).
10. Here Remizov references the Russian translation, but appears to be citing the original. The translation is in K. Shmitt (1998), 'Glossarii: zametki 1947–1951 g.', *Referativnyi zhurnal, Sotsial'nye i gumanitarnye nauki*, 1.

11. On Sergei Glazyev, and his links to the controversial American political activist Lyndon LaRouche, see Shekhovtsov (2017: 52–4).
12. During his lifetime, Schmitt advised his followers against citing his work. His biographer Mehring comments: 'for the actualisation of certain of Schmitt's theses it is necessary to simply avoid citing him. After 1945 he repeatedly advised his followers to do likewise, calling on them to avoid misunderstanding and not damage their career by mentioning his name. Whoever cites Schmitt is forced, alongside the obligatory systemic argumentation, to refer to further explanations and examples' (Mehring 2018: 34).

THREE

Sovereignty and the Exception

> What is the meaning of state sovereignty . . . ? It is above all a question of freedom, freedom of choice for every person, every people, every state [to decide] their own fate.
>
> Vladimir Putin (2015a)

The Centrality of Sovereignty

When Vladimir Putin won a presidential election in March 2004 with 71.4 per cent of the vote, he appeared to be entering his second term in office at the height of his political power. Putin had succeeded in turning the tide in the Chechen war, reasserted control over Russia's regions, tamed the media and parliament, and suppressed or co-opted powerful oligarchs. But by early 2005 the Kremlin 'felt like a besieged fortress', wrote Mikhail Zygar, and 'panic was beginning to set in' (Zygar 2016: 102). There was domestic unrest, as large protests erupted in Russian cities over pensioners' benefits. Neighbouring countries were rocked by 'colour revolutions' – popular protests that overthrew corrupt or authoritarian regimes. A 'Rose' revolution in November 2003 in Georgia was followed by an 'Orange' revolution in Ukraine in December 2004, and a 'Tulip' revolution in Kyrgyzstan in April 2005. Looking ahead to the next presidential elections in 2008, Vladislav Surkov worried about a possible 'colour revolution' in Russia itself. 'In 2008 we will either preserve our sovereignty or be ruled externally', Vladislav Surkov announced dramatically to a party meeting in Krasnoyarsk in November 2005 (Zygar 2016: 113).

The struggle to preserve and enhance Russia's sovereignty became the defining trope of Putin's second term in office, and a central pillar of the entire Putinist system. It was accompanied by an important debate about the meaning of sovereignty in the twenty-first century that owed much to the work of Carl Schmitt and his followers. Conventional accounts of sovereignty agreed that it is a contested concept with multiple meanings. A standard work by Krasner highlights four key meanings. International legal sovereignty refers to the formal recognition of states in the international system, while Westphalian sovereignty represents the 'exclusion of external actors . . . from the territory of a state'. Domestic sovereignty refers to the 'ability of public authorities to exercise effective control within the borders of their own polity'. In the era of globalisation, 'interdependence sovereignty' references 'the ability of public authorities to regulate the flow of information, ideas, goods, people, pollutants or capital across the borders of their state' (Krasner 1999: 3–4).

Schmitt's understanding of sovereignty goes beyond these meanings to explain sovereignty in a different way: both external and internal sovereignty can be defined in terms of decision-making, including the ultimate decision – the decision to declare the state of exception. Schmitt summarised his view in his famous aphorism: 'Sovereign is he who decides on the exception' (Schmitt 1985a: 5). Sovereignty therefore presupposes a willingness and a capacity to break the rules, to take a decision to step outside the law, not on a whim, but with the aim of restoring or maintaining a form of order. A genuinely sovereign state is able to relocate decision-making power back to its political leadership, and not allow it to be 'disaggregated' in multiple transnational networks, alliance structures or global institutions. Schmitt asserts that a sovereign state is one that can claim 'the monopoly to decide' (Schmitt 1985a: 13) when its vital interests are at stake, and not be constrained by the strictures of international law and norms or the objections of the 'international community', transnational civil society or multilateral institutions.

Almost every official document on Russian foreign policy, beginning with the 1993 Foreign Policy concept, contained a statement prioritising the defence of national sovereignty. However, sovereignty was initially understood primarily in a narrow sense related to the territorial integrity of the Russian Federation, corresponding to Krasner's 'international legal sovereignty'. In successive Russian military doctrines, the primary aim of the armed forces has always been 'to protect the sovereignty and territorial integrity of the Russian Federation and the inviolability of its territory' (Russian Federation 2014b). In his first presidential address to the Federal Council in 2000, Putin argued that Russia 'faced a systemic threat to its state sovereignty and territorial integrity' in Chechnya, and complained that other countries were engaged in 'attempts to violate the sovereign rights of states under the guise of "humanitarian" operations or, as it is now fashionable to say, "humanitarian" interventions' (Putin 2000d).

This renewed concern with sovereignty was seen as dated by many Western commentators, convinced that these defensive interpretations of sovereignty belonged in the past. Since at least the 1980s the concept of sovereignty had been challenged by the diffusion of authority within the state – to corporations, cities, regions and civil society – and internationally to institutions of regional and global governance, and transnational networks of experts and activists. Liberal scholars, such as Anne-Marie Slaughter, argued that old ideas of sovereignty, representing 'the fiction of a unitary will' (Slaughter 2004: 12), should be discarded, replaced by the idea of 'disaggregated' sovereignty (Slaughter 2004: 268). Many welcomed the passing of a historically contingent phase of sovereign states and embraced the emergence of post-sovereign orders, most evidently in the European Union (MacCormick 2010).

In Russia the debate was flowing in the other direction. In a semi-official book published in 2006, Alexei Chadaev described sovereignty as the 'key value' for Putin's ideology (Horvath 2011: 21), and sovereignty quickly became the central leitmotif of the Putin regime during his second term (Garadzha 2006; Morozov 2008; Ziegler 2012; Trenin 2015). An important work by Nikita Garadzha (2006) interpreted sovereignty not primarily in legal or functional terms, but as a means of resistance by which Russia could preserve its national identity in a hostile world (Bowring 2013). In a chapter of Garadzha's volume, Alexander Filippov introduced readers to Carl Schmitt's concept of sovereignty, and linked Russia's apparently uncertain international status to Schmitt's own conceptualisation of internal sovereignty as control of decision-making (Filippov 2006). For many Russian intellectuals, this became a highly productive reading, because fears of loss of external sovereignty in Russia were always bound up with deep concerns over internal sovereignty, the ability to assert political order across a vast territory, and the government's capacity to make decisions independent of other power centres.

The most influential effort to conceptualise this overlap of internal and external meanings of sovereignty came from Vladislav Surkov, the influential deputy head of the presidential administration.[1] Surkov argued that the 1990s – with its corrupt privatisations, fraudulent elections, acceptance of separatism in Chechnya and its financial indebtedness to the West – had left Russia 'on the verge of losing state sovereignty', using the term to reference both domestic and international meanings (Surkov 2006b). In 2006 Surkov began articulating a new ideological framework of 'Sovereign

Democracy' (Surkov 2006b; Averre 2007; Orlov 2008), an idea with strong affinities to Carl Schmitt's ideas (Svetlichnaja and Heartfield 2010; Bowring 2013; Morris 2019). Surkov defined Sovereign Democracy as:

> a form of the political life of society, where the authorities [*vlasti*], their organs and actions are chosen, formed, and directed exclusively by the Russian nation in all its diversity and integrity with the aim of achieving the material well-being of all the citizens, social groups and peoples which make up [the Russian nation]. (Surkov 2006a)

Russian political development, argued Surkov, must take place within the ideational parameters of Russian political culture, and reject the imposition of external ideological blueprints. At the centre of this political culture is 'a strong central state', which 'gathered, consolidated, and developed an enormous country [and] . . . conducted all significant reforms'. By contrast, any 'incautious and untimely decentralization' would weaken Russian democracy, allowing 'democratic' institutions to be replaced by 'oligarchic cliques and foreign organizations' (Surkov 2008: 84).

Although the term 'Sovereign Democracy' faded from official discourse in the 2000s, its essential principles – the exclusion of foreign ideological influences, the suspicion towards internal pluralism, and the recentralisation of decision-making within the Russian state – remained central pillars of the Putinist system. Moreover, the ideological framework of Sovereign Democracy recognised that internal order and international order were inextricably intertwined. Any weakening of Russia in the international arena would also undermine internal political order; and any internal unrest or political weakness would damage Russia's ability to make sovereign decisions internationally. This link between Russia's status in international affairs and domestic order remained a constant principle throughout Russia's subsequent foreign policy turns.

Sovereignty in International Affairs

Echoing a Schmittian understanding of sovereignty as the capacity to decide, Surkov's intervention in the debate reinforced an understanding of sovereignty as an assertion of Russian subjectivity in international relations (Averre 2007). Russia faced a world dominated by the United States, which 'aims to assert its sovereignty by refusing to others the right to be themselves' (Garadzha 2006: preface). In response to US hegemony, Russian understandings of sovereignty evolved to address issues of identity, status and subjectivity. Morozov argued that the 'idea of state subjectivity' was 'pivotal' for Putin (Morozov 2008: 162), and it emerged repeatedly in Putin's official speeches. Speaking at the UN General Assembly in 2015, Putin asked and answered his own rhetorical question: 'What is the meaning of state sovereignty . . . ? It is above all a question of freedom, freedom of choice for every person, every people, every state [to decide] their own fate' (Putin 2015a).

This understanding of sovereignty as 'freedom to choose' – the capacity to be a conscious, decision-making subject of international relations – was central to different strands of Russian conservative thought. Sergei Prozorov notes that the new understanding of sovereignty among conservatives in the early 2000s – heavily influenced by Schmitt's thinking – entailed 'precisely the declaration of independence from anyone and anything at all'. Unlike the critical approaches to sovereignty evident in many Western theories of international relations, Russian conservatives equated sovereignty with 'the freedom of the state(sman) to independently devise the course of policy and of the social actors to engage in their cultural practices in the face of the homogenising and universalising thrust of "globalisation"' (Prozorov 2004: 27).

The ideal model of sovereign power in international affairs for Putin appears to have been George W. Bush, towards whom Putin felt a mix of 'envy, respect and fear' (Zygar 2016: 108). Bush was able to both make and shape the rules-based order, and also break those rules at will. This understanding of sovereignty as freedom to make decisions unconstrained by norms or law is explicit in Putin's famous Munich speech in 2007 (Hill and Gaddy 2015: 317–19). Putin's outspoken remarks reflected long-standing concerns about the location of sovereignty in the international order, and the destabilising nature of a US-dominated international system:

> what is a unipolar world? However you dress it up, in the end it means in practice only one thing: one centre of power, one centre of force, one centre of decision-making. It is a world of one master, one sovereign. And in the end this is disastrous not only for everyone inside this system, but also for the sovereign itself, because it destroys it from within. (Putin 2007a)

This unipolar system under 'one master, one sovereign' involved 'unilateral and frequently illegitimate actions', which, far from resolving problems, 'became the generator of new human tragedies and created new hotbeds of tension'. As a result, the world was 'witnessing an almost unrestrained, hyper use of force – military force – in international relations, force that is plunging the world into an abyss of one conflict after another' (Putin 2007a). In this view, the United States and its allies were increasingly seen as encircling Russia with tightening circles of containment – the 'coils of the Anaconda', as one writer phrased it (Bartosh 2018). In this view, Russian sovereignty was threatened by NATO's pursuit of hybrid warfare against Russia, which was deliberately fomenting what Russian analysts refer to as 'managed chaos' along Russia's borders, using economic sanctions, 'color revolutions' and information warfare, with the aim of ultimately challenging Russian statehood and sovereignty (Bartosh 2018).

This interpretation of US foreign policy understood sovereignty as a zero-sum concept in which states are divided into subjects and objects of international affairs. Some insight into this worldview can be gained through Schmitt's analysis of the Allied occupation of the Rhineland after 1918, and the French invasion of the Ruhr region in 1923 to enforce payment of war reparations. The occupation prompted Schmitt to deliver the first of a series of critiques of the League of Nations – and by extension American foreign policy and 'liberal imperialism' (Kennedy 2004: 108). In April 1925 Schmitt gave a lecture about this transformation of the Rhineland into an 'object' of international relations, comprising a demilitarised zone, controlled by the Allied powers (Schmitt 2014b).

Rather than outright conquest, the new 'liberal' imperialism relied on new 'forms and methods by which a country and a nation are made an object of international politics' (Ulmen 2003: 12), such as sanctions, investigations, reparations and temporary occupations (Koskenniemi 2016: 598–9). Unlike outright annexation, these controls were vague and could be interpreted in different ways; in this way, complained Schmitt, 'words such as independence, freedom, self-determination, sovereignty lose their old meaning' (Schmitt 2014b: 34). Germany faced an 'in-between condition of nameless, ongoing, low-level warfare' in which 'hostilities . . . were indefinitely perpetuated through international sanction and propaganda directed at defeated, second-class states' (Balakrishnan 2000: 81).

Just such a condition of being an 'object' of international politics, suffering the effects of an ongoing, undeclared hybrid war – including ideological warfare and economic sanctions – was the perception of many in the Russian political elite. Sergei Karaganov, of the Higher School of Economics in Moscow, argues that the crisis in Russian–Western relations could be traced to 'the West's refusal to recognize a worthy place for Russia in European and global politics', and instead pursuing a policy akin to Versailles. The West avoided 'direct annexations and contributions', but did everything to limit 'Russia's freedom, spheres of influence and markets, while at the same time expanding the sphere of its own political and military interests through NATO expansion, and its political and economic pursuits through EU enlargement' (Karaganov 2014).

Whether this narrative of a 'second Versailles' represents an accurate portrayal of relations with the West in the early 1990s is beside the point: it has nevertheless become a central trope in official and semi-official discourse.[2] In his outspoken 2014 Valdai speech, Putin repeatedly complained that the West decided that it 'did not need to take account of Russia', instead doing whatever it wished, regardless of international law. In a colourful section, he argued that events in Crimea demonstrated that Russia would no longer acquiesce in this second-tier status:

> Remember that wonderful phrase: 'what is permitted to Jupiter, is not permitted to the bull'. We cannot agree with this formulation. Perhaps the bull is not permitted, but I want to tell you that the bear will not ask anybody for permission. He is considered the master of the *taiga* and I know definitely that he is not planning to move anywhere else, to different climatic zones – that would not suit him. But he will not give up the *taiga* to anybody. (Putin 2014b)

This conceptualisation of sovereignty as full subjectivity in international affairs ensures that the attainment of sovereignty becomes a question of existential identity, the assertion of a Russian 'I' in relation to the verbs of action of international relations. This association of sovereignty with identity reached an apogee after the annexation of Crimea in 2014. In his 'Crimea' speech in March 2014, Putin argued for sovereignty as a condition of existence, an existential question:

> While for many European countries national pride is a long-forgotten concept and sovereignty too great a luxury, for Russia real state sovereignty is an absolutely necessary condition of her existence ... either we will be sovereign, or we will disappear, and lose ourselves in the world. (Putin 2014c)

Russia's ambition to reclaim subjectivity in international affairs was already clear in the early 2000s, but its capacity to operate autonomously in international relations had been circumscribed by its economic and military weakness. In the 1990s, Russia became highly dependent on international financial institutions and foreign lending, culminating in the sovereign default and financial crisis of 1998. Russian officials complained of the humiliation of having to travel to Washington, DC to agree their annual budget with the IMF (Surkov 2006b). Putin identified Russia's reliance on external agencies as a key vulnerability for Russia, and began to pursue what Nigel Gould-Davies called 'sovereign globalization', an attempt to achieve sovereign decision-making power while remaining engaged with the global economy (Gould-Davies 2016).

Putin was lucky: an upturn in oil prices, the 1998 devaluation of the rouble and the impact of structural reforms kickstarted a period of high economic growth (averaging 6.75 per cent in 1999–2004). In a concerted effort to reduce dependence on external finance, Russia reduced its government debt/GDP ratio from more than 80 per cent to under 5 per cent between 1998 and 2005 (Gould-Davies 2016: 10). The government refused a new IMF agreement in 2001, and repaid $3.3 billion in IMF loans ahead of schedule in 2005. Even the 2008 financial crisis did not derail Russia's commitment to fiscal rectitude, which was driven as much by sovereignty concerns as by economic motivations. In February 2019 Putin announced that for the first time in history, Russia's $475 billion of reserves covered both public and private debt, which had fallen sharply since 2014 to $454 billion (RT 2019).

The Russian government continued to seek foreign investment, but after 2003 it no longer permitted foreign companies to own majority stakes in strategic sectors such as oil and gas. The threat that Mikhail Khodorkovsky might sell his Yukos oil company to Exxon Mobil was one of the motivations for his arrest and the effective expropriation of the company. A similar caution accompanied Russian participation in supranational legal regimes. Although Russia did finally join the WTO in 2012, its membership took a record nineteen years to negotiate, and it immediately faced accusations that its trade policy was subordinated to foreign policy goals (Gould-Davies 2016: 11). After the 2008 financial crisis, Russia's commitment to further integration into the global economic system slowed, and the ideological prioritisation of sovereignty increasingly placed strains on policies designed to attract foreign investment.

More liberal voices repeatedly pointed to the growing tensions between an emphasis on existential understandings of sovereignty and Russia's need to grow its economy through openness to the global economy. A 2017 report by the Centre for Strategic Research, a think tank headed by the leading 'systemic liberal', Alexei Kudrin, argued that

> The conflict with the West forces Russia to choose between sovereignty and security on the one hand and its participation in global cross-border activity on the other. In the paradigm that has emerged lately, addressing security issues is detrimental to Russia's participation in globalization

processes ... This paradigm does nothing to address the problem of Russia's backwardness, which is the key threat to the country's sovereignty. (CSR/RIAC 2017)

This conceptualisation of sovereignty in terms of economic prosperity and openness to foreign investment had little traction in the Kremlin, which continued to insist on the prioritisation of a zero-sum understanding of sovereignty over other values. At a meeting of government officials, Kudrin argued that Russia needed to lower geopolitical tensions to improve foreign investment and boost the economy. According to media reports, President Putin responded by saying that 'even if the country was lagging behind in some way, it had a thousand-year history and Russia would not begin to trade away its sovereignty' (Papchenko and Prokopenko 2016).

Russian leaders were not immune to the argument that sovereignty required both political will and material capacity. After 2008 Russia pursued a far-reaching programme of military reform that permitted it once again to project hard power outside its borders. The scale of decline in the military in the 1990s was greater than in almost any other sector of the Russian state – a multi-million-strong military with a budget of some $250 billion in the late 1980s had shrunk by 1994 to just one million men and spending of $14 billion (Trenin 2016). By the mid-1990s it was incapable even of overcoming a relatively limited insurgency in Chechnya. A series of proposed reforms were only half-implemented in the early 2000s, and the Russian military intervention in Georgia in 2008 again demonstrated serious weaknesses, with Russian forces hampered by ageing equipment and communication failures.

In response, the government launched the 'New Look' military reform policy, designed to transform the traditional Russian mass mobilisation army into a more flexible, better equipped – and better paid – force. There were extensive cuts to the cumbersome military bureaucracy and officer class, significant internal reorganisation and a huge $283 billion procurement programme promising at least 600 new aircraft, as many as 100 new surface ships and submarines and more than 2,000 new tanks by 2020 (Braw 2015). Internal reorganisation made the force an effective, if still patchy, fighting machine that proved itself in conflicts in Ukraine and Syria. A more effective military enabled Russia to intervene in Syria in 2015, thereby 'undermin[ing] the de facto monopoly on the global use of force that the United States has held since the collapse of the Soviet Union' (Trenin 2016). Russia's military reforms effectively restored Moscow's freedom to make choices and its ability to assert full sovereignty in international affairs.

Discursive Sovereignty

Richard Sakwa, commenting on Russia's declining relations with the West, argues that one of the problems is that in EU foreign policy, '[t]he political subjectivity of others is inevitably denigrated if they fail to subordinate themselves to the EU's logic of normative superiority, precluding the normal diplomatic intercourse between two sovereign entities' (Sakwa 2015b: 557). Russia's search for its own conception of sovereignty as subjectivity inevitably resulted in a clash with the West expressed in terms of values and norms, and in a constant struggle over language, information and meaning. This struggle over the production of knowledge and the interpretation of reality underpinned all Russia's material efforts to regain influence in international affairs.

Conservative intellectuals had long argued that Russia was under discursive attack (Østbø 2016: 214): Russian conservatives saw Russian society as defenceless against the language, discourses and information flows emanating from the West. Over time, these concerns also emerged in government policy. In 2016 the government published an 'Information Security Doctrine', which claimed that an information campaign was being conducted against the Russian Federation, including 'an increase in the volume of materials in foreign mass media containing a biased assessment of the state policy of the Russian Federation'. There was a deliberate attempt to undermine Russian culture and values. The 'information impact on the population of Russia, primarily on young people, is being increased in order to erode traditional Russian spiritual and moral values' (Russian Federation 2016).

'Information warfare' was often interpreted in the West as primarily involving the deliberate circulation of 'fake news' or the manipulation of media narratives. These were important tactics, but in Russian thinking this discursive challenge was about a much deeper conflict, involving a 'war of meanings', a struggle over fundamental concepts and the interpretation of events (Bartosh 2018). Consequently, reasserting Russia's discursive sovereignty was seen as not merely a welcome cultural goal, but as a central element in Russian strategic thought, and a precondition for a revival of Russia's great power status in international affairs. Yegor Kholmogorov called for Russia to become a 'sensocracy' (*smyslokratiya*), a regime which prioritised the 'sovereign' articulation of particular meanings of key concepts in ways that would exclude other interpretations (Kholmogorov 2005a, 2006a). In his 'Sovereign Democracy' concept, Vladislav Surkov called for Russian culture to be an 'organism of meaning-formation and ideational influence'. Surkov argued that 'Russia must say what it does, and not do what others say', becoming a 'coauthor and co-actor of European civilisation', involved in the 'production of meanings and images, interpreting pan-European values and articulating Russian goals' (Surkov 2006a).

The importance of language to the practice of sovereignty was central to Schmitt's understanding of international relations. For states without subjectivity, without sovereignty – the 'objects' of international relations – it would be for a foreign power 'to determine what is "Order"' and to define concepts such as 'peace' and 'war' (Schmitt 2014b: 34). Language and power in Schmitt's thinking were always deeply intertwined:

> It is one of the most important phenomena in the entire legal and intellectual life of humanity that whoever has real power is also able to appropriate and determine concepts and words. *Caesar dominus et supra grammaticam*: the emperor is ruler over grammar as well. (Schmitt 2011b: 44)

For Schmitt, the critical question about political concepts is always 'who interprets, defines and applies them; who says, by means of concrete decision, what is peace, what [is] disarmament, what [is] intervention, what [is] public order and security' (Schmitt 2011b). Elsewhere he comments:

> Words and names are never of secondary importance . . . The argument surrounding words like 'state,' 'sovereignty,' and 'independence' was the mark of deep-seated political debates and confrontations, and the victor not only wrote the history but also determined the vocabulary and the terminology. (Schmitt 2011a: 102–3)

Schmitt was always impressed by the capacity of the United States to master this use of concepts as a critical part of its arsenal of weapons in international affairs: 'The great superiority, the astounding political accomplishment of the United States reveals itself ever anew in the fact that it makes use of general, open concepts', writes Schmitt (Schmitt 2011b: 44). 'Such an elasticity, such an ability to operate with broad terms and to force the peoples of the Earth to respect them, is a phenomenon of world-historical significance', he claims (Schmitt 2011b: 44). By contrast, the defeated power – Germany – was unable to articulate its own vocabulary of international concepts and laws. It was for the victorious Allies to define what 'peace' or 'security' meant, not Germany, which was forced to use the conceptual language of the victor, 'like a beggar in rags speaking of the riches and treasures of others' (Schmitt 2011b: 44).

This effort to escape the discourse of liberalism was a profound challenge for Russian thinkers, brought up in a Western-centric education and worldview, in which liberalism continued to 'predetermine the structure of political discourse, both at the expert and at the ordinary level' (Remizov 2002: 8). Conservative Russian commentators often framed this process as equivalent to a decolonisation of knowledge and meaning production. 'Until now', explains Sergei Karaganov,

> we all lived in a world in which we saw ourselves and the world order to a significant degree through the eyes of the West and through the prism of theories, which the West gave birth to, including those that explain international relations.

But, concludes Karaganov, 'these theories no longer work' (Vasiliev 2017). Dmitry Yefremenko argued that in the contemporary international environment:

> Competition in the interpretation of reality, in the production of meaning, and the translation of values is becoming ever more intense. If the domination of the West in this area seemed very recently to be absolute, then now we are discovering that in discussions about meanings and values, the roles of teacher and pupil, or leader and the rest, are certainly not attributed once and for all to certain nations and models of socio-political organisation. (Yefremenko 2016)

Russia's ability to challenge what it viewed as a Western hegemonic discourse and articulate alternative narratives was later identified by Surkov as one of Putinism's most notable achievements. 'When everybody was still mad about globalization and shouting about a flat world without borders, Moscow clearly reminded [everybody] that sovereignty and national interests all have meaning', he wrote in 2019. In the same way, 'when everybody was praising the Internet as an untouchable space of unlimited freedom, it was Russia who awkwardly raised the question: "and who are we in this world web? Spiders or flies?"'. And when nobody was willing to speak out against American hegemony in world affairs, and 'the great American dream about world domination was almost achieved', and the end of history was nigh, 'in the gathering silence', writes Surkov, 'was heard the Munich speech' (Surkov 2019).

The problem for Surkov – and for other Russian conservatives – was that there was no social consensus within Russia on the meaning of key political concepts. Successfully challenging a hegemonic liberal discourse on the international stage did not mean that there was a broad social consensus over the meaning of ideas such as 'democracy' or 'freedom' at home. Although conservative ideas dominated Russia's political debates, Russian society also increasingly rejected the authorities' attempts to limit opposition voices and liberal ideas in society. While calling for a plurality of voices in the international arena, the Russian authorities suppressed pluralism of voices at home, reflecting Schmitt's long-standing assertion that while pluralism was appropriate between states, it was a highly destructive notion inside the state, where only a single sovereign decision-maker could maintain order.

Domestic Sovereignty: Deciding on the Exception

Schmitt's understanding of sovereignty also helps to explain the evolution of sovereign power inside Russia, and its interconnection with its role in the international system. As discussed above Schmitt defines sovereignty in terms of the declaration of the exception ('*Souverän ist, wer über den Ausnahmezustand entscheidet*'; Schmitt 1985a: 5), where the ambiguity of *über* suggests that sovereign power has a dual focus. It represents the capacity both to define what *is* the exception and to decide on what actions should be taken in response *to* the exception (Strong 2011: 34): '[The sovereign] decides whether there is an extreme emergency as well as what must be done to eliminate it' (Schmitt 1985a: 7). Schmitt characterises the exception as 'a case of extreme peril, a danger to the existence of the state, or the like', but it is a situation that 'is not codified in the existing legal order', and 'it cannot be circumscribed factually and made to conform to a preformed law' (Schmitt 1985a: 6). Thus the exception cannot be defined pre-emptively as having particular characteristics: it can only be recognised in its immanence, and only the sovereign can identify and react to it. The decision to declare the exception is made by the sovereign without constitutional or legal constraints; this, asserts Schmitt, is the defining act of sovereignty.

Instead of Weber's famous definition of the state as 'a human community that (successfully) claims the monopoly of the legitimate use of physical force within a given territory', Schmitt argued that it is rather *Entscheidungsmonopol*, the 'monopoly of decision', that defines the essence of the sovereign state (Meierhenrich and Simons 2016: 31). Schmitt writes: 'Therein resides the essence of the state's sovereignty, which must be juristically defined correctly, not as the monopoly to coerce or to rule, but as the monopoly to decide' (Schmitt 1985a: 13). In extreme situations, the sovereign must take whatever decisions are necessary to restore order, without reference to the courts, to parliament or to the provisions of the constitution. Such an understanding of sovereignty is not pure 'decisionism', nor should it be understood in the terms deployed by Zygmunt Bauman, as similar to the capricious, whimsical rule of God in the Book of Job, who may strike at will and owes nothing to his subjects (Ek 2006: 379, n 10; Bauman 2004: 6–7). Schmittian sovereignty is conceived as order-producing: the executive decision on the exception may be mistaken or ill-conceived, but in Schmitt's universe, it is never a matter of malicious caprice.

The assertion of sovereign power through the declaration of an emergency is not a temporary abrogation of the constitution, as in Schmitt's earlier conception of a 'commissary dictatorship', in which the dictator suspends certain laws for a defined period of time in order to protect the constitutional order (Balakrishnan 2000: 33–5; Agamben 2005: 32–5; Schmitt 2014a; Brännström 2016). A Schmittian sovereign is unrestricted by legal and constitutional constraints, and is not subject to temporal limits; sovereign power is only very weakly constrained by what Schmitt calls 'democracy', an ill-defined 'identity of governed and governing' (Schmitt 1985c: 14). Sovereignty is not a legal attribute of the state or of representative institutions but a political concept, which 'intermittently crystallizes if and when political crises and social disorder – liminal situations – escape constitutional norms' (Teschke 2011: 192).

This distinction became clear at the start of Russia's counterinsurgency in Chechnya in 1999, when Putin refused to declare a state of emergency in Chechnya, despite pleas from human rights activists to do so. The Russian Federation did not derogate from its obligations under the European Convention on Human Rights, as it would have been entitled to do had it legally promulgated emergency powers, and therefore all Russia's constitutional and legal protections of rights in theory remained intact (HRW 2000). The Russian government feared that a formal declaration would – paradoxically – allow for additional mechanisms of control to be exercised by parliament and other domestic agencies over Russian military forces on the ground (Memorial 1999).

In practice, Chechnya became a brutal space of exception, where constitutional rights and norms did not apply. According to Makarychev, 'Russia's military offensive in Chechnya . . . clearly created a state of exception uncontrolled and unregulated by any law' (Makarychev 2016: 120). Kahn termed it a 'legal blackhole in a geographic territory that, ironically, Russia claimed to be an integral part of the Russian Federation' (Kahn 2008: 527). Pohl writes that 'the entire republic of Chechnya . . . [was] turned into a special off-limits zone, a place where disappearances, torture, and violent death are commonplace experiences' (Pohl 2007: 30).

This contradictory construction of Chechnya as both unquestionably part of Russia while also being demarcated as exceptional, reflects the constitutive contradictions of the state of exception. As Schmitt writes, 'Although [the sovereign] stands outside the normally valid legal system, he nevertheless belongs to it, for it is he who must decide whether the constitution needs to be suspended in its entirety' (Schmitt 1985a: 7). This ambiguity of the sovereign power is summarised by Giorgio Agamben as '*Being-outside, and yet belonging*', reflecting a topographical uncertainty: 'the state of exception represents the inclusion and capture of a space that is neither outside nor inside' (Agamben 2005: 35).

In Chechnya Russian soldiers talked of *bespredel*, a sense of complete lawlessness (Reynolds 2000).[3] Such a characterisation might appear to contradict Schmitt's argument that although constitutional norms do not apply in the state of exception, it does not mean that the state of exception is a state of chaos (Brännström 2016). Schmitt argues that there is still an order in the exception:

> What characterises an exception is principally unlimited authority, which means the suspension of an entire existing order. In such a situation it is clear that the state remains, whereas law recedes. Because the exception is different from anarchy and chaos, order in the juristic sense still prevails even if it is not of the ordinary kind. (Schmitt 1985a: 12)

The exception is therefore not a situation of anarchy or chaos. Moreover, alongside the exception, a 'normal' situation must also exist, in which norms and law function according to constitutional and legal codes (Schmitt 1985a: 13). Agamben critiques Schmitt's argument, concluding that the exception is a 'space without law' characterised only by 'anomie' (Agamben 2005: 51). But in the most brutal and cruel sense, the *bespredel* in Chechnya still corresponds to Schmitt's conceptualisation of a different order, rather than the normlessness of Agamben's anomie, or what he terms 'a pure violence without *logos*' (Agamben 2005: 40). Although there is unpredictability in the way that violence is deployed, it remains within the bounds of what is understood by the Russian military to constitute a form of order, albeit one that is brutal and abusive in the extreme. There may not be clear legal rules, but there are multiple informal practices that produce new forms of order within the zone of exception. A form of order still prevails, even in the exceptional case.

The Sovereign Leader

For Remizov, writing in the early 2000s, the Russian experience was a constantly self-reproducing liminal experience, formed from 'multiple local sources of exceptionalism', and 'teeming with . . . extraordinary situations'

(Remizov 2002: 24–5). Russia had arguably been in a permanent state of exception since the late 1980s, not demarcated by constitutional provisions that defined a state of emergency, but evident in an informal and undeclared derogation from constitutional principles (Sakwa 2014b: 42). Formally, the 1993 Constitution effectively instituted a 'super-presidency' in Russia, in which 'the president is not one branch of power but is above all branches' (Shevtsova 2007: 17). This executive presidency faced few formal constraints from the legislature, the judiciary or from within the bureaucracy, and a very limited culture of accountability to the population at large (Fish 1997). Yet under Yeltsin it was clear that the president, despite his formal powers, had no monopoly of decision-making power, which instead was dissipated among multiple centres of authority.

Decision-making authority was distributed across a kaleidoscope of oligarchs, regional chiefs, criminal groups, non-state actors and external powers (Morozov 2008: 163). Russia was 'close to the state of nature, where anarchy rather than hierarchy prevails' (Volkov 2002: 26). Volkov argues that an image of the state as 'one private protection company among others' was a better characterisation of Russia's reality 'than a view of the state as the source of public power' (Volkov 2002: 26). Rather than the state exerting a monopoly of violence, 'there is competition and cooperation among different violence-managing agencies' (Volkov 2002: 155). Thus Russia in the 1990s corresponded to the weak total state that Schmitt found so unstable, in which multiple parties could claim sovereign decision-making powers, both inside and outside the state. As explored in Chapter 1, Schmitt views this dispersal of power away from the central state as deeply destabilising, in which the state 'simply transforms itself into an association which competes with other associations' (Schmitt 2007a: 44).

This challenge was most evident in the patchwork of de jure and de facto sovereignties among Russia's regions. Yeltsin had famously urged the regions to 'take as much sovereignty as you are able to swallow', and they had responded by claiming extensive autonomy. In his first term, Putin's central policy goal was the recentralisation of power, through a series of measures to force the regions 'to return everything that they had swallowed', as a journalist put it (Grigoreva 2005). New presidential plenipotentiaries were introduced and regional governors were removed from the Council of the Federation, and instead offered a symbolic role in an advisory State Council. Moscow set about correcting the multiple contradictions between regional and federal law in favour of the latter: about a quarter of more than 300,000 normative legal acts adopted by the regions violated federal laws (Ross 2005: 359). Declarations of sovereignty – present in the constitutions of many of Russia's ethnic republics – were also ruled unconstitutional. In

2004 Putin abolished direct gubernatorial elections, finalising the removal of sovereign decision-making power from regional leaders. Writing in 2005 after this latest round of political reforms, Makarychev commented:

> Putin's reforms in this sense rely on the logic of Carl Schmitt: both see that the essence of the problem lies in the state becoming one of many institutions (groups, associations) and as a result it enters into dependent relations with other entities. A relativisation of the state takes place: it is forced to take part in negotiations, to conclude formal or informal agreements with other institutions claiming political status. As a result, the image of the state becomes the product of the balance of forces among conflicting groups of interest, while the central power becomes only an 'arbiter' or a 'peacemaker'. (Makarychev 2005)

Putin's response to this challenge, argues Makarychev, is twofold. On the one hand, in abolishing elections for regional governors, Putin attempts to use 'depoliticised methods' 'to resolve the essentially political problem of the restoration of the subjectivity of the state'. On the other hand, Makarychev argues, the state is reasserting its monopoly over political decision-making:

> The political decision emerges from the will of the sovereign and is not directly written in the laws. The president, in this version, is a figure autonomous from other, much less influential players on the political stage, and independent from them in his actions . . . the president definitively is confirmed in the role not simply as the central source of power, but as the single politician, on whose decision everything depends. All other political players are seen in society as some symbolic attributes (if not accessories) of the presidential will. (Makarychev 2005)

This removal of sovereign decision-making power from other actors was the primary aim of the recentralisation of formal power in a 'power vertical' headed by the president. Tensions remained in the balance between central control and local legitimacy, and Russia's regional policy demonstrated a constant cycle between periods of more or less centralisation and localisation (Blakkisrud 2015). In 2012 elections were reintroduced for regional governors, albeit with a careful 'filtering' process for potential candidates, but tensions continued between local elites and the so-called 'varyagi' (incomers) who were regularly parachuted in from the centre as regional governors when local elites appeared to have developed too much autonomy. Yet these centre–region dynamics took place within a different paradigm from the 1990s: regional elites could undermine, disrupt or fail to implement central directives, but few were in any doubt that the ultimate decision-making power had been relocated back to Moscow.

The assertion of sovereign power at the centre of the political system should not be confused with achieving an effective centralised bureaucratic state, what Michael Mann (1984) terms 'infrastructural power', a system of state power that could ensure implementation of government policy across all of Russia's provinces, regions and republics. Sovereign power claims a monopoly of decision, but cannot guarantee the effectiveness of normal, everyday policy development and implementation. Schmitt is always less interested in effective institutional forms – at least in his pre-1933 work – than in ensuring that there is some – any – mechanism for taking the decision. The sovereign could be a personalised dictator, a monarch, or, potentially, a collective ruling body (Rasch 2000: 7–8), but the main point was to have a single decision-making body, and not to disperse power among different parties within the state. In his own historical context, of course, Schmitt is temperamentally committed to what in Russian is termed 'vozhdism' (Alekseeva 2009) – the idea that political life circulates around a dictatorial figure at the centre of the state, but in theory this monopoly of the decision could take on different institutional forms.

The definition of sovereignty in terms of the capacity for decision-making rather than a formal institutional position creates potential confusion in the political system. In these Schmittian conceptualisations of sovereignty, Vladimir Putin's status as sovereign does not necessarily derive from his formal position or from constitutional norms. Nor does it derive from his election by the people. Russian conservative thinkers candidly reject a literal interpretation of the claim in Article 3 of the Russian Constitution that the 'multinational people' of Russia is the 'bearer of sovereignty', instead identifying Vladimir Putin as the embodiment of sovereignty (Matveichev 2014). A consequence of this mode of thinking is that the succession process is fraught with political problems beyond the prosaic ones of policy continuity and immunity for the outgoing president. Putin's departure from office – for whatever reason – is interpreted by some conservative thinkers as tantamount to what is termed 'the desovereignisation' of Russia, a point neatly captured in this exchange between two conservative philosophers:

> M.M. Federova: 'Very well, and what if Putin flies off to the moon tomorrow, what will happen then?'
> O.A. Matveichev: 'That will be very bad, it will be some kind of process, which will seriously desovereignise Russia.' (Matveichev 2014: 165)

Consequently, when Dmitry Medvedev assumed the presidency in 2008, he did not automatically become the sovereign leader, in Schmittian terms, argues Matveichev (Matveichev 2014: 165). A similar point has been made more prosaically by Russian officials. Boris Gryzlov, then speaker of the State Duma, argued in late 2007 that 'Vladimir Putin will remain the national leader regardless of what official position he will hold' (Gryzlov 2017). In similar vein is then deputy chief of staff Vyacheslav Volodin's well-known quip that 'there is no Russia today if there is no Putin' (Moscow Times 2014).

Fish argues that 'Putin's authority stands independent not only of any organization or ideology, but also of the office he holds . . . If Putin chose to become minister of transport, the minister of transport would rule Russia' (Fish 2017: 70). Fish continues: 'As sovereign, Putin also stands above impersonal rules. He makes, alters, and ignores the law at will, and he retains the ultimate power to decide when other officials – and major economic actors – may flout its provisions with impunity' (Fish 2017: 70).

A picturesque analogy is offered by a Kremlin official, who described the position of Putin in the following way:

> the entire political system – the elite, the government, oligarchs – is Everest. And above Everest, flying at an unattainable height, is an aircraft – that is President Putin . . . There is no question of competition or rivalry, no need to account to anybody or make deals with anybody, our job is just to make sure that the aircraft does not lose height. (Gaaze 2018a)

The ideal sovereign leader in this Schmittian paradigm must at all times retain the capacity and will to take existential decisions in liminal moments. In extreme circumstances, argues Ostromensky, the leader is always faced with a binary choice: 'the sovereign is forced either to be the power, or to leave' (*Suveren vynuzhden ili byt' vlast'iu, ili zhe uiti*). He rehearses a well-worn trope in Russian political thinking, which clarifies this distinction between political leaders who retain and lose sovereignty:

> We can cite the Ukrainian experience of Viktor Fedorovich Yanukovich, who was unable to affirm his status as a sovereign; the Libyan experience of Colonel Muammar Gaddafi, who lost to a much stronger opponent, but remained a political actor and claimed the role of sovereign to the very end; the Syrian experience of President Bashar al-Assad, who continues to be a sovereign, confirming his status by four years of civil war. (Ostromensky 2016: 88)

This conceptualisation of political leadership through the prism of sovereignty idealises the moment of decision by the strong leader who is faced with an existential threat. The exception is the moment at which sovereignty is either revealed in the existential decision – or its glaring absence becomes clear. The presence or absence of sovereignty thus becomes, in some sense, a moral position. 'At the core of the political idea', writes Schmitt, is an 'exacting moral decision' (Schmitt 1985a: 65). Leo Strauss argued for the recognition of this moral quality to Schmitt's thinking, arguing that '[t]he affirmation of the political is in the last analysis nothing other than the affirmation of the moral' (Strauss 1976: 99).

But Strauss also highlights a complex tension between this view of morality and Schmitt's much more extensive critique of 'humanitarian morality', 'ideals' and 'normative prescriptions'; in essence, Strauss concludes, Schmitt offers 'a *moral* judgement on humanitarian morals' (Strauss 2007: 119). Schmitt does not recognise this apparent moral quandary, and would reject any idea of a duel between the decision to assert sovereignty (and save the political order) and the ethical assessment of the means required to implement the decision – the use of violence, killing or arbitrary arrest to disperse demonstrators and protesters, for example. In real political situations, however, just such a moral duel is encountered. In the Ukrainian context, the interpretation of Yanukovich's ousting from power is disputed by liberal and anti-liberal forces, but both agree that President Yanukovich is a moral failure. His failure to end the Maidan – to take the decision, to 'be power' – led to him being treated with contempt by Russian conservatives, while his actual, ineffectual use of violence against demonstrators made him a hate-figure in his own country and in the West (Walker 2017: 129).

The Sovereign and the Court

Schmitt's image of the sovereign leader acting as a largely unconstrained decision-maker is unconvincing for many analysts of Russian politics. For some, Putin is little more than 'a plaything in someone else's hands' (Felshtinsky and Pribylovsky 2008: ix), at most an arbiter among other powerful groups, a figure ruling through a collective decision-making process, a 'collective Putin'. Journalist Mikhail Zygar sees Putinism not as a one-man show, but as a monarchical court, in which Putin is largely the hostage of the personal and business interests of those around him: 'over 15 years the circle of confidantes [*priblizhenykh*], colleagues and friends closed around him ever tighter, ever more completely fencing him off from reality' (Zygar 2015: 401). By late 2017 Gleb Pavlovsky saw Putin as a weakening figure, surrounded by 'regents', competing to manage a transition to a post-Putin era (Pavlovsky 2017). Gudkov suggested that 'the real Putin personally depends on the circle of "decision makers" much more than they depend on him', and concluded that 'Putin is hardly in a position to determine the composition of this circle or limit access to it' (Gudkov 2011: 30). The evidence suggests that this view of Putin as a 'hostage' of his own court is ultimately misleading, but the relationship between the president and his entourage undoubtedly complicates any over-simplistic account of sovereign decision-making.

An influential model of presidential governance has been Minchenko's 'Politburo 2.0', a network model of Kremlin insiders (Minchenko. ru). Many of Putin's inner circle date back to the 1980s or earlier. Sergei Chemezov, for example, served with Putin in the KGB in Dresden, and became CEO of Rostec, a huge state corporation in the military-industrial complex. Yury Kovalchuk, chair of Rossiya Bank, a bank favoured by the Russian political elite, and with other business interests in finance and the media, was one of Putin's original friends from the 'Ozero dacha' cooperative in St Petersburg. Other St Petersburg friends included businessman Arkady Rotenberg (Minchenko 2017). Key officials included the prime minister Dmitry Medvedev, Sergei Sobyanin, the mayor of Moscow, and Anton Vaino, presidential chief of staff. Igor Sechin, head of Rosneft, was a dominant force in the energy sector. Nikolai Patrushev, secretary of the Security Council, led a security bloc, alongside Sergei Shoigu, defence minister, Alexander Bortnikov, head of the FSB and Sergei Naryshkin, head of the Foreign Intelligence Service (SVR).

Dubbing this group a 'politburo' suggests some quasi-formalisation of decision-making in a way that is misleading. As early as 2005, scholars argued, on the basis of interviews with officials, that 'the authority of the central executive is in practice devolved to a series of small and informal groups around the president himself', with Putin preferring to work through 'ad hoc groups that are not defined by institutional boundaries' (Kryshtanovskaya and White 2005: 1066). Putin used an informal and often-shifting geometry of consultation and decision-making to avoid both formal and informal constraints on his power. Different figures were involved in decisions in different areas of government policy, with the only constant presence in the room being Putin himself. Andrei Kolesnikov of the Moscow Carnegie Center comments that 'the most important question is who takes decisions and who is present when they are taken'. The key question, for Kolesnikov, is 'who was in the room when they took Crimea or decided to send forces into Syria?' The decision-making process is at best a 'situational Politburo on different questions', with a different format for different sectors of government policy (Kamyshev and Mukhametshina 2019).

Here Schmitt's distinction between exceptional decisions and the routine decisions that make up the norm is helpful: different members of the elite had extensive influence over government decisions in ordinary, everyday matters, and were certainly able to influence the outcomes of many policy processes and personnel appointments, but in all the key exceptional decisions of the Putin period, it is evident that the president had the freedom and capacity to make a decision. The focus on the exception is always revealing of real power dynamics. As Gopal Balakrishnan comments, 'emergency situations are like X-ray flashes which suddenly reveal the antinomies of legal reason' (Balakrishnan 2000: 45).

Nevertheless, the circle of influencers and gatekeepers inevitably has an impact on the decision-making process. An important theme in the evolution of Putin's mode of governance was the concern that his freedom of decision-making would be constrained by the influence of his political entourage and personal networks. In one of his Schmitt-inspired analyses of political power, Alexander Filippov explains the risk of power being dispersed within the elite: 'The sovereign . . . is surrounded by the heads of smaller, secondary pyramids of power', which leads to an inflation of power and 'an excess of power decisions, each of which has relatively less worth' (Filippov 2008b: 55, 56).

After 2015 Putin embarked on a major personnel reshuffle, apparently in an attempt to diminish some of these 'secondary pyramids', and to reduce the risk of such a dispersal of power. After August 2015, when long-time ally Vladimir Yakunin was dismissed as head of Russian railways, Putin demoted or dismissed half-a-dozen figures once thought to be close to the president, such as Viktor Ivanov, head of the Federal Narcotics Control Service; Andrei Belyaninov, head of the Federal Customs Service; and chief of staff Sergei Ivanov. According to Tatyana Stanovaya (2017), the new chief criterion for appointment was no longer loyalty to Putin, as it had been in his earlier terms (loyalty was already assumed), but managerial effectiveness: Putin sought new ways to make an often dysfunctional state machine work more effectively by appointing a new generation of technocrats (Stanovaya 2017). Yakunin was replaced as railways chief by the little-known deputy transport minister, Oleg Belozerov, Vladimir Dmitriev was replaced at VEB by Sergei Gorkov, a young manager from Sberbank, and so forth.

The dismissal of several of Putin's close allies was partly prompted, according to Minchenko, by 'the unwillingness of V. Putin to become a hostage of his inner circle' (Minchenko 2016: 3). His goal in these personnel changes was to ensure that he retained sovereignty, defined as freedom of action in extraordinary circumstances, including freedom from the influence of powerful figures and groups around him. According to Andrei Kolesnikov, 'Putin decided to bet not on his friends-cronies, but on technocrats and officials from the security services, who were more distant from him' (Kolesnikov 2017: 14). According to Kolesnikov, Putin's 'kitchen cabinet' was increasingly made up of 'those who cannot address him with [the familiar personal pronoun] *ty* and certainly cannot have a serious argument with him' (Kolesnikov 2017: 14). 'Russia's Solitary Man' was the headline on one analysis pointing to Putin's apparent self-isolation from his erstwhile inner circle (Whitmore 2016). Stanovaya portrays this shift as moving away from 'subject-subject relations' with advisers. Instead of regular meetings with these informal advisers,

> [a] new model of discussing decisions was formed, vertical, much more comfortable for the president, and the close circle of the head of state was no longer filled by advisers, but by their replacements – the implementers, who do not ask unnecessary questions and do not organise discussions. (Stanovaya 2017)

This self-isolation did not mean that Putin could – or wanted to – take decisions on all issues of policy. Many questions regarding appointments or allocation of resources were fought over and disputed among rival clans and networks without Putin's involvement. In some cases, Putin studiously avoided getting involved, or merely commented from the sidelines, as if playing the role of a neutral observer. Putin frequently did not make clear what his position was on a key issue, perhaps preferring to see bureaucratic interests fight it out (Anayev 2018: 43). But in matters of state, in key strategic decisions and above all in foreign policy, Putin fulfilled the role of a sovereign decision-maker.

Yet the claim of an autonomous sovereign decision-making agent raises complex questions, which trouble both Schmitt and his Russian disciples. In the Russian presidential system, influence is measured not by formal position, but by what has been termed '*dostup k tele*' (literally, 'access to the body' [of the president]), the ability to engage in formal and informal discussions with Putin on an individual basis. Hence power has an important element of spatiality, in which access to the physical corridors and rooms of power is much more important than any formal position in the hierarchy. And those who control access to this space – literally, the 'gatekeepers' – play a vital role. This categorisation of power in spatial terms defined by adjacency to the sovereign was also a preoccupation of Schmitt's later work. In a short dialogue published in 1954, Schmitt writes:

> In front of every space of direct power there forms an antechamber [*Vorraum*] of indirect influence and power, access to the ear, a corridor leading to the soul of the power-holder. There is no human power without this antechamber and without this corridor. (Schmitt 2008c: 23)

Whether it is 'the antechamber, the back stairs, the surrounding space [*Umraum*], or subspace [*Unterraum*]', this space forms a kind of 'dialectic of human power' (Schmitt 2008c: 23).

> Certainly in this antechamber of power during the course of world history a colourful and varied society could be found together. Here are assembled all the indirect [influences]. Here we meet the Minister and the Ambassador in full uniform, but also priests and personal physicians, adjutants and secretaries, valets and mistresses (Schmitt 2008c: 23–4).[4]

Schmitt's colourful historical vignette encapsulates his own doubts – never fully developed – about the possibility of a genuinely sovereign decision, given the role of courtiers, ambassadors, gatekeepers and mistresses. Is sovereign power possible if the holder of sovereignty is constrained, not by laws or external powers, but by his own physical frailties or by the filtered information he received from officials, lackeys and favourites? This is what Schmitt calls the 'dialectic of human power and powerlessness' (Schmitt 2003: 337, n 6), in which the exigencies of authoritarian rule create their own logic of isolation and vulnerability. The leader beomes obsessed with security, but this obsession comes at a price:

> From its compulsion to self-affirmation, daily and hourly power seeks to secure a dialectic whereby the ruler, in order to maintain this position, is compelled to organise new security systems around himself and to create new anterooms, corridors and accesses to power. The inescapable dialectic consists in the fact that, through such security measures, he distances and isolates himself from the world he rules. His surroundings thrust him into a stratosphere, wherein only he has access to all the others over whom he exercises power, and they no longer have access to him. (Schmitt 2003: 337)

As Putin moved among an archipelago of vast residences and palaces across the country, this sense of isolation and distance was surely inescapable. Putin was reputed to dislike the corridors and close spaces of the

Kremlin, perhaps viewing them as a form of entrapment and confinement. As Kate Marshall concludes in her study of corridors of power, 'the true struggle, after all, is for the occupation of antechambers and control of corridors' (Marshall 2013: 166), and this is understood not only in metaphorical terms, but in the spatiality of architecture, and in physical access to the president, the corridors to his inner sanctums. Marshall argues that 'the sovereign requires corridors, and corridors in turn reveal the form of that sovereignty, for in this world decision-making is always encoded in architecture, and it can always be seen' (Marshall 2013: 165).

In the Russian context, this problem of the physical limitations on a sovereign particularly concerns Filippov, who first translated Schmitt's 1954 treatise into Russian, and returns to the issue in several places in his work (Filippov 2006, 2007, 2008a, 2008b). He comments:

We say that [a leader] has power. But what happens when the power-holder [*vlastitel'*] falls asleep? Or when his memory fades? Or in those situations, when we are talking about transferring power from one power-holder to another. Or when there is too much information? What happens then? (Filippov 2006: 196)

More significantly, perhaps, a decision does not necessarily lead to the expected outcome – it may have very different consequences, questioning the very essence of the sovereign decision. Filippov partly addresses these objections, arguing that a lack of total control over the implementation of decisions does not mean that the state has no capacity to intervene in society effectively. But this problem of human limitation opens up a much more substantive critique of Schmitt's conception of the sovereign – that the political leader may make a decision that is mistaken, ill-informed or not committed to the public good. As Holmes notes in discussing the Schmittian sovereign, Schmitt 'completely neglects the distinction between intelligent and stupid decisions' (Holmes 1996: 47). Schmitt's own biography, as so often, provides the perfect example. 'At least a decision', wrote Schmitt in his diary on 30 January 1933. The occasion was Hitler's nomination as chancellor (Minca and Rowan 2015a: 274).

Putin appears to have been acutely aware of the possible constraints on the capacity of a sovereign to make adequate decisions in a situation of limited information and informal pressure from advisers. Businessman Vladimir Potanin told an interviewer: 'Putin likes controlling things. He does not like to not be in the loop. He likes details, he likes to know how things work' (Foy 2018). Information is the key to political control. Alexei Gromov, first deputy head of the presidential administration, and according to reports an informal 'curator' of Russia's main media outlets, produces a daily digest of news for the president (Rubin et al. 2019). Other information flows are believed to rely heavily on the intelligence services, including the Federal Security Service (FSB), the Foreign Intelligence Service (SVR) and the Federal Protection Service (FSO). According to one account, by journalist Ben Judah:

> The master begins his work day by reading three thick leather-bound folders. The first – his report on the home front compiled by the FSB, his domestic intelligence service. The second – his report on international affairs compiled by the SVR, his foreign intelligence. The third – his report on the court complied by the FSO, his army of close protection. He is obsessed with information. (Judah 2014)

Little is known for certain about this process of information gatekeeping. Soldatov and Rochlitz argue that the current system unduly privileges the FSB, which enjoys a 'near monopoly' on intelligence provision, and places remarkable power in the hands of the FSB chairman, who 'effectively controls what kind of information reaches Putin' (Soldatov and Rochlitz 2018: 102). According to Mark Galeotti, 'systems for evaluating intelligence and transmitting it to the president' are 'highly personalised', and therefore 'damage its quality and impact on policy' (Galeotti 2016: 2). The danger is that information flows reinforce rather than challenge misleading views: 'The agencies reinforce his assumptions and play to his fantasies rather than informing and challenging his worldview, as good intelligence services should' (Galeotti 2016: 5). Part of the official worldview no doubt stems from this particular framing of information. Gleb Pavlovsky comments that 'Moscow views world affairs as a system of special operations, and very sincerely believes that it itself is an object of Western special operations' (Macfarquhar 2016).

Exception, Norms and 'Manual Control'

A second major problem for the Schmittian paradigm of sovereignty is the difficulty of retaining exceptional decisions only for truly existential threats to the state, while ensuring an effective regime of regular bureaucratic practice to manage the mundane, normal situation. In practice, creating mechanisms that enable the sovereign to resort to exceptional measures risks undermining the institutions and rule-sets that are designed to ensure the effectiveness of decision-making processes. While

Putin retained the capacity to intervene in critical situations and make final decisions in almost any domain of the state, in many cases the system lacked institutions that would ensure effective implementation of policy decisions. Pavlovsky (2016) argues that 'despite his image as an all-powerful tsar, Putin has never managed to build a bureaucratically effective state' (Pavlovsky 2016: 10). The much-vaunted 'power vertical' was often more a rhetorical device than a functioning reality (Monaghan 2012), designed to remove decision-making power from other political forces, such as regional governors, but without putting in place effective institutional measures to implement presidential directives.

While the number of presidential decrees increased rapidly in Putin's first two terms, their implementation did not keep pace. In 2010–14 alone the number of presidential decrees was estimated to have risen by over 30 per cent each year, but fewer than 60 per cent were properly implemented (Polunin 2016). In May 2012, on resuming the presidency, Putin issued eleven 'executive orders' – the so-called May *ukases*. In his Federation Council speech in 2013, Putin complained that

> a year and a half has passed since the executive orders were issued. You know what I'm seeing? Either things are being done in a way that elicits a negative reaction among the public, or nothing is done at all. (Putin 2013b)

Effective implementation of presidential decrees 'depends on the cooperation of other players in the political arena' much more than on the constitutional powers of the president (Remington 2014: 4). A former official describes how even a high-level decision requires an official to go around knocking on doors – it requires what are informally termed 'legs' (*nogi*) – to make sure it is implemented (Anayev 2018: 43).

The response to this crisis of governance in Russia was twofold. First, Putin began issuing fewer presidential decrees after 2014 – only thirty-seven per month in 2014–16, compared with eighty-two a month on average in his first two terms (Anayev 2018: 45). Second, he began to circumvent government and formal institutions and instead revert constantly to exceptional methods. Much of the system had come to rely on a parallel system of governance, known as *ruchnoe upravlenie* (manual control), with officials often working through unofficial 'curators' to ensure effective implementation of decisions. Manual control is a system of 'exceptions from the rules' (Polunin 2016), extended to large parts of the state apparatus, in which executive officials bypass official bureaucratic processes to resolve particular social, political or economic problems in a more expeditious fashion.

Experts on local government note an increasing incidence of cases in which 'individual "subjects of governance" understand the "extraordinary situation" very broadly' and resort to methods of 'manual control' to achieve results (Shlychkov et al. 2016: 42). The result at the local level is 'a crisis of state and social institutions and the deformation of the existing model of Russian local government' (Shlychkov et al. 2016: 44). Nikita Maslennikov, an expert at the Institute of Modern Development, argued that 'the entire current Russian government has become used to working in this regime of "manual control"', and that to achieve any far-reaching change to the system will require a governance revolution (Polunin 2016).

Quick fixes to manage local government problems were only the beginning of this growing domain of exceptionality. The authorities increasingly relied on 'adventurous freelances', as Anayev (2018: 44) dubs them, to implement aspects of foreign and defence policy where the state wished to take a back seat. In foreign and military policy, semi-independent, para-state outfits, ranging from pro-regime oligarchs to paramilitary organisations, took on state functions. Yevgeny Prigozhin, who began his business career as the owner of a floating restaurant in St Petersburg, became a powerful businessman, the owner of the Concord group of catering companies, with close connections with the presidential administration. He established the Internet Research Agency (IRA), a 'trolling factory', which promoted fake social media messages during the 2016 US presidential election.[5] Prigozhin also rapidly expanded into Africa, promoting his political and economic interests in numerous countries, using a mix of private military companies (PMC), political technologists and business deals, primarily in the mining sector.[6] Prigozhin was believed to control the Wagner group, a state-sanctioned PMC (although formally PMCs were illegal in Russia). Wagner was involved in fighting on behalf of the Russian state in Ukraine and Syria, and reportedly was involved in training and other security work in several African countries (Marten 2019).

Other ostensibly non-state actors also operated in these grey zones on behalf of the Russian state. The Night Wolves, a 5,000-strong biker group led by Alexander Zaldostanov (nicknamed *khirurg* – the 'surgeon'), which enjoyed Putin's active patronage, were strong supporters of the Kremlin's agenda. In Ukraine members of the Night Wolves were involved directly in the secession of Crimea and the fighting in Donbas. Zaldostanov also led an anti-liberal anti-Maidan movement, which held pro-government demonstrations in Moscow in 2015 (MK 2015), but he lost government funding in 2017 as domestic policy priorities shifted (Laruelle 2019). There were many other non-state associations and organisations that had close links to parts of the state, but responsibility for their actions often became blurred. Business overlapped with political entrepreneurship in the networks of Konstantin Malofeev, for example, an ultra-conservative Orthodox oligarch, who reportedly funded volunteers in the Donbas rebellion and developed a network of pro-Russian NGOs and activists across the Balkans (Weaver 2014; Laruelle 2016a).

The Dual State

This array of institutions and practices of exceptionality raised the question of how they related to the normal functions and institutions of the state. One of Schmitt's arch-critics, Ernst Fraenkel – a Jewish lawyer who fled Germany in 1938 – attempted to theorise this distinction between norms and exceptions through his concept of a 'dual state' in a groundbreaking analysis of the Nazi regime first published in 1941 (Fraenkel 2017). He argued that the state was divided into two spheres: the first, a political sphere, was not governed by law and was regulated by 'arbitrary measures', forming a 'prerogative' state (*Massnahmenstaat*) (Fraenkel 2017: 3). Alongside the political realm, however, there was a normal sphere, governed by a 'normative state'. In this second domain, everyday life continues largely untouched by the exceptional practices of the prerogative state. 'Normal life is ruled by legal norms', notes Fraenkel, although at the same time exceptions are continually made by the prerogative state (Fraenkel 2017: 57). The result of this division is clear:

> In specifically political realms, power holders may directly apply administrative sanctions or extrajudicial force upon political adversaries, while they allow the rule of law to operate in less conflictive areas, such as the market or the repression of moderate opponents. (Barros 2002: 25)

Fraenkel was highly critical of Schmitt's decisionism and his conceptualisation of the political, which he claimed contributed to the development of a 'National-Socialist counter-state' (Meierhenrich 2018: 166). But Fraenkel follows Schmitt closely in his theory of sovereign power, defined as he who decides whether a case should be treated as a normal or exceptional case: 'whether the decision in an individual case is made in accordance with the law or with "expediency" is entirely in the hands of those in whom the sovereign power is vested' (Fraenkel 2017: 56). In this way, Fraenkel's dual state theory affirms Schmitt's division of the domains of state activity into 'the normal situation' and the 'state of exception'. The difference of course is that Schmitt largely approved of such an authoritarian order – at least in theoretical form – while Fraenkel had to flee for his life from the real-life implementation of the authoritarian dual state.

Several authors have used the dual-state thesis to analyse contemporary Russian politics. Richard Sakwa has used the framework effectively to analyse the functioning of the Putinist state, including in its relationship with Chechnya, the space of exception in the Russian periphery (Sakwa 2010a, 2010b). Sakwa contrasts the 'formal procedures of the constitutional state, together with the political practices of public competition between parties and other representatives of society' and the 'shadowy and opaque structures of the administrative regime, populated by various factions and operating according to the practices of Byzantine court politics and mafia dons' (Sakwa 2013: 70).

Sakwa argued that a 'full-blown' prerogative state did not emerge in Russia (2014a: 63), and that the 'state of exception has not become the norm' but 'coexists with the routine exercise of law' (Sakwa 2014a: 65). For Sakwa, this indicated that Russia remained a 'flawed' democracy 'trapped in the stalemated grey area between an administrative and a genuine constitutional state' (Sakwa 2014a: 66). Outside the state apparatus, however, social forces representing these two state types are 'locked in stalemate' (Sakwa 2014b: 44).

Such an account emphasises a constant tension between the prerogative and normative states, but in Schmitt's theorisation of the same distinction, the relationship between the norm and the exception is not primarily one of opposition. As Agamben argues, Schmitt 'complicate[s] the topographical opposition into a more complex topographical relation' between norms and the exception (Agamben 2005: 23). For Schmitt, alongside the exception, a 'normal' situation must also exist, in which norms and law function according to constitutional and legal codes (Schmitt 1985a: 13):

> Every general norm demands a normal, everyday frame of life to which it can be factually applied and which is subjected to its regulations. The norm requires a homogeneous medium . . . For a legal order to make sense, a normal situation must exist, and he is sovereign who definitely decides whether this normal situation actually exists. (Schmitt 1985a: 13)

In this way, for Schmitt, 'the exception can be *good* for the legal order, for it confirms its existence' (McCormick 1997: 226). According to McCormick, 'Schmitt asserts that the rule, in effect, defines the exception and that the exception, in turn, draws attention to the rule, hence, ostensibly restoring confidence in the importance and primacy of the norm-bound regular situation' (McCormick 1997: 226). Thus the norm and the exception are not necessarily binary oppositions or contradictions, but instead they constitute a particular form of authoritarian political order, in which the sovereign decision about what constitutes the exception and what constitutes the norm is the fundamental fulcrum around which politics revolves. This argument explains why Schmitt repeatedly returns to the importance of the exceptional case:

> The exception can be more important ... than the rule, not because of a romantic irony for the paradox, but because the seriousness of an insight goes deeper than the clear generalizations inferred from what ordinarily repeats itself. The exception is more interesting than the rule. The rule proves nothing; the exception proves everything ... In the exception the power of real life breaks through the crust of a mechanism that has become torpid by repetition. (Schmitt 1985a: 15)

The reality of the political order is not only starkly illuminated by the exception, but is effectively constituted by the distinction between the exception and the norm. The polity needs the exception to survive, in Schmitt's view, but he has no effective response to Fraenkel, who argues that the dual state is unbalanced by definition, with an inbuilt primacy for the political over the 'technical apparatus' of the state (Meierhenrich 2018: 163). This imbalance ultimately threatens to undermine the whole state, as the exception becomes the norm, and the distinction between the two becomes increasingly difficult to police. Since the distinction cannot be codified or institutionalised, but depends on the decision of the sovereign, modes of exceptional governance threaten to overwhelm the capacity of one person to continually make the decision about what constitutes the norm and what can be declared the exceptional case. In this way, sovereign power threatens once again to become dissipated in the state among diverse actors, each of which claims the sovereign right to declare the exception.

Notes

1. On Surkov's biography, see Sakwa (2011).
2. For accounts disputing the Russian narrative, see Applebaum (2014), Clark and Spohr (2015) and Shevtsova (2015).
3. Timothy Snyder argues that *bespredel* characterises Putinism as a system, meaning 'the absence of limits, the ability of a leader to do anything' (Snyder 2018: 81).

But this is an oversimplification – as I argue, Putinism is an order that is characterised by duality, by the presence of both the exception and the norm.
4. See also the translation into Russian by Filippov (2007), and the discussion in Filippov (2008b). Zhikharev et al. (2015) offer a translation and commentary on an Italian version of the text.
5. The IRA was investigated in the Mueller investigation, although this section was heavily redacted. See Mueller (2019: 14–35). See also MacFarquhar (2018).
6. The most detailed investigation of Prigozhin has been the reporting of Ilya Rozhdestvensky and Roman Badanin, 'Shef i povar', *Proekt*, 14 March 2019, and in three subsequent reports.

FOUR

Democracy and the People

> Weakness and muddle-headedness do not amount to democracy.
>
> Vladislav Surkov[1]

Putinism and Democracy

Early twenty-first-century Russia enjoyed all the institutions of modern democracy while gradually developing an increasingly authoritarian political system. This contradictory system suggested to many that Russia was a 'hybrid regime', in which authoritarian and democratic institutions co-existed (Hale 2010; Treisman 2011; Petrov et al. 2014), or an 'electoral authoritarian' regime, in which authoritarian leaders came to power through the ballot box, but governed as authoritarians (Schedler 2006). Yet Russia under Putin was neither a genuinely hybrid system nor a version of electoral authoritarianism, but a regime which combined an important role for popular opinion within a system comprising illiberal and authoritarian practices and institutions. Putinism was an authoritarian political system, which attempted to come to terms with the democratic spirit of the age, by representing the popular majority within the system, not through free elections, but through the assertion of a shared identity between the leader and the people.

Versions of this 'democratic' authoritarianism have become familiar across authoritarian polities, from Hungary's 'illiberal democracy' to China's 'populist authoritarianism' (Tang 2016). Its primary characteristic was the levering apart of 'liberal' and 'democracy', rejecting liberal norms and institutions but retaining an important role for mass popular opinion in a majoritarian form of democracy. Vladislav Surkov had led Russian discussions on this different understanding of democracy through his idea of 'Sovereign Democracy'. Many critics assumed that Surkov's model was a conceptual oxymoron, in which the assertion of sovereignty implied the negation of democracy (Prozorov 2009: 149). However, Surkov's slogan could also be read through Schmitt in a more productive way, defining a democracy not as a system of accountability and constraints on power, but as a 'democratic identity of governed and governing', in Schmitt's phrase (Schmitt 1985c: 14).

In Surkov's later vision of what he terms an 'ideology' of 'Putinism', outlined in a widely read article in 2019, the Russian people and the leader had formed an unmediated form of democracy, largely unconstrained by liberal principles of rule of law or parliamentary process. The people in this system plays a role as a kind of political sediment, which constrains the leader and acts as an inchoate veto-wielder over elite initiatives: the people 'constrains the fantasies of theoreticians, and forces practitioners to take concrete steps' (Surkov 2019). The Putinist system requires a sovereign leader, who is able to tune into the popular mood by listening and responding to the people. The ability 'to hear and understand the people, to see through it, into its depths, and to act accordingly – is the unique and important achievement of the government of Putin', claimed Surkov (2019). Institutions to mediate this relationship, needless to say, are sidelined.

Surkov's ideas of Putinism were met with considerable ridicule, both inside Russia and without. Yet his views, if overblown, reflected an important strand of opinion not only in Russian political thinking, but more widely in global politics, influenced in the first place by highly critical views of Western liberal democracy. For Surkov, liberal democracy in the West had been revealed as little more than a sham, in which the people have only an 'illusion of choice', while real power lies with a 'deep state', which recognised that, at heart, the state is still essentially 'a weapon of defence and attack'. These attacks on liberal democracy were commonplace in Russian political thinking, emanating from a mix of Russia's experience of flawed democracy in the 1990s, the failures of Western democracy-promotion programmes in the post-Cold War period, and the evident challenges faced by Western democracies, particularly after the 2008 financial crash.

These critiques – and Surkov's conceptualisation of Putinism as a form of 'democratic' authoritarianism – had much in common with Schmitt's theory of democracy. In a powerful critique that resonated in post-Soviet Russia, Schmitt argued that parliamentarianism is a sham. The liberal ideal of decisions being reached among independent representatives on the basis of informed parliamentary discussion became a mere 'empty formality', behind which stood 'social and economic power-groups calculating their mutual interests and opportunities for power'. Indeed,

> many norms of contemporary parliamentary law ... function ... like a superfluous decoration, useless and even embarrassing, as though someone had painted the radiator of a modern central heating system with red flames in order to give the appearance of a blazing fire. (Schmitt 1985c: 6)

The voters, meanwhile, were 'won over through a propaganda apparatus whose maximum effect relies on an appeal to immediate interests and passions' (Schmitt 1985c: 6).

Schmitt argues that true democracy and liberalism are incompatible: 'modern mass democracy rests on the confused combination of both' (Schmitt 1985c: 13). Liberal pluralism undermines the state, as already discussed in Chapter 1, and liberal forms of democracy effectively deny the importance of the political, attempting to erase conflicts through debate and compromise, rather than acknowledging and declaring the dividing line between friend and enemy (Scheuerman 1999: 44–5). Instead, Schmitt proposes an identitarian democracy, characterised by a 'series of identities', including the

> identity of governed and governing, sovereign and subject, the identity of the subject and object of state sovereignty, the identity of the people with their representatives in parliament, the identity of the state and the law, and finally an identity of the quantitative (the numerical majority or unanimity) with the qualitative (the justice of the laws). (Schmitt 1985b: 26)

To ensure the possibility of such an overlap of identities between the rulers and the ruled, Schmitt argues for an exclusionary political community that is marked by homogeneity and clear boundaries. Schmitt's assertion in 1926 that 'democracy requires ... homogeneity', and also, 'if the need arises – elimination or eradication of heterogeneity' (Schmitt 1985c: 9), never fails to disturb in the context of subsequent events in 1930s Germany, but – as we will discuss in the Russian case – his theoretical claim does not necessarily rely on ethnic homogeneity, but only on some 'quality of belonging to a people', which 'can be defined by very different elements (ideas of common race, belief, common destiny, and tradition)' (Schmitt 2008a: 258).[2] This leaves 'deliberately open' the definition of 'substantial homogeneity' (Bielefeldt 1998: 27). According to Mouffe, 'what is important for Schmitt is not the nature of the similarity on which homogeneity is based', but the possibility of demarcating clear boundaries of a community (Mouffe 1999: 41). A political community, argues Mouffe, borrowing a term from Derrida, requires a 'permanent "constitutive outside" ... an exterior to the community that makes its existence possible' (Mouffe 1993: 114).

This understanding of democracy opens up challenging ideas, not least that Schmitt's understanding of democracy can be perfectly compatible with dictatorship. Writing in 1926, Schmitt comments that 'Bolshevism and Fascism ... are ... certainly anti-liberal, but not necessarily anti-democratic' (Schmitt 1985c: 16). Indeed, Schmitt argues:

> in the history of democracy there have been numerous dictatorships, Caesarisms, and other more striking forms that have tried to create homogeneity and to shape the will of the people with methods uncommon in the liberal tradition of the past century. (Schmitt 1985c: 16)

Schmitt's argument is designed to make a final break between 'democracy' and 'parliamentarism', and to point to the foundational contradictions between 'liberalism' and 'democracy': 'democracy can exist without what one today calls parliamentarism and parliamentarism without democracy; and dictatorship is just as little the definitive antithesis of democracy as democracy is of dictatorship' (Schmitt 1985b: 32).

Schmitt claims that his understanding of democracy offers a more genuine mode of representation than a one-time vote in a parliamentary election, a representation that is emotive, affective and identity-constructing. 'Representation is not a normative event, a process and a procedure [but] ... something *existential*' (Schmitt 2008a: 243). In his vision, people identify with a sovereign leader in a way that is inconceivable in a liberal democracy. The 'idea of representation', in Schmitt's thinking, is 'completely governed by conceptions of personal authority' (Schmitt 1996: 21). This representation takes place through the mediums of language, ritual and symbolism, all of which are deficient in the technocratic, economistic thinking of liberalism: 'the understanding of every type of representation disappears with the spread of economic thinking', according to Schmitt (1996: 25). In a state reduced to a kind of technocratic machine, 'the personalism inherent in the idea of representation is lost or denied', ensuring that 'the fabrication of the authority of the political order becomes the central problem' (Bhuta 2015: 25).

The key point for Schmitt is that representation is both fundamental to politics, and also cannot be achieved in what he sees as the technocratic, soulless procedural politics of liberal democracy. Even thieves, argues Schmitt, can offer 'justice' or 'social usefulness', but they cannot represent a people as a political unity. A government that truly represents a people is 'something other than the power of a pirate' (Schmitt 2008a: 245).

A genuine government is much more than a technocratic version of Tilly's notion of the state as a formalised system of racketeering and organised crime (Tilly 1985): 'The difference lies in the fact that every genuine government *represents* the political unity of a people, not the people in its natural presence' (Schmitt 2008a: 245).

Schmitt is short on detail on the institutional procedures of such an illiberal democracy. He rejects democratic elections as a reliable calibration of the popular will: 'The method of the secret individual vote . . . is not democratic', he argues, since it only reflects the view of the citizen as a private person, and not of the people as a public entity (Schmitt 2008a: 273). The people is not a collection of individuals, to be represented at a distance through a parliament, but a collective public presence (Schmitt 2008a: 272). Rather than the secret ballot,

> the will of the people can be expressed just as well and perhaps better through acclamation, through something taken for granted, an obvious and unchallenged presence, than through the statistical apparatus that has been constructed with such meticulousness in the last fifty years. (Schmitt 1985c: 16)

In modern democracies, Schmitt concludes, 'public opinion is the modern type of acclamation' (Schmitt 2008a: 275). This is not, however, a carefully quantified calculation of the majority opinion on a particular issue, but something more fundamental and amorphous. On the one hand, Schmitt expects this public opinion to be unofficial, and unorganised, emerging spontaneously and not dictated from above (Rasch 2016: 330–1; Schmitt 2008a: 275). But Schmitt also recognises that 'everything depends on how the will of the people is formed' (Schmitt 1985b: 27). In dictatorships, which nevertheless claim to be representing the people's will, the central question is

> who has control over the means with which the will of the people is to be constructed: military and political force, propaganda, control of public opinion through the press, party organizations, assemblies, popular education, and schools . . . only political power, which should come from the people's will, can form the people's will in the first place. (Schmitt 1985b: 29)

Schmitt's understanding of the role of the people struggles to overcome this contradiction. Public opinion 'arises and exists in an "unorganized" form', but it is also 'influenced and even made by parties or groups' (Schmitt 2008a: 275). There is a danger that 'invisible and irresponsible social powers direct public opinion and the will of the people' (Schmitt 2008a: 275), but Schmitt assumes that a politically conscious nation, which 'can distinguish between friend and enemy', will not be vulnerable to such manipulation (Schmitt 2008a: 275).

The Decline of Parliamentarianism

Schmitt's critique of parliamentary democracy and his promotion of an illiberal alternative has many affinities with the political trajectory of post-Soviet Russia. The State Duma during its second and third convocations (1995–9, 1999–2003) provided ample evidence of Schmitt's claim that parliamentarianism was a sham. A rough price list was published in the media of informal services allegedly offered by parliamentarians: a phone call or a meeting with an official to represent a particular position cost $3,000–4,000; a vote on legislation would be charged at $30,000; and a legislative initiative to amend the law, $50,000 (Denisov 2010: 10).

Powerful oligarchs suborned the Duma in their own interests. John Browne, then head of BP, recalls a conversation during negotiations with the owner of Yukos, Mikhail Khodorkovsky:

> He began to talk about getting people elected to the Duma, about how he could make sure oil companies did not pay much tax, and about how he had many influential people under his control. For me, he seemed too powerful. It is easy to say this with hindsight, but there was something untoward about his approach. (Roxburgh 2013: 76)

According to German Gref, 'not a single draft [bill] went through without Yukos' say-so' (Roxburgh 2013: 76). The government was unable to implement new taxes on extractive industries, because of opposition from oil companies who were able to manipulate and bribe Duma deputies to vote down new legislation (Roxburgh 2013: 75–6). Few oligarchs were genuinely interested in political change. Most supported political parties and candidates purely as lobbyists for their own corporate interests. In short, Russian democracy in the 1990s was widely recognised as dysfunctional, preventing effective decision-making by the executive, and highly corrupted, representing the corporate and political interests of different business groups, oligarchs and corporations.

In response to this dysfunctional democracy, Russian political technologists began exploring new forms of democratic practice, often characterised as 'managed democracy', in which elections retained an element of competition, but skewed rules for registration and campaigning, and rigged voting practices ensured that results were always predictable and favoured the government. The management of elections was achieved through a set of laws and electoral regulations that sharply restricted the formation of new political parties, and favoured the United Russia ruling party (Gelman 2015: 78). At the same time, elected bodies were effectively stripped of their autonomy and of any substantive decision-making powers (Wegren and Konitzer 2007; Krastev and Holmes 2012). The basic pillars of this system of 'managed democracy' were instituted rather swiftly, ensuring that at the Duma elections in December 2003, United Russia won more than 300 of the 450 seats, and the whole process of Russian parliamentarism became a predictable and controlled mechanism for approving legislation, but not for representing interest groups or for debate.

The State Duma itself was transformed from a place of often rambunctious debate into a largely depoliticised organ, where the executive's control was near complete. Duma chair Boris Gryzlov famously argued in December 2003 that parliament 'is not a venue in which it is necessary to hold political battles, to assert political slogans and ideologies' (State Duma 2003). This was still more than just a 'rubber stamp' parliament, since discussions in parliament sometimes reflected intra-elite disputes and struggles between different bureaucratic forces and corporate interests (Noble and Schulmann 2018: 50). But after 2005 parliament's role largely 'disintegrated', according to corporate lobbyists, who decamped from the Duma to target key sectoral ministries, local authorities and the presidential administration, who were responsible for all the key regulatory work and legislative initiatives (Bekbulatova 2018). As a newspaper editorial concluded in 2015, 'deputies were transformed from autonomous politicians, capable of generating and adopting decisions, into an instrument used by other power institutions for the adoption of their own decisions'. Debates about bills 'increasingly took place between ministries or in quiet offices – anywhere except in the intended place for debates in parliament' (Gazeta.ru 2015). Any attempt to mount a genuine challenge to the executive from within the Duma was quickly suppressed. In 2012, when opposition deputy Gennady Gudkov attempted to filibuster a bill that increased punishments for unauthorised demonstrations, he was quickly stripped of his deputy's mandate (Noble and Schulmann 2018: 56).

Marginalising parliament and manipulating elections were necessary first steps in the construction of a managed, illiberal democracy, but were far from sufficient. Schmitt's democratic theory asserted the importance of mechanisms for the articulation of expressions of popular will, and their representation in the political system, primarily through an identity relationship with the political leader. The first step was to define and shape what was meant by 'the people', to assert the boundaries of the political community in ways that would construct a common voice and a common identity. Russia's creative political technologists sought to forge messages and parties that appealed to different constituencies while identifying them closely with Putin's leadership, and also seeking to shape 'the will of the people' through a sophisticated policy of media manipulation and control. In doing so, the regime sought to develop a national unity around three key ideological fulcrums: first, around national identity; second, around shared values; and third, around a common enemy, articulating the fundamental distinction highlighted by Schmitt between friend and enemy.

Constructing a Majority

At the heart of Schmitt's vision of illiberal democracy is the construction of political unity. This should not be understood as the pursuit of a vague consensus within the nation around a lowest common denominator, but as the formation of a popular majority driven by a particular coincidence of identity with a political leadership. Schmitt admits that there are different ways of constructing political unity, including a 'unity from above (through command and power) and unity from below (through the substantive homogeneity of the people' (Schmitt 1999: 201). Schmitt does not accept the clear binary in liberal thought between 'unity by force' and 'unity by consensus', in which only the latter is considered valid (Schmitt 1999: 202). Schmitt instead points out that 'every consensus, even a "free" one, is somehow motivated and brought into existence'. The point to be explored is 'who controls the means of bringing about the "free" consensus of the masses: the economic, educational, psychotechnical means of very different kinds with whose help, as we know from experience, one can achieve a consensus' (Schmitt 1999: 202). If this power to construct a consensus is in private hands, and not the state, then 'everything which officially still gets called "state" is at an end, and political power has become invisible and unaccountable' (Schmitt 1999: 202).

The problem for Russia was how to construct this unity in a state divided by ethnicity, ideology, socio-economic status, regional affiliation and other fractures. Sociologist Natalya Zubarevich famously described four Russias, defined by socio-economic status and geography. Some 30 per cent of the population lived in larger cities – many had middle-class lifestyles and aspirations, were informed about politics, had travelled outside Russia, and used the internet regularly. Life was very different in smaller, industrial towns, home to some 25 per cent of the population, and facing rapid outmigration by younger residents. Nearly 40 per cent of the population, many of them elderly, still lived in rural villages and small settlements distant from the concerns and aspirations of the big cities. Finally, some 6 per cent of the population lived in ethnic republics, distinguished from the rest of Russia by both ethnic and cultural differences and by difficult social and economic conditions (Zubarevich 2011). These diverse socio-economic groups were further divided by generational differences, political views, deep differences on cultural issues, religious and ideological views, and divergent opinions on Russia's relations with the outside world.

Russian Nationalism

Against this fragmented background, official discourse in Putin's Russia stressed the importance of promoting the unity of the people, but faced the challenge of discovering common concerns that united all Russia's citizens. Different answers to the questions 'what is Russia?' and 'what does it mean to be "Russian"?' have historically played a central role in political discourse in Russia, but took on existential importance in the post-Soviet period. The collapse of Marxist-Leninist ideology, the indeterminacy of Russia's new post-imperial statehood, and Russia's uncertain status in international affairs all contributed to what Viatcheslav Morozov called 'a situation of utter indeterminacy' in Russia, with 'the old structures of meaning swept away by the revolutionary change, and the urgent need to define the very foundations of political community' (Morozov 2008: 158).

The most obvious basis for constructing a homogeneous political community was nationalism, but Russian nationalism itself was a fractured and contradictory project. Geoffrey Hosking argued that the history of the Russian empire impeded the development of a Russian national consciousness, with empire and nation locked in a complex and often contradictory relationship (Hosking 1997: xix–xi). The Tsarist regime was long distrustful of the idea of nation, viewing it as implying popular representation, in the spirit of the French revolution (Pain 2016); in partial contradiction to such an ethnocentric concept, the Russian empire had always been extremely effective at absorbing and assimilating non-Russians into its ruling imperial elite. The Soviet system did nothing to resolve this dilemma of Russian national identity, offering instead a supra-national Soviet identity, which at times overlapped with Russian imperial sensibilities, but was also constrained by an internationalist and integrative element. The collapse of the USSR forced Russians to re-examine the boundaries and basis of their national community, a search for identity made more difficult by the truncated nature of the post-imperial state, which left millions of ethnic Russians outside the boundaries of the new Russian Federation.

In the 1990s constructivist scholars such as Valery Tishkov believed that a new Russian nation could be constructed within the frontiers of the new Russian state, based on a 'civic nationalism' to create a *'rossiiskii'* nation, uniting all the citizens of the Russian Federation without regard to ethnicity (Kolstø 2016c: 32–3). But most people viewed *rossiiskii* as primarily an official identity category related to citizenship, and for some it was a concept associated with the failed attempts to construct a democratic political community in the 1990s (Kolstø 2016a: 3). By contrast, nationalist strands of opinion only recognised the ethno-nationalist identity of *'russkii'*, but this school of thought was also sharply divided. Historian Elena Galkina divides nationalists into 'national patriots', with a more xenophobic, authoritarian stance, and so-called 'national democrats', whose ethnic nationalism also included a repudiation of the Soviet and imperial past (Pain 2016: 56). Laruelle has an expanded typology, identifying three concrete groups: the National Bolsheviks of Eduard Limonov, influenced by leftist and anarchist thought; an array of neo-Nazi and skinhead groups, often involved in racist violence; and the national democrat movement, which pursued a right-wing politics akin to European right-wing populist parties. The important point is that far from nationalism acting as a uniting factor, all these groups were virulently opposed to the regime and to each other (Laruelle 2017c).

The most important divide, however, was between ethnic nationalists, who saw themselves as fighting on behalf of the Russian people, and *gosudarstvenniki* (statists), who sought to uphold the supremacy of the Russian state. Kolstø argues that ethnic nationalists and 'statist' or 'imperialist' nationalists, 'distrust, even hate, each other', as they pursue very different political ends (Kolstø 2016a: 1). Statists such as Putin and the presidential administration were wary of ethnic nationalism as a source of legitimacy, understanding its potential for division within a multinational state (where 21 per cent of the population were non-Russians in 2010), but also conscious of its mobilisational power. Hence the complex relationship with Russian ethnic nationalism demonstrated by the Putinist regime in the aftermath of the Ukraine crisis of 2014. On the one hand, Putin appealed to ethnic nationalism in speeches about Crimea, and official discourse repeatedly emphasised Russia's commitment to defend ethnic Russians inside Ukraine. On the other hand, Moscow quickly abandoned the Novorossiya project, the dream of a Russian imperialist adventure that aimed to consolidate the whole of southern and eastern Ukraine under Russian control (Laruelle 2016a). And the Russian authorities clamped down on far-right nationalist groups inside Russia after 2014, concerned about their growing activism following the Ukraine events (Petkova 2017). The Kremlin was willing to use radical nationalist groups when necessary for its own agenda, but was always careful to prevent them developing any mass following that might threaten political stability.

In response, Russian nationalists once again moved in opposition to Putin, condemning his reluctance to embrace their radical, neo-imperialist vision (Kolstø 2016b). Alexander Dugin, an advocate of Russian conquest in Ukraine, argued that:

> In the spring [of 2014] he [Putin] acted freely, in the interests of the state, from the point of view of observing moral laws, saving people from genocide. Now he is bound hand and foot, hobbled by those who are called the sixth column inside Russia, who in more and more obvious ways are emerging as a part, a segment of the Atlantic, American network, acting in the interests of a global financial oligarchy. (Dugin 2014d)

These divisions, paradoxically, are on display every year on the 4 November 'Day of National Unity' holiday. As noted in Chapter 1, the struggles around this official holiday demonstrate many of the key tensions around Russian political identity. The official version of the holiday asserts three basic principles of unity: first, unity emerges from a struggle with the external enemy (the day celebrates the expulsion of Polish forces from Moscow in November 1612); second, the different social origins of the leaders of the revolt – the butcher Kuzma Minin and Prince Dmitry Pozharsky – offered a useful myth of national unity in place of the deep social divisions that had been at the heart of the October Revolution; third, the official celebrations were inclusive of non-Russian cultures and religions.

During the 2016 event, for example, President Putin, along with the patriarch of the Russian Orthodox Church, laid flowers on the statue of Minin and Pozharsky on Red Square, immediately followed by representatives of other traditional religions, Buddhist, Muslim and Jewish. The ritual offered a vision of unity in which other approved religions were represented, although Orthodoxy had the leading role, while unrecognised minority religions were absent. This is neither a truly civic identity – in which all are equal, and enjoy equal rights of representation – nor is it a narrow ethnicised form of unity, which excludes different ethnic groups or religions. It is rather a conservative, hierarchical relationship, which respects the cultural and religious diversity of non-Russian groups, but does not afford them law-based rights as ethnic minorities in the liberal sense.

By contrast, alternative, ethnic and xenophobic visions of Russian nationalism were also visible on the same day elsewhere in Moscow. The

4 November holiday had also become the occasion for mass nationalist rallies, under the banner of the 'Russian March', which united ethnic nationalists and far-right activists. The Russian March united people who despised the *'rossiiskii'* identity and official versions of Russian-ness, and instead argued against immigration from Central Asia and the Caucasus as 'diluting' the homogeneity of the Russian nation. In 2016 the marches were much smaller than in the early 2010s, when tens of thousands attended these rallies, and the marches were split among different groups, including far-right and neo-Nazi groups, Orthodox traditionalists and fundamentalists, and pro-Kremlin radical groups such as the Night Wolves (Sova 2016).

This internal division – between a narrow Russian identity and a more inclusive official identity – was compounded by Russia's 'spatial crisis'. A concept of Russia as a 'divided nation' highlighted the fate of the 25 million ethnic Russians who were left outside the Russian Federation after the collapse of the USSR. This discourse emphasised the divide between Russia's 'cultural body' of members of the Russian nation, and the 'territorial body' that is coterminous with the borders of the Russian Federation (Laruelle 2015a). Attempts to resolve this spatial challenge produced further divisions among nationalists, between rival conceptualisations of the space around Russia, particularly between the idea of 'Greater Russia' as an ethnically defined community overspilling its boundaries to take in neighbouring areas of ethnic Russian population and a less ethnocentric vision of 'Eurasia' that centred on Russian hegemony, but also emphasised historical and cultural continuities across a wider geographical space. I explore these spatial projects in more detail in Chapter 8, but divides in the nationalist community over the geographic extent of the Russian 'body politic' again pointed to the difficulty of relying solely on nationalist ideology as the basis for a united and bounded political community.

A Majority of Values

From the early days of his political career, Putin claimed to be a democratic politician, representing a majority of the population. In one of his first articles in 1999 Putin repeatedly referenced the importance of 'the majority' in his thinking: he laid out a set of ideas and goals that would be attractive 'for the overwhelming majority of Russians'. The 'overwhelming majority of Russians rejected radicalism, extremism and revolutionary opposition'; the 'majority of Russians', he argued, associated improvements in living standards with a paternalistic state, not with individual entrepreneurship. They were patriotic, but not in favour of an exclusive nationalism: for 'a majority of Russians' the idea of 'patriotism', which Putin claimed had come to be treated with irony in some quarters, 'has retained its original, completely positive meaning' (Putin 1999).

In Putin's speeches and electoral campaigns, he developed a certain populist appeal, in which a self-proclaimed 'outsider' to the establishment claimed to represent the views of the majority of Russians against a small elite minority of oligarchs and liberals, an undemocratic group who had almost destroyed the Russian state. The population came to be divided rhetorically into *nashi* (our people) and *chuzhye* (alien), in a discursive construct where *nashi* constituted a clear majority of the population. This majoritarian vision was partially constructed through Putin's various stunts in his early election campaigns. Hill and Gaddy argue that

> Putin's various performance pieces as a biker, an outdoorsman, a fireman, and his meetings with workers on factory floors or in factory monotowns simultaneously embrace different Russian groups and social classes as *nashi* and appeal directly to them for political support. (Hill and Gaddy 2015: 174)

After Putin's first term, the discourse shifted towards constructing the 'overwhelming majority' (*podavlyayushchee bol'shinstvo*) of the population as an ideological construct, often created on the basis of shared values and – in subsequent years – on a collective recognition of the image of the enemy. This discursive shift can be traced through what Pennycook calls the 'politics of pronouns', the way in which collective political identities are constructed through the use of 'we' and 'they' in public discourse (Pennycook 1994). As Yulia Galyamina has shown, Putin's conceptualisation of 'we' and 'they' in official speeches gradually evolved: in early speeches, 'we' represented primarily the collective government, but in later periods he increasingly constructed the all-encompassing 'we' of the majority, while 'they' is already identified as the external enemy, complemented by an internal 'fifth column' (Galyamina 2016).

This way of thinking about the politics of the majority was always more than just a clever electoral strategy – the attempt to conceptualise 'the majority' had been an important theme in conservative thought in the 2000s (Remizov 2010; Polyakov 2014). Mikhail Remizov, for example, wrote in 2010 that

> the main shortcoming of the [Russian political] system is not in the infringement of [the rights of] minorities, but infringement of the [rights of the] majority. And if we do not see that infringement, then that is only because we became used to it long ago. (Remizov 2010)

Remizov traces this minority–majority division to the 1990s, when a 'reformist minority' was intent on 'reforming' a majority of the population, who were perceived as resistant to democracy and market economics (Remizov 2010). The Russian political system was designed to achieve the *containment* of the majority, not its *representation*, argued Remizov. Although Russia had a dominant, majority party – United Russia – which received a majority of votes, the party did not form the government or even have any influence on government policy, complained another influential conservative Boris Mezhuev (Mezhuev et al. 2010). Remizov echoed a widespread slogan of the new conservatism globally – that the political majority had lost its subjectivity in politics, which became dominated by liberal and technocratic elites, most starkly in the case of the European Union (Remizov 2011). Conservatives viewed this form of liberal, elitist, technocratic modernisation as undemocratic, and sought to counter it, not only through the ballot box, but also by seeking a 'hegemony of the majority' – in a Gramscian sense – in which a formal democratic majority in formal institutions would also be accompanied by a hegemony of values and ideas in society (Remizov 2011; Polyakov 2014).

This majoritarian understanding of values was increasingly recognised, even by legal scholars, who might be thought to be resistant to such trends. According to the chairman of the Russian Constitutional Court, Valery Zorkin:

> In each society there is a majority that is the bearer of general moral values and rules which secure peace and stability in that society, ... so that every effective legal normativity should take into account the values and rules of the majority. (Cited in Antonov 2017: 183)

Zorkin claims that in the West it had been argued that 'the defence of the rights of minorities should become the basic function of legal institutions'. Consequently, European legal systems had begun defending minorities, which 'the social majority consider communities of "damaged morals", ... particularly sexual minorities'. Zorkin argues that 'the European social majority, which has preserved traditional values and moral-ethical orientations, rooted in Christian culture' will view such 'legal innovations' as 'catastrophic symptoms' of a moral breakdown at the level of the state (Zorkin 2015).

This majority was already being constructed along 'moral' lines in the 2000s, when issues such as LGBT rights became an important source of political mobilisation. In May 2006 pro-government groups beat up many LGBT activists who attempted to hold a gay pride parade in Moscow, prompting the nationalist writer Kholmogorov to write that that the 'whole "anti-gay" campaign [represents] a completely organised action to form in Russia a socially active "moral majority"' (Kholmogorov 2006b). Kholmogorov – like other conservatives – strongly supported this campaign, claiming that 'the struggle for a moral majority is an inseparable part of the struggle for a national majority' (Kholmogorov 2006b). Despite being a majority, this moral crusade cannot manage without violence and coercion. Kholmogorov argues that the appearance of a 'civil guard' on the streets – a motley collection of Cossack militias and Orthodox militants – 'allowed the silent majority to raise their voice at last' (Kholmogorov 2006b).

Gay rights became a particularly powerful issue for drawing dividing lines between majority and minority, between the major cities and the rest of the country, between liberals and conservatives, and between pro-Western and nationalist forces (Wilkinson 2014). In 2013 a new law prohibited 'propaganda of non-traditional sexual relations to minors', prompting criticism from Western politicians, celebrities and activists; it was accompanied by reports of increased violence and discrimination against gay people in Russia (HRW 2018). Wilkinson characterises these moves as part of a wider campaign for 'moral sovereignty', in which 'human rights are contingent on the observation, especially in public spaces, of local traditional values, which are seen to represent the values of the majority' (Wilkinson 2014: 366). This majoritarian conceptualisation of values was articulated most clearly by Putin in a speech at the Valdai Club in September 2013 when he criticised 'excesses of political correctness' in the West, which he claimed opened 'a direct path to degradation and primitivism'. Putin argued that while 'one must respect every minority's right to be different', nevertheless 'the rights of the majority must not be put into question' (Putin 2013a).

The political utility of the LGBT agenda for the formation of an active political majority based on a belief in traditional values was augmented by claims that LGBT campaigns inside Russia were linked to Western information campaigns against Russia and therefore were an instrument in a wider geopolitical competition (Foxall 2017). In a poll in 2018, 63 per cent of respondents expressed a belief that there is 'an organization which tries to destroy the moral values of Russians through the propaganda on non-traditional sexual relationships' (VTsIOM 2018). One activist, Sergei Alekseenko, who was convicted in January 2016 of violating the 2013 'gay propaganda' legislation, claimed that the targeting of the LGBT community was about creating enemies:

> To rally the people, it is necessary to create internal and external enemies: the external enemy is the United States and the internal one is the LGBT community. [They say that] LGBT activists are paedophiles or U.S. and European agents ... [B]laming the Americans and gays – it's a method of diverting people from the real issues. (Sheerin 2017)

As Gulnaz Sharafutdinova has argued, the idea of the 'moral majority' was further activated by the prosecution and trial of the Pussy Riot punk rock group in August 2012, when its members were convicted of 'hooliganism motivated by religious hatred', after they played a protest song in a church. Sharafutdinova argues that 'Putin appealed to this "overwhelming majority" in his speeches, positioning himself as the person who expresses and follows the wishes of that majority' (Sharafutdinova 2014: 617). Sergei Markov, a conservative commentator, argued that Pussy Riot highlighted a dividing line in society between 'an active minority, associated with capital cities, the middle class and cosmopolitanism' and a 'silent moral majority', a term that Markov borrows from the New Christian Right in America (Markov 2012). Markov argues that the silent moral majority views the Pussy Riot affair in a very different way from liberals. For the majority, Pussy Riot represents

> a strategic campaign to defile values that are sacred for the Russian people. The final goal of this campaign is the liquidation of the Russian people as a subject of world history. Of course, we are not speaking about physical liquidation but about depriving the Russian people of political subjectivity and civilisational identity ... [the people] demand that the authorities defend the sacred objects of the Russian people from abuse. This tongue-less Russia asks Putin 'Are you Russian, Orthodox? Do you have strength and power? Then defend that which is dear to us.' This is more of an existential demand than a political demand to Putin. (Markov 2012)

Markov floats the idea that Pussy Riot is 'not the stupidity of some girls', but 'part of a global conspiracy against Russia and the ROC [Russian Orthodox Church]'. If this is part of a wider conspiracy, then 'Putin is obliged not only to punish the three little idiots like a father, but to defend Russia from this conspiracy as strictly as possible' (Markov 2012). In Markov's construction, all the elements of Schmittian politics are present – the apparently voiceless majority, which finds its voice and agency only through the sovereign leader; the internal enemy, always closely linked to an external threat; and an existential fear of a loss of identity and subjectivity at the hands of the enemy, the West.

This construction of a moral majority was always articulated as a defence of democracy against the minority position of advocates of liberal values. At his Annual Address to the Federal Assembly in December 2013 Putin argued that advocacy of conservative values represented a democratic response to an unaccountable global liberalism. He argued that the

> destruction of traditional values from above not only leads to negative consequences for society, but is also in essence anti-democratic, since it is carried out on the basis of abstract, speculative ideas, against the will of the popular majority, which does not accept the changes occurring or the proposed revision. (Putin 2013b)

Putin goes on to claim that Russia's anti-liberal position has global support: 'We know that more and more people in the world support our position on defending traditional values, which for thousands of years have formed the spiritual and moral foundation of civilisation, of every people' (Putin 2013b). As Neil Robinson argues, this produces a particular vision of democracy, in which far from rejecting democracy, Putin claims to be 'its truest representative', who is

> articulating a truly populist position that is more in tune with societal aspirations than anything that can be uncovered through an electoral system, especially where elections, such as to parliaments, are designed to secure representation of sectional interests, that is, fractions of the people that destroy representation of the majority.

Putin's vision of democracy, claims Robinson, ensures that he represents the majority, which supports traditional values, and in this way he 'sets his version of democracy against the forms of democracy that are most common in Europe' (Robinson 2017: 361).

This 'democratic' underpinning to the conservative values agenda is an important element of its success. But this should not be understood as a campaign that emerged 'from below', driven primarily by popular opinion. The conservative values agenda had its genuine supporters and ideologues, particularly in the Russian Orthodox Church, and it had some popular resonance, but it was instrumentalised and controlled by the presidential administration and its ideological allies. Deputies in the State Duma promoted a new conservative turn in legislation, but many of these bills were drafted by executive bodies, including the presidential administration and the Security Council (Noble and Schulmann 2018: 65). The formation of a sense of political unity around moral values had its roots in genuine social attitudes and worldviews held by many Russian citizens, but these were moulded and shaped by the active use of the media, education and political initiatives. A sense of unity was deliberately forged through division and exclusion, in ways that not only created – at least temporarily – a new political majority in Russian society, but also identified its enemies.

This mode of discursive division spilled over into the political sphere during Putin's controversial re-election campaign in 2012. In a typical pre-election address in 2012 Putin attempted to align himself again with a popular majority, claiming '[t]he broad support of the overwhelming majority of citizens', which 'assisted in the struggle against terrorism, the restoration of territorial integrity of the country, . . . in overcoming the consequences of the global economic crisis'. In short, he concluded, 'everything we have done, we have done together' (Putin 2012c). But Putin was speaking in the aftermath of huge anti-government demonstrations in Moscow in December 2011, protesting against State Duma elections on 4 December, which were marked by widespread fraud. The mood had already soured after Putin and Medvedev's cynical announcement on 24 September 2011 that not only would Putin run again for president in 2012, but that they had planned this deliberate swap in roles, or *rokirovka* (referring to the castling move in chess), all along. Protests were held in Moscow on 6 December, after the elections, and quickly gathered numbers, with more than 50,000 attending a demonstration on 10 December, and some 100,000 later in the month (Greene 2014: 202–18).

Putin's immediate response as prime minister on 8 December was to blame foreign interference, claiming that US Secretary of State Hillary Clinton 'set the tone for some figures inside the country and gave a signal. They heard this signal and with the support of the US State Department began active work' (RIA-Novosti 2011b). His intervention reiterated the now familiar division in society between the 'overwhelming majority' and a minority of foreign-funded activists. He told leaders of the All-Russia People's Front: 'We and you are all adults, we all understand that some of the organisers are acting according to a well-known scenario, that they are pursuing narrowly mercenary political goals.' He called on an 'overwhelming majority of our citizens' to avoid chaos 'as in Kirgiziya and Ukraine' (RIA-Novosti 2011b).

As the protests developed, the government line hardened, cementing the dividing line between the 'adults', who form the 'overwhelming majority', who do not 'want chaos', and the protesters who are backed by foreign powers. By the time of mass arrests of demonstrators in Bolotnaya Square in Moscow in May 2012, those arrested – the 'Bolotnaya' protesters – were presented in official media as pawns of the West, but also as liberal, urban elites who had no respect for 'the people'. A typical headline in the pro-government press ran: 'Bolotnaya regard the people as cattle, slaves and shit' (Politonline.ru 2012). Following a protest organised by Alexei Navalny in 2017, conservative commentator Vladimir Solovyov claimed that the thousands of demonstrators represented only 2 per cent of the people out in central Moscow that day, yet this 'shitty 2 per cent think that they have the right to explain something to somebody in Moscow'. The protesters, he explained, were not against Sobyanin (mayor of Moscow) or Putin, but 'they went out against the people, against people with children!'. If it weren't for the police, he went on, 'the people would have torn these scum apart' (VestiFM 2017). In this way the regime constructed anti-government protesters as an undemocratic minority, who were against the people, and were – wittingly or not – on the side of the enemy.

Notes

1. Surkov (2008): 19.
2. It is worth noting, however, that Schmitt's writings in the first years of Nazi rule demonstrated little of this earlier ambivalence about the nature of identity. In 1933 he characterised Hitler's rule as reflecting an 'absolute species identity between leader and followers'. 'Only this species identity', claims Schmitt, 'prevents the Leader's power from becoming arbitrary or tyrannical' (Agamben 2016: 465–6). Thus the requirement for social homogeneity at the heart of Schmitt's democracy too easily passes into exclusionary racism, or what he terms 'the existential bond' formed by belonging to 'a species and a race' (Mehring 2014: 313).

FIVE

Defining the Enemy

> The friend, enemy, and combat concepts receive their real meaning precisely because they refer to the real possibility of physical killings.
>
> Carl Schmitt (2007a: 33)

Schmitt argues that political communities are not formed by the state, through legal citizenship, nor are they necessarily formed by ethnic belonging. Instead, they are shaped and moulded by a simple binary, the identification of a distinction between 'friend' and 'enemy'. This distinction, argues Schmitt, is the very essence, the defining feature of 'the political'. In Schmitt's famous aphorism: 'The specific political distinction to which political actions and motives can be reduced is that between friend and enemy' (Schmitt 2007a: 26). Liberal democratic states – always Schmitt's main political target for critique – have either forgotten or deliberately disguised their political origins, and live in denial of the violence of the foundational friend/enemy decision. But Schmitt repeatedly asserts that at the base of any political entity this distinction still exists, creating defining boundaries around the political community.

When defining the enemy, Schmitt does not have in mind any kind of personal enmity, nor is the enemy defined by any sense of moral or aesthetic judgement. The 'political enemy' is 'the other, the stranger; [. . .] he is, in a specially intense way, existentially something different and alien, so that in the extreme case conflicts with him are possible' (Schmitt 2007a: 27). The enemy is a public enemy (*hostis*), a concept derived from Roman law, which distinguishes adversaries against whom the polity can declare war from mere criminals, thieves and brigands (Schmitt 2003: 51). The public enemy is distinguished from the personal enemy – in Latin, the *inimicus*; the enemy is the entity that poses a potential existential threat to the state, not simply an unpopular or despised group or individual. Although war is not necessarily desirable or advisable, the enemy is always defined by the possibility that war might be declared. Schmitt argues: 'The friend, enemy, and combat concepts receive their real meaning precisely because they refer to the real possibility of physical killings. War follows from enmity. War is the existential negation of the enemy' (Schmitt 2007a: 33).

But how can a people decide on the identity of the existential enemy? Schmitt explains:

> Only the actual participants can correctly recognize, understand, and judge the concrete situation and settle the extreme case of conflict. Each participant is in a position to judge whether the adversary intends to negate his opponent's way of life and therefore must be repulsed or fought in order to preserve one's own form of existence. (Schmitt 2007a: 27)

Schmitt's main point here is to argue that the judgement about the identity of the enemy 'can neither be decided by a previously determined general norm nor by the judgement of a disinterested and therefore neutral third party' (Schmitt 2007a: 27). In practice, the political entity that makes the decision is the state: 'in its entirety the state as an organized political entity decides for itself the friend-enemy distinction' (Schmitt 2007a: 27). The state can declare the enemy and also mobilize forces to fight him: 'to the state as an essentially political entity belongs the *jus belli* i.e. the real possibility of deciding in a concrete situation upon the enemy and the ability to fight him with the power emanating from the entity' (Schmitt 2007a: 45).

Schmitt's second key point is that there is no way to escape the friend/enemy distinction. A liberal worldview that relies on friendship and cooperation is an illusory utopia. 'It would be ludicrous', writes Schmitt, 'to believe that a defenceless people has nothing but friends, and it would be a deranged calculation to suppose that the enemy could perhaps be touched by the absence of a resistance' (Schmitt 2007a: 53). Defining the enemy is an existential decision, which cannot be evaded through liberal ideas or pacifist programmes:

> a people [cannot] hope to bring about a purely moral or purely economic condition of humanity by evading every political decision. If a people no longer possesses the energy or the will to maintain itself in the sphere of politics, the latter will not thereby vanish from the world. Only a weak people will disappear. (Schmitt 2007a: 53)

The friend/enemy distinction thereby takes on an existential meaning. There is no possibility to abolish the political and replace it with a depoliticised, technocratic, economic order. Schmitt argues:

> If a people is afraid of the trials and risks implied by existing in the sphere of politics, then another people will appear which will assume these trials by protecting it against foreign enemies and thereby taking over political rule. (Schmitt 2007a: 52)

This existential nature of the political – the existence or not of the Russian nation – is a common trope in conservative discourse in Russia. This binary produced by a clear definition of friends and enemies provides every political move with a more profound meaning, and simultaneously ensures an attractive simplicity to political analysis and strategic decision-making. As Bauman explains:

> The friends/enemies opposition ... makes the world readable and thereby instructive. It dispels doubt. It enables one to go on. It assures that one goes where one should. It makes the choice look like nature-made necessity – so that man-made necessity may be immune to the vagaries of choice. (Bauman 1991: 144)

Finally, the enemy discourse defines the Self, seemingly providing a long-sought answer to the question of Russian national identity. 'The enemy is our own question as form [*Gestalt*]', writes Schmitt (2007c: 85, n 89), or more plainly, 'tell me who your enemy is and I will tell you who you are' (Schmitt 1991: 243).

Russia and Its Enemies

This requirement for the recognition of an enemy in post-Soviet Russia had long been articulated by radical conservatives. Discussing his teaching at the military academy in the 1990s, Alexander Dugin said of the officers that 'they were utterly lost, they had no concept of the enemy; they needed to know who the enemy was' (Clover 2016: 202). No doubt inspired by his readings of Schmitt, Dugin had the answer, which found a ready audience among Russia's confused generals:

> Imagine the shock they were feeling: they had always been told the US is our enemy. Suddenly, some democrats come to power and say, no, the US is our friend ... They were all confused ... And nobody offers them

anything. And I come to them and say, 'America is our enemy, we must aim our missiles at them', and they say, 'Yes that is correct'. And I explained why. (Clover 2016: 205)

Dugin was not alone in wanting to label the West as Russia's existential enemy. Russia's historically complex relationship with the West (Tsygankov 2006, 2007; Stent 2007; Neumann 2016) was fuelled during the 1990s by widely circulated conspiracy theories, claiming the West was intent on destroying the Russian state. Many of these were derived from a 'meta-narrative', labelled the 'Dulles Plan', a text supposedly authored by CIA Director Allen Dulles in the late 1940s, which describes a plan to break up the Soviet Union by undermining traditional values, and by encouraging immorality, corruption and inter-ethnic strife. The text is evidently a forgery, but its alleged content has been endlessly reproduced by nationalist writers, and referenced by – among others – Vladimir Zhirinovsky, presidential aide Sergei Glazyev, and nationalist film director, Nikita Mikhalkov (Plotnikova and Coalson 2016).[1]

The 'Dulles Plan' as published by Russian nationalists threatens to 'sow chaos in Russia', and to achieve 'the demise of the last unbroken nation on Earth, the final, irrevocable extinguishment of her national self-consciousness'. The plan would 'imperceptibly replace their [Russian] values with false ones', using a fifth column, 'our accomplices, helpers and allies in Russia herself'. These Western-influenced individuals will ensure that 'literature, the theatre and the cinema will all proclaim the basest of human feelings', and will 'hammer into the people's consciousness the cult of sex, violence, sadism and betrayal, in a word, immorality'. Alongside this campaign to undermine social values, the Dulles Plan would 'create chaos and confusion in the workings of the government', by encouraging 'bureaucratic stupidity and bribe-taking' and promoting 'indecency, betrayal, nationalism and strife between ethnic groups, and above all hatred for the Russian ethnos'. As is notable in many conspiracy theories, only a chosen few would be able to identify this process:

only the few, the very few, will guess or understand what's happening. But we'll put such people in a helpless situation, turn them into objects of ridicule. We'll find a way to slander them and declare them the dregs of society.[2]

The attraction of the Dulles Plan as a conspiracy theory is that it accurately describes the social, political and moral crisis of post-Soviet Russia, but relocates the causes of the crisis outside the boundaries of Russia, and clearly identifies the enemy behind the plot. It explains the political and geopolitical relevance of the 'assault' on traditional values, and thus combines the force of moral conservatism with geopolitical counter-hegemony. Moreover, as Julie Fedor notes, it also provides a convincing retelling of the Cold War, which reascribes moral superiority to a vanquished Russia, undermined by a dastardly, immoral plot conducted by Western intelligence services (Fedor 2011: 848).

These ideas remained marginal in the 1990s. Even in the early 2000s, officials portrayed the West not as an existential enemy, but as an economic competitor in a race that Russia seemed destined to lose. In June 2005 Vladislav Surkov told *Der Spiegel* magazine, with a tone of regret: 'we have understood that we are surrounded not by enemies but by competitors' (Sborov 2005). In another interview, he explained further:

> They are not enemies, but merely competitors. This makes it harder. When it's an enemy you can die heroically in battle, if you go head to head. There is something heroic and wonderful in that. But to lose in just a competitive race, that just means you're a loser. (Sborov 2005)

In the decade after 2005, the construction of the West in public discourse as an existential enemy gradually moved from the margins to the mainstream of Russian political discourse (March 2012). The identification of the United States as an existential threat to Russia was most clearly articulated in Putin's February 2007 Munich speech, reflecting Russian concerns about US withdrawal from the Anti-Ballistic Missile Treaty in 2002, the US military intervention in Iraq in 2003, the popular uprisings of the 'colour revolutions', and the accession of seven Central and Eastern European countries to NATO in 2004. These moves contributed to a personal sense of betrayal expressed by Putin, who had taken a pro-Western stance for much of his first term, particularly after the terrorist attacks in the United States in September 2001. Although Dmitry Medvedev's presidency was punctuated by attempts to improve relations with the West – including a so-called 'Reset' with the United States – progress was undermined by the Russian intervention in Georgia in 2008, the war in Libya, and the wider upheavals of the Arab Spring, in 2011–12.

Nothing Putin had seen during Medvedev's tenure as president convinced him that the West could be trusted. On the contrary, he returned to the presidency in 2012, trailing a 'wagon train of resentments, disappointments and recriminations' (Sakwa 2017: 107), with a clear willingness to 'declare the enemy'. The United States was now identified as the main opponent of Russia in the new Military Doctrine (December 2014), in an updated Security Strategy (December 2015) and in a new Foreign Policy concept (November 2016). The 2015 National Security Strategy, for example, argued that the 'build-up of the military potential' of NATO 'and the approach of its military infrastructure towards Russian frontiers create a threat to national security'. According to Article 12 of the Strategy, on a global scale,

> Russia's independent foreign and domestic policy has been met with counteraction by the US and its allies, seeking to maintain dominance in world affairs. Their policy of containment of Russia envisions the use of political, economic, military and information pressure. (Russian Federation 2015)

Hawkish officials espoused more extreme forms of anti-Americanism, which often overlapped with the conspiratorial views that circulated among nationalist and radical conservative networks. Mikhail Zygar claims that Nikolai Patrushev, the former head of the FSB, who was appointed Secretary of the Security Council in 2008, was the 'nerve center of most of Putin's special operations', including Crimea, and also one of the strongest proponents of an anti-American worldview (Zygar 2016: 342). Patrushev argued that the West was using the Ukrainian crisis as a means to achieve regime change in Russia and to 'dismember' Russia. He regularly referenced former US Secretary of State Madeleine Albright as the author of an apocryphal quotation that Russia has control of 'too much territory' and too many natural resources (Yegorov 2015). In 2017 Patrushev argued that the 'consolidated efforts of the West' were aimed at undermining 'integration processes, in which our country is involved, to devalue the idea of the "Russian World" in its entirety, threatening the security not only of Russia but of a whole range of states' (Yegorov 2017).

Constructing the Enemy Discourse

At the height of the wave of concern in Moscow about 'colour revolutions' in 2005–6, the Kremlin's strategists, led by Gleb Pavlovsky, began using the media more actively to promote a new counter-revolutionary politics, in which a constant theme was that the West now constituted Russia's enemy. The new television programmes used innovative forms and genres and high production values, but produced content that centred on the active cultivation of an enemy discourse. Talk shows such as *Real'naya politika* (Real Politics) articulated anti-Western political ideas in a highly partisan, but engaging way (Horvath 2011: 21). There was a new flow of state funding for films and television programmes devoted to the construction of the West as the enemy, such as a 2005 film entitled *Men's Season: Velvet Revolution*, which pitted Russian state security agents against a thinly disguised 'George Soros', who was attempting to plot a revolution in Russia (Horvath 2011: 21). A series of documentaries, such as *Barkhat.ru* (2007) by Arkady Mamontov, argued that Western intelligence agencies were plotting regime change in Russia as the latest in the chain of colour revolutions after Serbia, Georgia, Ukraine and Kyrgyzstan (Sakwa 2010b: 237). Similar 'patriotic' films were produced every year, on topics ranging from Syria to the work of Belarusian border guards, and many were shown at an annual Eurasia Film Festival (see www.eurasia.film). After 2012, the focus of this propaganda effort switched to prime-time television programmes such as Dmitry Kiselev's *Vesti nedeli* (News of the Week) or Vladimir Solovyov's talk shows, such as *Vecher s Vladimirom Solovyovym* (An Evening with Vladimir Solovyov) or *Kto protiv?* (Who Is Against?). These shows had prime-time slots on the main television channels, offering master-classes in anti-Western propaganda and also acting as a form of ideological steer for officials and other media professionals (MK 2019).

By the mid-2010s, much of the propaganda campaign was already moving to the Internet, to social media sites, and to video platforms, such as YouTube. The Internet became an arena of state and para-state activity, including the operations of so-called 'troll factories', which operated both internationally and domestically to influence online narratives and discourses (Chen 2015; Khachatryan 2015; Kurowska and Reshetnikov 2018). There was a flurry of new initiatives to promote anti-Western discourses after the Russian–Georgian war in 2008, when Russian commentators widely agreed that Moscow had lost the 'information war' (Fedor and Fredheim 2017: 168). Much of the technological creativity in favour of the regime was outsourced to groups such as the Nashi movement, a state-sponsored nationalist youth organisation, characterised by virulent anti-Western messaging. Nashi played an important role in online propaganda in 2008–11, initiating the practice of paying people to leave pro-government posts and comments online. Leaked emails explained that commenters had to be

> people with balanced language, who write well, not idiots [*debily*], [who are] capable of maintaining a debate, of developing it. They will comment on our posts, on forums – basically slandering the opposition and praising Putin . . . [creating] the impression that the majority supports us. (Cited in Fedor and Fredheim 2017: 165)

Initially, this policy appears to have been successful. Spaiser et al. demonstrate how a pro-Putin campaign in early 2012 after the protests following the Duma elections 'decisively contributed to changing the momentum of the discourse on Twitter', with the result that 'the pro-Putin camp was very successful in regaining control over a means of communication that initially seemed particularly favourable to the opposition' (Spaiser et al. 2017: 133). In this case a vital framing device on social media was the accusation that protesters were 'paid by the US'. An analysis of shifting sentiments in Twitter shows that a key event was a meeting between the newly arrived US ambassador Michael McFaul and opposition activists, which helped to delegitimise the protest movement (Spaiser et al. 2017: 147). In this case, it was Mikhail Leontyev's television show, *Odnako*, which picked up on this routine meeting in the US embassy with human rights activists, and turned it into an anti-American propaganda show.[3]

This interaction between social media campaigns and television programmes – such as *Odnako*, or Dmitry Kiselev's *Vesti nedeli* – created what Kurowska and Reshetnikov term 'trolling frames', a litany of narratives and interpretations, often contradictory, which 'despoils and precludes the very possibility of meaning' (Kurowska and Reshetniknov 2018: 346). Kurowska and Reshetnikov point to this as a mechanism of depoliticisation and desecuritisation, effectively preventing the opposition – or anybody else – from developing a clear narrative of events, which could define the regime as a security threat. Yet the messaging involved in these activities is more than simply a defensive depoliticisation achieved by sowing a post-truth confusion among different narratives. For example, following the murder of Boris Nemtsov in 2015, multiple interpretations were floated on social media, but there was also a constant, underlying thread suggesting that the killing of Nemtsov was a provocation being used for political purposes by the United States (Kurowska and Reshetnikov 2018: 355–7; see also Khachatryan 2015). Rather than desecuritising the issue, the state-sponsored social media activists and accompanying television shows resecuritised the murder as yet another event that affirmed the profound challenge to Russia from the external enemy.

Studies of online activism in Kazakhstan have demonstrated that some measure of ideological fluidity among activists does not prevent online posts and videos from confirming the basic pillars of a state discourse (Lewis 2016a). Fedor and Fredheim have shown how state-sponsored video producers are also careful to avoid overt propaganda, and operate with a 'very high degree of ideological fluidity' (Fedor and Fredheim 2017: 176). Although producers of 'state-commissioned "viral videos"' on YouTube primarily aim to crowd out alternative narratives, rather than promote particular content, they nevertheless reproduce a particular worldview, regardless of the 'post-modern' framing of their messages. The work of an influential video producer, Yuri Degtyarev, had a 'clear and explicit ideological dimension and drive', in which the main content is 'anti-Westernism, augmented with a dose of conspiracy theorizing' (Fedor and Fredheim 2017: 168). Despite being involved in what is dubbed 'post-ideological propaganda', Degtyarev and similar online activists 'are engaged in discrediting – and developing and legitimizing an authoritarian alternative to – liberal democracy' (Fedor and Fredheim 2017: 173, 174).

All of this discursive activity against the West had an impact on public opinion. In June 2016 some 78 per cent of Russians in a poll identified the United States as Russia's primary enemy (followed by Ukraine at 48 per cent and Turkey at 29 per cent) (Levada 2016). Attitudes to the United States had changed significantly in a five-year period, with only 26 per cent viewing the United States as an enemy in 2010, already a shift away from more positive attitudes in 2000.[4] In 2011, 71 per cent had a positive attitude towards the European Union, but this figure fell to 25 per cent in 2016 (Levada 2016). These shifts followed external events (the overthrow of the government in Ukraine in 2014, the annexation of Crimea and subsequent imposition of Western sanctions against Russia), but there is little doubt that the impact of these events was magnified and interpreted through the deliberate use of television propaganda and online activism. Lilia Shevtsova concluded that 'the amazingly successful military-patriotic Kremlin mobilization of the Russian society after the Crimea annexation has confirmed the sad truth: Russian state and national identity is still based on the search for the enemy' (Shevtsova 2014).

The Enemy Within: The Fifth Column

In October 1992 Alexander Prokhanov, editor of the nationalist *Den'* newspaper, published a list of names under the headline 'Fifth column in Russia', including Boris Yeltsin, Yegor Gaidar, Mikhail Gorbachev, Andrei Kozyrev and others (Dunlop 1995: 300). Nationalists repeated claims by the leader of the August coup in 1991, Vladimir Kryuchkov, the last head of the KGB, who believed that the fall of the USSR was the result of a Western plot, prepared using 'agents of influence' at the highest levels of the Soviet state (Fedor 2011: 851). At the time, such calls were dismissed as fringe talk by marginalised polemicists, but the increasing influence of ultra-conservative thinking in the early 2000s – including in the State Duma – began the process of normalisation of the discourse of 'aliens amongst us'.

Figures such as former KGB general Nikolai Leonov, a parliamentary deputy from the nationalist Rodina party, regularly attacked Russian human rights activists as working for foreign powers. Some were simply 'parasites living on Western grants', while other were 'almost undisguised conduits of an alien policy, largely oriented towards the weakening of the Russian state, the violation of the rights of the Russian people, and a schism in the Orthodox church' (Leonov 2003). Writing in 2003 Leonov called for such groups to be registered as 'foreign agents', a call that appeared extreme at the time, but was implemented by the government only a decade later.

In the mid-2000s, following the colour revolutions in Serbia, Georgia and Ukraine, the term 'fifth column' became common currency for pro-Kremlin groups, such as the Nashi youth group. Its annual Lake Seliger youth camp, a hotbed of nationalist agitation, organised a 'fifth column award' for 'liars, falsifiers, and those who blacken our homeland's reputation' (Ioffe 2010). But the term crossed into mainstream public discourse only after the Ukraine conflict of 2013–14, when it was used to label public figures opposed to the Crimean annexation. The faces of five opposition leaders appeared on huge banners draped across buildings in central Moscow in the spring of 2014, with the caption: 'The Fifth Column: Aliens Among Us'. One of the faces was that of Boris Nemtsov, an outspoken critic of Putin, who commented that 'hanging such banners on bookshops could be imagined in 1930s Germany', but 'was impossible to imagine even in the late Soviet Union' (Masyuk 2015).

In his political diaries on 15 March 2014, after an opposition march in Moscow, Alexander Dugin wrote:

> A march of the fifth column in Moscow. This is no longer a joke. This is support in our own country of our militarily armed opponent. This is no longer simply ideological opponents or people who think in a different way – this is a parade of traitors. They have risen up against the Russian people, against our State, against our history. They defend murderers, occupiers, Nazis and NATO. All participants in the march of the fifth column are sentenced (by history, by the people, by us). (Dugin 2015: 95)

Dugin was one of the chief theoreticians of the 'fifth column'. He provided a simple definition: 'The enemies inside Russia – Westernisers, liberals, the network of agents of influence in all spheres – is the fifth column' (Dugin 2015: 162). These enemies, for Dugin, are only enemies because they are the agents of the true, geopolitical, existential enemy – the combination of actors and ideas that Dugin terms 'Atlanticist' ('The US, NATO, the European Union, liberalism, technocracy, globalism, the global financial oligarchy') (Dugin 2015: 162). For Dugin, this fifth column is

> the most effective weapon of Atlanticism. It was the fifth column that destroyed the USSR. And it was the fifth column that came to power in the 1990s, engendered oligarchy and introduced liberalism at all levels of the Russian political elites, and until now controls the most important spheres in economics, politics, culture and education. (Dugin 2015: 163)

Not content with a simple fifth column, Dugin develops the notion of a 'sixth column', a kind of internal opposition within Russia's power structures. The sixth column, unlike the overt oppositionists of the fifth column, is firmly ensconced within the corridors of power, comprising 'systemic liberals, effective state managers, loyal oligarchs, executive bureaucrats, active officials and even some "enlightened patriots"' (Dugin 2014c). For other nationalist writers, this group is the most dangerous, comprising 'influential figures from Medvedev's cabinet', and regional businesspeople and officials, driven by financial motives (Kalashnikov 2015). Dugin dubs these apparently loyal allies of the regime 'the most important existential enemy of Russia', arguing that '[i]n the world of networked wars it is just this kind of snake-like body of influence, infiltrated into the structures of power, that becomes decisive in the deconstruction of political regimes and the overthrow of rulers' (Dugin 2014c).

It is this apparently ubiquitous 'sixth column' that concerns Dugin most, perhaps because it represents the difficulty of Russia ever achieving the kind of political and cultural sovereignty of which Russian conservatives dream. For Dugin, the cloying embrace of the West is always around him:

> The West is inside us in all senses, including our consciousness, analysis, system of relationships, meanings and values. Contemporary civilisation is not yet completely Russian, this is not a Russian world, it is only something that could yet become a Russian world. (Dugin 2014c)

In this telling analysis, the fifth column becomes a genuine internal enemy, one that is inside each individual's psyche. Schmitt too had some sense of this problem. As he hints in a diary entry after the war, the definition of the enemy may only provide us with a warped mirror-image of ourselves: 'The enemy is he who challenges me. Who can challenge me? Basically, only myself. The enemy is he who defines me', concludes Schmitt (1991: 217). In this way the fulfilment of a national mission for Russia becomes deeply entwined with the psychological fulfilment of the self, ensuring that the struggle with the existential enemy becomes imbued with all the affect and emotion of a deeply personal psychological challenge.

For a long time this kind of talk of the 'fifth column' could be dismissed as marginal activity by over-enthusiastic 'patriots', but in the euphoria following the Russian incorporation of Crimea into the Russian Federation, President Putin himself gave the phrase official blessing in his March 2014 speech on the incorporation of Crimea into Russia:

> Some Western politicians are already threatening us not only with sanctions but also with the prospect of worsening domestic problems. I would like to know what they have in mind: actions by some kind of fifth column, all sorts of 'national traitors', or do they think they can worsen the social and economic situation of Russia and in that way provoke public discontent? (Putin 2014a)

Speaking to the nationalist youth camp at Lake Seliger in 2014, Putin also delved into history to help formulate this distinction, telling young people that the 'extra-systemic' opposition in Russia was similar to the Bolsheviks, who 'openly wished their motherland be defeated in the First World War', and who were 'rocking Russia from the inside and this rocking caused the country to engineer its own defeat. It was a nonsense, a delirium, but it did happen. It was a betrayal of national interests' (RT 2014).

During a press conference in December 2014, journalist Natalya Galimova asked Putin if he felt responsible for reintroducing the term 'fifth column' into the 'active political lexicon'. Putin conceded that he might have to be more careful with his choice of words, but then asserted that 'sometimes you have to call things by their names'. He went on: 'It is difficult, probably, to give a scientific definition of where the opposition ends and the "fifth column" begins' (Putin 2014e). Putin continued with a short monologue on this subject, discussing why Mikhail Lermontov was still considered a patriot, despite being an opponent of the Tsar. He concluded:

> the divide between oppositionists and the 'fifth column' is internal, it is difficult to see from outside. What is the difference? An oppositionist, even the most strident, in the end will fight for the interests of his Motherland to the end. And the 'fifth column' – it is those people who carry out what is dictated by the interests of another state, they are used as an instrument to achieve political goals that are alien to us. (Putin 2014e)

But the discourse of the fifth column was not just an intellectual game. On 27 February 2015 a gunman murdered Boris Nemtsov on the Bolshoi

Moskvoretsky bridge a few hundred yards from the Kremlin. In the 2010s nationalists had regularly labelled Nemtsov as a leading member of the 'fifth column'. Although five Chechen men were convicted in a subsequent trial, the real story of the murder remains murky. Nemtsov's family demanded an investigation into Ramzan Kadyrov, the Chechen leader who regularly railed against 'enemies of the people' and 'traitors', while journalistic investigations pointed to inconsistencies in the official account and implicated state security forces in a cover-up (Reuters 2017; Dunlop 2019).

Civil Society and Foreign Agents

Official references to the 'fifth column' declined after 2015–16, but the underlying friend/enemy paradigm remained in place.[5] While the language was sometimes more cautious, the institutionalisation of the discourse continued through a series of legal and regulatory constraints on organisations, with international links. As far back as his address to the Federal Assembly in May 2004, Putin had criticised foreign-funded non-governmental organisations (NGOs), and in April 2006 a new law imposed strict registration requirements on NGOs, which led to many being forced to close, and a reduction in NGO activities more widely (Crotty et al. 2014). In 2007 Putin had criticised 'non-governmental organizations', which were 'financed by foreign governments', and noted that 'we consider this as an instrument of foreign states in their policy towards our country' (Putin 2007a). Alongside these new restrictions, the government also began funding loyal NGOs, encouraging a very different relationship between civil society and the state from that promoted by Western civil society advocates (Hemment 2012; Chebankova 2013a, 2013b; Cheskin and March 2015). It also supported the creation of 'uncivil society' – new, illiberal movements, such as the nationalist youth group Nashi, which Putin described as a 'shining example of civil society' (Zygar 2016: 100), or the virulently nationalist biker group, Night Wolves. Just as Schmitt sought a politics of order that could engage with the age of mass democracy, so the creation of groups such as Nashi was a political technologist's response to the global politics of networked protest and regime change: 'Nashi was a Putin-era repackaging of the civil-society concept that proposed its own solution to the "problem" of the crowd and (youthful) bodies on streets' (Hemment 2015: 216). Its most important goal was always to remove subjectivity from the streets, and to ensure that the regime, not its opponents, controlled the political agenda.

The attacks on NGOs intensified further after the protests of 2011–12, when groups such as the electoral monitoring organisation Golos had played a key role in uncovering fraud in the Duma elections. In December 2011 Putin promised that there would be new legislation to tackle an 'unacceptable' situation, where 'internal organisations, which are supposedly our own national [organisations], are essentially working for foreign money and performing to the tune of a foreign state' (RIA-Novosti 2011b). This was the impetus for a new law on 'foreign agents', enacted on 21 November 2012, forcing all NGOs in receipt of foreign funding and engaged in political activity (defined loosely to cover almost any public advocacy activity) to register as 'foreign agents'.

Subsequently, in June 2014, the legislation was further tightened, permitting the Justice Ministry to unilaterally confirm the 'foreign agent' status of an NGO. As a result, by June 2018 the Justice Ministry had designated 158 organisations as foreign agents, ranging from well-known human rights groups such as Memorial to small environmental organisations. About thirty groups closed or suspended their activity to avoid the listing, and some were later delisted after they stopped receiving foreign funding (HRW 2018). It was clear that the term 'foreign agent' was used to imply connections to foreign intelligence services and to permit the identification in public discourse of these NGOs as part of a 'fifth column' (although such an interpretation was denied by Russia's Constitutional Court).

A second strand of legislation sought to identify 'enemies' among international organisations. In May 2015 President Putin signed a law on 'undesirable' international organisations (defined loosely as those that posed a threat to Russia's security or constitutional order) which gave the General Prosecutor the right to ban such organisations from undertaking any activities inside Russia (Interfax 2015b). This identification of the enemy through new laws and regulations became commonplace in multiple areas of political and social life. With the so-called 'Dima Yakovlev' law, Russia banned US citizens from adopting Russian orphans in 2012, in retaliation for the US adoption of the Magnitsky Act. The government also imposed new restrictions on foreign travel for civil servants, essentially securitising many public-sector positions, even those without any access to state secrets (Lipman 2015). In April 2014 even junior employees among the 1.3 million workers in the Interior Ministry lost the right to travel internationally, along with two million people working in the Defence Ministry, more than 60,000 employees of the Prosecutor General's Office, and more than 30,000 working at the office of the Federal Migration Service. In total, some four million government employees are estimated to have lost the right to travel internationally, an unprecedented shift in freedom of movement for Russian citizens in post-Soviet Russia (Ryzhkov 2014).

The End of Consensus

For a short period following the annexation of Crimea, all these efforts to build unity came together to form the 'Crimean Consensus', which successfully combined Russian nationalist sentiment (both ethnic and statist), a majoritarian agreement over values and beliefs, and a general identification of an existential enemy that posed a threat to the well-being of Russians, their identity and the Russian state more widely. For a while something akin to a Schmittian identification 'between rulers and the ruled' could be seen in practice, in which the political leader embodied the collective desires of the vast majority of the population. Yet the Crimean consensus was ultimately short-lived, as its discursive construction soon began to unravel.

Above all, one of the main strands of the Crimean consensus – the enemy discourse – appeared to lose some of its traction in domestic politics. In polls, most Russians still had little compunction in identifying the United States as their main enemy. A poll in June 2019 found that the United States was still cited by most respondents as Russia's number one enemy, followed by Ukraine, the United Kindom and Poland (Levada 2019). But the over-use of the discourse of the enemy and the fifth column in domestic politics began to grate. Part of the problem was the use of this discourse to disguise the unpopularity of local officials, in ways that merely reinforced their weak position.

In August 2016, in the run-up to Duma elections in September, Samara governor Nikolai Merkushkin argued that the CIA was targeting Samara oblast', and that opposition leader Alexei Navalny 'was trained in the United States', was 'devoted to Uncle Sam' and was carrying out the 'Dulles Plan' (Plotnikova and Coalson 2016). (He was dismissed as Samara governor in 2017.) In Sevastopol in Crimea, Governor Sergei Menyailo claimed that discontent with poor local governance was provoked by 'foreign enemies of Russia' – notably the United States – and claimed that protesters and political opponents were affiliated to the US State Department (Nikiforov 2015). Menyailo also lost his position, and was dispatched as presidential envoy to Siberia. These attempts to use the discourse of the external enemy to fight local political battles often prompted a mocking backlash: one of Menyailo's opponents responded witheringly that 'it is not the Americans who dumped all the rubbish [in Sevastopol]' and 'turned [it] into a garbage dump' (Nikiforov 2015).

Moreover, many protests could no longer credibly be linked to external forces. A wave of protests in 2019 – against corruption, against church construction in public spaces, for free elections, or against new waste-disposal sites in rural areas – all had clear origins in social and political discontent.

When large protests were held in Moscow in August 2019 after opposition candidates were barred from local elections, only 26 per cent of those polled believed government claims that the demonstrations were stirred up by 'Western interference' (Vedemosti 2019). Declining real wages and continued evidence of local and national corruption contributed to the decline in support for the government, and for Putin personally. The days when Putin could present himself as the leader of a silent majority, ranged against a minority of corrupt oligarchs and officials, had long gone. Paradoxically, by asserting his own sovereignty within the political system, all problems – pension reform, poverty, inequality – ended up as his responsibility.

By the time of contested regional elections in September 2018, Konstantin Gaaze concluded that 'the notorious Crimean consensus is dead' (Gaaze 2018b). A 'golden age' of Russian authoritarianism, which began with the Crimean annexation, had ended, and 'the largest coalition of support for the regime in modern history ceased to exist'. For Gaaze, this suggested that the government had little alternative but to revert to more repressive measures and 'stage show trials against the country's vigorous "fifth column"' (Gaaze 2018b).

Carl Schmitt's biography provided its own warnings of his theories. Schmitt's theoretical advocacy in the 1920s of the friend/enemy distinction as the foundation of a political community became all too real after Hitler's rise to power. In 'Die Deutschen Intellektuellen', published in May 1933, and described by his biographer as 'among the worst excesses Schmitt ever published' (Mehring 2014: 296), Schmitt put into polemical prose the violent reality of the friend/enemy distinction, justifying book-burning and launching a vicious attack on Albert Einstein and other intellectuals who had fled Germany. Labelling Einstein a 'poison-filled German-hater', Schmitt denied that any of the exiled intellectuals had 'ever belonged to the German people'. Schmitt concluded that 'Germany spat them out for all eternity' (Meierhenrich and Simons 2016: 8).

Putin and his advisers had always stepped back from the full repressive implications of the friend/enemy distinction. Yet its deployment had already polarised Russian society. The warped polarised television talk shows, the conspiracy theories of the Dulles Plan, or the myth of foreign support for revolution all conjured up a simplistic discursive framework that left Russian elites facing a difficult choice. Either to retreat from the path of continued polarisation and enemy construction, but without an alternative ideological framework, or to continue to shape Russian politics within a dangerous framework that divided the population into friends and enemies.

Not only does a friend/enemy analytical gaze oversimplify the complex reality of relationships, but the categories themselves are misleading. Galli writes that Schmittian thinking 'only manages to conjure up a trick of the eye: enemies and friends are actually ghosts and projections, who feed on *desiderata* and aggressive nostalgia' (Galli 2010: 20). The Russian intellectual landscape became full of such ghosts, the blurred images of invented enemies, the projections of unfounded conspiracy theories, undermining the very national unity which the friend–enemy distinction had once promised to create.

Notes

1. There is no archival source for any kind of 'Dulles Plan' – it most likely derives from a fictional plot in a 1981 Soviet novel by Anatoly Ivanov, *Vechnyi zov* (The Eternal Call). Authors claiming to cite the 'Dulles Plan' often also cite various genuine US government texts, which have little in common with the text of the plan used by Russian nationalists (Fedor 2011). There are multiple sources in Russia that challenge the authenticity of the Dulles Plan. See, for example, 'Plan Dallesa: Tekst i ego analyz' <http://sakva.ru/Nick/DullPlan.html> (last accessed 17 December 2018). For a 'standard' Russian-language version of the text, see Khlobustov (2005).
2. This account cites one of the earliest versions of the 'Dulles Plan', by Ivan Snichev (Metropolitan Ioann of St Petersburg and Ladoga), presented in an article, 'Bitva za Rossiyu', in *Sovetskaya Rossiya*, 20 February 1993. Republished in Snichev (2011), and cited here from the translation available at: <https://web.archive.org/web/20041204191242/http://eairc.boom.ru/icon/battle_for_russia.html> (last accessed 1 November 2018).
3. The programme is available online at: <https://www.1tv.ru/news/2012-01-17/102215-analiticheskaya_programma_odnako_s_mihailom_leontievym> (last accessed 4 October 2019).
4. In a poll in 2000, 8 per cent of those polled had very good feelings towards the United States, but 62 per cent had basically good feelings, with only 6 per cent having 'very bad' sentiments towards America (cited in Shevtsova 2003: 175).
5. Writing in late 2015, Tatiana Stanovaya noted: 'Even the negative connotations with regard to the "fifth column", "national traitors" and liberals have disappeared . . . Of course, the internal enemies in his understanding have not disappeared. It is simply that this [issue] is also delegated to those who are responsible for it' (Stanovaya 2015).

SIX

Dualism, Exceptionality and the Rule of Law

Auctoritas, non veritas, facit legem [Authority, not truth, makes law]
                                                            Thomas Hobbes, *Leviathan*

When President Putin won his first presidential elections, in 2000, he promised voters a revolution in legality, the creation of a law-based state (Putin 2000c). He wrote in 2000 that 'the law should govern all of us, from the representatives of power to the ordinary citizen'. From now on, the police, prosecutors, politicians and oligarchs would all be subject to the same rules (Putin 2000c). Relations between the state and powerful oligarchs would be no different from relations with 'the owner of a small bakery or a shoe-repair shop' (Putin 2000c). A new criminal code was introduced in 2001, judges' salaries were increased, courts were reformed and better funded. Businesses increasingly turned to the courts rather than criminal gangs to resolve disputes (Gans-Morse 2017). In many areas of everyday law, local courts were efficient and reasonably fair (Hendley 2017), while at the highest level of the judiciary, the Russian Constitutional Court frequently challenged unconstitutional laws and decrees (Trochev and Solomon 2018: 201).

Despite these apparent successes, in the World Justice Project's Rule of Law Index, Russia was listed in 89th position out of 113 countries, and was one of the worst-ranked states in relation to its GDP.[1] Russia scored among the lowest 20 per cent of all states for rule of law in the Worldwide Governance Indicators (WGI) dataset.[2] Perceptions of Russia's judiciary were coloured by a series of highly politicised cases against Mikhail Khodorkovsky, Alexei Navalny and other political opponents of the Putin regime. Thousands of Russians flocked to the European Court of Human Rights

(ECtHR) in Strasbourg to seek redress unavailable in the Russian judicial system (Mälksoo and Benedek 2017). Unwilling to trust Russian justice, Russia's oligarchs and business leaders became lucrative clients for London law firms and the English courts. President Dmitry Medvedev admitted that Russia was plagued by 'legal nihilism' (Medvedev 2008).

This chapter explores these apparent contradictions, building on a growing literature that considers law in Russia as a dualistic domain (Sakwa 2010a, 2010b, 2013; Hendley 2017; Trochev 2017; Paneyakh and Rosenberg 2018; Trochev and Solomon 2018). While many 'normal' cases in Russian courts were decided in accordance with proper judicial procedures and codified rules and laws, a much smaller number of 'exceptional' cases were resolved effectively through extra-legal – and sometimes nakedly political – decisions (Sakwa 2010a, 2010b; Hendley 2017; Trochev 2017; Paneyakh and Rosenberg 2018: 220; Trochev and Solomon 2018).

In this legal dualism, Russia mirrors many other contemporary authoritarian regimes, which combine both legalism and political decisionism in a single system. These regimes are 'legalist in that their authoritarianism is open to legal reasoning and legal disputing', but also 'decisionist in that the sovereign will of their authoritarian ruler(s) is limitless and supreme' (Meierhenrich 2018: 245). Jayasuriya explored this dualism between 'legalism in the economic sphere and a regime of exception in the political domain' in East Asia, explaining how authoritarian states have achieved economic growth while restricting political pluralism, because 'the "rule of law" applies to the economy but not to the political arena' (Jayasuriya 2001: 124). This approach delineated particular economic domains where legalist reasoning would be the final arbiter, in special economic courts or in demarcated zones.

In most authoritarian states, however, there is no formal distinction between the exception and the norm. Indeed, as Schmitt informs us, there is no possibility of codifying this distinction without constraining political sovereignty. In Russia the judicial and legal systems reflect both legalist and decisionist logics, which are often in tension with each other, but nevertheless form a single, functioning system of authoritarian law. I assess this duality of law with reference to Carl Schmitt's understandings of law, based on two of his most important binaries: first, the familiar distinction between the norm and the exception; and second, Schmitt's attempts throughout his career to theorise the distinction between the concept of 'legality' and the idea of 'legitimacy', to assert an incompatibility between liberal understandings of the rule of law and the popular and sovereign will in an illiberal democracy (Schmitt 2004b).

Law in Russia

Russian has two words for law, *zakon* and *pravo*, which reflect an important distinction between 'legality' and 'legitimacy' (Agamben 2016: 458). *Zakon* refers to written law, to written legislation and codified regulations, and is the basis for what Schmitt terms a 'legislative state', a state in which impersonal norms govern all decisions, without scope for personal discretion by officials or judges. In such a state, writes Schmitt, '"laws govern", and not men, authorities or unelected governments' (Schmitt 2004b: 3–4). The alternative term for law, *pravo*, has a different meaning, closer to Schmitt's use of the term legitimacy. *Pravo* implies a certain scepticism about the written law (*zakon*), as it 'asks whether the law in question is just and whether it represents the will of the people' (Hendley 2017: 20). From *pravo* are derived the Russian words *spravedlivost'* (justice) and *prava cheloveka* (human rights). It is a concept which is much broader than simply adherence to written rules, and may be in contradiction with codified law.

Variants of this conceptual dualism can be traced throughout a Russian legal tradition stretching back to the judicial reforms of 1864, which introduced a new class of independent-minded lawyers and judges in city courts, while whole sections of the population – notably the peasants – continued to rely heavily on customary law in rural courts (Hendley 2017: 7–9). A different type of dualism emerged in the Soviet period (Berman 1963; Feifer 1964; Sharlet 1977). Far from the law 'withering away', as socialists had argued it would in a classless society, the Soviet legal system became a huge regulatory apparatus, although always subordinate to the writ of the Communist Party (Kahn 2006). Robert Sharlet pointed to a duality between the concept of *zakonnost'* (legality) and *partiinost'* (party orientation) in the Soviet justice system (Sharlet 1977: 155–6), reflecting essentially the same concerns as Schmitt's distinction between legality and legitimacy, between codified rules and the imperatives of the socio-political environment. It remained the case, as Peter Solomon notes, that 'Stalinist law, like the tsarist and Bolshevik before, assumed that law was subordinate to political power', and it also 'implied no restrictions on the use of extralegal coercion or terror' (Solomon 1996: 153). For Stalinist Commissar of Justice Nikolai Krylenko, there was no difference in essence 'between a court of law and summary justice', except in one important aspect, speed and efficiency: 'A club is a primitive weapon, a rifle is a more efficient one, the most efficient is the court' (Kahn 2006: 380).[3] For Krylenko, the courts were political weapons, and a judge was 'a politician', a 'worker in the political field' (Trochev and Solomon 2018: 203).

Yet even dictatorships require everyday regulation and law that is not subject to constant political interference. Harold Berman's ground-breaking work on Soviet law in 1950 highlighted the important role played by everyday law in the USSR, prompting a reviewer to conclude that 'we are confronted with the phenomenon of the "dual state", in which a stabilized legal sector co-exists with a fluid sphere of unlimited prerogative' (Bodenheimer 1952: 160). Even the Stalinist state required a set of regulations and norms which were applied more or less equally in everyday civil matters, such as divorce, adoption, inheritance, property sales or leasing, and reasonably impartially in minor criminal and administrative violations. At the same time, the state reserved the right to intervene at will in judicial processes for political reasons. These interventions came to be known as 'telephone justice' – orders transmitted to the judge by a direct line from the Party. In the 1970s Alexander Solzhenitsyn wrote that 'in his mind's eye the judge can always see the shiny black visage of truth – the telephone in his chambers. This oracle will never fail you, as long as you do what it says' (Solzhenitsyn (1973: 521). In contemporary Russia the essential principles of 'telephone justice' have been retained from the Soviet period, even if the technology has evolved (Solomon 2007: 126; Ledeneva 2008; Esakov 2012: 669–70).

In the late 1980s and 1990s, post-Soviet Russia made significant strides in reforming the Soviet-era judiciary and overcoming this legacy of dualism between constitutionalism and arbitrary rule. In 1991 a Constitutional Court was founded with the right of judicial review. In 1995 Russia ratified the European Convention on Human Rights (ECHR) and acknowledged the jurisdiction of the European Court of Human Rights (ECtHR) in Strasbourg in domestic law. Limited budgets, low salaries and a lack of a tradition of judicial independence undermined the ability of courts to develop genuine independence, either from the state or from oligarchs, business, local governors or powerful security agencies. The result was a contrast between what Kahn termed 'a melange of extraordinarily rapid statutory reform of Russia's civil, political, economic, and legal institutions' and 'painfully slow reform of attitudes and norms of behavior in each of those spheres' (Kahn 2006: 393–4).

Putin's initial rhetoric about developing a law-based state was accompanied by a good deal of 'ambiguity and complexity' in his approach to legal reform (Kahn 2008: 512). On the one hand, there were clear procedural and technical improvements in court operations. Budgets and salaries improved significantly. Jury trials – although still limited in extent and scope – became an accepted part of judicial procedures, despite attempts to restrict their use (Esakov 2012). Despite ongoing controversy about its role in domestic jurisprudence, the decisions of the ECtHR had many positive impacts on

Russian legal decisions and processes (Mälksoo and Benedek 2017; Trochev 2018; Bowring 2019). The wider Council of Europe architecture also had an impact, such as promotion of norms on the treatment of national minorities, or through the activities of the European Committee for the Prevention of Torture (CPT), which regularly visited places of detention in Russia, and had a positive impact on prison conditions (Bowring 2019). Russian conservatives often criticised the ECtHR as undermining Russian sovereignty, but government officials and judges continued to emphasise the extent to which Russia's legal development remained intertwined with the judgments of the ECtHR (Bowring 2019).

The impact of the courts on business was particularly notable. Use of the courts by Russian firms rose dramatically, from some 200,000 cases in 1994 to over one million in 2010 (Gans-Morse 2017: 339). Paneyakh and Rosenberg note a quadrupling of cases in *arbitrazh* courts in 1994–2013 (Paneyakh and Rosenberg 2018: 223). The figures partly reflected increased business activity, but they also demonstrated a substantive shift as businesses moved their disputes from shoot-outs on the streets to the court room. Business-related violence declined sharply in Russia after 2001. The number of businesspeople murdered annually in Russia's Central Federal District, for example, fell from 213 in 1997 to just 33 in 2005 (Gans-Morse 2012: 268). Russian business came to rely on courts and lawyers, rather than shady mafia outfits, to protect their businesses and to ensure that contracts were enforced (Gans-Morse 2017: 341).

Legal reforms did not only affect business disputes. According to a detailed study by Kathryn Hendley, people who used justice-of-the-peace courts felt that they had been fairly treated; she concluded that 'courts operate fairly normally when it comes to mundane cases' (Hendley 2017: 224). Moreover, research by Alexei Trochev demonstrated that citizens who sue the state – usually on the grounds of wrongful actions by officials or failure by federal organs to fulfil their obligations – won 87 per cent of cases (Paneyakh and Rosenberg 2018: 223). The conventional view that Russian justice is irredeemably politicised ignored 'the increasing successes that firms and citizens have had over the past two decades in using the courts to defend themselves against the state' (Paneyakh and Rosenberg 2018: 225). Hendley (2017) pointed out that Russian courts hear over 16 million cases a year, but that this 'everyday law' is routinely ignored by researchers, who are primarily interested in high-profile political cases (Hendley 2017: 2).

This emerging trend in Russian legal studies deplored the 'disproportionate attention to high-profile clashes involving owners of Russia's largest conglomerates', which 'has perpetuated Russian capitalism's lawless image' (Gans-Morse 2017: 339). Focusing on these well-known cases, argues Gans-Morse, 'offers a skewed and unrepresentative portrayal of modern-day Russian business practices' (Gans-Morse 2012: 264). Political cases probably constitute 'much less than 1% of the total', according to Paneyakh and Rosenberg (2018: 220), and Maria Popova argues that politicised prosecutions, such as the prosecution of Mikhail Khodorkovsky, were the exception and not the rule (Popova 2012: 166). This literature is a useful corrective to one-sided views of the Russian judicial system, but this strand of research runs the risk of underplaying the significance of politicised justice, or treating it as a temporary aberration rather than as a constitutive part of the system. Hendley recognises the key question about dualistic systems, which is how to conceptualise 'legal systems that pay attention to the law most of the time but ignore or manipulate it in spectacular fashion in a small number of cases' (Hendley 2017: 3).

In a study of dualism in the Russian Constitutional Court (RCC), Trochev and Solomon characterise the distinction between norm and exception as between 'constitutional' decisions and 'politically expedient' judgments (Trochev and Solomon 2018: 202). The RCC had a long and complex relationship with the Russian authorities, but managed to extend its jurisdiction into many areas of political and social life, retained a certain independence in its judgments, and continued to act as the main judicial interlocutor with the ECtHR (Trochev 2017; Trochev and Solomon 2018). The RCC often declared particular laws unconstitutional – indeed, in 2016, for the first time in the court's history, not a single law reviewed by the RCC was declared constitutional (Trochev and Solomon 2018: 210). It also often ruled in favour of individual complainants, including in matters of political or civil rights. Out of nineteen decisions on political rights in 2010–15, twelve were won by the complainant, and out of fifty decisions on personal rights, thirty were won by complainants (Trochev and Solomon 2018: 211).

Yet on the major political decisions, the court always sided with the executive. The court's chairman, Valery Zorkin, argued that the RCC had to consider both 'the spirit of the Constitution and the spirit of life', a diplomatic nod to the Kremlin's demands for compliance (Kommersant 2013). The court prioritised the question of incorporation of Crimea into Russia in 2014, and unanimously approved the move. It refused to enforce several judgments of the ECtHR against Russia, most notably in the December 2014 judgment ('OAO Neftyanaya Kompaniya Yukos v. Russia'), in which the ECtHR awarded almost €1.9 billion in favour of Yukos shareholders; the RCC ruled in January 2017 that the judgment was impossible to implement because it violated the Russian Constitution.

The RCC also refused to consider a complaint by Alexei Navalny about his being barred from running in a presidential election (Trochev and Solomon 2018: 210). As Solomon and Trochev concluded,

> the Court was effectively forced to decide politically sensitive matters favourably to the Kremlin and provide unconditional support of Putin's key policies . . . but in matters where the Kremlin does not have a clear interest, the RCC has been able to involve other actors and decide cases impartially. (Trochev and Solomon 2018: 209)

For Solomon and Trochev, this political 'pragmatism' leads them to conclude that 'the RCC of today displays many positive features', although it has been unable to slow the development of authoritarianism in Russia (Trochev and Solomon 2018: 213).

Conceptualising Dualism

Viewing this dualistic system as simply a clash between political pragmatism and constitutionalism underplays the constitutive role of the exception in the Russian authoritarian system. As discussed in Chapter 3, the dualist theories of Fraenkel and Schmitt help to provide more substantive readings of this apparently contradictory system of law. For Fraenkel, the contestation is between a political sphere, which is regulated by 'arbitrary measures', thus forming a 'prerogative' state, and a normative state, where law prevails (Fraenkel 2017: 3). Schmitt's conceptualisation of law, on the other hand, is grounded in a profound critique of liberal theories of the rule of law, particularly legal positivism – and his own advocacy of a jurisprudence rooted in 'legitimacy'. He defines this as an understanding of law as being in accordance with an existing 'concrete order', a specific socio-political environment, in which judicial decisions are taken with regard to shared cultural, social and 'democratic' imperatives. Moreover, within this system there is the possibility for the sovereign to act outside the law, and to declare the exception. This produces the same dualism identified by Fraenkel, but in Schmitt's understanding it produces sustainable order, and – most importantly, in Schmitt's view – ensures a space and role for the political.

Schmitt's critique of liberal theories of law has two stages. First, he argues that – like parliamentary democracy – the rule of law is essentially a sham. Far from being the liberal ideal of a 'neutral domain', it instead 'camouflag[es] its violent uses of force under the fig leaves of rule and norm' (Rasch 2000: 3). The court-room is simply a façade that disguises the underlying conflicts and power relations in society. Schmitt consistently argues for a concept of jurisprudence that recognises the essentially political nature of the law, akin to the Marxist understanding of law as the reflection of existing power relations in society. Legality is not a neutral arbiter among competing factions in a pluralistic order, but 'has become a poisonous dagger, with which one party stabs the other in the back' (Schmitt 1990: 70).

Second, legality acting as a 'free-floating order' is not only 'deceptive', but also 'impotent' (Rasch 2000: 3). Law requires some kind of underlying political decision to give it authority, and to produce a viable legal order. A free-standing set of norms and laws cannot be the basis for the legal system's own legitimacy:

> The norm or rule does not create the order; on the contrary, only on the basis and in the framework of a given order does it have a certain regulating function with a small degree of validity independent of the facts of the case. (Schmitt 2004a: 49)

Schmitt is 'ideologically hostile' to any 'idea that cognitively derived normative orders could be the foundation for political orders' (Bhuta 2015: 10). A legal system based only on 'free-floating' norms is not sustainable. Instead, '[l]ike every other order, the legal order rests on a decision and not on a norm' (Schmitt 1985a: 10). Any attempt to make law sovereign – to make it the decision-making subject of political affairs – only produces a kind of 'ersatz sovereign' which is unable to produce order, but instead is a source of political instability (Meierhenrich and Simons 2016: 30). Law should not attempt to replace the political. Schmitt was strongly opposed to the politicisation of the judiciary, through the idea of judicial review, for example: the judiciary should not become 'a lawgiver with a highly political function'. Even in 'critical and turbulent times', it was not for the judiciary 'to decide social and political conflicts' (Mehring 2014: 213).

There is a fundamental tension, Schmitt claims, between legality and legitimacy: 'legality and legitimacy cannot be the same: indeed they stand in contradiction to each other' (Strong 2007: xv). Legality 'has the meaning and purpose of making superfluous and negating the legitimacy of either the monarch or the people's plebiscitarian will as well as of every authority and governing power' (Schmitt 2004b: 9). A rule of law based on abstract norms binds and constrains sovereign power in ways that Schmitt views as unacceptable. Consequently, there is a profound opposition between 'the system of legality of the parliamentary legislative state and that of plebiscitary-democratic legitimacy'. This is not merely an opposition between different bodies and institutions, but 'a struggle between two forms of law' (Schmitt 2004b: 66).

Instead of the rule of law, Schmitt effectively argues for the 'rule of men', an assertion that an effective legal order is based not on a set of abstract norms, applied without regard to time or place, but on decisions rooted in a particular society and culture. Schmitt argues – building on the ideas of the nineteenth-century German jurist Friedrich Carl von Savigny – for a concept of law that is derived from a particular order and a particular culture, and located in a specific place (positivism, by contrast, 'knows no origin and has no home'; Schmitt 1990: 56). A Schmittian understanding of law always has a spatial aspect, a close binding to place and culture that also ensures its legitimacy. 'All law', writes Schmitt, 'is "situational law"' (Schmitt 1985a: 13). Jurisprudence had to be grounded in the idea of 'concrete order' and not rely on a free-floating normativism (Schmitt 2004a: 54–5):

> Legal and jurisprudential thinking occurs only in connection to a historical, concrete, total order. It cannot also rely upon free-floating rules or free-floating decisions. Even the fictions and illusions of such 'freedom' and such 'floating' belong, as an accompanying symptom, to a specific condition of a disintegrated order and are only comprehensible within it. (Schmitt 2004a: 73)

In other words, universal norms, divorced from a specific political or historical context, and set up as a system of domestic legal norms, would undermine, not reinforce, political order.

This appeal to legitimacy, however, should not be understood as indicating full autonomy for the courts, in the liberal conception of separation of powers, since the judiciary is always circumscribed by the power of the sovereign to declare this or that issue as an exceptional case. Attempts to develop a 'gapless' legality that will cover all eventualities – including exceptional circumstances – will limit or constrain sovereign power, in a way that undermines the state's ability to defend itself from attacks on the constitutional order. In this way of thinking, the exception is not an aberration from the law, but a way of asserting and confirming the normal situation; in effect confirming the existence and validity of the wider legal order (McCormick 1997: 226).

In the normal situation, however, where there is no exceptional case, judges and courts must act in accordance with codified rules and procedures and make fair and robust decisions in accordance with the existing laws, statutes and regulations. Consequently, the Schmittian legal system becomes a dualist system, bifurcated between the normal situation and the exception, a system policed and demarcated not by law or custom, but by the decisions of a sovereign power. In Schmitt's thinking, at least, this is not a hybrid system, or one marked by constant contestation between the exception and the norm, but one in which the exception and the norm constitute each other, in a coherent, sustainable form of order. Yet, as in other domains of social and political life, this exceptionality requires concrete mechanisms to allow for political interventions into judicial processes. The nature of these mechanisms makes it very difficult to maintain the demarcation of norm and exception. Instead, exceptional cases that undermine the rule of law begin to extend throughout the system.

Politicised Justice

On 6 June 2019 Ivan Golunov, an investigative journalist, was arrested in Moscow. Police claimed to have discovered the synthetic drug mephedrone in his backpack and to have uncovered more illegal drugs in his apartment. After an unprecedented outcry, Golunov was freed and charges were dropped. Yet his case was remarkable only because of the publicity, and because he was released. There were thousands of so-called *'zakaznye dela'* (prosecutions-to-order) where the police and the courts connived to give individuals long prison sentences on trumped-up charges, either simply to reach a quota of arrests, or to punish a political opponent, a business rival or an ex-lover. Planted drugs were a simple mechanism with serious consequences: long prison sentences were routinely imposed in such cases. In other incidents, businesspeople faced false charges of fraud, tax evasion or money-laundering.

For many people, including officials working inside the system, the Golunov case was the last straw. Olga Romanova, the head of the NGO Rus Sidyashchaya (Russia Behind Bars), a prisoners' rights organisation, wrote:

> People are sick of the fact that like Golunov, any one of us could have drugs planted on them; [and] ... be beaten and tortured with impunity; ... that a major TV channel would show a fictitious report about them during prime time; that they could explain all of this in court ... and hope for a judicial enquiry, but none would come: the judge doesn't care. They have heard this a thousand times before. The judge doesn't doubt that the complainant was beaten, but can't and doesn't want to do anything about it. (Romanova 2019)

The growing exceptionality in the Russian judicial system was not simply a case of widespread and endemic corruption, or the unintended consequences of quota-driven policing. These were important systemic factors, but at the heart of the problem was the use of law as an instrument to achieve political goals. A growing literature on law in authoritarian states explains how the law is used by political regimes to police elites, to discipline potential opponents and to form and maintain a rent-seeking coalition that supports the political regime.

Douglas North has argued that in countries without effective rule of law, political order is dependent on maintaining a coalition of elites who benefit sufficiently from rents to avoid reverting to violence or attempting to destabilise the regime. Such a system also requires a constant policing of the authoritarian coalition: some groups need to be excluded from benefits to ensure sufficient returns for the elites who have access to this privileged club (North et al. 2009). The pattern of high-level corruption and frequent arrests of businesspeople typical of Russian-style authoritarianism produces a certain type of order for the ruling regime, one in which economic and political power are almost synonymous, and where the law is routinely used for political purposes. Maria Popova concludes that '[i]n Putin's Russia, the sovereign uses the law and legal institutions to fulfil political goals, to communicate them to society, and to manage the authoritarian coalition that helps the president govern' (Popova 2017: 65).

The emphasis in recent studies of Russian justice has been on the 'normality' of Russian judicial and legal processes, but this normal situation has been punctuated from the beginning by a series of high-profile political cases, which are a central, defining feature of the system. Putin's first use of politicised justice came just four days after his inauguration as president, when masked men raided the headquarters of Vladimir Gusinsky's Media-Most corporation. Gusinsky was arrested in June 2000, and by the end of that month he had left the country for permanent exile, having been forced to cede control of his critical television channel NTV in exchange for his freedom.

The raid on Gusinsky set the tone for all subsequent state raids: the uncovering of potential legal violations, easy to discover in Russia's opaque criminal and tax codes; the use of criminal – not civil – prosecutions against top executives, with the threat of long prison terms to encourage compliance; and the use of informal mechanisms behind the scenes to resolve the dispute not through the courts, but through an essentially political deal. Tax investigations soon targeted other major corporations, including state or para-state companies, such as Gazprom, where Rem Vyakhirev was ousted from his personal fiefdom in favour of close Putin allies (Yaffa 2017: 50). Personal and financial interests no doubt played a part in all these moves. But this was not primarily about the enrichment of Putin's cronies: the moves against the 1990s oligarchs realigned power within the business world with the Kremlin, rather than permitting semi-independent fiefdoms to be ruled by mini-sovereigns.

For any entrepreneurs who had not yet understood the implications of the Gusinsky affair, the prosecution and imprisonment of Russia's most powerful oil tycoon Mikhail Khodorkovsky in 2003–4 was the clearest evidence that a new system was in place. Khodorkovsky was arrested in October 2003, after he had demonstrated an unwillingness to play by the new rules of the game; his criticism of Putin, his support for opposition parties and his apparent political ambitions all demonstrated that he was refusing to acknowledge that sovereignty was now monopolised by a new leader, and was no longer the preserve of individual oligarchs (Sakwa 2014b). Otto Luchterhandt, a lawyer who observed Khodorkovsky's first trial, called it 'an extraordinary scandal of justice', in which 'the Prosecutor General's Office and the courts fabricated a criminal case, during which basic principles of legality were systematically and cynically violated' (Luchterhandt 2006: 1).

Whatever its legal shortcomings, the case was presented in Russia as essentially legitimate, both in political terms and as a reflection of popular opinion. Khodorkovsky's actions in funding opposition parties had confirmed the widespread view in the presidential administration that the existence of independent businesspeople with political interests would inevitably lead to the kind of political pluralism that they viewed as potentially destructive. Moreover, often uncritical Western support for Khodorkovsky reinforced suspicions in the Russian government that businesspeople with extensive links to the West were a potential threat to their understanding of Russian sovereignty: Khodorkovsky, after all, had previously been in talks to sell a share in Yukos to US oil company Exxon Mobil. The subsequent long-running legal cases in international courts against Russia on behalf of Yukos shareholders confirmed the problems Russia faced in managing its economic elites in a world where transnational finance was increasingly accompanied by transnational legal processes.

Moreover, Khodorkovsky – along with all those who had become incredibly wealthy during the 1990s – was extremely unpopular in Russian society. Only 28 per cent of respondents were prepared to tell opinion pollsters in 2011 that the second trial of Khodorkovsky in 2010 was unfair (although most lawyers agreed that it was even more egregiously unjust than the first); the same proportion believed it to be fair, while many could not answer. Only 4 per cent of respondents would have definitely freed the defendants immediately. Perhaps more significantly, a large proportion (41 per cent) believed that the authorities had put pressure on judges to reach a guilty verdict, suggesting that many saw politicised justice as 'legitimate', even if – in Schmitt's distinction – it was not 'legal' (Levada 2011b).

The prosecution of Khodorkovsky became the prototype for many other similar prosecutions. After Alexei Navalny published reports about high-level corruption in the Russian government, prosecutors began investigating his involvement in a timber business deal while he was working in Kirov as an adviser to regional governor Nikita Belykh. Navalny was subsequently charged with embezzlement of some $500,000 worth of timber from the Kirovles state timber company (ECtHR 2016: para 30). According to a report in the *New Yorker* magazine, 'Navalny was accused of doing something that was both impossible and absurd' (Gessen 2016). In more diplomatic language, the ECtHR concluded that his actions were 'indistinguishable from regular commercial middleman activities', but that 'the criminal law was arbitrarily and unforeseeably construed to the detriment of the applicants, leading to a manifestly unreasonable outcome of the trial' (ECtHR 2016: para 115). On 18 July 2013 the court sentenced Navalny to five years in prison, subsequently suspended. A retrial in 2017 ordered after the ECtHR ruling merely confirmed the previous conviction.

To take on the regime directly, as Navalny had done, was to be forced to operate exclusively within the domain of the exception, to operate outside the realm of norms and rules. Individuals connected too closely to Navalny also entered this Kafkaesque space. According to a report by the journalist Masha Gessen, '[e]very single person on the [Fund for the Struggle against Corruption (FBK)] foundation's staff has been called in for interrogation', and several faced unfounded criminal charges (Gessen 2016). His brother Oleg Navalny was imprisoned as part of the case against him. Alexei Navalny complained that his brother was being used as a hostage to try to limit his own political activities. In this way, the collective around Navalny was gradually drawn into the world of exceptionality, in which every act, however innocent, can be construed as criminal.

This set of exceptional practices gradually became a normal part of political and business life. In June 2015 the respected Russian human rights organisation Memorial published a list of fifty individuals that it characterised as 'political prisoners'. It argued that

> In the new politically-motivated prosecutions various instruments of such prosecutions that are typical for similar cases are employed: direct falsification of evidence, arbitrary and expanded interpretations of the statutes of criminal law, the use of illegally or irresponsibly worded statutes of legislation, the unfounded criminal interpretation of factual circumstances, and combinations of these instruments. (Memorial 2015)

The existence of these methods to declare the exceptional case in political cases inevitably led to their use at almost every level of law enforcement and every level of government, in both political and economic cases. Indeed, in many prosecutions the mix of political, personal and economic motivations was inextricably blurred. When these cases involved the takeover or dismemberment of a company, they were part of a process termed *reiderstvo* (raiding), a term originally derived from the highly aggressive takeovers of companies that were common in the 1970s and 1980s in the United States, but distinguished in its Russian variant by the use of illegal or semi-legal means. According to one estimate, there may be 70,000 cases of illegal corporate raiding every year in Russia, most of which involve the use of prosecutions to order (Ruvinsky 2011). In a speech in December 2015 President Putin gave even higher figures, noting that in 2014, while the investigative authorities opened some 200,000 cases related to 'economic crimes', only 46,000 cases were taken to court and only 15 per cent resulted in a conviction, but 83 per cent of businesspeople investigated in these cases lost their business partially or entirely. As Putin admitted, 'they got intimidated, robbed and then released' (Putin 2015c).[4]

Scholar Mariya Shklyaruk divides such cases into two types: first, those in which the prosecution is based on events that actually happened, but where that activity would not normally be considered criminal; and second, cases in which evidence is blatantly forged or fabricated (Shklyaruk 2016). The problem in the first place, as argued by Kirill Titaev and Irina Chetverikova, is that 'actions which are part of normal business turnover or the result of insignificant mistakes in the economic activity of enterprises, organisations and citizens, can be qualified and are qualified as criminal acts' (Titaev and Chetverikova 2017).

While such cases were once 'ordered' by businesses and organised criminals to dispossess other businesses, gradually the main threat to business became state officials and law enforcement agencies themselves. The agencies that once operated according to outside orders or in response to political demands also had the capacity to use the justice system for personal gain. Konstantin Dobrynin, a senior Moscow lawyer, called this a shift from 'prosecutions-to-order' (*zakaznye dela*) to 'bureaucratic prosecutions' (*prikaznie dela*). 'Now the law enforcement agencies themselves act as the initiators of the attack – they don't need somebody else to give the order [*zakazchik uzhe ne nuzhen*]', he told *Kommersant* newspaper (Kommersant 2019).

Mechanisms of Exception

This politicised and corrupted justice system became an accepted – almost naturalised – part of the Russian political and economic system. It was the consequence of multiple factors, including historical and structural causes, but it also played an important functional role in regime maintenance. A system of exceptionality in politics requires the subordination of the legal system to sovereign political will: powerful elites need to have the capacity to suborn the police, to order the security services and the procuracy to violate laws and regulations, and to control the functioning of judges and courts at will. These mechanisms are both formal – direct presidential control over the security services, the Investigative Committee and the *prokuratura* – and informal, through the use of patronage networks, 'curators' who manage courts, and the institutions of court chairs and other mechanisms to ensure that 'telephone justice' remains effective. The whole system has evolved in such a way as to ensure that in every case where it is deemed necessary by the authorities, particular legal outcomes can be assured.

There are numerous institutions involved in this interlocking justice system, but I highlight three organisations that are central to the functioning of the system, particularly in its role of political consolidation and 'elite management': first, the *prokuratura* or procuracy, along with its newer offshoot, the Investigative Committee (*Sledstvennyi komitet*, often known as *Sledkom*); second, the investigative organs and special departments of the Federal Security Service (FSB), particularly those responsible for investigating 'economic crimes'; and finally the court system, which should provide a check on exceptional power, but in reality always facilitates it.

Prokuratura

The institution of the procuracy has a remarkably consistent history in the Russian state. Founded in Russia by Peter the Great in 1711, it was designed as an institution of surveillance for the Tsar over his growing bureaucracy (Greenberg 2009). Yury Chaika, prosecutor-general from 2006 to 2020, continued to see the institution in this light, arguing that 'the fundamental task . . . of the Russian procuracy is to be the eye of the sovereign' (Greenberg 2009: 15). Abolished briefly by Lenin in 1917, it was quickly reconstituted and went on to become a central instrument of repression in the Soviet system, gaining worldwide notoriety for its role in the 1930s show trials. Largely unreformed during the 1990s, in 2005 the Venice Commission called it

> an organization, which is too big, too powerful, not transparent at all, exercises too many functions . . . but which nevertheless, despite its powers, remains vulnerable to presidential and political power . . . As it stands, the system . . . raises serious concerns of compatibility with democratic principles and the rule of law.[5]

The procuracy acts simultaneously as an investigative organ, a prosecutorial agency and an institution mandated with oversight over other state bodies. In this latter role, it was largely ineffective in upholding adherence to constitutional norms and civil liberties. The dual nature of the procuracy, acting as both the chief prosecuting body and as an organ of judicial oversight, inevitably led to contradictions, and provided the conditions for corrupt practice and ordered prosecutions. The procuracy continued in its role as an instrument of political prosecution subordinate to the executive, and has frequently been used in highly politicised cases against regime opponents. Burger and Holland argue that in cases where there are high-level political implications, the procuracy '(1) selectively fails to investigate; (2) selectively prosecutes; (3) facilitates expropriation of private property; and (4) leads illusory anti-corruption efforts' (Burger and Holland 2008: 162).

After 2011, many of Russia's high-profile political cases were pursued by the Investigative Committee, which had been established in 2007 under the aegis of the procuracy, but eventually became an independent body, reporting directly to the presidential administration. The new body was headed by Alexander Bastrykin, a former university classmate of Vladimir Putin, ensuring both a formal and informal chain of command. Subsequently, the Investigative Committee became the leading instrument of the regime in controversial prosecutions. It oversaw the multiple investigations of Alexei Navalny and his supporters. It also managed the prosecutions of more than thirty demonstrators and protesters who were arrested in Bolotnaya Square in 2012, and many other cases viewed as politically motivated. Investigative Committee investigators were trained to be ruthless and take shortcuts to get their target. Unscrupulous methods became the norm, precisely because the system was designed to ensure that the Investigative Committee would be a powerful instrument that could bypass any judicial constraints and target political opponents or business rivals at will.

When Prosecutor-General Yury Chaika took up his post in 2006, he promised to clean up corruption inside the agency, having discovered twenty criminal cases 'initiated without sufficient grounds' in the Central Federal District – in other words, prosecutions-to-order (Newsru 2006). But the logic of the system – and its requirement for continued access points for political influence – ensured that corruption continued to flourish in the system. The Investigative Committee, in particular, was dogged by allegations of corruption and links to organised crime (Kommersant 2016). In the most notorious case, in 2016 several Investigative Committee officials were arrested, alleged to have received bribes from one of the leading mafia bosses in Russia, Zakhary Kalashov, more widely known by his nickname 'Shakro Molodoy' (Young Shakro) (Moscow Times 2018).

Security Services

Although the police – the criminal investigation departments of the Interior Ministry – played an important role in almost all investigations, it was the prosecuting authorities or the internal security services that had the key decision-making roles in high-profile cases. The FSB became the lead agency in pursuing crimes in three areas characterised by frequent cases of exceptionality – elite business and property disputes; crimes associated with extremism and terrorism; and crimes against the 'constitutional order'. In all these areas the number of investigations and prosecutions rose sharply after 2012. For example, the number of terrorist crimes investigated by the FSB rose by eight times between 2013 and 2015, despite an overall decline in terrorist attacks in Russia (Rogov and Petrov 2016). A wave of investigations and prosecutions were initiated against cultural and political figures, such as theatre director Kirill Serebrennikov, in which the FSB's 2nd Department reportedly took a lead role (RBK 2017).[6]

The cases with the most serious political impact, however, were economic cases. Following a series of inter-agency battles in the 2010s, including the arrest of senior officials in the Interior Ministry's once-powerful Department for Economic Security in 2014, the FSB emerged as the lead agency for investigations into high-level economic crimes. The FSB formed the core of an increasingly powerful 'security vertical', with wide latitude to investigate and prosecute political and business elites, accountable only to the president and his most powerful allies. Not surprisingly, the number of economic crimes investigated by the FSB rose from fewer than 2,000 in 2012 to almost 5,000 in 2018 (Rogov 2019: 55).

The lead role in these investigations was played by one of the FSB's most powerful departments, the Economic Security Service (SEB), which had effective control over the most powerful financial and industrial groups in Russia, leading it to be dubbed the 'main department for control of oligarchs' (Dobrolyubov 2016). It was heavily involved in all the key operations against Gusinsky, Berezovsky, Khodorkovsky and other powerful business interests, and was responsible for 'control over the managerial and economic elite' of Russia (Rogov and Petrov 2016). In short, as one article put it, 'whoever controls the SEB of the FSB controls the entire finances of the country' (Dobrolyubov 2016).

Perhaps the most important directorate within the SEB is Directorate K (officially the 'Counterintelligence Department for Securing the Financial-Credit Sector of the Economic Security Service of the FSB'), which acts as a watchdog for the entire banking and financial sector in Russia. A report in the *Financial Times* asserted that Department K

> is one of the most controversial departments of Russia's new security elite, and figures prominently in some of the biggest scandals facing Russia today . . . In May 2007, Viktor Voronin, head of Directorate K, issued a finding that companies belonging to Hermitage Capital, at the time Russia's largest portfolio investor, had underpaid taxes. That led to a search of Hermitage offices, which in turn precipitated an alleged $230m tax fraud, and the death of one of Hermitage's lawyers, Sergei Magnitsky, in prison. (Clover 2011)

Directorate K is tasked primarily with cases of state-level significance or of personal interest to powerful individuals in the political elite. The head of Directorate K, Ivan Tkachev, in post since 2016, presided over a series of high-profile cases, including the prosecution of former minister of economic development, Aleksei Ulyukaev; minister of open government, Mikhail Abyzov; and the owners of the Summa group of companies, the brothers Ziyavudin and Magomed Magomedov (Sergeev and Sergeev 2019). Officers of Directorate K were involved in high-profile cases against the Taganskaya organised crime group, the head of Yugra bank, Aleksei Khotin, and the controversial prosecution of Michael Calvey, a US investment banker, whose detention was protested by many Russian business leaders (Nikolskii 2019).[7] In short, the Directorate became the instrument of choice to discipline the elite, and to decide which high-ranking businessman or minister would next fall into the zone of exception.

Courts and Judges

The prosecutorial and investigatory organs of the Russian state had tremendous power, but were not checked by any judicial processes. Once a prosecution was launched in an exceptional case, the chances of acquittal were close to zero. Even without any political interference, defendants faced an uphill struggle in Russian courts. If private prosecutions are excluded, only 0.2 per cent of criminal prosecutions in 2008 resulted in an acquittal (Paneyakh 2016: 139).[8] Esakov (2012: 693) has slightly higher calculations, but still concludes that acquittals in the judicial system did not exceed 1.5 per cent in any year in 2004–11. Jury trials produce a much higher level of acquittals – around 18 per cent on average in the years 2004–11

(Esakov 2012: 693), but trial by jury remained rare, reportedly used in only about 600 cases out of more than one million trials (Barry 2010).[9]

Many judges are former prosecutors, and prosecutors are also able to influence the career of judges, so a close relationship between the two is not surprising. Moreover, an acquittal by judges is almost automatically appealed by prosecutors, with a high likelihood of being overturned, resulting in a black mark against a judge's career. Almost 25 per cent of acquittals were annulled or changed at a higher court in 2008 (fewer than 4.5 per cent of convictions are annulled or changed on appeal) (Paneyakh 2016: 143). Even without an appeal, a judge who appears too lenient can face career-threatening sanctions. Alexander Melikov lost his judgeship in 2004 after his superiors concluded that he had issued sentences that were too lenient (Finn 2005).

In normal cases, there are still ways in which a judge can show leniency, by shortening sentences or imposing a suspended sentence (Paneyakh 2016). But in cases identified as having particular political implications, or involving powerful business interests, a judge has no such leeway. In such cases, the Soviet tradition of 'telephone justice' comes into play. State Duma member and chair of the Association of Lawyers of Russia, Pavel Krasheninnikov, commented: 'certainly the role of the law has increased somewhat in recent times, but unfortunately, sometimes a telephone call as before remains a much more effective mechanism than some legal norm' (Rossiiskaya gazeta 2010). According to the former chief justice of the Higher Arbitrage Court, Anton Ivanov, 'you can be an excellent expert and speaker, but if there is an order [from above] to decide the case not according to law, you cannot overcome this [order]' (Trochev 2017: 128).

'Telephone justice' is seldom as crude as that reported in Chechnya, where Vakhid Abubakarov, a judge, recused himself from hearing the case of Suleiman Edigov. He had concluded that Edigov was illegally detained by the police for over a month and tortured, but the judge said:

> A person who introduced himself as the internal affairs minister, Lieutenant-General Ruslan Shakhaevich Alkhanov, called me from an unidentified phone and said he is certain that the defendant is guilty and warned me against acquittal. After the intervention of an official of such a high level . . . any sentence . . . will look like a concession in case of a guilty verdict or a demonstration of courage in acquittal. (ICG 2015: 31)

In most cases, there is no need for such a direct intervention. The system itself ensures that exceptional cases are directed to compliant judges.

A vital role is played by court chairs, who typically oversee several courts and groups of judges, control rewards and sanctions for judges, and are able to award a case to any judge, picking the most 'reliable' individuals to oversee complex or controversial cases (Ledeneva 2013; Solomon 2008). Solomon explains:

> In the post-Soviet world chairs of courts are especially powerful, often controlling discretionary perks and benefits for their judges, and in a position to help their judges get promotions or hurt them through disciplinary initiatives including recommending their dismissal. At the same time, chairs represent a conduit for requests from the outside regarding particular cases, and they often control the assignment of at least important or hard cases. (Solomon 2008: 1–2)

A judge in the Volgograd regional court, Marianna Lukyankovskaya, claimed that she was forced to resign after she released a detainee charged with extortion, citing serious procedural violations in an earlier court hearing. She later claimed that the case had been a prosecution-to-order. After her resignation, she explained to the media the ways in which the court chair could influence decisions:

> In our court we have the following custom: every Monday we meet after lunch with the chair of the Collegium of Criminal Cases . . . and agree our positions on all cases which we are to hear during that week. I know that this is a direct violation of the independence of the court. But we have this custom. (Newsru 2009)

These different informal mechanisms in the court system, which leave judges vulnerable to political pressure, are not merely a question of poor practice or corruption. They are structurally necessary to preserve the possibility for powerful actors to intervene in the exceptional case. This produces an inevitable contradiction. The ability to manage the prosecutions of Khodorkovsky, Navalny and other political threats to the regime opens up the judicial system to wider abuse by multiple powerful individuals who use similar methods to apply pressure on judges. On the one hand, the regime understands the need for wider applicability of legal rules and impartial processes, for the development of a 'law-based state'. On the other hand, it consistently asserts the informal, unwritten right to intervene in the judicial process when it sees fit to protect what it views as important principles of the political and social order, interpreted with the interests of the regime and its close allies in mind.

The Exception Becomes the Norm

The challenge for courts, lawyers, plaintiffs and defendants, from the Constitutional Court downwards, was to identify and manage the dualism in the Russian justice system between the normal situation and the exception. Schmitt's simple answer – that the sovereign decides whether a normal situation or an exceptional case applies – fails to recognise the complex reality of the delegated powers and institutional mechanisms required to ensure that exceptions can be made in the normal application of legality. The result was the continuing spread of exceptionalism throughout the system in ways that could not help but hinder the development of any kind of rule of law. By 2019 some analysts worried that the system was beginning to break down as intra-elite arrests, *zakaznye dela* and inter-agency rivalry threatened to spiral out of control (Stanovaya 2019).

As Hendley (2017) has argued, ordinary Russians became adept at recognising the exceptional case 'from below', and where possible avoiding any involvement in any such cases. A court case can safely be categorised as 'routine', suggests Hendley, if 'it involves parties of approximately the same station in life and the outcome is of interest only to those parties'. Such cases are likely to be resolved according to normal procedures. But 'as a case edges away from the ordinary to the extraordinary, the risk of telephone law increases' (Hendley 2017: 224). Hendley admits to the 'fuzziness' of the 'dividing line' between the norm and the exceptional cases, but argues that many Russians feel able to distinguish between such cases (Hendley 2017: 224).

However, identifying the dividing line does not prevent ordinary citizens from being drawn into the shadowy world of the exception against their will. The operations of the extrajudicial exception in small-town life are brilliantly demonstrated in Andrei Zvyagintsev's film *Leviafan* (Leviathan) (2014), a tale of small-town tyranny in rural Russia, in which an ordinary man faces the untrammelled power of the local boss, who seeks to take over his property illegally. Zvyagintsev's title both points to the profusion of multiple would-be sovereigns across Russia, while also offering an implicit critique of Hobbesian notions of political order. The ability of the political leader to act outside the law provides the opportunity for others to do likewise, threatening to produce not Schmitt's ideal of sovereign decision-making as the basis for order, but what Rigi terms the 'chaotic mode of domination' (Rigi 2012). The achievement of Schmittian modes of sovereignty – of unconstrained power to operate in the domain of the exception – can only be at the expense of the everyday institutions that ensure legal order when the exception is not invoked. As power becomes concentrated among the unaccountable few, the institutions of the judiciary become hollowed out, and the distinction between the exception and the norm becomes increasingly strained.

Notes

1. http://data.worldjusticeproject.org/#/groups/RUS
2. http://info.worldbank.org/governance/WGI/#reports
3. In a stark illustration of his own premise, Krylenko was himself executed in 1938, after a twenty-minute trial.
4. In a later analysis, a *Vedemosti* investigation argued that these figures were exaggerated. Analysts calculated some 128,000 'economic crimes', not all of them related to business. See Shklyaruk and Chetverikova (2016).
5. European Commission for Democracy Through Law, 'Opinion on the Federal Law on the Prokuratura (Prosecutor's Office) of the Russian Federation', Opinion No. 340–2005, CDL-AD(2005)014.
6. The 2nd Department was responsible for cultural affairs, and had oversight over museums and theatres. According to an FSB spokesperson, it was staffed by specialists 'who understand what is culture and what is art'. The spokeperson warned that 'cultural institutions can be used by the enemy for propaganda as structures producing hostile attitudes to the Russian Federation' (RBC 2017).
7. The Directorate was not immune to investigations. In 2019 one of its departmental heads, in charge of overseeing the banking sector, Kirill Cherkalin, was arrested on charges of fraud. See Sergeev and Sergeev (2019).
8. It is worth noting that in many Western judicial systems acquittal rates are also very low, but prosecutors also have stricter criteria for bringing cases to court in the first place. See Titayev (2013).
9. Despite their rarity, conservative law-makers and judges criticised the use of jury trials from the beginning and sought to reduce their use, particularly in terrorist cases (Kahn 2006: 395).

SEVEN

The Crimean Exception

> Our western partners, led by the United States of America, prefer not to be guided by international law in their practical policies, but by the rule of force.
>
> Vladimir Putin (2014a)

The decision to incorporate Crimea into the Russian Federation in March 2014 was a stark example of exceptionalism in foreign policy. It was a decision that violated the rules of international order, but gained the support of the majority of the Russian and Crimean population. Viewed internationally as an illegal annexation and a blatant violation of international law, in Russia it was portrayed as profoundly legitimate, meeting the demands of historical justice and democracy. Russia's decision to incorporate Crimea was presented as a step towards a reformed international order, in which Russian subjectivity would be restored, and where Western manipulation of international law in their own interests would no longer be possible. In this way, the geopolitical contest between Russia and the West became also 'a struggle for the nature of international law' (Müllerson 2014: 133), a contest between a cosmopolitan vision of universal norms, and an idea of law as embedded organically in local cultures and civilisations, a plurality of laws to reflect a multipolar world.

The Crimean case brings together two fundamental themes of Schmitt's thought, which some scholars have tended to separate, but which overlap in important ways (Galli 2010). First, it provides a further instance in which sovereignty is revealed through the exceptional decision, in this case with regard to international law and international norms. Russia was internationally isolated after Crimea, but had successfully demonstrated its full sovereignty, understood in Moscow as the ability to take a decision outside the rules and in the face of Western opposition: 'Geopolitically she is alone, but free', concluded Dmitry Trenin (2019). Although the decision on Crimea violated international legality, it was nevertheless legitimated in Russian thinking by appeals to democratic support, articulated both in a formal referendum in Crimea, and in the broader 'Crimean consensus' that emerged among the Russian population in support of the annexation. The sovereign decision was viewed as reflecting the will of the people, even if it violated international legality.

Second, studying the annexation of Crimea reminds us that Schmitt is a spatial thinker, one who sees politics and law not as abstract, universal norms unrooted from culture and geography, but as concepts intimately related to concrete spaces, underpinned by an attachment to land and territory, defined by the physical markers of division: walls, barriers, boundaries and frontiers. Instead of universal, detached, abstract norms, which Schmitt interpreted as little more than a veiled pretext for US imperialism (Schmitt 2011b), he argued for an idea of law as rooted in territorial possession – even, in an almost mystical sense, in the earth. 'In mythical language', he writes in *The Nomos of the Earth* (1950), 'the earth became known as the mother of law . . . [the] root of law and justice' (Schmitt 2003: 42). Ultimately, law is not a set of spaceless, cosmopolitan norms, but 'the unity of order and orientation' (Schmitt 2007c: 69), a unity forged by the appropriation of land and its demarcation from the enemy.

The annexation of Crimea was the first forcible 'land appropriation' in Europe since 1945. In the contemporary period, when scholars assumed that the norm of territorial conquest had long been eliminated (Stiles and Sandholtz 2009), Schmitt's theory of land appropriation (*Landnahme*) as the basis for international order appears as a conceptual and theoretical shock. The Crimean decision took place in a unique set of circumstances, and may yet prove to be an isolated case. Yet it highlighted much broader tensions between Russia's search for what it viewed as historical justice and the legal rules of the international system. Russia is far from the only country to articulate this fundamental tension between the legal norms of international law and 'legitimate' claims to territories or borderlands; consequently, Schmitt's long-standing claim that this distinction is fundamental to legal and political order is worth examining once more.

Crimea: The Sovereign Decision

On the night of 22 February 2014, at his presidential residence at Novo-Ogarevo, outside Moscow, Vladimir Putin called a meeting with a small group of advisers: defence minister Sergei Shoigu, Security Council secretary Nikolai Patrushev, head of the FSB Alexander Bortnikov, and head of the presidential administration Sergei Ivanov (Zygar 2016: 275). In Ukraine, after weeks of protests in Kiev's main square, the Maidan, a negotiated agreement to hold early elections had broken down. Angry protesters once again took to the streets, shouting 'death to the criminal' and 'out, bandits', forcing President Viktor Yanukovich to flee the city (Higgins 2014). In Moscow's suburbs, Putin and his advisers spent all night overseeing a mission by Russian special forces to rescue Yanukovich, despite the contempt towards the Ukrainian leader felt by many Kremlin officials.[1] At seven o'clock in the morning of 23 February, with Yanukovich safely in Russian hands, Vladimir Putin – alone, according to his own account – took the decision to organise the incorporation of Crimea into Russia.[2]

Putin's own account of the decision might be treated with scepticism, but subsequent reports have repeatedly constructed this image of a solitary Putin as the sole decision-maker. He said later in an interview: 'Do you know what our advantage was? It was that I managed this personally' (RIA-Novosti 2015). When asked by US academic Daniel Treisman whether he had consulted his advisers, Putin responded: 'No, I told them we will do this and then that. I was even surprised at how well it went!' (Soldatov and Rochlitz 2018: 101, n 12). The presidential spokesperson Dmitry Peskov agreed that 'it was a personal decision of the head of state. He was the only person who could and had to make it and who made it.' Peskov claimed that 'there was no collective discussion' (TASS 2014).

An initial decision appears to have been tested over the next couple of weeks as public opinion evolved: Putin later said that he took a final decision on Crimea only after an opinion poll showed 80 per cent support for annexation, possibly referring to a poll taken 8–11 March, a week ahead of the formal referendum (Toal 2017: 222). Yet in the end, the sovereign decision, the decision to declare the exception, belonged to Putin. According to the well-connected editor of *Russia in Global Affairs*, Fedor Lukyanov, 'it seems the whole logic here is almost entirely the product of one particular mind' (Myers 2014). Former State Duma deputy Denis Voronenkov, who fled Russia and was subsequently assassinated in central Kiev, agreed that 'the decision on annexation was taken by one person. All normal people were against. Including his inner circle' (Kashin 2017). Mikhail Zygar's account suggests that only defence minister Sergei Shoigu urged caution, with Patrushev and Bortnikov assuring Putin that secret opinion polls suggested that Crimeans would support incorporation (Zygar 2016: 275–6).

Once a decision had been made, all subsequent collective decisions were simply formal political performances by institutions that lacked sovereign decision-making power. Putin gained official approval from the Federation

Council on 1 March for a possible deployment of Russian troops in Ukraine, but in reality special forces had already been deployed (Karagiannis 2014). On 11 March 2014 the Supreme Council of Crimea and the City Council of Sevastopol declared independence from Ukraine. In a referendum on 16 March, according to official figures, some 97 per cent of voters (on a turnout of 80 per cent) in Crimea, and 96 per cent of voters (86 per cent turnout) in Sevastopol, voted in a referendum to 'rejoin' the Russian Federation. In reality, turnout was almost certainly much lower: Crimean Tatars had boycotted the vote, and there were numerous violations of procedures during the referendum (McDougal 2015).[3]

The Supreme Council of Crimea formally declared independence on 17 March, a decision recognised by the Russian government the same day. This decision was immediately followed by the signing of the 'Treaty on Accession of the Republic of Crimea to Russia' on 18 March. This document in turn was ratified by Russia's State Duma (with just one dissenting vote) on 20 March and unanimously approved by the Federation Council on 21 March. This rapid and choreographed sequence of events demonstrated both a recognition of the importance of formal legal and constitutional process, and the complete lack of autonomy of any institution in the Russian political system outside the presidential administration.

There is a formal basis for unilateral presidential decision-making on foreign policy in Russia's constitution. Article 85 gives the president the sole right to 'govern the foreign policy of the Russian Federation' (Constitution of the Russian Federation 1993). As a consequence, 'the country essentially has only one decider when it comes to serious international issues . . . In foreign affairs and security policy . . . Putin has to make all the important decisions himself, with others essentially advising him or implementing his decisions' (Trenin 2015: 34). Vladimir Frolov also concludes that 'in the sphere of foreign policy, the Russian leadership [*Rossiiskaya vlast'*] is absolutely autonomous and accountable to no one' (Frolov 2017). Yet, in the case of Crimea, the decision went far beyond simply the exercise of formal constitutional powers. The emphasis in subsequent official accounts on Putin's complete autonomy in the decision is an important narrative, since it seeks to reaffirm Putin's individual sovereignty, not simply the formal powers of his office. The exercise of genuine sovereignty, in Schmitt's thinking, *requires* the sovereign leader to act outside the constitutional order in the exceptional case. Paradoxically, it is only by disregarding international law that Putin could demonstrate his own sovereign power and assert Russia's restored subjectivity in international affairs. The Crimean case finally provided Putin with an opportunity to exercise full sovereignty, understood in Russia as an existential freedom, including the freedom to break the rules.

Putin's first-hand account of the decision to intervene suggests that there was something compelling in the decision-making process itself, an existential, affective moment that is difficult to explain solely through rationalist accounts. The Crimean decision was equivalent to what Schmitt understood as a moment of 'pure conviction and executive will, unconstrained by any rules' (Dyzenhaus 1998: 11). For Schmitt, history is not made by inexorable social or economic forces, but by the historical event, the historical decision: 'History is not the realization of rules or regularities or scientific, biological, or other types of norms. Its essential and specific content is *the event* that arrives only once and does not repeat itself' (Koskenniemi 2004: 502). It is this event, this decision, which is 'the carrier of all that is meaningful' (Koskenniemi 2004: 502). In this sense, the decision becomes an end in itself, a conscious claim to be a subject of history, to declare the exception, simultaneously revealing and reasserting Putin's sovereign power.

This is not to deny the importance of a wider political and geopolitical context, or to suggest that there was no deliberative process of decision-making, which weighed and assessed different factors. The decision was heavily influenced by strategic concerns, particularly the status of Sevastopol, home to the Russian Black Sea fleet; domestic political considerations in Russia also no doubt played some role (Allison 2014; Karagiannis 2014; Treisman 2016). Yet a Schmittian reading of the Crimean decision suggests that it is not unreasonable to answer the question, 'Why did Putin annex Crimea?', with the almost facile response: 'Because he could', or, more accurately, because the annexation declared that Russia's sovereignty, embodied in its president, had finally been regained. The significance of Crimea was not only in its immediate territorial and strategic impact, but as a symbolic moment indicating that a quarter-century of humiliation and capitulation was finally over. The most emotional speech of Putin's career – his 'Crimea speech' in March 2014 to the entire Russian elite in the vast, chandeliered St George's Hall in the Grand Kremlin Palace – is also his most vivid articulation of a litany of two decades' worth of grievances against the West and an attempt to justify not only the incorporation of Crimea into Russia, but the entire conservative turn of Russian foreign policy after 2012. Perhaps its emotional tenor also reflected his own personal journey, that long, historical arc from the powerless humiliation of Dresden in 1989 to the proof of his own sovereign power in the annexation of Crimea.

Legality as Imperialism

The decision to incorporate Crimea became the starkest illustration in Russian foreign policy of Schmitt's constantly reiterated distinction between 'legality' and 'legitimacy'; the decision clearly violated international law, but Russian officials and jurists alike proclaimed it as a legitimate act, in accord with both historical justice and the will of the people. An extensive literature has examined how Crimea's secession from Ukraine and unification with Russia violated international law (Allison 2014; Burke-White 2014; Marxsen 2014; McDougal 2015). The annexation violated Article 2(4) of the UN Charter, prohibiting 'the threat or use of force against the territorial integrity or political independence of any state', and flouted the provisions of the 1975 Helsinki Final Act of the Conference on Security and Cooperation in Europe, which committed signatories to the inviolability of frontiers and territorial integrity, principles reaffirmed in the 1990 Charter of Paris and other agreements of the Organisation for Security and Cooperation in Europe (OSCE) (Burke-White 2014; Marxsen 2014; McDougal 2015).

It seems evident that Russia violated the 1997 bilateral Treaty of Friendship, Cooperation and Partnership between Russia and Ukraine, which committed the two countries 'to build their mutual relations on the basis of the principles of mutual respect for their sovereign equality, territorial integrity, inviolability of borders, peaceful resolution of disputes, non-use of force or the threat of force'.[4] Russian troops in Crimea also violated Article 6 of the 1997 bilateral status of forces agreement relating to the Russian Black Sea Fleet in Sevastopol (extended in 2010 for a further twenty-five years), which committed Russia to 'respect the sovereignty of Ukraine, obey its laws, and not allow interference in the internal affairs of Ukraine' (Allison 2014: 1263; McDougal 2015: 1847). Russia's actions went against the 1994 Budapest Memorandum on Security Assurances, signed by the United States, the United Kingdom and Russia, in which the three powers promised to 'respect the Independence and Sovereignty and the existing borders of Ukraine' and affirmed 'their obligation to refrain from the threat or use of force against the territorial integrity or political independence of Ukraine'.[5]

Russian officials responded to these multiple claims that they had violated international law in several, sometimes contradictory ways. First, they made the argument that Russia had the right to intervene because of an unconstitutional seizure of power in a 'coup' by 'fascist' forces in Kiev, which allegedly posed a threat to Russian-speaking communities; Russia therefore had a right and a duty to protect the human rights of the people of Crimea (Issaeva 2017: 89). A statement from the Russian Ministry of Foreign Affairs on the third anniversary of Crimea's annexation argued that the decision was 'a legitimate exercise of the right of the people of Crimea to self-determination', in the face of 'mayhem wreaked by radical national forces', using 'terror and intimidation on both political opponents and the population of entire regions of that country' (MFA RF 2017). The Ukrainian government was labelled a US-backed puppet regime, with – according to Sergei Lavrov – 'Nazi and neo-Nazi characteristics', which was intent on expanding NATO up to the Russian frontier (Kommersant 2018).

This narrative of 'humanitarian' intervention often had a contradictory element: on the one hand, it was justified by the claim that a new, aggressive regime in Kiev threatened the people of Crimea; on the other hand, it was justified because the Ukrainian state had effectively collapsed, and in legal terms no longer existed (for a discussion, see Hilpold 2015: 256–8). In an original interpretation, which had no basis in international law, Tolstykh argued that a fracturing of the social contract in Ukraine resulted in 'the return of the Crimean population to its natural state', allowing it to choose unification with Russia (Tolstykh 2014: 881). Stanislav Chernichenko, a law professor at the Russian Diplomatic Academy, argued that the Russian intervention was justified because 'in a legal sense, there was no public authority in Ukraine', consequently, the Russian government 'could only by guided by the expression of will of the Crimean population' (Issaeva 2017: 95). Similar views emerged in articles by other Russian scholars of international law (Pursiainen and Forsberg 2018). This line echoed official statements: in March 2014 Putin had claimed that 'there is still no legitimate executive authority in Ukraine' (Putin 2014a).

Alternative opinions were rare among legal scholars in Russia, reflecting both the dominance of official narratives and, according to some Russian scholars, the weakness of Russian international law scholarship. In a rare critique, Davletbaev and Issaeva criticised the 'archaic language' of Russian diplomats, which they described as full of 'clichés', and accused legal scholars of acting as though the entire post-war development of international law had passed them by (Davletbaev and Issaeva 2014). Tolstykh pointed to problems of 'scholasticism, false theories, and incompetence' among his colleagues in a critical review, and lamented that many Russian legal scholars did not discuss the Crimean problem in any depth (Tolstykh 2019). A Russian lawyer noted that 'among Russian international legal scholars there were almost no critical voices willing to assess Crimea's annexation as at least questionable under international law'. Instead, the majority of Russian scholars 'spoke or wrote on the matter feverishly defending Russia's actions' (Issaeva 2017: 87). In a typical example, Professor Anatoly Kapustin, president of the Russian Association of International Law, wrote an open letter mounting a far-reaching critique of Western actions in Ukraine, attacking its 'hypocrisy' with regard to international law and 'disrespect of the will of the people of Crimea' (Kapustin 2014).

At first glance, these views appeared to contradict long-standing positions from Russian officials and legal scholars on the legality of the use of force in international affairs, the principle of non-interference and the right to self-determination (Allison 2017). Yet the basis for such a divergence of positions had long been latent in Russian scholarship on international law, which continued a Soviet tradition of distinguishing between 'Western' and 'Russian' interpretations of international law, and increasingly prioritised the latter at the expense of alternative views (Mälksoo 2017: 87–92). A critique of Western interpretations of international law in turn laid the basis for an increasingly influential Russian 'native' school in international legal scholarship, which reflected Russian official positions on key legal concepts such as intervention or sovereignty, and critiqued the West as a hypocritical violator of international law (Mälksoo 2017: 88–9).

Claims of Western hypocrisy in relation to international law became an organising frame for almost all official and scholarly responses. Putin's speechwriters outlined the argument in the Ukrainian context:

> How is it possible . . . to support the armed seizure of power, the violence and murders? . . . How is it possible to support the subsequent attempts to use armed force to suppress people in the south-east who disagreed with this lawlessness? I repeat, how is it possible to support this? And all accompanied by hypocritical conversations about the defence of international law and human rights. This is simply pure cynicism. (Putin 2014c)

In an earlier speech, Putin had highlighted what he believed was an evident double standard, by referencing the precedent of Kosovan independence, citing the 2010 ruling of the UN International Court of Justice in favour of Kosovo's right to declare independence. Russia was strongly opposed to Kosovo independence, but Putin complained that 'for some reason, what is permitted to Albanians in Kosovo . . . is forbidden for Russians, Ukrainians and Crimean Tatars in Crimea' (Putin 2014a). For Putin this proved the wider point: 'This is not even double standards; this is a kind of remarkable, primitive, straightforward cynicism. One should not try so crudely to make everything suit one's interests, calling the same thing today, white, and tomorrow, black' (Putin 2014a).

For Putin, the Crimean case came after a long history of Western violations of international law, beginning in Yugoslavia, and continuing in Iraq and Libya. According to the president:

> They act as they please: here and there, they use force against sovereign states, building coalitions based on the principle 'If you are not with us, you are against us.' To make this aggression look legitimate, they force the necessary resolutions from international organisations, and if for some reason this does not work, they simply ignore the UN Security Council and the UN overall. (Putin 2014a)

In this critique of the post-Cold War liberal order Russian officials echoed Schmitt's concerns about the use of a universalist conceptualisation of international law to justify Western neo-imperialism, characterised by 'expanding patterns of interventionism justified through the language of "space-disregarding universalizations" such as "humanity"' (Minca and Rowan 2015a: 275). The 'concept of humanity', argues Schmitt, is 'a useful ideological instrument of economic expansion', a cynical misuse of a concept to justify an expansionist foreign policy. His view was summed up in a famous quip: 'Whoever invokes humanity wants to cheat' (Schmitt 2007a: 54). Yet, it is not only a cynical misuse, according to Schmitt, but potentially destructive, because 'to confiscate the word humanity, to invoke and monopolize such a term', risks labelling the enemy as inhuman, and thus justifying 'the most extreme inhumanity' (Schmitt 2007a: 54). Schmitt constantly criticises attempts to develop universal legal norms, beginning with the Hague Peace conference in 1899 and culminating in the failure of Versailles and the League of Nations. For Schmitt:

> Universalism . . . is the representation of the international scene as a smooth and homogenous space that is morally and legally malleable [but this] space is actually functional for those in power (the Anglo-Saxons and their economic potential) who act politically through the moral disqualification of their enemies. (Galli 2010: 4)

Consequently, the universal, abstract norms that constitute international law are not universal at all, but are the particularistic norms of Anglo-American civilisation promulgated on a global scale, 'a kind of imperial universalism' (Koskenniemi 2016: 598). This is an international law imbued with a 'false universalism', because 'self-interested liberal great powers (e.g. the United States and United Kingdom) skilfully exploit it in order to pursue their specific power interests' (Scheuerman 2007: 70). International law, as developed in the inter-war and post-1945 periods, lacks a spatial element that would limit its scope, and is an irredeemably liberal project, which masks the political and economic interests of its American authors (Brown 2007: 47).

Such views of the Western misuse of international law echoed throughout Russia's defence of the Crimean annexation, but left Russia with an awkward dual argument that both critiqued the West in its violations of international law, while simultaneously deflecting criticisms of Russia's own legal violations in Ukraine.

Russia's most radical argument in favour of the Crimean decision goes beyond a traditional interpretation of international law and instead argues that whatever the legality of the decision, it was legitimate because it represented the popular will. This argument is the most far-reaching and the most radical in terms of international law, with the potential to justify irredentist claims around the world in terms not only of current popular opinion, but also of historical justice. In his March 2014 'Crimea speech', Putin argued for the correction of an anti-democratic decision in the past, the transfer of the Crimean ASSR and Sevastopol to the Ukrainian SSR in 1954. According to Putin,

> this decision was made with clear violations even of those constitutional norms that were in place then. The decision was made in secret, behind the scenes. Naturally, in a totalitarian state nobody bothered to ask the citizens of Crimea and Sevastopol. They were simply confronted with the fact. (Putin 2014a)

Moreover, the 1991 separation of Russia and Ukraine was also carried out without regard to the will of the Crimean population, according to this narrative. According to Putin, speaking in 2014:

> Now, many years later, I heard residents of Crimea say not long ago that back in 1991 they were passed from hand to hand like a sack of potatoes. It is difficult to disagree with this. And what about the Russian state? What about Russia? It hung its head and went along with it, and swallowed the insult. This country was going through such hard times then that realistically it was incapable of protecting its interests. (Putin 2014a)

Other commentators referenced the referendum held in March 1991, in which Crimean residents voted by an overwhelming majority to preserve the USSR. An academic argued that:

the Reunification of Crimea with the Russian Federation that took place on 21.3.2014 became a practical realization of the initial will and aspiration of the people to live in one single democratic and constitutional state, which was clearly stated in the Soviet Union Referendum on 17.3.1991 and was clearly expressed again in the Crimean Referendum on 16.3.2014. (Salenko 2015: 166)[6]

In the contemporary period, the March 2014 referendum in Crimea was presented as the clear legitimising device for Russia's actions, but references to the referendum result were bolstered by the citation of popular support in Russia itself. Putin claimed that 'the absolute majority of our people clearly do support what is happening', and cited opinion polls showing that 'some 95 percent of citizens think that Russia should protect the interests of Russians and members of other nationalities living in Crimea', and that 'more than 83 percent think that Russia should do this even if it will complicate our relations with some other countries'. Putin also cited polls showing that '86 percent of citizens of our country believe that Crimea is still Russian territory, Russian land', and that 'almost 92 percent support Crimea's unification with Russia' (Putin 2014a). Putin concluded: 'Thus the overwhelming majority of residents of Crimea and the absolute majority of citizens of the Russian Federation support the reunification of the Republic of Crimea and the city of Sevastopol with the Russian Federation' (Putin 2014a). The decision is a political decision for Russia alone to make, argues Putin. And 'it can only be based on the will of the people, because only the people are the source of any power' (Putin 2014a).

Valentin Tolstykh, Chair of International Law at Novosibirsk State University, argued that while Western scholars favoured arguments against secession based on sovereignty and human rights, Russia followed a Rousseauian argument that the decision should reflect the 'general will' of the population (Tolstykh 2015: 138). Even if there were a number of shortcomings in the referendum campaign, this did not invalidate the result, since it reflected the broad desire of the mass of the Crimean people (Tolstykh 2015: 134). The presence of Russian troops in the peninsula also should not invalidate the outcome, since they did not interfere with the expression of the 'general will'. On the contrary, Tolstykh argues that it is interference from other, third states – what he calls 'penetration' – which

> is a violation of natural laws of the political organism; it inevitably causes imbalance, division, separation of the political organism, distancing of its elements from each other, and, in extreme cases, the decay of the organism or the atrophy of its elements. (Tolstykh 2015: 132)

Tolstykh argues that 'the general will (its formation and implementation) cannot be influenced by third states' (Tolstykh 2015: 132). These ideas demonstrate an affinity with Schmittian ideas regarding the need for spatial boundaries to law, to defend against the use of international law and international norms by Western powers as a weapon for penetrating 'alien' spaces.

Rather than technical interpretations of international law, this claim to be representing the popular will infuses much of the Russian discourse on Crimea. For example, on a talk show led by the nationalist commentator Artem Sheinin, devoted to the third anniversary of the referendum on 14 March 2017, many of the commentators repeatedly articulated this appeal to democracy and the will of the people (Izborsky club 2017). This democratic aspect of the exceptional case is recognised in Schmitt's claim that the true sovereign has a democratic mandate for extraordinary decision-making, understood as a coincidence of identities between the leader and the people. David Dyzenhaus comments on the 'democratic' nature of the exception:

> when we call the content of what is asserted in that moment democratic, what we really mean is that its success depends on its recognition as an authentic expression of identity by a substantial proportion of the population of a given, that is, geographically bounded, territory. (Dyzenhaus 2016: 503)

This sense of an 'authentic expression of identity' becomes more important than any technical shortcomings in the referendum. The decision has an existential character, which is shared by the vast majority of the people as an expression of identity, and is articulated through the collective sense of emotion and solidarity later termed the 'Crimean consensus'. Claims about international legality would always struggle to compete against the legitimacy claimed by this kind of collective emotional affirmation.

Despite all the violations in the referendum, a majority of residents probably did support unification with Russia, with the significant exception of Crimean Tatars, many of whom did not vote and remained suspicious of the new Russian authorities (O'Loughlin and Toal 2019). Although polling in Crimea faces obvious challenges, outcomes of opinion surveys have been consistent. In a December 2014 poll, 84 per cent of respondents supported annexation by Russia (O'Loughlin and Toal 2019), almost identical results to a 2015 poll, in which 82 per cent supported Crimea's unification with Russia, with only 4 per cent opposed (Bershidsky 2015). A more substantive survey in 2017 did not ask this direct question, but only 2.4 per cent said that they would vote differently (Sasse 2017: 17). O'Loughlin and Toal (2019) conclude that

> there is no indication that a majority of current residents of the peninsula question or regret the annexation. . . . irrespective of the controversial means by which Crimea became part of Russia, the majority of its residents appear happy about this fact and want it to stay there. (O'Loughlin and Toal 2019: 18–19)

Order and Orientation

The claim of legitimacy through democratic support also invokes a spatial aspect to law – for Schmitt, law reflects the popular will of a specific people in a specific place, not an abstract, globalised concept such as 'humanity'. In contrast to the 'free-floating' universal norms of liberalism, Schmitt's understanding of law always invokes geographic place and space, and the inevitable divisions that implies. In Schmitt's work, spatial division is the only sustainable mechanism for international order: 'if managing conflict is the aim of order, then spatial division is the means of ordering' (Minca and Rowan 2015a: 274). Meierhenrich and Simons (2016: 36) argue that Schmitt's theory of international law is 'deliberately vague and incomplete', but 'hinged on what he called the "unity of order and orientation" (*"Einheit von Ordnung und Ortung"*)'. International order depends on spatial determination, an orientation in accordance with actual physical control of land and the division of the world into Great Spaces – *Großräume* – the spheres of influence of great powers.

For Schmitt, international order – or what he terms *nomos* in his later work (Schmitt 2003) – is not a legal order, but refers to 'a political form', brought into being through 'originary violence', and constituting a 'concrete order oriented not by harmony but by a "cut" that creates political space, instituting normality derived not from law (*nomos* is not law) but from a concrete act of differentiation' (Galli 2010: 14). An international order based on merely technical or legal agreements – evident in many contemporary ideas of global governance based on cosmopolitan norms – is vulnerable to revolutionary upheaval, because such an order refuses to recognise the fact that 'the central problem of world order is always a political problem' (Schmitt 1995: 599). Schmitt insists on the presence of the political in international order, and by insisting on the political, he ensures that order is produced not through cooperation and global governance, but through clear lines of amity and enmity between different states and spaces.

At the foundation of this vision of international order is not international law or a set of norms, but land appropriation and division. Schmitt explains that *nomos* should not be translated as law (*Gesetz*), in the sense of statute or regulation:

> *Nomos* comes from *nemein* – a [Greek] word that means both 'to divide' and 'to pasture'. Thus, *nomos* is the immediate form in which the political and social order of a people becomes spatially visible – the initial measure and division of pasture-land, i.e., the land-appropriation as well as the concrete-order contained in it and following from it ... *Nomos* is the *measure* by which the land in a particular order is divided and situated; it is also the form of political, social, and religious order determined by this process. Here, measure, order, and form constitute a spatially concrete unity ... In particular, *nomos* can be described as a wall, because, like a wall, it, too, is based on sacred orientations. (Schmitt 2003: 70)

Thus the appropriation and division of land, the marking of boundaries and the building of walls, all precede and shape international law. The seizure of land is the 'reproductive root in the normative order of history' (Schmitt 2003: 48). Land appropriation 'constitutes the original spatial order' and acts as the 'source of all further concrete order and all further law' (Schmitt 2003: 48). In this interpretation, international law is not an abstract, universal body of law, disconnected from time and place, derived from certain foundational norms, such as ideas of universal human rights. Law is rather carved out in geography, in the earth, through an original act of land appropriation: 'The great primeval acts of law remained territorial orientations: appropriating land, founding cities, and establishing colonies' (Schmitt 2003: 44). This insight, argues Schmitt, confirms the spatial nature of law, and of order:

> Every fundamental order is a spatial order. One speaks of the constitution of a country or a piece of earth as of its fundamental order, its Nomos. Now, the true, actual fundamental order touches in its essential core upon particular spatial boundaries and separations, upon particular quantities and a particular partition of the earth. At the beginning of every great epoch there stands a great land-appropriation. In particular, every significant alteration and every resituating of the image of the earth is bound up with world-political alterations and with a new division of the earth, with a new land-appropriation. (Schmitt 2015)

Schmitt's portrayal of land appropriation can be read as a reminder of the violent origins of the European state, a corrective to the naturalisation of the liberal democratic state in the modern era; or as a post-colonial reading of international law that makes visible the violence that underpinned the legalisation of European expansionism (Koskenniemi 2016: 604). In these ways, the argument can be read as a powerful critique of liberal order, but it must be remembered that it emerged alongside – and in support of – policies of Nazi expansionism and territorial conquest. Teschke reminds us that Schmitt's ideas also reflected 'a fascist concept of territorial Landnahme (land capture) – brute acts of seizure and occupation that repartition the world – in which . . . unities of space, law, and political order were forged by wars of conquest, establishing radical titles to land' (Teschke 2016: 369).

This stark reminder of Schmitt's own personal history and historical context is suggestive of a fundamental contradiction in his work, highlighted by Hannah Arendt, among others, 'namely that he both embraces conquest and repudiates imperialism' (Jurkevics 2017: 346). Jurkevics sees Schmitt as 'in contradiction with himself regarding conquest and imperialism' (Jurkevics 2017: 354), but Schmitt is clear that there is a distinction between the spaceless, normative imperialism that he ascribes to America, and a space-forming, order-producing division of land that is an act of resistance against US power. In the same way, contemporary Russian thinking places these 'imperialisms' in fundamentally different categories, arguing for distinct assessments of Russian and US military actions that violate state sovereignty (Allison 2017). Western 'humanitarian intervention' is presented as fundamentally different from Russia's own form of intervention, which is designed to protect Russian citizens, and prevent the intervention of Western powers in Russia's spatial realm. Western interventions are 'penetrative' – in Tolstykh's formulation – forcing open closed realms and deconstructing spatial orders. Russia's interventions are protective, space-forming, designed to create the conditions for the will of the people to be heard. As Putin points out, 'Russia created conditions – with the help of special armed groups and the Armed Forces, I will say it straight – but only for the free expression of the will of the people living in Crimea and Sevastopol' (Putin 2014f). In Putin's articulation, Russia's interventions are democratic interventions, both protecting compatriots and allowing their voice to be heard, free of the pressure of external powers.

Russia's interventions into neighbouring countries assert new boundaries, build frontiers and transform the principles of land division. The division of land is at the heart of Schmitt's *nomos*, because for Schmitt the role of the land in political and juridical thinking is fundamental: 'Every ontonomous and ontological judgement derives from the land' (Schmitt 2003: 45). The land is related to law in three ways, claims Schmitt: through a 'reward of labour', extracting and processing its resources; through 'fixed boundaries' and divisions, which produce the political basis for law; and through the built environment, whereby 'the solid ground of the earth is delineated by fences, enclosures, boundaries, walls, houses, and other constructs' (Schmitt 2003: 42).

After the war, Müller argues (1997: 30), 'Schmitt finally moved to a full-fledged mysticism of the soil, in which his concerns for concreteness and order converged in a unity of order and location *(Ordnung und Ortung)*'. Schmitt argues that 'a concrete truth is never utopian; it has a piece of earth under it, a soil, from which it emerges; it is located in the full sense of the word' (Schmitt 1995: 514). However, this attachment to the soil is not necessarily articulated as nationalism or ethnicity. Although Schmitt's talk of peasants, *Heimat*, and soil bears an uncomfortable resemblance to Nazi slogans, such as Darré's infamous *Blut und Boden* (1930), there is not necessarily a racial aspect to his understanding of attachment to the land (although this conclusion must also be qualified in the context of Schmitt's rampant anti-Semitism: for Schmitt the Jews are the archetypal 'spaceless' people, who lack spatial and territorial order [Gross 2016]).[7] As Hannah Arendt noted in the margins of her copy of *Nomos*: 'Poor Schmitt: The Nazis said blood and soil – he understood soil. The Nazis meant blood' (Jurkevics 2017: 345).

For Schmitt, this mystical – but nevertheless political – relationship to the land also acts as the foundation for an ongoing source of resistance to a totalising and despatialising liberal order. Schmitt's figure of the partisan, developed in *The Theory of the Partisan* (1963), offered 'resistance to the despatialization and absolutization of enmity that grew from universalist political thought' (Minca and Rowan 2015b: 237). The partisan was spatially bound, committed to the defence of the land on which he lived, against a real enemy. This 'telluric' partisan 'defends a piece of land with which he has an autochthonous relation. His fundamental position remains defensive, despite the intensive mobility of his tactics' (Schmitt 2007c: 92). The partisan is rooted, not only in space, but in history. He is 'the last sentinel of the earth as a not yet completely destroyed element of world history' (Schmitt 2007c: 71). But partisans defending their land can develop a wider ideological message, particularly when supported by a third party, such as a state, which transforms their local war into a wider struggle against an international order. In this ideological turn, their struggle, it might be said, is against legality itself, but in favour of legitimacy.

Koskenniemi points to this argument in the context of global terrorism: 'Against formal legality, the terrorist – like the partisan – relies on a deeper legitimacy from the perspective of which the law (North Atlantic Treaty Organization, United Nations, the coalition) is the crime and legality itself the enemy' (Koskenniemi 2016: 606).

In a similar, way the Russian intervention in Ukraine defied legality in favour of a legitimacy embedded in a particular historical narrative and a belief in the deeper connection of the Russian people to the Crimean land. In other disputed areas, Russia had refused to permit the incorporation of territories such as South Ossetia or Abkhazia into the Russian Federation, preferring them to occupy a precarious no-man's land as de facto states recognised only by Russia and one or two allies. In the Crimean case, however, a new territorial element was introduced to Russia's official discourse. Putin described Crimea as a sacral land in Russian history, and inscribed its territory with a mythical geography:

> Here is ancient Khersones, where Prince Vladimir was baptised. His spiritual victory, the acceptance of the Orthodox faith, predetermined the common cultural, moral and civilisational principles, which united the peoples of Russia, Ukraine and Belorussia. In Crimea are the graves of Russian soldiers, by whose courage Crimea was taken in 1783 by the Russian state. Crimea is Sevastopol – the legendary city, a city with a fateful history, a fortress city and the birthplace of Russia's Black Sea Fleet. Crimea is Balaklava and Kerch, Malakhov Kurgan and Sapun Ridge. Each one of these places is sacred for us, symbolising Russian military glory and outstanding valour. (Putin 2014a)

In a speech in December 2014, Putin went further, arguing that 'For Russia, Crimea, ancient Korsun, Kherson, [and] Sevastopol have an enormous civilisational and sacral meaning. Just like the Temple Mount in Jerusalem for those who follow Islam or Judaism' (Putin 2014c). The resonance of these names, their constant reiteration in public events and ceremonies, serves to reassert the significance of the land. Articulating names provides a 'third orientation of power . . . the tendency to visibility, publicity, and ceremony' (Schmitt 2003: 349). Schmitt writes of 'the relation between *Nahme* and name, power and name-giving, and . . . the formative, even festive processes of many land appropriations that are able to make *Nahme* a sacred act' (Schmitt 2003: 348). The names of places underpin ritual and reinforce the idea of a concrete place, in historical time. By contrast, argues Schmitt, 'Law is still not a name. Humanity and reason are not names' (Schmitt 2003: 349).

The land was named discursively as 'ours' in the popular meme '*Krym-Nash*' (Crimea Is Ours), but also repeatedly codified in Russian laws, regulations, documents and maps. At the same time, it was physically divided and bounded in new ways. Since 2014 Russia has redrawn Crimea's geography, building new border infrastructure, military installations and transport connections. In 2018 FSB border guards constructed a 60-km fence equipped with movement sensors and night-vision cameras along the peninsula's northern boundary with the rest of Ukraine, thus giving physicality to this unrecognised border (BBC 2018). Russia constructed a new 20-km bridge in 2018 over the Kerch Strait to link the peninsula to the Russian mainland. The Crimean bridge acts both as a physical connection to Russia and as a new de facto boundary for Ukraine, limiting access for larger vessels to the Sea of Azov and to the Ukrainian ports of Mariupol and Berdyansk. Russia asserted territorial claims over the waters around Crimea and the Kerch straits, leading to clashes with Ukrainian naval vessels in November 2018. Since 2014 Russia has militarised the Crimean peninsula, expanding the Sevastopol naval base, building a new military garrison, and installing new radar systems and anti-air and anti-ship missile systems all around the coast (Sukhankin 2017).

The militarisation of these new boundaries emphasises their role as external lines of enmity, which define the land in terms of a distinction between friend and enemy. The annexation is further determined by the fundamental political decision that distinguishes the 'friend' from the 'enemy', and creates boundaries between the interior and the exterior: Schmitt's work reminds us that 'the friend-enemy distinction is mapped against, or rather "situated" at, the borderline of an inside/outside relation' (Minca and Rowan 2015a: 273). The Crimean peninsula became a frontline in a new struggle against NATO and its allies, and the Black Sea the latest virtual battle-ground with the West. However, in a stark illustration of the dangers of Schmittian concepts of the political, this friend–enemy distinction maps all too easily onto historical myths of collaboration among communities inside Crimea. Russian commentators have argued that the United States and Ukraine supported the Crimean Tatars as part of a 'hybrid war' against Russian control of Crimea (Mukhin 2015). This discourse revived Soviet portrayals of the Crimean Tatars as a 'fifth column', accused of collaboration with outside powers.

After 2014, the new Russian authorities immediately demonised the role of Refat Chubarov, the head of the Crimean Tatar Mejlis, as a security threat accused of working on behalf of the West to destabilise Crimea (Mukhin 2015; Wilson 2017). The Mejlis, as a body with aspirations to sovereignty, was outlawed by Russia in 2016 as an 'extremist organisation' and Crimean

Tatars faced serious human rights abuses and constraints on their ability to organise politically (HRW 2017). Moscow promoted loyalist Crimean Tatar organisations, such as the Milli Firka grouping, to replace the Mejlis and other independent Tatar organisations, in an extension of the Putinist system of a depoliticised 'managed democracy', which rejects a genuine pluralism of political subjects.

Russian official discourse emphasised that 'Crimea is a unique blend of cultures and traditions of different peoples' in which 'Russians and Ukrainians, Crimean Tatars and representatives of other ethnic groups have lived side by side on Crimean soil, retaining their own identity, traditions, language and faith' (Putin 2014a). Yet, this inclusive rhetoric was belied by the simplistic monologic *KrymNash* discourse, which asserted a narrow sense of belonging that disguised the complexity and violence of Crimea's history. Since the mid nineteenth century Crimea has been constructed in Russian myth-making as a sacral Russian heartland, from which Crimean Tatar history has been eroded or – in the most extreme case of the Tatars' physical deportation – completely effaced. The 1944 physical deportation of the Crimean Tatars was followed by a campaign in which they were 'discursively cleansed' in a 'campaign of censure and slander that erased their ethnonym from the pages of print media and their toponyms from the face of the earth' (Finnin 2011: 1093). After their deportation, 'efforts were made to cleanse all traces of them from the Crimean landscape' (Uehling 2015: 3).

The annexation of Crimea has reasserted a narrow, ahistorical and exclusionary discourse. In Landa's study of the Crimean poet Maximilian Voloshin, he argues that 'Putin's new religious, nationalist and Biblical myth of Crimea is very different from how Russians saw Crimea before the annexation' (Landa 2015: 190). This post-annexation discourse undermines multinational and cosmopolitan views of Crimea, occludes its complex and contested history, and downplays the special relationship of indigenous Crimean Tatars to the land. In this sense, the view of the Schmittian partisan becomes confused, and contested. Instead of a single figure standing on their land against a totalising world order, the land is always contested between different orders, different sovereignty claims, and different histories. Yet within a Schmittian worldview, there is no mechanism for managing this pluralism of claims to memory, identity and territory within society, except for state violence and erasure, and enforcing social homogeneity within a bounded space, characterised by exceptional practices and defined by its external enemies.

Russia did make a number of formal concessions to the Tatars after 2014, including making Crimean Tatar a state language, which had not been the case in the Ukrainian state. Yet of much greater significance were measures taken to silence Crimean Tatar voices and discourses. The authorities closed an independent Crimean Tatar television channel and the popular Radio Meydan, which specialised in 'Eastern' music and attempted 'to carve out space for a "Crimean publicness" . . . in tension to the dominant Russo-Slavic public sphere' (Sonevytsky 2019: 100). Maria Sonevytsky explores how something as mundane as Radio Meydan's music, playing in a *marshrutka*, contributed to a clash of competing 'sovereign imaginaries', each of which viewed the radio station's programming as reinforcing or negating their own political desires. Many Russian Crimeans saw the annexation as 'a restoration of proper juridico-political sovereignty to the Russian state', and an overcoming of the 'unsettled sovereignties of preannexation Crimea'. For many Crimean Tatar communities, however, it was a smothering of their own visions, and a negation of an emerging post-colonial sovereign imaginary that had offered a more pluralistic vision of Ukraine, in which Crimean Tatars could once again regain a genuine subjectivity (Sonevytsky 2019: 103, 112).

The problem of Russia's post-annexation politics in Crimea is the problem that Schmitt consistently ignores: diversity and heterogeneity within societies either require channels and mechanisms for political resolution, or demand a hegemonic, coercive state to suppress alternative visions and subjectivities. The clash is not a simple binary between the autochthonous, telluric partisan and a despatialised liberal order, but between different visions of spatial order, law and sovereignty within the same territory. Schmitt denies the possibility of pluralistic politics within the state as a mediating institution for managing difference, permitting the political only to appear along an enmity line along the border, effectively negating the idea of public politics inside the state and removing any agency from the people themselves. Hannah Arendt complains that Schmitt's obsession with the soil leaves him indifferent to the people who actually inherit the earth (Jurkevics 2017: 349). Schmitt's concept of law as emerging from the earth, from territory, overlooks 'the content of laws and their orientation (Richtung) towards the people'. As a consequence, argues Arendt, Schmitt's concept of law is somehow contentless, and aims 'to remove justice from the content of the law' (Jurkevics 2017: 350).

In the end, Schmitt is always more interested in the boundary of spaces than in their content. Land appropriation is ultimately about constructing international order, not addressing the needs of the local population. In this context, Schmitt identified two types of land appropriation. One type takes place '*within* a given order of international law', in which it will 'readily receive the recognition of other peoples'. A very different type, exemplified by the Crimean annexation, will 'uproot an existing spatial order and establish a new *nomos* of the whole spatial sphere of neighbouring peoples' (Schmitt 2003: 82). In this latter interpretation, the annexation of Crimea was a first step towards a new spatial order, achieved through territorial change. As a headline in *Russia in Global Affairs* phrased it: 'A total but peaceful battle over Ukraine, for a new world order' (Bordachev 2014). Visions of this emerging world order in Russian conservative thought bore striking affinities with the international thought of Carl Schmitt, who proposed a new *nomos* of the earth, in which universal ideals of equal justice for all would be supplanted by the spatialised, localised norms of a multipolar, multi-order world.

Notes

1. In Russia Yanukovich was seen as indecisive and incompetent, while in Ukraine, according to British journalist Shaun Walker, '[e]ven the oligarchs who supported him and benefited from him found his extreme avarice distasteful'. Walker comments: 'Yanukovich was a useless democrat; he was also a useless autocrat. He specialized in crackdowns which were brutal enough to radicalize more Ukrainians into action, but not brutal enough to subdue the revolutionary impulses with fear. He was held in contempt by Western leaders for his undemocratic impulses, and by Moscow for his unwillingness to take them far enough' (Walker 2017: 123, 129).
2. This is the version provided by Putin himself in the propagandistic film *Krym: Put na rodinu* (Crimea: The Way Home). For a reading of the film as 'an improvised rescue fantasy', and its role in a 'drama of affected geopolitics', see Toal (2017: 217).
3. The US State Department argued that the referendum 'occurred under duress of Russian military intervention' and 'under threats of violence and intimidation from a Russian military intervention that violates international law', and was therefore not legitimate (White House 2014). The OSCE refused to monitor the vote, and its chair argued that 'the referendum . . . is in contradiction with the Ukrainian constitution and must be considered illegal' (Dahl 2014). The Council of Europe's European Commission for Democracy Through Law (Venice Commission) ruled that the referendum violated the Ukrainian constitution. See: 'Whether the Decision Taken by the Supreme Council of the Autonomous Republic of Crimea in Ukraine to Organise a Referendum on Becoming a Constituent Territory of the Russian Federation or Restoring Crimea's 1992 Constitution is Compatible with Constitutional Principles, Opinion', European Commission for Democracy Through Law (Venice Commission), 98th Plenary Session, Opinion No. 762/2014, 21 March 2014.
4. 'Treaty on Friendship, Cooperation, and Partnership between Ukraine and the Russian Federation', 31 May 1997, Article 3. Cited in Marxsen (2014: 371).

5. Budapest Memorandum, 5 December 1994, paras 1–2. Cited in Marxsen (2014: 371). For the Russian response, which argued that in Budapest, 'Russia did not undertake to force part of Ukraine to stay in it against the will of the local population', see MFA RF (2014).
6. This argument ignores the approval by a majority of voters in Crimea for the Act of Declaration of Independence of Ukraine later in 1991, albeit on a low turnout. The level of support in Crimea (the Crimean Autonomous Soviet Socialist Republic) was 54 per cent, and in Sevastopol 57 per cent. These figures were considerably lower than in other regions.
7. Raphael Gross has argued that anti-Semitism was central to Schmitt's theories, and that 'Jewishness' became 'virtually a code for all that he rejects in the world' (Gross 2006: 102). Bendersky claims that Gross's claims over-reach: 'nowhere, including his anti-Semitic private notes, does Schmitt ever provide the kind of theoretical analysis of Jews Gross attributes to him' (Bendersky 2010).

EIGHT

Großraum Thinking in Russian Foreign Policy

If I could stand above the heavens,
I would draw my sword
And cut you in three parts:
One piece for Europe,
One piece for America,
One piece left for China.
Then peace would rule the world.

Mao Zedong[1]

A World of Great Spaces

At a tense press conference with German Chancellor Angela Merkel in May 2015, President Vladimir Putin was asked about his attitude to the 1939 Molotov–Ribbentrop Pact. 'We could discuss this all night', he began, before justifying the pact as an agreement that enhanced the USSR's security, and trying to diminish the significance of the Soviet invasion of Eastern Poland and the Baltic States by also noting Poland's annexation of the Zaolzie region (Teschen Silesia) of Czechoslovakia in October 1938 (Putin 2015b). This was not Putin's first controversial foray into the history of the Molotov–Ribbentrop Pact – officially the 'Treaty of Non-aggression between Germany and the Union of Soviet Socialist Republics', signed on 23 August 1939. At a meeting in 2014 with young historians, Putin asked rhetorically 'what was so wrong?' about the Molotov–Ribbentrop Pact, before going on to justify it as a breathing-space for the USSR to modernise its army ahead of the German invasion (Putin 2014d).

Russian conservatives, such as historian Andrei Dyukov and polemicist Natalya Narochnitskaya, had long questioned the dominant Western argument that the pact was both deeply immoral and the primary cause of the war (Benn 2011). But Putin's remarks reflected a hardening of Russian official interpretations of history. Popular opinion in Russia largely followed.

In a poll in August 2017, 45 per cent approved the signing of the pact, with only 17 per cent opposed; some 38 per cent did not know about the pact or struggled to answer (Levada 2017).

The rehabilitation of the Molotov–Ribbentrop Pact in Russia was not only a dispute over history, but also a tacit debate about contemporary international relations. Attempts to rehabilitate the Molotov–Ribbentrop Pact as a defensible act of great power diplomacy were part of a much wider rethinking of Russia's foreign policy, in which the ideas of 'spheres of influences' and geopolitical blocs were once more in vogue. Influential foreign policy gurus promoted new conceptualisations of international order based on 're-legitimis[ing] geopolitical spheres of influence as an organising principle of international life' (Liik 2014: 15). Elements of this thinking were inspired by traditions in Russian thought or classical realist accounts of international relations, but these emerging views of world order also echoed the influence of inter-war German geopolitics on Russian foreign policy thinking, including the Schmittian idea of a world ordered into Great Spaces – a *Großraum* order.

For Schmitt, the Molotov–Ribbentrop Pact was in clear accord with his own spatial theory of international relations. The pact demarcated the spatial boundaries between Nazi Germany and the USSR in a way that enacted many of the principles that underpinned his emerging theory of the *Großraum*, which he had articulated in a 1939 lecture (Schmitt 1995: 269–71, 2011a). In 1940 he argued that his *Großraum* concept was

> in accord with the formulation of the German-Soviet border and friendship agreement of 28 September 1939, which establishes in the sharpest terms the principle of exclusion of intervention by alien powers [*raumfremde Mächte*] and at the same time speaks of 'the mutual state interests' and [those] of the peoples on both sides. (Schmitt 1995: 259–60)[2]

One aim of Schmitt's lectures and articles on international affairs in 1939–40 was undoubtedly to legitimise Nazi Germany's military conquest of Eastern Europe,[3] although Schmitt's theory of *Großraum* is distinct from the Nazi policy of a racially defined *Lebensraum* (Müller 1997; Nunan 2011; Minca and Rowan 2015a: 277).[4] Despite attempts to distinguish his work from that of Karl Haushofer, Schmitt's thinking had clear overlaps and forms an important contribution to the notorious school of German inter-war geopolitics (Barnes and Minca 2013). But his thinking on international relations had much wider implications than its emergence in the context of Germany's historical experience, and did not end with the demise of the Third Reich, but became an important strand in a much broader critique of the post-war liberal international order.

Schmitt's thought on international relations is based on three basic premises. First, the old European order, a long-standing community of sovereign states bound in a rules-based order, underpinned by a set of homogeneous norms, had ended, and could not be resurrected. Second, in the modern era, the nation-state could no longer be considered the sole actor in international relations: 'The state as a model of political unity, as the bearer of the most astounding of all monopolies, namely the monopoly of political decision ... has been dethroned' (Schmitt 1963: 10). Third, any kind of cosmopolitan alternative, or attempt to form a world government or universal order, would merely reflect the power politics of a dominant hegemon, veiling Anglo-American power behind liberal, universal values. Such a universalist order would be both highly destabilising and also represent a negation of something fundamental to humanity – the role of the political, the ability of political communities to distinguish between friend and enemy, and therefore, ultimately, to preserve their separate identities.

This argument allows Schmitt to present us with his favoured theoretical device – the conceptual binary – which here posits 'a clear dilemma between universalism and pluralism, monopoly and polypoly' (Schmitt 2003: 243). Schmitt asserts a bare choice between a universalist cosmopolitanism, which he views as a mask for US hegemony, and a multipolar global order based on *Großraum* thinking, comprising 'a combination of several independent *Großräume* or blocs [which] could constitute a balance, and thereby could precipitate a new order of the earth' (Schmitt 2003: 355). The question, for Schmitt, was whether the world is ready 'for a global monopoly of a single power, or whether a pluralism of coexisting *Großräume*, spheres of interest, and cultural spheres determine the new international law of the earth' (Schmitt 2003: 243–4). In Schmitt's argument, both cosmopolitan ideas of global governance and Westphalian concepts of state sovereignty are destined to be replaced by a new spatiality, a multipolar world of regions dominated by hegemonic great powers (Kervégen 1999; Mouffe 2005b; Rasch 2005; Axtmann 2007; Elden 2011; Legg 2011; Salter 2012; Minca and Rowan 2015a, 2015b).

In his April 1939 lecture Schmitt found his conceptual foundation for ideas of international order in the 1823 Monroe Doctrine, US President James Monroe's assertion that any further European colonialism or interference in the affairs of the Americas would be deemed 'the manifestation of an unfriendly disposition toward the United States'. Schmitt saw this normative and geopolitical demarcation of the Old World from the New as the archetype of a *Großraum*. He claimed that 'the original Monroe theory of 1823 is the first declaration in the history of modern international law that speaks of a Großraum and erects the principle of the non-intervention of spatially foreign powers' (Schmitt 2011a: 86).[5] In Monroe, Schmitt sees the defining features of his new spatial conceptualisation: 'Here is the core of the great original Monroe doctrine, a genuine principle of Großraum, namely the conception of politically awakened nation, political idea, and a Großraum ruled by this idea, a Großraum excluding foreign interventions' (Schmitt 2011a: 87).

Schmitt does not wish simply to create a German version of Monroe (in one place he writes that whether there could be a 'German Monroe Doctrine' is 'terminological hairsplitting'; Schmitt 2011c: 52); rather he argues that 'this core, this concept of a *Großraum* order of international law, is translatable to other spaces, other historical situations, and other friend-enemy groupings' (Schmitt 2011a: 87).[6] His criticism of US policy is not that it advocated liberal, democratic ideas within the Western hemisphere, but that it extended these principles outside the boundaries of the American sphere of influence as the founding principles of a global order. The globalisation of American ideals produced a blurring of divisions and a disorderly breakdown of spatial boundaries. As Schmitt wrote, 'an economic imperialism had enveloped the Monroe Doctrine in fog', turning a 'reasonable logic of spatial separation [*Raumabgrenzungsgedanke*] into an ideological claim to world interference' (Schmitt 2011c: 52).

After 1945 Schmitt continued to develop his conception of a post-Westphalian international order designed to produce stability, not through international cooperation and interdependence, but through clear lines of division among great powers and their associated grand spaces (Schmitt 2003). This new 'Nomos of the Earth' retains Schmitt's precondition for order, the presence of the political – the ability to define clear boundaries of a political entity through the distinguishing of friend and enemy. Schmitt's *nomos* is a fundamental critique of 'a de-territorialized model of world unity' (Teschke 2011: 181). Instead, it reintroduces the importance of land division, as discussed in the previous chapter, and promotes a pluriverse of demarcated spaces. Schmitt's great fear was that an emerging post-Westphalian international order would produce spaces without the necessary order-producing antagonism of the political.

He revisits the division between Land and Sea as a way of emphasising this point (Schmitt 2015). There can be no spatial order on the sea, no land appropriation or land division. This leads to a fundamentally distinct understanding of order and space, to the 'universalism of the Anglo-Saxon sea-based hegemony that transcends space, is foreign to the land [*landfremd*], and is therefore limitless' (Schmitt 1995: 320, as cited in Hell 2009: 301). He viewed 'post-political' ideas of cosmopolitan global governance as antithetical to international order, precisely because they attempt to deny the salience of the political: 'all of Schmitt's speculations around the spatial concepts of *Großraum*, *Reich*, and *Nomos* were ultimately linked to his ontological preoccupation of filling up space with politics' (Barnes and Minca 2013: 676).

Schmitt foresaw the possibility of a victory for the United States in the Cold War, which would lead to 'an ultimate, complete unity of the world – the last round, the final step . . . in the terrible rings to a new *nomos* of the earth' (Schmitt 2003: 354). Schmitt argues that such an order will give rise to totalising wars, infused with the righteous indignation of liberal ethics, which will prove more damaging than any limited inter-state wars in a multipolar world. But Schmitt's pluriverse is more than simply a realist mechanism to avoid total war. Schmitt claims that this plural vision of international relations is also a preservation of something fundamentally human – expressed in the divisions of the political – against the vision of a 'technical unity' of the world: 'no matter how effective technical means may be they can destroy completely neither the nature of man nor the power of land and sea without simultaneously destroying themselves' (Schmitt 2018: 354–5).

Russia's Spatial Crisis

The Schmittian paradigm of international relations helps to explain the challenges faced by Russian elites in forging a viable foreign policy in the face of what came to be viewed as a hostile liberal international order, in which a post-imperial Russia struggled to find an appropriate role. After a short-lived period in the early 2000s, when a new partnership with the West appeared possible, the Russian leadership came to perceive in US foreign policy the combination of monopolistic power politics and the hypocritical façade of humanitarianism that Schmitt had warned against. American advocacy of liberal values was interpreted as little more than a bid for unipolar power, from the invasion of Iraq in 2003 to the promotion of regime change in the Middle East and former Soviet Union in 'colour revolutions' and the 'Arab Spring'. In this dominant foreign policy paradigm in Russia, there appeared to be no role for Russia in the post-Cold War liberal order, except as a weak mimic of Western values and Western order, or as the target of Western policies of regime change and international isolation.

The exploration of new forms of international order was therefore the logical culmination of the search for a new role for Russia in the post-Cold War world (Sakwa 2015b; Monaghan 2016). Russian elites gradually shifted towards a newly assertive Russian foreign policy, which was widely interpreted in the West as a neo-imperialist policy towards its neighbours (Grigas 2016), or as a 'revisionist' turn in relation to the global 'rules-based international order'. The 2018 US National Defense Strategy, for example, argued that 'China and Russia are now undermining the international order from within the system by exploiting its benefits while simultaneously undercutting its principles and "rules of the road"'.[7] From Moscow's perspective, the 'liberal international order' had itself increasingly embraced revisionist norms and practices, beginning in 1999 with the NATO air campaign against Yugoslavia, an event which marked a turning point for many Russian intellectuals in their attitudes to the West (Prozorov 2004: 14).

This rethinking of Russian foreign policy involved a rich debate in Russia across a wide spectrum of realist and conservative positions. The basic premise of Russian realist thought – that Russia was, is and must remain a 'Great Power' – was widely accepted across the political spectrum (Smith 2016). Even during Russia's cataclysmic decline in the 1990s, Russian officials continued to insist on Russia's status as a great power (Lo 2002). In 2000 Putin asserted in an interview: 'Russia is not claiming a Great Power status. It is a great power by virtue of its huge potential, its history and its culture.' He concluded that this was an existential question for Russia: 'either Russia will be great, or it will not be at all' (Shevtsova 2003: 175). An important corollary of 'Great Power thinking' was a relegitimisation of ideas of 'spheres of influence', viewed as an essential precondition for the status of a great power in international relations. The idea that Russia plays a special role in the territories of the former Tsarist empire and the USSR united almost all of Russia's elites, from liberal Westernisers to ultra-conservative neo-Eurasianists (Lynch 2016: 109; Prozorov 2009). Russia's identity crisis after the Cold War consequently became deeply intertwined with a litany of spatial projects attempting to define its relationship with its historical neighbourhood (Clowes 2011; Lewis 2018a). But in the era of liberal internationalism, not only did many of Russia's neighbours reject a continued Russian hegemony, but a normative West rejected the very idea of 'spheres of influence' in international relations as outmoded and illegitimate (Sakwa 2017: 70–2).

Beyond these common premises, a lively debate among Russian intellectuals developed between more centrist, mainstream realist positions and more radical stances, characterised by anti-Westernism and civilisational thinking. These positions mapped quite closely the contours of the debate between liberal and radical conservatives outlined in Chapter 2. Kuchins and Zevelev used the terms 'great power balancers' and 'nationalists' to recognise a significant divide between these more mainstream and radical positions (Kuchins and Zevelev 2012). Andrei Makarychev argued for a distinction between a 'realist' school and a position he terms 'normative conservatism', which promotes conservative values and norms, while also espousing an enmity towards the West (Makarychev 2013). Tsygankov's (2006) widely cited typology identified 'statist' and 'civilisationist' positions, alongside a 'Westerniser' school, the latter now marginalised in Russian discourse after a brief flourishing in the early 1990s.

Statists accepted the main premises of mainstream realist international relations theory, although refracted through Russia's historical experience (Tsygankov and Tsygankov 2010). This realist school deployed a familiar set of concepts and theoretical assumptions, such as great power management, balance of power and spheres of influence (Makarychev 2013: 243–5). They considered the state to be the key actor in international relations, and viewed the world primarily through the prism of potential external threats to Russian statehood. Statists promoted 'equidistant' relations with both Western and non-Western powers, and sought a flexible, multi-vector foreign policy based on a pragmatic understanding of Russian national interests. While not inherently anti-Western, they sought respect and recognition of Russia's role as an independent great power. As part of their understanding of 'great-powerness', they pursued recognition of Russia's unique role in the former Soviet space (Tsygankov and Tsygankov 2010: 673–5).

While statists viewed spheres of influence primarily through the framework of balance of power politics, civilisationists viewed the multipolar world as divided into large regions, centred on great powers, considered to be the bearers of certain civilisational values and histories (Auer 2015; Linde 2016; Tsygankov 2016). Conservatives in Russia cite Schmitt as an important inspiration for this emerging ontology of international relations based on cultural–civilisational spaces (Chebankova 2013a: 301–2), although a wider literature – both Russian and Western – that views civilisations as constituent elements of world order has also been highly influential. The civilisation thesis was promoted through the post-Soviet tradition of cultural studies (*kulturologiya*) in Russia (Scherrer 2013), and follows an intellectual lineage that includes the work of Nikolai Danilevsky in the 1860s, which promoted the 'inevitable struggle of Europe and Russia'; the often esoteric work of Lev Gumilev, with his ideas of 'passionarity' and super-ethnos; and Western writers, including Oswald Spengler and Arnold Toynbee, and, more recently, Samuel Huntington's much-cited 'Clash of Civilisations' thesis (Scherrer 2013; Clover 2016; Mjør 2016). Such views were once largely confined to neo-Eurasianist and other conservative geopolitical thinkers, but have become increasingly mainstream, informing a 'civilisational turn' that characterised Putin's third term in office (Scherrer 2013; Linde 2016). Even in international law, the notion of the 'civilisational space of Russia', a concept with no basis in the UN Charter or other legal codes, has been deployed by a leading legal scholar, V. M. Shumilov (Mälksoo 2017: 143–4).

The geopolitical implications of civilisational thinking were interpreted both through the classical ideas of Halford Mackinder (Bassin and Aksenov 2006) and through German geopolitical thinkers, such as Karl Haushofer and Carl Schmitt. A framework that both Schmitt and Mackinder shared was the division between 'Land' and 'Sea' as defining features of geopolitics, determining political and military outcomes in a constant struggle between land and sea powers. This division has often been viewed in Russian geopolitics as directly consequential, understanding Russia as a powerful land-based power ranged against the maritime powers of Britain and America (Dugin 1997b). Schmitt's reworking of the land/sea distinction goes further, linking a geographical divide to an ideological distinction, and constructing a theory of international relations on a foundational, almost mystical dynamic of world history, primarily between the European telluric powers and the sea powers of Atlanticism ('thalassocracies') (Schmitt 2015). A recent textbook in Russia echoes Schmitt's land/sea distinction by contrasting the 'solid' civilisation of the Russian World with the 'liquid' ideology of the West, which has the 'ability to easily move, to leak and to flood the land' (Kotkina 2017: 66). In this way, the land/sea distinction also produces boundaries and walls, preventing the spacelessness of liberal thought from spreading around the globe.

The theoretical groundwork for this geopolitical turn in Russian foreign policy thinking was at least partly laid by Alexander Dugin. His reworking of Schmitt in the 1990s for a geopolitics of contemporary Russia produced extreme conclusions, even for many conservatives (Dunlop 2001; Ingram 2001: 1036). Dugin called for a 'new Eurasian empire', arguing that 'the existence of the Russian people as an organic, historical entity is unthinkable without empire-building and continental creation. Russians will remain a people only in a New Empire' (Dugin 1997b: 121–2). Attempts to reduce Russia to the status of a regional power or a European nation-state would be tantamount to 'suicide' for the Russian people (Dugin 1997b: 109–10, 113).[8] 'Russians seek to avoid such an outcome at any price' and instead are prepared 'to make unthinkable sacrifices and deprivation in order to realise and develop the national idea, the great Russian dream. The boundaries of this dream, the nation sees, at a minimum, in an Empire' (Dugin 1997b: 110). This empire should be expansive in scale: 'Eurasian', 'great-continental' and even 'global' (Dugin 1997b: 122).

For Dugin, the whole Soviet period can be understood – and perhaps legitimised – in terms of *Großraum* theory. Like Schmitt, Dugin admires the simple spatial distinctions embodied in the Molotov–Ribbentrop Pact, and views it as a 'missed opportunity' of *Großraum* theory (Dugin 2009: 212).

Dugin is at pains to differentiate Schmitt from the racist model of expansion espoused by Hitler, arguing that 'Schmitt's Großraum is based on cultural and ethnic pluralism, on broad autonomy, restricted only by strategic centralism and total loyalty to the highest institution of power' (Dugin 1997b: 46). Indeed, for Dugin, these ideas of *Großraum*, far from recalling Nazi geopolitics, 'anticipated the basic principles of modern integration policy' (Dugin 1997b: 46).

Dugin uses Schmitt's *Großraum* theory to envisage four Great Spaces, or 'empires': an Atlantic 'empire', centred on the United States, an Asian 'empire' around China, a European space and a Eurasian 'empire'. Three of these spaces – in Europe, Eurasia and a Sinocentric Asia – are expanding, while the 'Atlantic space, which today claims a universal and global nature, will have to shrink' (Dugin 2009: 214). This prospect leads Dugin to conclude that 'Carl Schmitt's Grosraum theory . . . is the most reliable platform for a multipolar world, for anti-globalism and the national-liberation struggle against American global domination' (Dugin 2009: 214).

When Dugin published his original work on geopolitics in 1997, this grand scheme of a modern Russian *Großraum* seemed, as Clover puts it, 'completely insane' (Clover 2016: 235). But it was not necessary to accept all of Dugin's most far-reaching conclusions to absorb the important ontological argument, that the essential, decision-making subjects of a new international order would be a small group of major powers at the heart of Great Spaces, opposed, by definition, to a global universalising liberal order. Such views were at least implicit in Russia's long-standing commitment to a multipolar global order, which had become a central theme in Russian foreign policy under Yevgeny Primakov in the second half of the 1990s.

Such views on evolving global order became central to Russia's post-2012 'Eurasian turn' in foreign policy. A report by the Institute of National Strategy on Conservatism argued that '[g]eoeconomic confrontation more and more clearly is shifting from the inter-state level to the level of struggle between macro-regions'. For Russia, 'this defines the principal importance of the activation of efforts to pursue its integration project in the Eurasian space' (Institute of National Strategy 2014: 110–11).

Similar versions of this worldview began to appear in official discourse, also justifying the idea of Eurasian integration. President Putin, speaking in 2013, argued that 'the 21st century promises to become the century of major changes, the era of the formation of major geopolitical zones, as well as financial and economic, cultural, civilisational, and military and political areas'. Integration in Eurasia 'would be a chance for the entire post-Soviet space to become an independent centre for global development, rather than remaining on the outskirts of Europe and Asia' (Putin 2013a). In 2017 he reiterated this claim:

> Today in the world new centres of influence and models of growth are emerging, new civilizational alliances and political and economic associations are being formed. This diversity does not lend itself to unification. Regional organizations in Eurasia, America, Africa, the Asia-Pacific region should act under the auspices of the United Nations and coordinate their work. But each association has the right to function according to its own ideas and principles that correspond to their cultural, historical, geographical features. (Putin 2017a)

While rejecting 'a division of spheres of influence in the spirit of classical diplomacy', Putin argued for 'the institutionalization of these [regional] poles, the creation of powerful regional organizations and the development of rules for their interaction'. In the aftermath of the clash of Eurasian and European projects in Ukraine, he asserted that 'in order to develop . . . a dialogue, we need to begin with the [idea] that all regional centres, which have formed integration projects around them, should have equal rights to development' (Putin 2014b).

In a multipolar world of macro-regions, each great power can only survive if it can become the dynamic force at the heart of one of these Great Spaces. This particular understanding of multipolar order made attaining great power status for Russia as a centre of a new or revived space an existential question. Sergei Glazyev argued that 'Russia is facing a clear choice: either become a powerful ideological and civilizational centre in its own right . . . or integrate with one of the existing power centres and lose its identity' (Glazyev 2015: 84). Conservatives argued that the Eurasian project could become a 'third centre of power and influence that will be able to become a counterweight to the two already existing ones led by the U.S. and China', and thus avoid any agreements between those two powers at Russia's expense (Podberezkin et al. 2013: 109). Dugin puts the choice starkly: 'either neo-Eurasianism will become the basic worldview of Russian elites, or occupation awaits us' (Dugin 2009: 214). For Surkov, it comes down to a simple binary: whether Russia is a 'spider' or a 'fly' in the 'global spider's web' (Surkov 2006b: 69).

This existential view of world order has far-reaching consequences. Taken to its logical conclusion, Russia's identity – and even its survival as a nation – has become bound up with a spatial revision of international order, although there can clearly be maximalist and minimalist versions of this position. Richard Sakwa emphasises a minimalist position, in which

Russia's stance amounts to 'neo-revisionism', in that it does not challenge the 'secondary institutions' of international society, such as the United Nations and other bodies of global governance, but only opposes their subordination to a liberal, Western hegemony (Sakwa 2017). Sakwa views this as an anti-hegemonic stance, the aim of which is not merely to displace the United States, but to 'question hegemonic leadership itself' and to replace it with a more equal international order (Sakwa 2017: 52). Missing from this account is the possibility that hegemony – dethroned at the global level – would merely be reproduced at other scales of the international system. As Schmitt would have predicted, just as Russia and China resist hegemony at the global scale, they attempt simultaneously to create new forms of hegemony within their respective regions.

Großraum theory offers a framework though which to rethink the dilemmas faced by Russia in its evolving response to a dominant international liberal order. The ideas of *Großraum* thinking suggest four key claims about Russian foreign policy. First, Russia cannot be confined by the boundaries of a modern nation-state but can only assert its identity through the articulation of a greater space, which does not coincide with its formal state borders. Second, within this space, Russia acts as the 'politically awakened' nation, whose sovereignty is assured, but whose influence extends into a space occupied by other states, who therefore enjoy only partial sovereignty. Third, in this grand space, Russia is the bearer of a 'political idea', a set of values and ideas that unite peoples across the wider region in ways that transcend ethnicity. Fourth, this Russian-dominated *Großraum* is one from which it will endeavour to exclude the ideological, political and military presence of foreign powers.

Russia's Spatial Projects

At a prize-giving for schoolchildren organised by the Russian Geographical Society in December 2016, President Putin indulged in a characteristic aside. 'Where do Russia's borders end?', he asked one of the schoolboys, before answering himself: 'Russia's borders do not end anywhere.'[9] 'It's a joke', he explained to a cheering audience, but a discourse of Russia as unbounded by conventional borders has long historical roots, influenced by Russia's almost continual expansion into neighbouring territories from the fifteenth to the nineteenth centuries (Tolz 2001: 162–3). This sense of historical 'boundlessness' was compounded by the loss of empire and the collapse of the USSR. Consequently, Schmitt's first condition for the construction of a *Großraum* order – the idea that a state's identity is associated with a greater space beyond its formal borders – forms a central element in almost all discourse on Russia since the collapse of the USSR. Russia's post-Soviet identity has been articulated through a succession of geopolitical projects that promote alternative spatial visions that extend beyond the boundaries of the Russian nation-state (Clowes 2011; Shevel 2011; Lewis 2018a).

One incarnation of this spatial thinking was the discursive and political project known as *Russkii mir* – 'Russian World' (Zevelev 2014; Laruelle 2015a, 2015b; Feklyunina 2016; Kotkina 2017; Suslov 2018). Suslov traces the evolution of the idea in three stages that emphasise its shifting spatial register: early versions during the 1990s emphasised cultural ties within a spatial archipelago, which emphasised difference and hybridity among Russia's extensive diaspora. A second incarnation placed the Russian state at the hub of a network of influence among loyal diasporas, an idea influenced by Vladislav Surkov's notion of 'Sovereign Democracy'. A third version was an irredentist concept which asserted a new post-sovereign civilisational space incorporating neighbouring territories in Ukraine and Belarus, an idea which

> looks to radically reform ideas of sovereignty from a juridical (law governed) notion of statehood and international order into a cultural notion of sovereignty in a world of states composed of regions – i.e. a world of new 'spheres of influence'. (Suslov 2018: 18)

However, as a spatial project to frame Russia's 'great-powerness', the Russian World concept had clear limitations, both in its emphasis on ethnicity and language, and its lack of geopolitical scale. For ambitious geopolitical thinkers in Moscow, 'the concepts of "compatriots abroad," "the Russian world," and "a divided people" were... too narrow for Russia's positioning on the world stage as a great power' (Zevelev 2014). Moreover, the Russian World concept had little popular appeal outside ethnic Russian communities, particularly among non-Russian peoples in Central Asia and the Caucasus, who had once formed part of the USSR. When President Putin spoke of Kazakhstan 'remaining within the spaces of a Greater Russian World', he provoked a predictably adverse reaction from Kazakh intellectuals and officials (Kalikulov 2014). In Ukraine, too, the Russian World concept had a polarising rather than unifying effect (Feklyunina 2016). Some 90 per cent of residents in Crimea considered themselves part of the Russian World (O'Loughlin et al. 2017: 17–20), but in most of south-eastern Ukraine a sizeable majority in each region rejected the idea (O'Loughlin et al. 2017: 13). The Russian nationalist project of 'Novorossiya', a proto-state that nationalists imagined might emerge from the Ukrainian state in eight southern and eastern regions of Ukraine, faded quickly in 2015. Its proponents admitted that they had overestimated the 'unity of the Russian World', as an expected pro-Moscow 'popular uprising from Lugansk to Odessa' failed to materialise (Vladimirov 2014).

A much more productive spatial project for Russian foreign policy was 'Eurasia', which had become a central trope in mainstream and official foreign policy thinking in Russia by the 2010s. Eurasia was a vague, polysemous concept, used in different ways to devise diverse geopolitical imaginaries. As originally conceived in the 1920s by George Vernadsky, Nikolai Trubetskoi, Petr Savitsky and other Russian exiles, Eurasia identified a geographical zone, centred on 'the region of the desertic steppes that extend in an uninterrupted stretch from the Chinese Wall to Galicia' (Savitsky 1927, cited in Laruelle 2015b: 17). This region constituted a spatial, historical and cultural unity, which demarcated it from both Europe and from Asia. The ideological content of Eurasianism has varied, but in most formulations Eurasia is imagined playing a counter-hegemonic role against the West, in which Eurasia 'was reinvented as a colonized country, a potential leader of the uprising of the colonized against the colonizers' (Glebov 2015: 48).

This anti-colonial element of Eurasianism had little in common with the emancipatory decolonisation paradigms of the developing world, but aimed instead 'to sustain the unity of the imperial space, to disarm local nationalisms, and ... to articulate a non-European subjectivity of the Russian imperial space' (Glebov 2015: 49). In this lay its defining conceptual contradiction, between Russia as an imperial power, intent on continuing its dominance over other states in the region, and Russia as the would-be subject, attempting to emancipate itself from a hegemonic Western ordering of the world. This contradictory stance is summed up by Viatcheslav Morozov's description of Russia as a 'subaltern empire', experiencing the identity of both coloniser and colonised (Morozov 2008), which in turn reminds us of Arendt's critique of Schmittian geopolitics as both embracing conquest and opposing imperialism (Jurkevics 2017: 346).

Many different political thinkers have used this historical Eurasianist tradition with a wide variety of different meanings (Laruelle 2008, 2015d; Vinokurov and Libman 2012: 12–23; Dugin 2014a: 131–4; Bassin et al. 2015). One version – based on readings of Gumilev, who stressed his respect for nomadic and Turkic culture – downplays Russian hegemony as a central feature of neo-Eurasianism, and instead emphasises Turkic–Russian historical and cultural ties. Such views can be found in Kazakhstan, in particular, and among Turkic peoples inside the Russian Federation (Bassin 2016: 273–305). A technocratic vision of Eurasianism, or what Vinokurov terms 'pragmatic Eurasianism', promotes an ideal of cross-border trade and freedom of movement that draws its inspiration from EU-style regional integration (Vinokurov 2013). This neo-liberal Eurasianism emphasises openness to globalisation, strong economic ties to Europe and the West, and economic and technological modernisation. This is the approach that informs the framework of the Eurasian Economic Union (EAEU), a customs union set up in 2014, which unites Russia, Belarus, Kazakhstan, Kyrgyzstan and Armenia. However, as has been frequently noted, the EAEU itself can be interpreted as both a technocratic initiative and a geopolitical enterprise (ICG 2016).

The most significant version of contemporary Eurasianism is the articulation of Eurasia as a geopolitical space, dominated by a hegemonic Russia. There are more and less radical versions of this position. Dugin and other ultra-nationalist geopolitical thinkers interpreted Eurasia as a neo-imperial project, characterised by a radically anti-Western agenda (Dugin 2014a: 132–3). But even more moderate Eurasianists promoted geopolitical projects which relied on continued Russian hegemony, and were constructed in tension with the West (Tsygankov 2016). The emergence of Eurasia as a defining trope in Russian foreign policy thinking after 2012 was prompted by the failure of Russia's European project. For Fedor Lukyanov, the end of hopes of a 'Greater Europe' left Russia with no choice but 'to participate in the construction of a new Eurasian space' (Lukyanov 2016). Speaking in 2015, former foreign minister Igor Ivanov talked of the 'sunset' of Greater Europe, bemoaning the missed chance of a united Europe, and instead identifying an inevitable shift towards a Eurasian orientation for Russia (Ivanov 2015).

The original conception of 1920s Eurasianism can be understood as a 'geographical ideology', in which territory and environment acted as determining factors on political outcomes (Laruelle 2015e). The geography of modern versions of Eurasia, however, was always secondary to geopolitical and political drivers: Dugin's work, clearly influenced by Haushofer, initially advocated a continental space on a Berlin–Moscow–Tokyo axis, and was marked by a distancing of Russia from China, at least in his earlier work (Laruelle 2017a). By contrast, the idea of 'Greater Eurasia', which emerged in official speeches after 2016, promoted an imagined space premised on a strong axis between Moscow and Beijing, linking Russia, China, Central Asian states, India and possibly Iran, in a new network of economic, political and security ties (Lewis 2018a). At a summit in Beijing in May 2017, Putin argued that 'Greater Eurasia is not an abstract geopolitical scheme, but without any exaggeration, a genuinely civilisational project, directed towards the future' (Putin 2017b).

The importance of all these spatial projects is not in their often vague geographical reach or limited institutionalisation, but in the ways in which they are viewed as building-blocks for a new world order. As such they reflect a paradigm among Russian foreign policy thinkers which has moved beyond Westphalian thinking, but also rejects liberal, cosmopolitan ideas of international order, instead arguing for a world order of great powers, surrounded by spheres of influence. Foreign policy analyst Sergei Karaganov argues that 'our European friends hoped that they could reject concepts such as a sphere of interests, a sphere of control, but they were unsuccessful. That world view is falling apart' (Vasiliev 2017). The importance of these ideas was not in the exact geographic boundaries of particular spatial projects, but in the consistent agreement that Russia could only achieve subjectivity and sovereignty in the international order by acting as a military and ideological hegemon in a wider post-Westphalian space.

As the Russian World and Eurasian projects encountered increasing difficulties in the 2010s, some authors cautioned against this continuing search for a sphere of influence. Dmitry Trenin argued that the project of constructing Russia as the centre of a reintegrated group of post-Soviet states had failed: Russia had lost influence in much of the former Soviet space, and its most important neighbour, Ukraine, was actively hostile. Consequently, for Russia a period of 'geopolitical loneliness' awaited, but one which Moscow could use very effectively. Without the entanglements of alliances, Russia would be free to exercise its sovereignty and achieve a rare status in international politics – the capacity to be free (Trenin 2019). Trenin's ideas echoed the original insights of Vladislav Surkov in a 2018 article, which had also predicted 'a hundred years (or possibly two hundred or three hundred) of geopolitical loneliness', in which Russia – characterised by 'double-headed statehood, hybrid mentality, intercontinental territory and bipolar history' – would be allied only with itself (Surkov 2018).

This idea of Russian 'geopolitical loneliness', however, should not be understood necessarily as a negation of *Großraum* thinking, the idea that Russia can only find its identity in a wider geopolitical space. Its genealogy can be traced to Vadim Tsymbursky's concept of 'Island Russia', which accepted the civilisational space as the most important unit in history, but welcomed Russia's withdrawal to the 'island' of its post-Soviet boundaries (Tsymbursky 2007; Østbø 2016). Yet in Tsymbursky's account, Russia was still divided from Europe by space, by a set of buffer states in what he termed the *limitrof*, meaning an expanse of space between two empires or civilisations. These Eastern European lands, according to Tsymbursky, attain meaning only as peripheral regions of one civilisation or other, or, as Østbø puts it, 'are reduced to being a battlefield for Russia's desires and complexes' (Østbø 2016: 90, n 61). In this sense, Russia still retains a spatial barrier around itself, a kind of ideological moat around the Russian island, to preserve itself against universalist Western ideas and apocalyptic designs (Østbø 2016).

Russia as Hegemonic Power

Within the *Großraum*, argues Schmitt, not every state is equal: one power – 'a political active nation' – is required to exercise full sovereignty as the hegemon. In a multipolar world order based on grand spaces and great powers the Westphalian equality of sovereignty is replaced by a distinction between *Staaten* and *Reiche*, between ordinary states and hegemons, small states and great powers. At the centre of every *Großraum*, according to Schmitt, 'are the leading and bearing powers whose political ideas radiate into a certain *Großraum* and which fundamentally exclude the interventions of spatially alien powers into this Großraum' (Schmitt 2011a: 100). Schmitt is careful to point out that 'the Reich is not identical with the *Großraum*, but the *Großraum* is also something different from an enlarged small space' (Schmitt 1995: 260). As Balakrishnan explains, the hegemon in a *Großraum* is not simply a large state; indeed it is not a 'state in the conventional sense, as its field of political action extended far beyond its own territorial borders' (Balakrishnan 2000: 237).

The key distinction between hegemons, which enjoy full sovereignty, and ordinary states, which have a form of conditional sovereignty, is fundamental to understanding the internal dynamics of the *Großraum* (Schmitt 2011a). This differentiated sovereignty does not necessarily indicate direct control or any kind of territorial conquest. Schmitt described US economic dominance in Latin America as the archetype of this mode of external control, despite the continued existence of formal state sovereignty. As Schmitt explains:

> The external, emptied space of the controlled state's territorial sovereignty remains inviolate, but the functional content of this sovereignty is changed by the guarantees of the controlling power's economic *Großraum* . . . The controlling state . . . was free, at its discretion, to interfere in the affairs of the controlled state. Its right of intervention was secured by footholds, naval bases, refuelling stations, military and administrative outposts, and other forms of cooperation, both internal and external. (Schmitt 2003: 252)

'Obviously', summarizes Gary Ulmen, 'relations among nations or empires within a *Großraum* would be different from relations among *Großraüme*' (Ulmen 2003: 24), so much so that Schmitt is unsure whether the ordering of these relations inside the *Großraum* should even be considered as a form of international law (Ulmen 2003: 24). At the very least, it introduces two layers of legal relationship among states: those among states within a *Großraum* are defined with an emphasis on the superior rights of the hegemonic power, while relations among hegemons are marked by equality and the principle of non-interference (Koskenniemi 2016: 601).

The distinction between the hegemon in a *Großraum* and other states can be understood in terms of sovereignty, defined not in formal, legalistic terms, but in Schmittian terms by its right to define the enemy, and thus its relations with other *Großraüme*. In Schmitt's theory, the Reich was not a traditional empire – it would 'respect the difference of internal nations' – but 'it would reserve for itself the ultimate right to sovereignty, defined precisely by its ability to identify the enemy' (Minca and Rowan 2015a: 276). Other countries in the hegemon's sphere of influence do not have the right to define their friends and enemies, and therefore have diminished sovereignty. They enjoy legal, external sovereignty, but they lack subjectivity in international relations, above all marked by the right to choose alliances, partners and enemies. Schmitt argues that *Großraum* thinking embraces the 'principle of mutual respect for every nationhood' and rejects notions of 'assimilation, absorption and melting pots', instead aiming to protect the 'unique volkish nature of every national group'. But this 'protection' is not from the dominant, hegemonic power at the centre of a *Großraum*, but from alien interventions and 'Western ideas of assimilation' (Schmitt 2011a: 98).

This differential understanding of sovereignty is central to all post-Soviet Russian geopolitical imaginaries, whether expansionist neo-Eurasianism or Tsymbursky's neo-isolationism. They all envisage a belt of states around Russia, which lack subjectivity in international affairs. As Vladislav Surkov phrased it, presumably talking about states such as Ukraine:

> unlike . . . many other countries we were always the bearer of a state idea. It is clear that some states, who declared their national idea to be entry into the European Union . . . have never been sovereign for a single day in their history. (Surkov 2006b: 60–1)

Russia must be fully sovereign, but its neighbours lack the historical and political basis for full sovereignty: they can only enter the spatial orders of others. This does not mean that such states will lose their external form of sovereignty, but that in varying degrees they lack important attributes of sovereign choice in international relations – they are not, as Surkov frames it, the 'bearer of a state idea', or as Schmitt puts it, a 'politically active nation'.[10]

This conceptualisation of sovereignty in *Großraum* thinking helps to explain some apparent contradictions in the Russian understanding of sovereignty, not only in political discourse, but even in scholarly debates over international law (Mälksoo 2017: 100–4). Ruth Deyermond identifies 'two working models of sovereignty in Russian foreign policy: a "Westphalian" and a "post-Soviet" approach' (Deyermond 2016: 958). Outside the former Soviet space, Russia has become 'the most prominent defender of the Westphalian model in response to the Western-led shift to a post-Westphalian conception of sovereignty' (Deyermond 2016: 962). Among the former Soviet states, however, a very different model applies, which derives more from the Soviet experience of dealing with constituent republics of the USSR rather than in accordance with normal rules of international diplomacy. Such a bifurcation has three objectives: it 'helps to secure Russian national interests at domestic, regional, and international levels'; 'it acts as a form of balancing against the US and its allies'; and, significantly, 'it acts as a marker of "non-Western" power identity in an emergent multipolar order' (Deyermond 2016: 958–9). These different conceptualisations of sovereignty mark out a distinct space, within which Russia believes that it – rather than the United States and its allies – retains hegemonic power.

Russia's view of sovereignty within its sphere of influence has been evident in its military interventions in Georgia and Ukraine, but Russia also asserts power throughout the region in indirect ways. Russia retains military bases in the unrecognised states of Abkhazia and South Ossetia, and in Moldova, Armenia, Kyrgyzstan and Tajikistan, and radar stations in Kazakhstan and Belarus. Russia continues to exercise political influence among its neighbours, both directly through close ties with local political and business groups, and through ethnic Russian diasporas and other proxies. Russia has also used economic pressure, including its role as a dominant energy actor, its position as a host country for millions of labour migrants and its capacity to impose informal and formal economic sanctions. Finally, Russia has attempted to construct integrative institutions, with varying success, such as the Commonwealth of Independent States (CIS), the Collective Security Treaty Organisation (CSTO) and the Eurasian Economic Union (EAEU) (Lewis 2018b). Despite this array of structural power and direct levers of influence, Russia has often failed to assert its desired policy outcomes among its neighbours, most obviously in Ukraine in 2013–14, when Moscow's attempts to persuade Ukraine to join the EAEU rather than a rival European Union trade agreement resulted in political turmoil and armed conflict.

The Ukrainian case demonstrates that hegemony is a constantly shifting relationship, in which all parties have agency. Hegemony can be seen as 'negotiated' in the former Soviet space, with small states also exercising a certain freedom of foreign policy choices, and asserting their own sovereignty in important policy domains (Costa Buranelli 2018). Moreover, while some post-Soviet states, such as Georgia or Ukraine, have developed a national project in opposition to Russian hegemony, in other states, such as Kyrgyzstan, statehood has been constructed through 'entanglements with Russia, rather than constituted in opposition to it' (Ortmann 2018: 13). Stefanie Ortmann explains how 'a variety of practices of identifying and associating with Russia construct a Kyrgyz sensibility of sovereignty, rather than by asserting difference' (Ortmann 2018: 14). This sense of what Ortmann calls Russia's 'seductive power' produces a differential understanding of sovereignty that ensures that 'representations of Kyrgyz statehood imperilled by foreign penetration of space are much less frequent with regard to Russia', as opposed to the West (Ortmann 2018: 12).

Ikenberry and Kupchan (1990) point to the dualist character of hegemonic power, which combines material incentives with ideational activities to persuade leaders to 'internalise the norms and value orientations espoused by the hegemon and accept its normative claims about the nature of the international system' (Ikenberry and Kupchan 1990: 286). Hegemony, in other words, requires some evidence of legitimacy, a shared set of ideas and a common discourse, and thus requires a multifaceted foreign policy operating in different domains. These ideational aspects of hegemony have become increasingly important as Russia has put more emphasis on initiatives that it terms 'soft power', such as funding of NGOs, media and educational initiatives (Lewis 2015). Russia, it seems, has understood Schmitt's assertion that the hegemon in any geopolitical space requires also a political idea.

The Political Idea

Schmitt's third condition for a sustainable multipolar order is that a *Großraum* should be 'governed by one "great political idea" represented by the political body in which sovereignty would be located' (Hell 2009: 294). One of Schmitt's most important theoretical moves is to reject a neutral, positivist understanding of space, and instead link the notion of space to the realm of ideas:

> Seen from the standpoint of international jurisprudence, space and political ideas do not allow themselves to be separated from one another. For us, there are neither spaceless political ideas nor, reciprocally, spaces without ideas or principles of space without ideas. It is an important part of a determinable political idea that a certain nation carries it and that it has a certain opponent in mind, through which this political idea gains the quality of the political. (Schmitt 2011a: 87)

In the case of Nazi Germany, the core idea of the *Großraum* was a racist philosophy, but as noted previously many critics argue that Schmitt was sceptical that a *Großraum* could be based purely on a nationalist idea (Müller 1997: 29).[11] In any case, the important point for Schmitt is not the content of this *Weltanschauung*, but that 'a set of ideas and principles' excludes the intervention of foreign powers (Müller 1997: 29). The idea must be 'carried by' the hegemonic nation and have 'a certain opponent in mind', giving it the 'quality of the political'. As shown by his enthusiasm for the Monroe Doctrine, Schmitt's objection to liberalism is not to its existence in the American hemisphere, but to its transformation from a spatially bounded idea to one that aspires to universalism. The philosophical content is not primary for Schmitt; the point is that it is contained within the space within which it was first promulgated. Attempts to universalise ideas risk supporting a dangerous imperialism.

In the 1920s Schmitt's argument was directed against the 'penetration' of Wilsonian liberalism into Central-Eastern Europe, arguing that liberal-universalistic notions of the protection of ethnic minorities are simply geopolitical interventions in an alien geopolitical space:

> The underlying liberal-individualistic and therefore universalistic construction of minority protection became the foundation for the spatially alien Western powers' exercise of control and intervention in the Eastern European space, a development anticipated by the universalistic Geneva League of Nations. (Schmitt 2011a: 98)

Schmitt argues that the articulation of minority rights as a universalistic norm occludes the obvious power politics that inform Western claims. Moreover, although promulgated as 'universal', these claims in reality have a spatial boundary, being directed only towards a specific region in which Western powers have specific interests:

> The geographical zone of the expansion of minority protection under the international law of Geneva and Versailles is limited to and runs from the Baltic Sea to the Mediterranean in a belt of land that resulted from a certain historical development; indeed, a belt that amounts to an arena of interests and claims. (Schmitt 2011a: 97)

By contrast, claims for 'minority protection' could not be directed against Western powers themselves: 'Because they stand as true free legal and constitutional states, no minority protection under international law may ever be brought to discussion against them; among the Western democracies, there conceptually cannot exist any minorities in need of minority protection' (Schmitt 2011a: 97). As a result, universal principles are used in a unilateral fashion to legitimise external intervention by external powers into a particular geopolitical space.

Remarkably similar accusations of geopolitical ambitions disguised as advocacy of minority rights would be traded in discussions between the West and Russia in the early twenty-first century in the Organisation for Security and Cooperation in Europe (OSCE), a multilateral organisation which promoted liberal values and practices, such as democratic elections and civil rights, including minority rights. Russia claimed that these commitments were monitored and disciplined selectively, in a space 'East of Vienna', which targeted the OSCE's non-NATO members (Morozov 2005: 70–1; Lewis 2012; Kropatcheva 2015: 13–14; Sakwa 2016: 120–1). Russian foreign minister Sergei Lavrov argued that the West attempted 'to reduce [the OSCE] to the monitoring of democratic processes and the observance of human rights in the post-Soviet space'. The European Union and NATO promoted their own values, but 'the OSCE will only monitor the adoption of these organizations' values by countries that have remained outside the EU and NATO' (Lavrov 2005). In 2007 Putin accused the West of 'trying to transform the OSCE into a vulgar instrument designed to promote the foreign policy interests of one or a group of countries', and of using human rights norms as a means of 'interfering in the internal affairs of other countries, and ... determining how these states should live and develop' (Putin 2007a). Although Russia remained a member of the OSCE, these fundamental disputes about norms and space dominated the organisation's agenda and blocked any possibility of the OSCE emerging as the framework for a pan-European security system.

For Schmitt, it was not sufficient to oppose the penetration of alien ideas; an aspiring great power had to bear its own political idea, an ideology to unite the *Großraum*. As discussed earlier in this book, when Putin first came to power, he often argued that Russia did not need a 'national idea', but there was an important ideational aspect to Russia's 'counter-revolution' of 2006–8, which was further developed in reaction to the Arab Spring, the wave of protests in Russia in 2011–12 and subsequently the Ukrainian events of 2013–14. Consequently, the idea of Russia as the bearer of a 'new political idea' emerged as a central feature of the official discourse of Putin's third term in office (2012–18).

The exact content of this 'political idea' was more difficult to identify. As discussed above, the idea of a Russian World had little resonance with non-Russians in Eurasia, and its promotion tended to reduce rather than increase Russia's influence. The Russian Orthodox Church (ROC) promulgated a set of conservative ideas and norms as part of what has been termed 'Orthodox geopolitics' (Sidorov 2006). In tandem with the Russian state, the ROC promoted traditional values, while strongly opposing Western liberal ideas and the beliefs of 'non-traditional religions' and missionary activities (Payne 2010: 4). The Sixteenth World Russian National Assembly, a body chaired by Patriarch Kirill, in October 2012 asserted the concept of 'humanitarian sovereignty', defined as 'the aggregate of cultural, religious, worldview-related, and sociopsychological factors that enable a nation and a state to assert their identity and avoid sociopsychological and cultural dependence', an idea that mapped easily onto the notion of 'Sovereign Democracy' (Suslov 2014: 72). In this way, the ROC acted to oppose universal values, instead reifying a space imbued with alternative norms, those promulgated by the Orthodox Church.

The ROC played an important role in the promotion of a wider set of conservative ideas, many of which became central to a new narrative about Russia's place in the world. There were two strands to this new conservatism in foreign policy. One strand promoted so-called 'traditional values', sometimes labelled 'Christian humanism', and opposed to a 'post-human future', which conservatives claimed eroded clear boundaries that define sexual, psychological and biological identities (Institute of National Strategy 2014: 106). Although conservative activists and State Duma deputies were the most radical promoters of this agenda, it soon became a staple of official discourse, both as a means to distinguish Russia from the West, and to assert an alternative civilisational space around Russia. In a speech in Valdai in 2013, Putin argued that

> many of the Euro-Atlantic countries have effectively gone down the path of rejecting their roots, including the Christian values that constitute the basis of Western civilisation. [They] reject moral principles and any traditional identities: national, cultural, religious and even sexual. Policies are being implemented that equate large families with same-sex partnerships, and belief in God with belief in Satan.
>
> The excesses of political correctness have reached the point that [people] talk seriously about registering political parties whose aim is to promote paedophilia. People in many European countries are ashamed or are afraid to talk about their religious affiliation. Holidays are even abolished or called something different, hiding in shame the very essence of the holiday, the moral basis of these holidays.

Not only is this damaging Western civilisation, argued Putin, but 'people are aggressively trying to impose this model on everybody, on the whole world. I am convinced that this is a direct path to degradation and primitivism, to a profound demographic and moral crisis' (Putin 2013a).

Russia's conservative agenda played an important role in supporting a more assertive turn in Russian foreign policy and differentiating Russia from the West (Keating and Kaczmarska 2019). When the United States challenged Uganda in 2013 over anti-homosexuality legislation, Ugandan president Yoweri Musaveni responded by saying he would 'want to work with Russia' (Ayoub 2017: 86). Closer to home, Russia generated support for anti-LGBT views in many societies in the former Soviet space, even in countries such as Georgia, where political attitudes were traditionally opposed to Russian influence (Amighetti 2017). A range of Russian proxies – NGOs, ROC-linked networks and para-state organisations – all promoted anti-LGBT policies and so-called 'Eurasianist' values in the former Soviet republics (Lutsevych 2016). Russian scholars argued that there was widespread support across Eurasia for 'absolute values' that appealed to a variety of cultural and religious conservative beliefs, whose holders were united in a view of the West as 'the centre of sin and depravity' (Lukin 2014: 54). Russian activists were assisted in promoting conservative values in the region by international networks such as the American conservative advocacy group, the World Congress of Families, which had long-standing connections to Russia, but also promoted their anti-liberal agenda in states such as Georgia and Ukraine (Michel 2017).

Russian diplomats were increasingly found promoting such ideas in international bodies. In the field of human rights, for example, Russian conservative activists sat alongside Russian diplomats in the UN Human Rights Council (HRC) in Geneva to denounce universal ideas of human rights, promoting instead particularistic notions of 'traditional values'. On 27 September 2012 the HRC adopted a Russian-backed resolution on the importance of traditional values in a vote of twenty-five to fifteen, supported by traditional Russian allies such as India, Belarus, China, Kyrgyzstan, Syria, Uzbekistan and Vietnam (Horvath 2016: 887). Schmitt had argued that the articulation of international law in terms of universal human rights 'only introduce[d] a vocabulary that sustains the policies of those (liberal) actors well-placed in the diplomatic institutions that decide what they are to mean in concrete cases' (Koskenniemi 2004: 504). Russia was determined to reshape the vocabulary of human rights, and to influence 'what they are to mean', constantly challenging Western human rights accusations against sovereign states in bodies such as the HRC and the UN Security Council.

A second strand of conservative ideas used in Russian foreign policy were those that prioritised ideas of state sovereignty, regime security and strong states (Keating and Kaczmarska 2019). Russian commentators claimed that what they viewed as a US strategy of 'managed chaos' was becoming increasingly 'unmanageable' (Institute of National Strategy 2014: 107). In the context of the Middle East, Karaganov argued that 'any weakening of statehood, especially in such a vulnerable region, is a proven evil' (Karaganov 2017a). Against the challenge of 'colour revolutions', viewed as a political technology for regime change promoted by the West, Russia provided diplomatic and material support for authoritarian leaders across the post-Soviet space, in the Middle East, Venezuela and some African states.

Like Schmitt, Russian conservatives promoted international pluralism among the subjects of international relations. Karaganov, for example, advocated 'the rights of every people and country to choose their own path of development, way of life, support for the freedom from external interference, for cultural pluralism, religious belief and religious tolerance' (Karaganov 2016). But, like Schmitt, he is unenthusiastic about pluralism within the state. Karaganov argues that

> the prevalent social-political system of the future will not be Western European or American-style liberal democracy, which is in crisis almost everywhere, but illiberal strongman democracy (*neliberal'naya liderskaya demokratiya*) prevailing in the rising states of the non-West. (Karaganov 2015)

This recognition of and support for hierarchical political systems fell short of any kind of active 'autocracy promotion' (Burnell and Schlumberger 2010; Tansey 2016). It did, however, reflect a kind of 'Moscow Consensus' that emerged in many states regarding the legitimacy of authoritarian rule (Lewis 2016c), and reflected a firm belief among many Russian officials that political systems should reflect underlying political cultures, not universal norms. This anti-universalist position also contributed to an illiberal turn in other areas of international policy. For example, Russian policy positions challenged liberal approaches to peacebuilding and conflict resolution in favour of statist repression and violent counterinsurgency campaigns (Lewis et al. 2018).

There was an obvious contradiction in this emerging set of ideas. On the one hand it promoted – as Schmitt had advocated – a set of ideas bounded by space, a civilisational set of values and principles for the Eurasian continent. On the other hand, Russian activists also promoted traditional values as having universal meaning, relevant not only for Russia but for Europe, the United States, and even the globe. Boris Mezhuev recognised this problem in discussion in 2014: 'On the one hand we appeal to European conservatives, we say that as our partners, they are also against gay marriage, just as in Russia . . . On the other hand, our geopolitics are formulated in civilizational categories' (Minakov 2014: 29). This is a fundamental – and unresolved – contradiction within Russian conservative thought that dates back to at least the nineteenth century, but it is also a challenge to Schmitt's claim that space and ideas are bound together: as Schmitt's own reading of the Monroe Doctrine proved, political ideas were impossible to contain within a geopolitical space.

In practice, Russian intellectuals viewed conservative values in potentially contradictory ways: as a reversion to traditional European values, as a set of principles that underpinned a Eurasian space, but also as ideas that competed with Western norms globally. Karaganov claims that Russia's advocacy of the principles of sovereignty, of 'freedom of political and cultural choice' and of what he terms 'the normal values in social and personal life that took root during many thousands of years of human history' was a source of soft power for Russia (Karaganov 2017a). A manifesto of conservatism as 'soft power', published by the Institute of National Strategy, explains that advocacy of conservative values was aimed not at the 'political beau-monde' of Western countries, but at their ordinary citizens, who were talking about these issues. For people in the non-West, in 'the countries of Latin America, Asia, the Middle East, Russia has planted hope in many of those who today are asserting their civilizational identity and are not ready to be "ground" by the millstones of modern neo liberalism' (Institute of National Strategy 2014: 105).

Some analysts argued that the conservative agenda was not a real ideological offensive, but was more of a 'Potemkin conservatism', a form of political technology without real ideological commitments, a creed that was hardly reflected in the everyday mores of Russian elites or wider society (Rodkiewicz and Rogoża 2015). Certainly, genuine conservatism had only limited traction with many in the Russian elite, but perhaps that missed the point. A set of often inchoate conservative values offered Russia the outline of a political idea that supported Russia's claim to be a great power at the centre of a broader region, and to offer an ideological space of resistance to the universalising tendencies of liberal norms.

Exclusion of Foreign Powers

Schmitt's final condition for the *Großraum* is that it excludes external powers, or what he terms *raumfremde Mächte* ('powers alien to the space'), borrowing from the central principle of the Monroe Doctrine, which aimed to curtail European involvement in the Western hemisphere. The exclusion of external powers from the *Großraum* is critical to Schmitt's conceptualisation of a pluralistic international order. By confining great powers – and their ideological influence – to well-defined spaces, Schmitt believes that a form of sustainable international order can be constructed. Having clearcut boundaries between these spaces ensures the successful reproduction of the distinction between friend and enemy at a global level, and therefore underpins the principle of 'the political' in international affairs.

The exclusion of Western military, security and normative influence from the region considered by Russia to be its sphere of influence has been a central goal of Russian foreign policy since the early 1990s. Russia's 1993 Foreign Policy Doctrine envisaged 'an order centred on and largely determined by Russia, in which the roles of external powers and external institutions were limited' (Macfarlane 2003: 201). As Macfarlane argued, this hegemonic regionalism was not simply a reflection of strategic or economic interests, but was rooted in a rights discourse about the role of great powers in the international system (Macfarlane 2003: 201). In the post-2000 period Russia has retained its consistent assertion of a special role in the region, but has gradually developed a coherent neighbourhood doctrine, asserting three red lines in its regional policy: first, it strongly opposed any suggestion that post-Soviet states (outside the Baltics) would join Western military alliances such as NATO; second, it sought to exclude any Western military bases in the former Soviet space, such as US bases in Central Asia; and third, it aimed to prevent any regime changes that would result in a shift towards an overtly more pro-Western foreign policy orientation.

Russia's opposition to NATO expansion was the most obvious manifestation of its attempts to exclude alien powers from its sphere of interests (for discussion, see Sakwa 2017: 77–90). Early attempts to cooperate with NATO, including establishing the NATO–Russia Council in May 2002, did not prevent NATO agreeing to include the Baltic states in 2004 and fuelled a growing sense in Moscow that cooperation did not produce any concessions from the West. The international environment had changed markedly by April 2008, when NATO made promises to Georgia and Ukraine at the Bucharest Summit that their aspirations for membership in NATO would one day be fulfilled. Although Germany's objections delayed agreement on their membership, the further expansion of NATO to the east still seemed likely, until the Russian military interventions in Georgia in 2008 and in Ukraine in 2014 ended any immediate prospects of NATO membership for either country.

This dispute over the exclusion of NATO as a military alliance from the former Soviet space took on a wider, civilisational meaning. The struggle for Ukraine became a struggle over fundamental values and norms, identified by the West as universal, and by Russia as associated with the civilisation of the 'Russian World'. As Schmitt argued, ideas became potent when associated with space, and the attempt by Russia to exclude alien powers translated into a broader, regional battle against liberal norms, civil society and democratic values. The shift to a normative struggle also ensured that non-military spatial projects, such as the EU's Eastern Partnership, were also increasingly viewed in Moscow as intruding on this Russo-centric space.[12] Russia's development of the EAEU made the European Union's power projection into the region more threatening to Russia's interests, producing a spatial clash between two geopolitical and ideational orders, which ultimately resulted in military conflict in Ukraine.

Since the Ukraine crisis, Russia has not opposed other forms of partnership and cooperation with the European Union, such as an Enhanced Partnership and Cooperation Agreement (EPCA) signed between the European Union and Kazakhstan in December 2015, or a Comprehensive and Enhanced Partnership Agreement (CEPA) agreed between the European Union and Armenia in November 2017. Russia also acquiesced in the development of China's Belt and Road Initiative (BRI) across much of the former Soviet Union, at least rhetorically. In practice, Russia was cautious about its potential impact on its sphere of influence, and promoted its own EAEU project as a counterpart to the BRI. In May 2015, at a summit between Xi Jinping and Vladimir Putin in Moscow, the two sides agreed to form a 'conjunction' or '*sopryazhenie*' between the EAEU and the BRI. In reality, however, China's economic influence in Central Asia – coupled with growing political and security ties – posed a long-term threat to Russia's sphere of influence across Eurasia.

Military bases are the most potent signifiers of hegemony in international relations. Russia initially acquiesced in the establishment of temporary US military bases in Uzbekistan and Kyrgyzstan in 2001–2 to support the American military campaign in Afghanistan, but became increasingly concerned when they remained in place long after the initial intervention. From July 2005 onwards Russia and China repeatedly called in the Shanghai Cooperation Organisation (SCO) for the closure of US military bases in the Central Asian region. Uzbekistan's turn away from the West following the killing of protesters in Andijan in 2005 led to the closure of the US base at Karshi-Khanabad (Lewis 2008). The US airbase at Manas, Kyrgyzstan, was only closed in 2014, after a change of government in 2010 and under strong pressure from Russia. By the end of 2015 the last Western military base in the region, a German base in Termez, on the Uzbek–Afghan border, was also closed; a French airbase in Dushanbe had been terminated in 2014 (RFE/RL 2015).

As Russia reasserted its role in the region, Western military and security ties in Central Asia came under growing pressure. Central Asia had played an important role as the resupply route for NATO forces in the Northern Distribution Network, in which Russia was also involved through a logistics centre in Ulyanovsk. The logistics centre at Ulyanovsk was strongly criticised by nationalist deputies in the State Duma as a 'NATO base' in the heart of Russia. As relations worsened with the West, the Russian government ended the arrangement in May 2015 (Vladykin 2015). Russian diplomats strongly criticised an apparently innocuous transit agreement between Kazakhstan and the United States to allow military goods to be transported across the Caspian en route to Afghanistan. A Russian diplomat told *Kommersant* newspaper that the Americans 'needed [the agreement] [to develop] a presence on the Caspian, so that their infrastructure could appear here' (Solovyov 2018).

This heightened concern about any American military presence was evident in an agreement on the legal status of the Caspian Sea reached in 2018. After more than two decades of negotiations, all the littoral states – Azerbaijan, Iran, Kazakhstan, Russia and Turkmenistan – signed an agreement – the Convention on the Legal Status of the Caspian Sea – on 15 August 2018 setting out principles for joint governance of the Caspian. Article 3 of the convention committed littoral states to 'ensuring security and stability in the Caspian Sea region', through the 'non-presence in the Caspian Sea of armed forces not belonging to the Parties' and the 'non-provision by a Party of its territory to other States to commit aggression and undertake other military actions against any Party'. Article 11 of the convention restricts 'navigation in, entry to and exit from the Caspian Sea exclusively by ships flying the flag of one of the Parties'.[13] The agreement establishes exactly the principle of exclusion of powers 'alien to the space', and instead reinforces the strategic position of Russia, which thereby enhanced its already dominant military position in the sea. The main advantage of the agreement for Russia, argued conservative commentators, was 'the prevention of the appearance of Americans there, a guarantee of the "absence of their presence"' (Starikov 2018).

A third strand of Russia's exclusionary policies has been to combat what it views as Western political interference in the region. Popular revolts forcing changes in government in Georgia (2003), Ukraine (2004) and Kyrgyzstan (2005) played a critical role in crystallising the Russian belief that the flow of ideas – promoted by international NGOs and Western-funded democracy initiatives – was part of an interventionist geopolitical agenda, which used the mechanism of 'colour revolutions' for political ends. Russia's negative reactions to 'colour revolutions' intensified after the Arab Spring of 2010–11 and the second round of political upheavals in Ukraine in early 2014. At a session of the Russian Security Council in 2014, Putin called these events 'simply state coup d'états, provoked and financed from outside' (Russian Federation 2014a). In a typical intervention, in June 2014 CSTO Secretary-General Nikolai Bordyuzha warned that the West was intent on 'further destabilization of the post-Soviet space and break-up of the international collective institutions created there' and was using 'the well-drilled know-how of "colour revolutions" to bring pro-Western puppet regimes to power' (Interfax 2014).

Always absent from Schmitt's theories of international relations is the agency of small and middle powers, whose sovereignty is necessarily constrained by their inclusion in a *Großraum*. Russia has also repeatedly underestimated or miscalculated the potential for post-Soviet states to assert their own agency. Ukraine has offered the clearest example of Russian miscalculation, the result of poor intelligence and a worldview that underestimates the significance of domestic political dynamics in post-Soviet states. Even in states with historically close relations with Russia, such as Tajikistan, Moscow has been increasingly forced to compete for influence, with China, with the West and with the Gulf states. Azerbaijan, Uzbekistan and Turkmenistan all shifted away from the Russian sphere of influence in the 1990s, although Russia still retained considerable influence in Central Asia and the southern Caucasus. The war in Afghanistan ensured that Russia remained an important security actor across the region, and the lingering Nagorno-Karabakh conflict and Russia's base in Armenia left Russia with a leading strategic role in the Caucasus.

Despite clear limitations on its influence, Russia nevertheless clearly articulated its three red lines related to the exclusion of foreign powers from what it claimed as a sphere of special interests: the presence of foreign military bases; overtly pro-Western political regimes; and membership in Western military alliances. The Russian leadership always acted in cases where these red lines seemed likely to be violated, in two cases using military force. At other times, Russia used political, military and economic means to signal its displeasure over pro-Western foreign policy stances by post-Soviet states. Over time Russia's spatial vision for the region and its understanding of Russia's place within it may change. In the late Putinist period, however, the need for a greater space within which Russia would construct its role as a great power remained central to Russian foreign policy thinking.

The New Schmittians

Writing in the 2000s, some critics argued that Schmitt's view of international relations had little relevance to understanding a global politics that was dominated by interdependence and globalisation. Galli argued that

> The complexity of today's world is necessarily lost on Schmitt ... He could have known nothing of multilevel governance, neomedievalism, nor of the complex spaces and political forms that are not hierarchical and Westphalian, but multilateral and characterized by widespread political power. (Galli 2010: 19)

Galli suggests that 'attempts to form order based on resolution, exception, restoration of space, and the creation of borders are diluted and even liquefied in globalization' (Galli 2010: 20). Minca and Rowan concur:

> [Schmitt's] two attempts to conceive of a new political form capable of respatializing the political, the *Großraum* order and the telluric partisan, failed to gain traction in political reality and seemed theoretically bankrupt. Investing hope in the idea that marginal localized struggles could produce a new global spatial order was arguably the sign of a chastened intellect. (Minca and Rowan 2015a: 284)

The empirical evidence of a changing world order suggests that these critiques were premature. It is exactly 'attempts to form order based on [the] ... restoration of space, and the creation of borders', in Galli's words, that are the most important political dynamics in contemporary international relations. From 'marginal localized struggles' in the Russian borderlands, new forms of order indeed began to emerge, marked not by multilateral and multilevel governance, but by efforts to respatialise power through new, militarised boundaries and frontiers.

Far from being theoretically bankrupt, the principles of *Großraum* order were shaping a new generation of foreign policy thinkers, not only in Russia but elsewhere. As Schmitt himself would have predicted, neo-liberal globalisation provoked a political and popular demand for anti-liberal ideologies, predicated on clear boundaries, concrete spaces and lines of amity and enmity. Whether the slogans were Brexit, the 'Russian World', 'America First', the rise of Hindutva in India or the 'China Dream', the geopolitical visions of the twenty-first century deliberately reduced the complexity of multilateral, globalised order to a simpler vision of bounded cultural and political spaces. Instead of movement, fluidity and creolisation, the Schmittian paradigm demanded hard borders, clear distinctions and fixed identities. Far from acquiescing in the emergence of a world of 'liquid modernity', as Zygmunt Bauman characterised it, Schmitt's disciples in the early twenty-first century sought to combat hybridity and liquidity with the reassertion of forms of solidity, of land, and walls, and new divisions in international relations.

Notes

1. Cited in Schmitt (2007c: 59).
2. The September German–Soviet Boundary and Friendship Treaty was a supplement to the August pact. It delineated the new frontiers between Germany and the USSR and the exchange of nationals between the two new occupied zones.
3. 'Schmitt pursues the dual strategy of developing a conceptual counter-vocabulary to rewrite international history geopolitically as a series of "spatial revolutions", inserting Hitler's Großraumpolitik into a transhistoricized continuum of "land-appropriations"; and, inversely, mobilizing this reconstructed history to ascribe historical legitimacy and direction to Nazi-Germany's wars of conquest' (Teschke 2011: 86).
4. Müller (1997: 29) argues that 'Schmitt's geopolitical conception was different from the biologically-based *Lebensraum-strategy* of the Nazis, since it aimed at the preservation of the political in a pluriversum of *Grossraume*, rather than at a limitless expansion of the Reich based on essentialist notions of the German *Volk*.' On the links, see also: Barnes and Minca (2013) and Elden (2011); and Bassin (1987) on the wider ideological tensions between German geopoliticians and National Socialism.
5. The English translation cited here is of what Schmitt refers to as a fourth edition of his April 1939 lecture. See Schmitt (2011a: 75) for the publication history.
6. In the specific historical circumstances of 1939, Schmitt did argue for a *Großraum* in Central Europe, analogous to the Monroe Doctrine in the Americas, an idea quickly picked up also by Hitler (Balakrishnan 2000: 235). In 1939 Schmitt approvingly cited Hitler's speech of 28 April 1939, in which Hitler attacked President Roosevelt's criticism of the German invasion of Czechoslovakia, saying: 'We Germans advocate exactly the same [Monroe] doctrine for Europe, but in any case for the region and the affairs of the Great German Reich' (cited in Schmitt 2011c: 52). Schmitt commented: 'With this the idea of a neat and peaceful distinction between Großräume is expressed in plain sobriety and the confusion removed with which an economic imperialism had enveloped the Monroe Doctrine in fog, in that it bent [the latter's] reasonable logic of spatial separation [*Raumabgrenzungsgedanke*] into an ideological claim to world interference' (Schmitt 2011c: 52). See also Kervégen (1999: 64).
7. <https://www.defense.gov/Portals/1/Documents/pubs/2018-National-Defense-Strategy-Summary.pdf> (last accessed 6 October 2019).

8. This rejection of a regional status for Russia has become a key trope in mainstream thinking. Dmitri Trenin writes that Russia 'refuses to accept the rank of a middle power with merely a regional role. It sees itself as a global actor, playing in the big leagues' (Trenin 2011: 230).
9. <https://web.archive.org/web/20161125102851/https://www.youtube.com/watch?v=hTcYwM0chnE> (last accessed 6 October 2019).
10. At times Schmitt's formulation of the 'politically active nation' has some similarities with Lev Gumilev's idea of *passionarnost'* (passionarity), an idea that a form of cosmic energy drives the rise and fall of civilisations and nations (Bassin 2016; Clover 2016). The idea has become commonplace in Russian public discourse. In his 2012 Address to the Federal Assembly, President Putin said: 'Who leaps ahead, and who remains an outsider and inevitably loses their independence, will depend not only on economic potential but above all on the will of each nation, on its internal energy; as Lev Gumilev said, on its *passionarnost'*, its ability to move forward and to change' (Putin 2012a).
11. Alexander Dugin also rejects this association between Great Spaces and race. According to Ingram (2001: 1034), 'Dugin repeatedly criticizes the Nazis for their prioritization of race over space, again enabling him to avoid the narrow fascist label, and side with the "dissidents of fascism"'.
12. For early signs of Russian concern over the impact of the Eastern Partnership, see 'Vostochnoe partnerstvo: problemy realizatsii i vozmozhnye posledstviya [The Eastern Partnership: problems of implementation and possible consequences]', Council of the Federation of Russia, November 2009, pp. 33–7.
13. 'Convention on the Legal Status of the Caspian Sea', <http://www.mid.ru/en/problematika-bassejna-kaspijskogo-mora/-/asset_publisher/FX0KRdXqTkSJ/content/id/3319235> (last accessed 16 November 2018).

NINE

Apocalypse Delayed: Katechontic Thinking in Late Putinist Russia

> For when they shall say, Peace and safety; then sudden destruction cometh upon them.
>
> St Paul, 1 Thessalonians 5:3

Russia's post-Cold War marginalisation in international affairs during the 1990s only temporarily suspended a powerful strand of exceptionalism and messianic thinking in Russian foreign policy discourse. By the late 2000s official discourse often reflected conservative ideas about Russia's 'indispensable' role in the world, and its engagement in a civilisational struggle, reflected in disputes over values and status in a contested international order (Lo 2015: 49–50). Putin's third term became identified with a 'civilisational turn', in which Russia claimed to represent a post-Westphalian 'state-civilisation', with a special role to play in international affairs (Chebankova 2013a; Linde 2016; Tsygankov 2016). Russia's international role was increasingly expressed in exceptionalist terms, reviving a long historical tradition of messianic thought in Russian political philosophy and spiritual thinking.

This messianic discourse characterised Russia as a civilisation fated to play an essentially tragic role in an imperfect world, a bulwark against the chaos and destruction unleashed by the dangerous excesses of American liberalism. Russia saw itself 'as a unique restraining factor in the world of increasing chaos' (Engström 2014: 362). The sources of this worldview can be traced to historical ideas of Russian exceptionalism, particularly reworkings of the theory of Moscow as the 'Third Rome' (Duncan 2000; Poe 2001; Østbø 2016). Since the 1990s these traditional Orthodox eschatological frameworks have been retheorised by radical conservatives through a variety of traditions, including Carl Schmitt's secular reworking of the Biblical figure of the *katechon*, portraying Russia as 'the restrainer', the power that holds back the apocalypse and maintains an imperfect order in a sinful world.

Schmitt and the Katechon

Schmitt's view of history denounces a liberal teleology, an idea of continual progress towards a better world, instead favouring a Christian eschatology, in which the world is inexorably moving towards the end times and humanity is continually threatened by a descent into chaos and disaster (Arvidsson 2016; Lievens 2016). Global conflict can be understood as a secularised version of the constant struggle between Christ and the Antichrist, in which '[t]he meaning of history . . . is not "progress" or unity, but *salvation*' (Koskenniemi 2004: 501). In 1932 Schmitt turned to the Biblical figure of the *katechon* (from the Greek τὸ κατέχον, 'that which withholds', sometimes translated as 'the restrainer') to represent a force that holds back evil and chaos (Hell 2009; Prozorov 2012; Agamben 2016; Arvidsson 2016; Lievens 2016; Meierhenrich and Simons 2016). The textual source of the *katechon* in the Bible is St Paul's Second Letter to the Thessalonians, where Paul writes of the *katechon* as a force that stands between the world and the apocalypse, a figure that restrains the emergence of the antichrist:

> 3. Don't let anybody deceive you in any way, for [that day will not come] until the rebellion occurs and the man of lawlessness is revealed, the man doomed to destruction . . .
> 6. And now you know what is holding him back [the *katechon*], so that he may be revealed at the proper time.
> 7. For the secret power of lawlessness is already at work; but the one who now holds it back [the *katechon*] will continue to do so till he is taken out of the way.

In traditional Christian thought, the *katechon* 'restrains *anomos* [the Wicked] and keeps the world from plunging towards its End' (Arvidsson 2016: 225). Schmitt reinterprets it as a secular concept, although, as he concluded in his post-war *Glossarium*: 'I believe in the katechon; for me he is the sole possibility for a Christian to understand history and find it meaningful' (cited in Meier 1998: 22). It may be right that it was partly the 'vagueness and ambiguity' of the concept that Schmitt found so appealing (Meierhenrich and Simons 2016: 47), because he could use the concept in reference to different historical epochs and different political regimes and institutions. But Schmitt's preoccupation with this passage also reflects a long history of contested interpretation of 'one of the most intensely political texts in the Western tradition' (Prozorov 2012: 484).

Schmitt applies the concept in different ways in different texts, and seldom defines it clearly. The role of *katechon* 'would fall in different historical moments on different actors, and the important political decision would be to apprehend what or who at any moment plays it' (Koskenniemi 2004: 502). At times, Schmitt refers to the Roman Empire and its Christian successor, the Holy Roman Empire, as the *katechon*: '"Empire" in this sense meant the historical power to *restrain* the appearance of the Antichrist and the end of the present eon' (Schmitt 2003: 60). The Eastern Roman Empire also took on this role: 'Byzantium was a true "forestaller," a "Katechon," as one calls it in Greek; it "held out," despite its weakness, for many centuries against Islam and thereby hindered the Arabs from conquering all of Italy' (Schmitt 2015).

Elements of a *katechontic* order could be identified in Europe before the French Revolution, which had been characterised by a 'fixed orientation in terms of space and land', above all in the medieval kingdoms, in 'a monarchy grounded in a country and its people' (Schmitt 2003: 64). In the post-war period, Schmitt argues that European jurisprudence, 'the legacy of Roman law, and the customs established over the centuries' (Ulmen 2003: 25), constituted a *katechon*, which acted to restrain the 'total functionalization' of law. 'Schmitt was seeking to reconstitute European jurisprudence in opposition to bureaucrats and technocrats, who systematically reduce it to regulations and procedures' (Ulmen 2003: 25). Against an 'empty, legalitarian technicism', jurisprudence offers a defence of an 'indestructible core of all law against all destructive enactments', an institution to preserve 'legal principles' that underpin 'the basis of a rational human existence' (Schmitt 1990: 67). Throughout these different characterisations of the *katechon*, it acts as a device for him to structure history in a way that shifts the theoretical perspective from the liberal vision of teleological progress to that of 'Order-thinking', a view of history that prioritises the suppression of chaos and the production of order, however flawed that might be.

In these different forms, Schmitt viewed the *katechon* as 'an institution that averts chaos and has the capacity to re-establish a concrete social order' (Meierhenrich and Simons 2016: 48, citing Günter Meuter). In some contexts the *katechon* can be understood as a 'caretaker', 'an individual or institution that ensures order' and acts as a guarantor of the constitution (Meierhenrich and Simons 2016: 35). Such a view is what Prozorov terms 'the Hobbesian-Schmittian tradition' of the 'secularized katechon', representing 'a force that wards off the natural anomie and thus the end of the social order as we know it' (Prozorov 2012: 488). This is the interpretation that has been consistently promoted within Russian Orthodox Christian thinking, and by contemporary Russian conservatism. Giorgio Agamben has a very different interpretation of the *katechon*, instead claiming that it is the *katechon* that is a device for the preservation of illegitimate power, justified as the 'lesser evil' of authoritarian order to prevent the 'greater evil' of chaos; in short, for Agamben, the *katechon* is the Antichrist, which must be removed (Prozorov 2012: 488–9):

> While for the Hobbesian–Schmittian orientation the restraining function of the katechon stabilizes the existing terrain of the political as 'all there is' and its disappearance is only thinkable as the self-destruction of humanity, Agamben's messianic approach insists on the removal of the katechon as the condition of possibility of life beyond the familiar coordinates of the political, defined by the logic of sovereignty. (Prozorov 2012: 489)

These two interpretations of *katechontic* order represent two fundamental paradigms of political thought in contemporary Russia (and indeed more widely): either the legitimation of Putinist Russia as an authoritarian order, which acts as a conservative bulwark against global chaos; or an interpretation of Russia's domestic authoritarianism and aggressive foreign policy as threatening both domestic peace and international order.

Schmitt rejects this second version, arguing that *katechontic* thinking is not merely another way of representing a simplistic conservatism, a pseudo-theological legitimation for any authoritarian political order. Schmitt explicitly warns against 'turn[ing] the word into a general designation for merely conservative or reactionary tendencies' (Lievens 2016: 418). In his later work, writes Lievens:

> the *katechon* appears time and time again as a force that has to ward off the possibility of a world without politics, be it in the form of cosmopolitan world unity, nihilistic centralization, total functionalization of law, or eschatological paralysis. (Lievens 2016: 415)

The *katechon* is the guarantor of the political, of open-endedness in history, the figure that stands against the end of history, however that might be manifested: 'its polemical aim is to ward off the idea that humans can definitely judge over the world, history, and morality and announce the end of history' (Lievens 2016: 418). This interpretation of the *katechon* – as a bulwark against the 'dangerous illusion of salvation through the final struggle of humanity' (Lievens 2016: 418) – takes on renewed significance in the context of the hubris of the post-Cold War period of universalist liberalism, not least in the version of Francis Fukuyama (1992), which proclaimed a teleological end of history, interpreted by some conservative thinkers as a goal to be achieved primarily through the defeat of the historical *katechon*, Russia.

In recent studies on Schmitt, the concept of the *katechon* as the producer of order acts as a metaphysical fulcrum for much of Schmitt's thinking, linking Schmitt's ideas of sovereignty and exception and the friend/enemy distinction with an eschatological theory of history (see Hell 2009; Lievens 2016; Meierhenrich and Simons 2016). In the context of Russia, however, the *katechon* takes on a meaning of much greater significance than simply acting as a somewhat esoteric theoretical device. Schmitt did not understand the *katechon* as an unworldly device that would distract political leaders from necessary decisions in this world. Schmitt's world is an 'emphatically worldly world' in which the *katechon* produces 'a concrete order' (Arvidsson 2016: 225). Indeed, Schmitt's reinterpretation of the *katechon* asserts it as the guarantor against what Schmitt terms an 'eschatological paralysis', a tendency to forget about the worldly here and now in favour of a focus on the end-of-times (Lievens 2016: 418). For radical conservative thinkers, Schmitt's *katechon* provides a concept that updates and retheorises Russia's messianic role in world history, but also informs a clear vision of Russia's place in the world and its strategic direction. As with other Schmittian concepts, Russian historical political culture provides fertile ground for the regeneration of these ideas in the contemporary political environment.

Russian Messianism

In *The Russian Idea*, Nikolai Berdyaev claimed that 'Messianic consciousness is more characteristic of the Russians than of any other people except the Jews' (Berdyaev 1947: 8). Perhaps Russia's extraordinary geography played a part, or the unique historical role of Russian Orthodox Christianity in Russian state formation, but Russian thought has lent itself to the idea of Russians being a chosen people, with a special historical role, not only in relation to the Russian nation, but in relation to humanity in general (Sinitsyna 1998; Duncan 2000; Billington 2004). Vladimir S. Solovyov defined this messianic trait as a 'conviction of the special advantage of a given people, as the chosen bearer and perpetrator (*sovershitel'*) of the historical fate of mankind' (Duncan 2000: 7).

Such beliefs appeared early in Russian intellectual history, stimulated at least partly by the fall of Constantinople in 1453, after which Russia (along with Georgia) remained as the only Orthodox Christian community not under Islamic rule (Sidorov 2006). Peter Duncan suggests that there were two types of messianism: first, a 'state-oriented messianism', or 'nationalist messianism', which is 'linked with the idea of Moscow's domination of other peoples'; second, a 'people-oriented' and 'universalist messianism', which is associated with 'the idea of the Russian people as being a model for other nations to follow' (Duncan 2000: 3). Both these traditions of messianism can be traced to the famous invocation of Moscow as the 'Third Rome' in 1511 by the priest Filofei:

> The Church of old Rome fell because of the impiety of the Apollinarian heresy; the Church of the Second Rome, Constantinople, was smitten under the battle-axes of the Agarenes; but this present Church of the Third, New Rome, of Thy sovereign empire . . . shines in the whole universe more resplendent than the sun. And let it be known to Thy Lordship, O pious Czar, that all the empires of the Orthodox Christian Faith have converged into Thine one empire . . . For two Romes have fallen, and the Third stands, and a fourth shall never be, for Thy Christian Empire shall never devolve upon others. (Cited in this version from Duncan 2000: 11)[1]

Historically, different ideological reworkings of the myth emerged over time. There is no evidence that Filofei's formulation had any direct impact on the foreign policy of Muscovy, and most scholars accept that it initially had a primarily eschatological meaning (Sinitsyna 1998; Sidorov 2006). However, Engström reminds us that the idea of the 'Third Rome' and the notion that Russia had a special mission to struggle against the Antichrist was not only influential in foreign policy thinking, but also informed domestic political culture. The people should also guard against 'the internal Antichrist, which is no less dangerous than the external one' (Engström 2016: 363). At various times, schismatics and revolutionaries saw the autocratic state, beginning with Peter I, as the instantiation of the Antichrist, as the usurper of true Orthodoxy and the promoter of alien values and ideas.

Spiritual interpretations of the 'Third Rome' doctrine, however, often became intertwined with a political reading of Russia's place in the world, through the idea of the *katechon*, whereby the sacral role of Russia also took on an inevitable geopolitical aspect. Sidorov summarises this view:

> In Orthodox theology, the Third Rome, the Orthodox Russian Empire, came to be seen as a third embodiment of what in the Bible (2 Thessalonians 2:6–8) is called 'hold back', 'restraining' power (in Greek, catehon) against the coming rule of lawlessness. Therefore, the Russian Empire had a sacral

meaning, with its fall, Filofei wrote, the Christian world would be over because the rule of lawlessness, of Satan, would prevail and there could be no 'Fourth Rome' to restrain it. That would be the Latter Times, the apocalyptical time of the Second Coming of Jesus Christ. . . . This understanding could be called eschatological; its geopolitical ideal was a protected and protecting Russian Orthodox empire-catehon. (Sidorov 2006: 323)

Doctrines based on 'Third Romeism' largely disappeared from Russian thought during the seventeenth and eighteenth centuries, but Russia's nineteenth-century wars against Turkey and against France were accompanied by a revival of Russian exceptionalism. The historian Vladimir Ikonnikov was among those who reinterpreted the Third Rome doctrine as a mode of legitimation for a Muscovite imperialist mission (Poe 2001). Pan-Slavists reworked its tenets to support an activist role for Russia in the geopolitics of the Eastern Question, notably with regard to Constantinople (Sidorov 2006: 323). Eschatological interpretations and the *katechon* concept were marginalised in this nineteenth-century reworking of the 'Third Rome' doctrine, when, as Berdyaev put it, 'the pure messianic idea of the Kingdom of God, the kingdom of right, was clouded by the imperialistic idea, by the will to power' (Berdyaev 1947: 194–5).

A different reading of Russian history, albeit one that also reflected a *katechontic*, messianic sensibility, interpreted Russia not as the all-conquering imperial power, but as the tragic, long-suffering defender of Europe and Christianity against an external Eastern 'Other'. This idea of Russia as the 'shield' of Europe against external foes, from the Mongol conquests onwards, became an 'unofficial Russian national ideologeme' (Kholmogorov 2005a: 275), a recurring trope in Russian thought and literature. Its most famous articulation is in a letter from Pushkin to Petr Chaadaev in 1836, where Pushkin writes that '[t]he barbarians did not dare to leave an enslaved Rus in their rear and returned to their Eastern steppes. Christian enlightenment was saved by a ravaged and dying Russia'.[2]

Versions of this reading of Russian history are often encountered in school textbooks, official political statements and conservative polemics, despite a highly contested historical basis for this claim (Kholmogorov 2005a: 275; Lavrov 2016; Yanov 2016). In this ideological framing, Russian interventions in European wars served to preserve order from 'ambitious and insurrectionary' threats, both internal and external (Kholmogorov 2005a: 276). Such a view could be applied to the Russian victory over Napoleon under Alexander I, the suppression of European revolution after 1848, or victory against Nazi Germany in 1945. In the portrayal of these historical events, the sense of Russian suffering for the good of Christianity, Europe and the world has been central to Russian messianic thinking (Duncan 2000).

Anti-Communist writers often used the ideas of Russian messianism to interpret the USSR as historically expansionist, driven by long-standing cultural and psychological traits; in this reading communist ideology was merely a new incarnation of a long-standing messianic mission (Barghoorn 1955). A very different interpretation of history emerged among Russian nationalist writers in the 1970s, however. Vadim Kozhinov, writing in the early 1970s, wrote of Russia's 'national and universal [*obshchechelovecheskii*] mission', which had saved humanity from Genghis Khan, Napoleon and Hitler: 'We came out three times in history as a unique force, able to save all the other nations from a grandiose war machine which was striving to crush them' (Duncan 2000: 95). In 1980, at the 600th anniversary of the Russian victory over Mongol forces at Kulikovo, this role of Russia became a central motif in the celebrations. Patriarch Pimen noted the importance of Kulikovo 'for the peoples and states of Europe, which at the cost of huge losses for Rus' were saved from alien invasion' (Duncan 2000: 80). Feliks Kuznetsov linked the Russian and Soviet roles, comparing historical victories over the Mongols with Soviet victory over the Nazis and what he viewed as Soviet attempts to save the world from nuclear destruction, thus offering a new and original twist on Russia's role as *katechon* (Duncan 2000: 81).

Russia as Contemporary *Katechon*

The collapse of the USSR undermined any concept of Russia as the indispensable power in international affairs and marginalised messianic thinking in mainstream political thought. Among Russian conservatives, however, the idea of the Third Rome, and the notion of Russia having a mission – both spiritual and geopolitical – soon began to re-emerge in the work of Alexander Dugin, Natalya Narochnitskaya, Yegor Kholmogorov, Mikhail Nazarov and others. One strand of thought largely followed Orthodox conceptions of Russia as *katechon*. Orthodox publicist Mikhail Nazarov offered a fundamentalist Orthodox version, combining apocalyptic conspiracy theories about the coming of the Antichrist with a concept of Russia as the *katechon*. In his work, writes Sidorov, 'the fate of the world is dependent on the Third Rome, its *catehon*, restraining, hold-back power of the Russian empire to provide humanity with a lighthouse for salvation' (Sidorov 2006: 327). Nazarov criticises Dugin's Eurasianism, instead emphasising a pan-Slavic vision, but one which also seeks to correct the territorial losses Russia is thought to have suffered in the post-Soviet period, writing that 'we must tend to restore the Third Rome in its historically just boundaries because we can't leave aside our compatriots on the lost territories (including our ancient, truly Russian lands)' (Sidorov 2006: 327).

In this tradition, Orthodox Christianity is located not on the periphery of Europe but as its 'cultural foundation', argues Suslov, reinforcing 'the role of Russia as the force that saves the West and all mankind from degradation and from falling under the power of the Antichrist' (Suslov 2014: 75). Similarly, Conservative Orthodox thinkers such as Natalya Narochnitskaya argued that the liberal world order is 'the kingdom of the beast, of the Anti-Christ' (Horvath 2016: 875).

Yegor Kholmogorov offered a more clearly political reading of *katechontic* thinking, by emphasising the 'shield ideology' as 'a very important addition to and interpretation of the idea of the "Restrainer"', the secularised version of the *katechon* (Kholmogorov 2005a: 275). A Russian order emerged from *katechontic* thinking, what Kholmogorov calls a 'Pax Rossica', directed primarily at the 'structuring of the surrounding geopolitical space' rather than internal development. Kholmogorov drew a contrast between the 'second' and 'third' Romes: 'if the Roman "katechon" restrains internal collapse, then the Russian [katechon] [restrains] the external enemy' (Kholmogorov 2005a: 275). For Kholmogorov, Russia as *katechon* must engage in geopolitics; in that role

> she must address the geopolitical tasks that are necessary to strengthen Russia's position as a great power, playing the role in the global system of a force constraining the establishment of a world order that is equivalent to world lawlessness. (Cited in Østbø 2016: 215)

Alexander Dugin followed a traditional Orthodox reading in arguing that the Eastern Roman Empire, in its Byzantine incarnation, was cast in the role of *katechon* for its more than 1,000 years of history, from the founding of Constantinople in 330 to its fall to the Ottomans in 1453 (Dugin 1996: ch. 45). The Orthodox empire was the obstacle 'in the path of the coming Antichrist', that which 'does not let him be revealed', the 'Restrainer' or 'the katechon' (Dugin 1996: ch. 45). The fall of Constantinople meant the retreat of the *katechon*, a threat that the Antichrist would come; Moscow's acceptance of the role of *katechon* was seen by many believers as merely a delay to the coming of the end times, and such a belief was repeated in Russian history during subsequent periods of political upheaval. But it transformed the geopolitical role of Russia:

> the fall of Byzantium meant . . . the dawn of apostasy and the universal rejection of Christianity. Moscow [became] the capital of an essentially new state: not national, but imperial, soteriological, eschatological, and apocalyptical. It is the last outpost of salvation, the Ark, the ground prepared for the descent of the New Jerusalem. (Dugin 2014b: 12)

In a 1997 article on *'Katechon* and Revolution', Dugin wrote that 'the imprint of the Third Rome is in the soul of every Russian. This is the central paradigm of our historical consciousness' (Dugin 1997a). Many other conservative thinkers picked up on this argument, or developed it independently. Conservative ideologue Sergei Kurginyan offered a typical example of this worldview:

> Many things are clouding around Russia; the evil is approaching from all directions; from the Middle East, from the Far East; it is clouding around Europe and the whole world. We know that the circle of evil is tightening around us. We remember that Russia is Katechon, that is, the withholder of peace. (Cited in Engström 2014: 367)

In this way, the concept of *katechon* gradually escaped its traditional Orthodox framing and became a central element in secular conservative thought, reflecting a much wider 'messianic turn' in contemporary conservatism in Europe, explored in work by Giorgio Agamben, Alain Badiou, Slavoj Žižek and others (Prozorov 2012: 483). Contemporary messianic thinking does not share an association with any tradition of historical messianism, but shares 'a sense of exigency about the advent of a radically different world' (Prozorov 2012: 483–4).

It is this sense of impending, fundamental change that informs *katechontic* thinking among a wide range of conservative voices in Russia, not only those in the Orthodox camp. An influential manifesto of Russian conservatism prepared by Mikhail Remizov's Institute of National Strategy in 2014 talks of 'the traditional conception among Russian conservatives of the role of Russia as *Katekhon* – the "Restrainer" [*uderzhivaiushchii*], preventing on the one hand, global anarchy, and on the other global monopoly and hegemony, both of which . . . risk apocalyptic consequences' (Institute of National Strategy 2014: 25). In this context, the role of *katechon* is viewed as a principled justification for the institution of 'balance of power', a central concept in the realist thinking that is associated with Russian foreign policy (Institute of National Strategy 2014: 25).

The circulation of the concept of *katechon* among these different strands of Russian conservatism reflects diverse intellectual sources and differences in nuance, but the essential geopolitical image of Russia that different schools of conservative thought construct is strikingly similar. Many advocates of Russia as a conservative, balancing force in international relations supported the international radical conservative website, Katehon.com. Orthodox conservative oligarch Konstantin Malofeev, presidential adviser Sergei Glazyev and Leonid Reshetnikov, Director of the Russian Institute of

Strategic Studies, were all members of the board; featured authors include both Russian conservatives and European far-right politicians such as Marine le Pen. The website describes their principles:

> We, at Katehon, clearly defend the principle of a multipolar world, and thus we fundamentally support a pluricentric worldview defined by an international balance of powers; we reject and challenge any kind of unipolar world order and global hegemony. Therefore, we pay special attention to global multipolar associations such as BRICS and the Shanghai Cooperation Organization (SCO). All of our fellow contributors hold firm to the main principles of the continentalist school of geopolitics . . . We . . . view the world as being a global space in which there will always be permanent and distinct civilizations or 'civilizational spheres' . . . In particular, we are engaged in studying the following 'great spaces' which comprise the majority of all world civilizations – North America, South (or Latin) America, Europe, Russia-Eurasia, China, India, the Islamic world, Africa, and the Pacific.[3]

This Schmittian worldview unites the Katehon.com community. Katehon.com is published in English, and appeals to radical conservative movements across Europe and beyond. But the underlying principle of *katechontic* thinking has developed beyond radical conservative networks to become a familiar trope in the discourse of the wider Russian political elite. Russian radical conservatives have been quick to praise what they see as *katechontic* thinking in Putin's speeches in his third term in office (Engström 2014). His 2013 Valdai speech, in particular, was seen as a turning point, in which Putin describes Russia as standing alone as a bulwark against European liberal values, which he views as a 'threat to Russia's identity' and 'a direct path to degradation and primitivism' (Putin 2013a).

Engström (2014) argues that the Foreign Policy Doctrine of 2013 describes a Russia that sees itself as 'as a unique restraining factor in the world of increasing chaos' (Engström 2014: 362). The Doctrine argues that 'imposing one's own hierarchy of values' will lead to 'chaos in world affairs'. Peace is threatened by 'attempts to manage crises through unilateral sanctions and other coercive measures, including armed aggression, outside the framework of the UN Security Council'. In this unstable world, Russian foreign policy is 'consistent and continuous and reflects the unique role our country has been playing over centuries as a counterbalance in international affairs and the development of global civilization'. Russia is 'fully aware of its special responsibility for maintaining security in the world both on the global and regional levels . . . [and] will work to anticipate and forestall events and remain prepared for any scenario in global affairs' (Russian Federation 2013).

In his December 2013 address to the Federal Assembly, Putin further developed this conservative ideological stance in foreign policy, quoting Nikolai Berdyaev to argue that 'the meaning of conservatism is not that it prevents movement forward and upward, but that it prevents movement backwards and downwards, into chaotic darkness and a return to a primitive state' (Putin 2013b). From Moscow's point of view the 'end of history' promoted by Western thinkers after the Cold War has only resulted in a threat of 'chaotic darkness' across the North Caucasus and the Middle East, evident in the barbarism of the Islamic State, and resulting in a refugee crisis and numerous terrorist attacks in Europe. Modern counter-terrorist campaigns in Chechnya, Afghanistan and elsewhere are interpreted through this lens: 'As terrorism increasingly takes on the features of a global barbarism, so Russia . . . will inevitably gain (and is already gaining) the image of an antiterrorist, who again and again restrains a global evil' (Kholmogorov 2005a: 276).

Even in 2000, in the early days of the Second Chechen War, Putin articulated a version of Kholmogorov's 'shield ideology', arguing that 'Russia is really standing at the forefront of the war against international terrorism. And Europe ought to fall on its knees and express its great thankfulness that we, unfortunately, are fighting it alone' (cited in Souleimanov and Ditrych 2008: 1199). In an interview with *Paris Match* on 6 July 2000, Putin claimed that 'we are witnessing today the formation of a fundamentalist international, a sort of arc of instability extending from the Philippines to Kosovo'. He added that 'Europe should be grateful to us and offer its appreciation for our fight against terrorism even if we are, unfortunately, waging it on our own' (cited in Russell 2005: 109). Russia was fighting in Chechnya to protect 'Europe and the whole world' from the 'terrorist abyss', according to Putin's spokesperson (cited in Gilligan 2016: 1053). This mode of thinking was influenced by a collective memory in the Putin-era elite of a much longer battle against Islamist extremism, from the Soviet experience in Afghanistan to the insurgency in Chechnya (Dannreuther 2015: 81). During all these episodes Russia was either actively opposed by the West militarily (most notably in Afghanistan) or experienced political criticism from the West, as in its counter-terrorism campaign in Chechnya.

This sense of Russia acting as an isolated, misunderstood bulwark – the *katechon* – against chaos and barbarism became a regular trope in official foreign policy discourse. In an article in 2016 in *Russia in Global Affairs*, foreign minister Sergei Lavrov's exposition of Russia's historical role in the world again returned to Pushkin's famous quotation about the salvation of

Europe by 'a ravaged and dying Russia'. For Lavrov, historical events testify to 'the special role Russia has played in European and world history' and contradict what he sees as 'the widespread belief that Russia has always been on the margins of Europe as a political outsider'. On the contrary, Russia was the critical 'balancer' in European relations who maintained stability. Lavrov resurrects the idea of Russia as the bulwark constraining the excesses of other powers, here understood as the United States and its unipolar model of international order, which has proved, in Lavrov's argument, so deeply destabilising in the Middle East (Lavrov 2016).

This discourse proved significant in determining the Russian response to the evolving situation in the Middle East after 2011. The official Russian response to the Arab Spring was informed by a number of domestic factors, including anti-government protests in Moscow 2011 that shook the Kremlin. In an article in 2012, Putin noted that 'the Arab Spring was initially received with hope for positive change', but that it quickly degenerated: 'instead of asserting democracy, and instead of the defence of minority rights, [we saw] overthrows of opponents and coups, when the domination of one force was replaced with the even more aggressive domination of another' (Putin 2012b).

A critical turning point occurred in March 2011, when there was an outbreak of rare public dissent between President Dmitry Medvedev and Prime Minister Putin over Libya. Medvedev ordered Russia's abstention in the UN Security Council vote on Resolution 1973, which permitted the use of force to impose a no-fly zone over Libya and ordered the use of 'all necessary means to protect civilians'. Prime Minister Putin, symbolically visiting a ballistic missile factory, immediately criticised Medvedev's decision, claiming that 'the resolution is defective and flawed. It allows everything. It resembles medieval calls for crusades' (Bryanski 2011). Medvedev criticised Putin's remarks, saying: 'it is inadmissible to say anything that could lead to a clash of civilisations, talk of "crusades" and so on. This is unacceptable' (Medvedev 2011). Yet UN Resolution 1973 resulted in an active Western campaign for regime change, which ended with the murder of Gaddafi and a chaotic civil war. As Putin saw it, 'a number of states, acting under the cover of humanitarian slogans, with the help of air power settled accounts with the Libyan regime', ending with the gruesome murder of Gaddafi (Putin 2012b). These events confirmed Putin's suspicions about Western intentions, and portrayed Medvedev as the naive victim of Western machinations.

The Libya debacle was a key turning point in Russia's relations with the West (Monaghan 2016: 62). Dannreuther is probably right to argue that this was the moment at which Medvedev's chance to win a second term as president evaporated (Dannreuther 2015: 83). For Putin, Russia's failure to veto UN Resolution 1973 surely appeared as a lapse in Russia's restraining role, a clear violation of its mission to prevent the violence and chaos that had emerged after previous Western military campaigns in the Arab world. After the Iraq War, Putin had responded to the killing of Saddam Hussein by calling it 'a barbaric execution' (Putin 2007c). Now the graphic images of the mob lynching of Gaddafi – recorded and broadcast around the world – clearly had a major impact on Putin. He repeatedly criticised what he termed 'the revolting scene of not just medieval but primeval slaughter of M. Gaddafi' (Putin 2012b). In October 2011 he commented:

> They killed almost the entire family of Gaddafi. His corpse was shown on all global [television] channels. It's impossible to watch without revulsion. What is this? They show a person covered in blood, wounded, still alive and they are finishing him off. All this is rolled out on our screens. (RIA-Novosti 2011a)

In December he went further, commenting:

> On the screens of the entire world they showed how he was killed, all covered in blood. Is that democracy? And who did this? Drones, including American ones, hit his convoy, and on the radio, [foreign] special forces – who should not have been there on the territory [of Libya] – brought in so-called oppositionists, militants. And they killed him without a court or investigation. (RBK 2011)

Other politicians echoed this language about Gaddafi's death and the Western intervention. Igor Barinov, deputy chair of the State Duma Defence Committee, commented: '[i]t is sad that the methods of fighting Gaddafi and the recent reaction of Western leaders reminds us more of the darkest episodes of the Middle Ages than modern operations to "build democracy"' (Barinov 2011). In the Libyan debacle and in the emerging civil war in Syria, the Russian authorities began to develop a discursive frame that promoted a narrative of Russia as the bulwark of order and civilisation, marking out a distinction between modern and medieval, order and chaos, and civilisation and barbarity.

Katechontic Thinking and the Syrian Intervention

In February 2012, while Western states continued to view the emerging conflict in Syria as primarily a struggle between an authoritarian regime and a democratically minded opposition, Russian ambassador to the United Nations Vitaly Churkin warned of a 'worsening of the crisis and its plunging into the chaos of a full-scale conflict', which 'would not only be a tragedy for the Syrian people, but would also inevitably destabilize the neighbouring countries and further stir up the strategically important region of the Middle East' (UN 2012a). From the very beginning, Russia asserted a simple binary between Russian-backed 'order' and Western-inspired 'chaos', and consistently constructed its policies, both in the United Nations and on the ground, in accord with this discursive and ideational framework. Speaking in 2013 about countries in the Middle East, Putin asserted that 'attempts in recent years to force other countries to adopt a supposedly more progressive model of development in reality turned into regression, barbarity and much blood' (Putin 2013b). As Roy Allison notes, 'Russian officials have frequently justified their position in the Syria crisis as a bulwark of international and regional order against the threat of state collapse, chaos and the spread of transnational Islamist networks' (Allison 2013b: 809).

In 2013, in one of Putin's most telling interventions on the Syrian issue, he referred to a recent online video of a rebel leader in Syria, who had publicly eaten the heart of one of his enemies. At a news conference in London, Putin commented:

> You will not deny that one does not really need to support people who not only kill their enemies, but open up their bodies, eat their intestines in front of the public and cameras. Are these the people you want to support? (Anishchuk 2013)

He continued: 'is it them who you want to supply with weapons? Then this probably has little relation to humanitarian values that have been preached in Europe for hundreds of years' (Anishchuk 2013).

During the Syrian conflict, the dichotomy between 'barbarism' and 'civilisation' became a discursive frame through which Russia sought to simplify a complex conflict. In 2013 Putin condemned 'a barbaric terrorist act' near the Russian embassy in Damascus (Putin 2013c). In 2016, he described ISIS as being involved in 'barbaric looting' in Palmyra (Putin 2016b). On hearing of the ISIS capture of Palmyra, and reports that the famous Roman amphitheatre had been destroyed, Sergei Lavrov commented: 'What can I say? Barbarians are barbarians. This ideology and practice are absolutely unacceptable for the modern civilization' (TASS 2017). In an address to the Valdai conference in 2017, Putin criticised Western policy in the Middle East, saying that 'instead of promoting progress and democracy, radical elements gain freedom of action, extremist groups which reject civilisation itself, and attempt to plunge it into archaism, chaos and barbarism' (Putin 2017a).

In March 2016 Syrian troops – backed by Russian air power and mercenaries – liberated Palmyra from ISIS forces. On 5 May 2016 Valery Gergiev conducted the Mariinsky Theatre orchestra in a concert in the famous Roman amphitheatre in Palmyra. The event was replete with symbolism. Mikhail Piotrovsky, director of the Hermitage Museum in St Petersburg, drew parallels with the siege of Leningrad, commenting that 'Our Northern Palmyra had resurrected after the deadly blockade by fascist Germany during the Second World War; now it is time to revive the Syrian Palmyra, replete with bleeding wounds' (Makarychev and Yatsyk 2017: 553). Vladimir Putin gave an address by video link, expressing hope 'not only for the renaissance of Palmyra', but also for 'contemporary civilization to be relieved of this terrible plague of international terrorism' (Putin 2016c). The *Economist* wrote that 'the music's message was clear: there is civilisation and there is barbarism; stand with Russia on the side of the good' (*Economist* 2016). The music (Bach, Schedrin, Prokofiev) was 'replete with a pathos of the supremacy of the forces of good over evil' (Makarychev and Yatsyk 2017: 553).

The West, in Russia's view, was either ambivalent towards, or even directly responsible for, this emerging barbarism. Culture minister Valery Medinsky, speaking in Palmyra, compared Russia's twenty-first-century mission with its historical experience of saving European culture from Nazi Germany in the Second World War. Contemporary Russia was continuing a long-standing historical role as the preserver of European culture against barbarism. The West, on the other hand, stood accused of helping the terrorists: 'Barbarians are assured of impunity as long as they have "sympathisers" and well-wishers, who attempt to "understand and forgive" the barbarian', he claimed. They gain support from 'contemporary political elites of "civilised" Western countries, who cultivate terrorists and connive with them in [pursuit of] their own petty goals' (Medinsky 2016). By comparison, the Russian soldier 'never ceas[es] to defend the sacred places of the world', as demonstrated by the concert in liberated Palmyra. 'Today', concluded Medinsky, 'in May 2016, the Russian soldier returns culture and civilization to a land torn apart by the savages and barbarians of the 21st century. That is what he has always done. This, it seems, is the "Russian's burden"' (Medinsky 2016).[4]

This discourse of barbarity against civilisation, a civilisation informed by 'European values', became a legitimating device for Russia's diplomatic (and subsequently military) intervention in support of President Assad. Russia re-emerged not only as a 'self-assertive subject with military strength . . . and political will . . . but also as a self-appointed universal signifier for civilization/humanism against barbarity and inhumanity' (Makarychev and Yatsyk 2017: 550). The most powerful instrument for Russia as the *katechon*, a Russia with the mission to hold back chaos, was Russia's power of veto in the UN Security Council. For Moscow, the choice was very clear. Russia had failed to live up to its mission in permitting the intervention in Libya in 2011. It would not repeat its mistake in relation to Syria. In this case,

> the international community had to jointly make a fateful choice: either to descend into further erosion of the foundations of the world order, the triumph of the law of force, the law of the fist, and the multiplication of chaos, or to make responsible decisions collectively. (Putin 2013b)

Its failure to do so, according to Putin, left Moscow with no option except to use its UN Security Council veto in February 2012, backed by China. What followed, according to Putin, was 'an extremely sharp, almost hysterical reaction to the Russian-Chinese veto'. Putin accused the West of taking actions that threatened to

> further unbalance the entire system of international security, and undermine the authority and central role of the UN. Let me remind [you] that the right to veto is not some whim but an inalienable part of the world order fixed in the UN Charter incidentally, at the insistence of the US. (Putin 2012b)

The third Russian veto in relation to Syria in June 2012 was accompanied by harsher language. An attempt to pass a Security Council resolution under Chapter VII of the UN Charter, which authorised military action, immediately recalled the Libyan precedent. Ambassador Churkin did not hold back: he accused the West of 'fan[ning] the flames of extremists, including terrorist groups', calling them 'Pharisees [who] have been pushing their own geopolitical intentions, which have nothing in common with the legitimate interests of the Syrian people', leading to 'an escalation of the conflict' to 'tragic proportions' (UN 2012b). In May 2014, with more than 160,000 people already killed in the war, Russia vetoed an attempt to refer the Syrian regime to the International Criminal Court (ICC). Russia saw the resolution as 'an attempt to use the ICC to further inflame political passions and lay the ultimate groundwork for eventual outside military intervention', citing a similar resolution in the Libyan case (UN Resolution 1970) in 2011, which 'did not help resolve the crisis, but instead added fuel to the flames of conflict'. Ambassador Churkin called upon the West 'to abandon their futile, dead-end policy of endlessly escalating the Syrian crisis', quoting the Russian proverb 'a bad peace is better than a good quarrel' (UN 2014). Russia used the veto seven times during 2012–17, with the express aim of limiting 'the further expansion of global chaos', as Putin termed it (Putin 2014b). While Western nations condemned Russia's use of the veto as an illegitimate defence of the mass human rights abuses of the Syrian regime, for Russia the power of the veto was presented as a *katechontic* instrument, preventing a further decline into chaos.

When Russia finally announced a military intervention in Syria, in September 2015, the move was justified through the same principles of stabilisation, defence of civilisation, and 'order-production'. Putin argued that the intervention was aimed at 'stabilising the legitimate authorities, and creating conditions for finding a political compromise' (Interfax 2015a). Putin used the now familiar dichotomy between order and barbarism to justify the alliance with the Assad regime: 'without active participation by the Syrian authorities and military, without participation by the Syrian army . . . you cannot expel terrorists from this nation, . . . you cannot protect the multi-ethnic and multi-faith people of Syria from elimination, enslavement and barbarism' (Putin 2015d).

According to Sergei Karaganov, 'the Syrian example demonstrates that a powerful Russia is able to stop the harmful expansion of the West and thereby prevent the spread of local conflicts onto more and more territories' (Khairemdinov 2017). In this way, Russia has a revived international mission, legitimised by a moral argument about international order and international peace. In performing this mission, Russia has also enhanced its own international influence and significance. Karaganov argued that '[r]egardless of how the Syrian civil war ends . . . Russia's victory alongside the forces of the legitimate government in Aleppo has confirmed its status [both] as a key regional power in the Middle East and as a global power'. This is not just for Russia's prestige, however, but as a mechanism to reintroduce balance into the world order: 'The global balance is restored . . . and despite all the many dangers, the world is becoming a safer place' (Karaganov 2017b).

In Syria, then, Russia legitimises itself as the defender of order, against an irresponsible West and against the forces of chaos and barbarism. Yet its *katechontic* role is tragic, since it is able to produce order only through the use of force; it restrains barbarism only through a resort to measures that are themselves barbaric – connivance with a regime that uses barrel bombs, chemical weapons and mass executions and torture to remain in power. This paradox is at the heart of the idea of the *katechon*, which makes 'relative evil possible', as Lievens puts it, 'by suppressing its radical counterpart' (Lievens 2016: 418).

The *katechon* should not be considered as an actor that is defined by any moral purity in actions. Indeed, although it 'restrains' the ultimate evil, the *katechon* is not a force which must follow a moral code or laws. 'In a certain way', writes Lievens, citing work by Virno, 'the katechon keeps humans being bad: it restrains evil by tolerating it' (Lievens 2016: 417). Virno rejects Schmitt's 'appropriation of *katechon* on behalf of authoritarian political thought' (Virno 2008: 58), but recognises that the *katechon* is a force that cannot avoid 'mingling with what must be restrained' (Virno 2008: 56). It 'safeguards the "radical evil" that it has engendered: the antidote, here, is no different from the poison' (Virno 2008: 189). Just as the sovereign declares the exception to maintain order in society, so the *katechon* uses violence to preserve the political, preventing the end of the world from an impending apocalypse, but only through means that are unethical and immoral.

These readings of the *katechon* reflect a long-standing concern in Russian messianic thought that Russia's mission might – in reality – induce it to violate the very morality that it proclaims. Vladimir Solovyov, in his critique of Slavophilism, wrote that its sin

> was not that it ascribed to Russia a higher vocation, but that it insufficiently insisted on the moral conditions of this vocation . . . let them proclaim still more decisively the Russian people as the gathering Messiah, so long as they remember that the Messiah must also act like a Messiah, and not like Barabbas. (Cited in Duncan 2000: 45)

The contradictions of *katechontic* thinking became increasingly evident in Russian foreign policy, where the narrative of 'good against evil' in the Syria war was constantly undermined by accusations of war crimes against Russian forces and their Syrian allies. The *katechontic* framework provided a form of moral justification for these ethical violations, since the ultimate goal – the restraint of a greater, radical evil, or what Russian officials termed 'global chaos', an 'abyss of violence', the 'erosion of global order', etc. – seemingly justified the short-term tragedy of war and repression, with its moral shortcomings, human rights abuses, violence and suffering. For liberal thinkers, this represented an unacceptable approach to managing conflict, but in Schmittian terms, it offered the only way to ensure the construction of order in an imperfect world. This does not mean that Russian policies had no moral constraints, or that they only relied on the use of violence and military force. Moscow consistently combined the use of arms with asymmetric peace negotiations, initiating talks with opposition groups from a position of strength, in the Astana political process, for example. But the discourse of Russia as the ultimate conservative bulwark, standing against a decline into chaos and destruction, provided a legitimation for Russia's military campaigns, even when its *katechontic* stance risked producing a far worse evil than that which it opposed.

This moral contradiction is also coupled with a second paradox, that *katechontic* thinking, while attempting to restrain an imperial power, nevertheless reproduces an imperial vision. The *katechon* serves as the kernel of a new imperial formation, born out of the ruins of the old. In its defeats, Russia finds a path to rebirth. 'First defeat, then the victory of the defeated', wrote Schmitt after the war. 'Only that provides the momentum to go out and conquer the world' (cited in Hell 2009: 293). Hell reminds us that 'defeat intensifies enemy-friend constellations, imperial ideologies, and the acute awareness that all empires will eventually end' (Hell 2009: 293). Russian military campaigns in Syria, Ukraine and Georgia, although articulated as preserving order and maintaining spatial boundaries, also reproduced imperial spaces. Schmitt, as paraphrased by Hell, argued that 'the *katechon* is the instance that brings about a successful process of imperial mimesis by maintaining the "identity of space" while changing the content of this very space' (*Glossarium* 61, cited in Hell 2009: 290). As the *katechon*, the empire is reborn.

The result, argues Hell, is *katechon* representing 'a kind of ruin-gazer scenario: the imperial sovereign – empire or emperor – who, with its or his eyes fixed on the end of time, prepares for a political battle to delay that very end' (Hell 2009: 290). This gaze, argues Hell, is an imperial gaze, and the *katechon* represents 'a reconceptualization of the trope of imperial decline' and acts to 'delay the empire's end' (Hell 2009: 311). Around Russia's periphery a series of ruins act as symbolic representations of Russia's modern imperial battles: Grozny, Tskhinvali, Donetsk, Aleppo. For Russia's critics, these are the bitter legacy of a neo-imperialist, expansionist foreign policy, which has left destruction in its wake. For Moscow, however, the ruins are metonymic representations of its stand against the disorder brought on by the totalising ambitions of its enemies; they represent the battles fought to preserve Russia as a subject of history, as a genuine sovereign state, a state-civilisation and the centre of a Schmittian 'Great Space' in a hostile world.

This reading of *katechontic* thinking as a revival of empire helps to explain why it represents much more than a theologised version of a realist plea for military restraint and a warning against attempts to engineer radical social and political change. By viewing international conflicts within this mode of thinking, everyday ethical demands are increasingly marginalised as incommensurate with the scale of the messianic task. Esoteric notions of the *katechon* risk converting all political conflicts into existential struggles, in which violence is legitimised as a means to prevent an apocalyptic vision of the end of history. Former Kremlin adviser Gleb Pavlovsky argues that this mode of thinking is increasingly widespread in Moscow:

> Deprived of a vision for the future, Russia's elites are tempted by conspiracy theories and apocalyptic announcements . . . The Kremlin is populated not by mere survivors of the post-Soviet transition but by survivalists, people who think in terms of worst-case scenarios, who believe that the next disaster is just around the corner, who thrive on crises, who are addicted to extraordinary situations and no-rules politics. (Krastev 2015)

The concept of the *katechon* in Russian thought is beset by ambiguity, on the one hand holding back chaos and destruction, but in doing so marking as undesirable or impossible any progress for humanity. In this reading, *katechontic* thinking can justify the imposition of oppressive political order or the waging of brutal counterinsurgency in the name of a greater good, to overcome some deeper, greater chaos. This mode of thinking not only identifies counterinsurgencies in Chechnya and Syria as essential means to construct order, but also justifies almost any means to bring about victory. By framing each struggle within a messianic worldview, dominated by a struggle against a secular Antichrist, there is no moral requirement to be concerned about the means used to bring about a successful vanquishing of the enemy. Paradoxically, Schmitt's concern to bracket war, to avoid a totalising conflict inspired by messianic liberalism, risks being undermined by the secular theology of his *katechontic* principles. The invocation of the *katechon* aims to preserve the political from dangerous utopian thinking, but in so doing Schmitt risks a political world forever characterised by unending conflict and human suffering.

Notes

1. On the origins of the Third Rome myth, see Østbø (2016: 47–9).
2. This version of the quotation was in Alexander Pushkin's letter to Pyotr Chaadaev (1794–1856) of 19 October 1836: 'Without doubt, the Schism separated us from the rest of Europe, and we did not participate in all the great events that stirred it, but we did have a special destiny. It was Russia and its limitless territory that absorbed the Mongolian invasion. The Tatars did not dare going to our Western borders, leaving us in their rear. They retired to their deserts and the Christian civilization was saved . . . our martyrdom saved the energetic development of Catholic Europe all the trouble.' Engström notes

that this quotation became well-known in Lavrov's generation through the 1974 Andrei Tarkovsky film *The Mirror*, when the quotation is read off-screen in a famous scene.
3. www.katehon.com.
4. In reality, this narrative was undermined by the reality of Russia's war. Palmyra had been liberated not by regular Russian soldiers, but partly by a group of mercenaries operating as a private security company called Wagner. The name 'Wagner' was apparently chosen by their commander Dmitry Utkin because of 'his adherence to the aesthetics and ideology of the Third Reich' (Korotkov 2016). My thanks to Kimberley Marten for drawing attention to this strange conjunction.

CONCLUSION

... Straining Order into Tyranny.

William Godwin

Is Schmitt relevant to understanding the rise of an authoritarian regime in contemporary Russia, and its wider impact on global politics? Some scholars argue that using Schmitt, a proven anti-Semite and a defender of the Nazi regime, to illuminate the present is both misleading and inappropriate. Sitze, for example, writes of 'the illusion that Schmittian thought is adequate for the task of naming our experience today' (Sitze 2010: 66). For Sitze, our aim should be 'to read Carl Schmitt so completely, so carefully, and so loyally, that we *therefore* close the book on him, turning now to face a set of crises about which Schmitt has, precisely, nothing to say' (Sitze 2010: 66). Galli argues that at best Schmitt's work is partially effective 'in its *pars destruens*' to critique contemporary politics, but 'in the *pars construens* – in the combination of decision and concreteness at the interior, and of war and spatiality at the exterior – it seems confused and inapplicable' (Galli 2010: 21). Jens Meierhenrich and Oliver Simons compiled the excellent 800-page *Oxford Handbook of Carl Schmitt*, only to conclude that 'it is important to read Schmitt, but not in order to understand the present' (Meierhenrich and Simons 2016: 58).

Yet even as scholars attempt to close the book on Schmitt, his influence on contemporary political thought is inescapable. The rise of far-right and authoritarian politics around the globe owes much to Schmittian paradigms of thought. A global reaction against neo-liberal technocracy and economic and cultural globalisation has often taken political forms that reflect Schmitt's anti-liberalism: a politics that seeks to fix identities, polarise societies and build walls around communities; a view of democracy as defined by majoritarian identification with a leader, not by parliamentary process and the rule of law; and an international system dominated by the geopolitics of great powers, not global institutions and international law. Schmitt provides a coherent theory of anti-liberal politics that helps us to understand better these growing challenges to liberal thinking in the twenty-first century.

In this book I have attempted to show the relevance of Schmitt for understanding contemporary authoritarianism in Russia. Political thought in the Putinist period was dominated from the beginning by a search for order, both domestically and internationally, a response to the breakdown of order after 1991 that traumatised an entire generation. The definition of what order is and how it could be achieved became the central intellectual and political challenge of the age, but the answers to these questions were sought almost exclusively within conservative political thought. Radical conservative ideas, many of which were heavily influenced by Schmitt, became influential not only among conservative polemicists, but could also be identified in the discourses and practices of many officials in the current Russian political elite. For the most part, these were not direct borrowings from philosophy, but a blurred *Weltanschauung* that was strongly influenced by various tenets of a Schmittian paradigm of illiberal thought.

Schmittian thinking can be identified in five conceptual pillars that underpinned the Russian political system during two decades of Putinist rule during 1999–2019. First, a search for sovereignty of decision-making, defined as the freedom from both domestic and international constraints on political action, was evident throughout political and social life in Russia, expressed above all by the declaration of the exception. From Chechnya to Crimea, from the workings of the law to electoral politics, the exceptional case came to define Russian politics under Putin.

Second, the experience of a weak, flawed democracy in the 1990s contributed to a distrust of political pluralism, and its replacement by a form of authoritarian politics in which a sovereign leader monopolised decision-making power to the detriment of other institutions, but also sought a democratic mandate, albeit one shaped by constant media manipulation.

Third, the difficulties of developing a viable post-Soviet Russian identity encouraged a definition of the Russian political entity in terms of a Schmittian friend–enemy distinction. Anti-Westernism became a constitutive discursive element in a new state identity project for Russia, which also produced an internal politics of division and marginalisation of political opponents, at times expressed in extreme terms as a 'fifth column'.

Fourth, Russian foreign policy struggled to find a viable status in a world order still dominated by American power, but its search for great power status at the centre of a wider region contributed to a succession of spatial projects in Eurasia, which often demonstrated affinity with aspects of Schmitt's theory of *Großraum* geopolitics. Russia's spatial crisis – its struggle to forge a viable state project within its post-imperial borders – and its attempts to construct alternative geopolitical spaces caused serious international tension and conflict.

Finally, as Russia gained influence after 2015 outside Eurasia, in the Middle East, and even in Africa and Latin America, Russia's historical messianism was increasingly in evidence, in which Moscow saw itself as the *katechon*, the bulwark of order in a world of chaos. Many officials and intellectuals in Moscow viewed Russia as once again on the right side of history, defending civilisation against barbarism.

Two decades after Putin came to power, this mode of thinking about political order achieved some successes. A form of centralised order was imposed on Russia's unruly regions, its organised criminal gangs and its Wild-West capitalism. The economy grew rapidly in Putin's first decade, and survived the 2008 financial crash and the wave of post-2014 sanctions better than many expected. In international affairs, Russia was once again a major player, at the centre of negotiations over a swathe of conflicts from the Middle East to East Asia. In its own neighbourhood, Russia had turned the tide of Western expansion into its sphere of influence, forcing out US military bases from Central Asia and blocking the eastward spread of NATO membership. Although Russian foreign policy was strongly criticised in the West, and had attracted extensive economic sanctions, Russia's brand of conservatism – a mix of traditional values and hierarchical politics – had a wider following in Europe and beyond.

In many cases, these successes were fragile, and came at a high cost. Russia also faced serious challenges, many of them reflecting exactly the same problems consistently identified by critics of Schmitt's conceptualisation of political order in earlier historical periods.

The first problem was that Russia's search for order in opposition to liberal norms evolved into a kleptocratic, repressive authoritarianism in which violations of ethics were justified by the existential threat to the state. Schmitt never resolved the potential problem of sovereign power unrestrained by law becoming a brutal tyranny, despite the fact that he had seen the outworking of this obvious theoretical problem in the all too real experience of the Nazi state. He continued to advocate an authoritarian mode of democracy, a manipulated majoritarian order, in which an overlap of identity between ruler and ruled replaces representative democracy, without properly recognising the need for institutional limits on the sovereign.

Schmitt did at least partially acknowledge the problem. In 1938 he published his treatise on Thomas Hobbes's *Leviathan* (Schmitt 2008b). Written after Schmitt's fall from favour with the Nazi Party, he later claimed that his interpretation of Hobbes was an 'act of resistance' against the Nazis (see Strong 2008: xxi), but his reading also exemplified the contradictions that bedevil his political thought. Schmitt rejected the criticism that Hobbes justifies tyranny:

> Hobbes' theory of the state would certainly have been a peculiar philosophy of state if its entire chain of thought had consisted only of propelling poor human beings from the utter fear of the state of nature only into the similarly total fear of a dominion by a Moloch or by a Golem. (Schmitt 2008b: 71)

He goes on to argue that Hobbes is actually claiming that

> to a rational state power belongs the assumption of total political responsibility regarding danger and, in this sense, responsibility for protecting the subjects of the state. If protection ceases, the state too ceases, and every obligation to obey ceases. The individual then wins back his 'natural' freedom. (Schmitt 2008b: 72)

Although Schmitt partly recognises the contradiction, he has no conceptual framework to explain at what point 'protection ceases', and a state becomes a danger to its own citizens. The violence of the state towards its own citizens is too easily legitimised as violence designed to produce order, unrestrained by political institutions or democratic procedures. For Schmitt, it is boundaries, decisions and events that constitute the political, but he is always reticent on the content bounded by these liminal elements. As Slavoj Žižek complains, 'the concrete content of the imposed order is arbitrary, dependent on the Sovereign's will, left to historical contingency – the principle of order, the *Dass-Sein* of Order, has priority over its *Was-Sein*' (Žižek 1999: 18).

This lack of any positive content, argues Žižek, is a central feature of modern conservatism, which reverts to 'decisionist formalism' to counter 'legal normative formalism' (Žižek 1999: 18–19). In a different philosophical tradition, Hannah Arendt has the same critique, accusing Schmitt of creating 'formal-technical' generalisations, within which 'any content becomes acceptable'. Schmitt's *nomos* is effectively 'contentless', lacking any consideration of justice or morality: 'By grounding all law in the soil, he disregards the content of laws' (Jurkevics 2017: 350). At its simplest, in Schmitt '[t]he question of right and wrong is completely disregarded' (Arendt, cited in Jurkevics 2017: 350). Crucially, Arendt argues that Schmitt has no place for humans in his account of politics and law. Instead, argues Jurkevics, the demarcations of the earth are necessarily those of friend and foe, resulting in the inevitable conflict that such a construction of international relations entails (Jurkevics 2017: 349).

Second, Russia demonstrates very clearly the systemic duality involved in constructing a system around exceptionality. The system inevitably spawns not one sovereign deciding on the exception, but a whole system in which sovereignty threatens to disperse in multiple 'Leviathans' across the country. Paradoxically, the assertion of exceptionality as the basis of sovereignty – and therefore of political order – has the effect of undermining order in the normal sphere, in everyday judicial processes, business transactions and security operations. The exceptional case in Chechnya was to be spatially bound within the republic, contained within its filtration camps and *zachistka* operations. Instead, the sovereign power struggled to limit the extension of exceptionality beyond Chechnya. The paradox is that – *contra* Schmitt – the exception threatened to undermine the very political order it was designed to create.

Akhutin and Filippov argue that 'all more or less relevant criticism of Schmitt revolves around this question: What does the sovereign dictator create: order, or a permanent war to destroy that which he himself has brought into being?' (Akhutin and Filippov 2013: 42). Russian policy-makers repeatedly faced this intellectual and political challenge, in which the distinction between exception and norm became increasingly blurred, and in which the sovereign appeared often unable to ensure that the distinction is maintained. The culture of exceptional extrajudicial killings spread beyond the spatial limitations of Chechnya, to the streets of Moscow, Istanbul and Vienna, where Chechen exiles were killed, and to central London and the suburbs of Salisbury, where Russian exiles in the United Kingdom – Alexander Litvinenko in 2007 and Sergei and Yulia Skripal in 2018 – were attacked by Russian agents. In a similar way, the use of manual control and informal mechanisms domestically soon spread to foreign and defence policy, with para-state mercenaries such as the Wagner group operating in a range of conflicts on behalf of the Russian state.

Third, the identification of an existential distinction between friend and enemy was – at least for a short time – a highly effective means of mobilising society, as evidenced by the success of anti-Western propaganda in Russia after 2014. However, this attempt to define the boundaries of the political community along lines of enmity creates as many problems as it appears to resolve. By locating 'the political' at the boundaries of the political community, internal cleavages and disputes are deliberately occluded in an attempt to produce homogeneity. The assumption that political pluralism undermines political order mandates the assertion of an artificial unity that can only be ultimately maintained through manipulation and violence. There can be no genuine political dissension inside such a political community. As Žižek phrases the question: 'is not the relationship to an external Other as the enemy a way of disavowing the *internal* struggle which traverses the social body?' (Žižek 1999: 39).

Paradoxically, the location of the political at the edge of the community depoliticises society inside its boundaries. The political only reappears in the context of a friend/enemy distinction, in which internal political and social antagonisms are mapped onto the external identification of the enemy, thereby encouraging the search for the internal enemy. The mania for identifying 'fifth columnists' may have peaked in 2014–15 in Russia, but 'fifth-column thinking' remained active in attitudes to civil society, to scholars and universities, resulting in the increasing isolation of parts of Russian society from international connections. Moreover, the friend/enemy distinction, designed to provide some fixity to identities, in reality destabilises a national identity based on territory and citizenship, thus inhibiting state-building and challenging principles of state sovereignty in the neighbourhood.

Fourth, the spatial thinking that emerges from the friend/enemy distinction contributes to a re-emergence of a version of Schmitt's *Großraum* thinking, a form of hegemonic multipolarity in which Russia acts as the central pole in a Eurasian space. *Großraum* thinking offers the temptations of civilisational scale, a post-imperial form that nevertheless challenges both cosmopolitan universalism and the Westphalian state. Continental spatial thinking overcomes the complex politics of building a Russian state within its formal post-Soviet boundaries, but only at the expense of the sovereignty of its neighbours. Russia finds the strategic military reach of the United States into its sphere of influence intolerable, but the Ukrainian case demonstrates the difficulty of maintaining influence through traditional mechanisms of Russian hegemonic control. While Western attempts to institutionalise spatial influence in Ukraine through NATO enlargement were undoubtedly myopic, Russian military intervention had the paradoxical outcome of strengthening Ukrainian national identity, and making a reassertion of Russian influence in Kiev much more unlikely in the long term. The more Russia pushed for greater influence in its neighbourhood, the more its neighbours hedged their positions, balancing Moscow with stronger relations with China, the West and with each other. Moreover, although the concept of a world order built on *Großräume* offered some intellectual appeal to a part of the Russian elite, in practice there was little coherent thinking on what such a post-Westphalian world order might imply for an economically weak and over-extended Russia.

Finally, the eschatological bent in Russian politics provided an important emotional and spiritual element in Putinist foreign policy, constructing discursive binaries between order and chaos, civilisation and barbarism, and proposing Russia as the balancing force, the *katechon*, to hold back chaos. In the context of a period of US policy thinking that severely undermined global institutions and was so destabilising in the Middle East, the attractions of *katechontic* thinking in Moscow might appear evident. However, *katechontic* order-building also poses enormous risks, not least of which is the acceptance of everyday violence and oppression in favour of a kind of meta-order, the order that, in spiritual terms, restrains the Antichrist, and in secular terms, imposes a sterile, oppressive stability on whole cultures, states and peoples. As long as *katechontic* thinking continually invokes a coming apocalypse as the outcome of political liberalisation, it is able to legitimise its preventative violence. Yet, the grand projects of global order that are invoked in Schmitt's concepts of *Großraum* and *katechon* struggle to come to terms with a world in which fixed identities, essentialised views of cultures and the sacral spaces of Schmitt's mythical partisan are increasingly contested.

Finally, it is worth reminding ourselves that one of Schmitt's most important insights is the recognition that politics is not merely a rule-based form of technocracy, but an affective practice that engages with people's profound emotions. Sovereign power creates an illusion of empowerment for a wider population through a populist moment of identification with a leader. Schmitt's conceptualisation of democracy as 'an identity of governed and governing' was politically flawed, but it correctly identified a potential moment of psychological identification, which had emotional resonance for at least part of the population. Understanding the emotional impact of this moment of identification with a leader is critical to understanding why the Putinist state was so resilient – and so popular – for so long. The problem for liberalism, argued Alexander Filippov, was not that its ideas were unconvincing, but that they were 'dull' (Engström 2014: 359). Schmitt – and many of his Russian followers – found the everyday world of constitutional and parliamentary procedures mundane and uninspiring. The exception was always more exciting than the norm (Schmitt 1985a: 15). Liberal philosophy only seemed to offer evolutionary improvements in technocratic administration, designed to make human existence less dangerous and more comfortable. Even Russian government officials, like Sergei Lavrov, argued against 'the monotony of existence within the uniform, Western frame of reference' (Lavrov 2016). Instead, Russian policies offered a rollercoaster of sovereign geopolitics, a dramatic, existential story, characterised by conflict and crisis on an almost daily basis.

This rejection of the mundane, the orthodox and the everyday explains why Schmittian thinking is distinct from a traditional conservative philosophy (Lievens 2016). Instead, Schmittian thought easily evolves into visionary ideas, or the enunciations of a prophet – not one who will seek 'to revive the ghosts of dead religious ideas', but instead one who will 'state a new vision that can harness the impulses which causes such ghosts to haunt us'. The Schmittian prophet 'will make politics victorious over legalistic rationality . . .[,] shatter the [Weberian] cage and construct an idea of the *Volk*, "the people", which can impart meaning to the lives of individuals' (Dyzenhaus 1998a: 11). The Schmittian sovereign offers not only a form of authoritarian state order, but more significantly, it offers an emotional, affective connection with the people that provides a sense of representation that goes beyond the flaccid mechanics of the ballot box.

Vladimir Putin has often been compared with Nicholas I, the Tsar who also presided over a politics of order at home and abroad, and whose adventurous foreign policy ultimately culminated in the disaster of the Crimean War. The most famous indictment of Nicholas's rule came from A. V. Nikitenko, who concluded that 'the main failing of the reign of Nicholas Pavlovich was that it was all a mistake'. Putinism may eventually face the same judgement. The attempt to produce a viable political order through authoritarian politics was an understandable response to the decline of post-Soviet Russia. Yet the search for order through sovereignty and exceptionality rather than through institution building was always likely to prove fragile.

The attempt to construct political order in Russia gradually descended into an illusory search for absolute sovereignty that resulted both in an increasingly destabilising Russian foreign policy and growing repression and discontent at home. Russian conservatism, heavily influenced by Schmitt's philosophy, appeared to offer an escape from an unequal international order and the dysfunctions of Western democracy. Yet the illiberal solutions of the Putinist model to the challenges of the liberal order proved unable to manage the challenges of a complex and rapidly changing world. In the end, Russia's new authoritarianism faced the same fundamental contradictions encountered by Carl Schmitt in his own long and troubled philosophical journey.

BIBLIOGRAPHY

Acemoglu, D. and J. A. Robinson (2006), *Economic Origins of Dictatorship and Democracy*, New York: Cambridge University Press.

Agamben, G. (2005), *State of Exception*, trans. K. Attell, Chicago: University of Chicago Press.

Agamben, G. (2016), 'A jurist confronting himself: Carl Schmitt's jurisprudential thought', in J. Meierhenrich and O. Simons (eds), *The Oxford Handbook of Carl Schmitt*, Oxford: Oxford University Press.

Akhutin, A. V. and A. F. Filippov (2013), 'Perepiska o Shmitte i politicheskom', *Sotsiologicheskoe obozrenie*, 13(12): 34–47.

Aleinikova, L. G., S. A. Mel'kov, V. O. Miiyukov and A. N. Perendzhiev (2017), 'Teoriya partizana: prodolzhenie teoreticheskoi problematizatsii', *Vlast'*, 3: 143–55.

Alekseeva, T. A. (2009), 'Karl Shmitt: avtonomiya politicheskogo', in M. M. Federova, (ed.), *Politicheskoe kak problema: Ocherki politicheskoi filosofii XX veka*, Moscow: Ideya-Press, pp. 23–50.

Allison, R. (2013a), *Russia, the West, and Military Intervention*, Oxford: Oxford University Press.

Allison, R. (2013b), 'Russia and Syria: explaining alignment with a regime in crisis', *International Affairs*, 89(4): 795–823.

Allison, R. (2014), 'Russian "deniable" intervention in Ukraine: how and why Russia broke the rules', *International Affairs*, 89(4): 795–823.

Allison, R. (2017), 'Russia and the post-2014 international legal order: revisionism and realpolitik', *International Affairs*, 93(3): 519–43.

Amighetti, E. (2017), 'In pictures: Russia looms large over Georgia's LGBTQ community', Politico.eu, 14 May, <https://www.politico.eu/interactive/in-pictures-russia-looms-large-over-georgia-lgbt-community/> (last accessed 22 June 2019).

Anashvili, V. (2009), 'Kak byt' s naslediem natsional-sotsializma? Revolutsiya sprava v predelakh tol'ko akademii', *Russkii zhurnal*, 4 May, <http://www.russ.ru/Mirovaya-povestka/Kak-byt-s-naslediem-nacional-socializma> (last accessed 22 September 2019).

Anayev, M. (2018), 'Inside the Kremlin: the presidency and the executive branch', in D. Treisman (ed.), *The New Autocracy: Information, Politics and Policy in Putin's Russia*, Washington, DC: Brookings, pp. 29–48.

Anishchuk, A. (2013), 'Putin warns West not to arm organ-eating Syrian rebels', *Reuters*, 16 June, <http://www.reuters.com/article/us-syria-crisis-putin-idUSBRE95F0AE20130616> (last accessed 18 November 2018).

Antonov, M. (2017), 'Philosophy behind human rights: Valery Zorkin vs. the West', in L. Mälksoo and W. Benedek (eds), *Russia and the European Court of Human Rights: The Strasbourg Effect*, New York: Cambridge University Press, pp. 150–87.

Applebaum, A. (2014), 'The myth of Russian humiliation', *Washington Post*, 17 October, <https://www.washingtonpost.com/opinions/anne-applebaum-nato-pays-a-heavy-price-for-giving-russia-too-much-credit-a-true-achievement-under-threat/2014/10/17/5b3a6f2a-5617-11e4-809b-8cc0a295c773_story.html> (last accessed 1 October 2019).

Artamoshin, S. V. (2009), 'Problema politicheskogo v konservativnoi publitsistike Karla Shmitta', *Vestnik TGU*, 7 (75): 350–6.

Arvidsson, M. (2016), 'From teleology to eschatology: the *katechon* and the political theology of the international law of belligerent occupation', in M. Arvidsson, L. Brännström and P. Minkkinen (eds), *The Contemporary Relevance of Carl Schmitt: Law, Politics, Theology*, Abingdon: Routledge, pp. 223–36.

Auer, S. (2015), 'Carl Schmitt in the Kremlin: the Ukraine crisis and the return of geopolitics', *International Affairs*, 91(5): 953–68.

Averre, D. (2007), '"Sovereign democracy" and Russia's relations with the European Union', *Demokratizatsiya*, 15(2): 173–90.

Axtmann, R. (2007), 'Humanity or enmity? Carl Schmitt on international politics', *International Politics*, 44(5): 531–51.

Ayoub, P. M. (2017), 'Protean power in movement: navigating uncertainty in the LGBT rights revolution', in P. J. Katzenstein and L. A. Seybert (eds), *Protean Power: Exploring the Uncertain and Unexpected in World Politics*, Cambridge: Cambridge University Press, pp. 79–99.

Baisswenger, M. (2004), 'Konservativnaya revolutsiya v Germanii i dvizhenie evraziitsev: tochki prikosnoveniya', in A. Yu. Minakov (ed.), *Konservatizm v Rossii i mire*, vol. 3, Voronezh: Voronezh State University, pp. 49–73 [republished in *Forum noveishei vostchno-evropeiskoi istorii i kultury*, 2 (2009): 23–40].

Balakrishnan, G. (2000), *The Enemy: An Intellectual Portrait of Carl Schmitt*, London: Verso.

Barbashin, A. and H. Thoburn (2014), 'Putin's brain: Alexander Dugin and the philosophy behind Putin's invasion of Crimea', *Foreign Affairs*, 31 March, https://www.foreignaffairs.com/articles/russia-fsu/2014-03-31/putins-brain (last accessed 2 October 2018).

Barghoorn, F. C. (1955), 'Great Russian messianism in postwar Soviet ideology', in E. J. Simmons (ed.), *Continuity and Change in Russian and Soviet Thought*, Cambridge, MA: Harvard University Press, pp. 531–49.

Barinov, I. (2011), 'Kaddafi, skoree vsego, prosto "ubrali"', 24 October, *Edinaya Rossiia*, <http://er.ru/news/64044/> (last accessed 26 May 2019).

Barnes, T. J. and C. Minca (2013), 'Nazi spatial theory: the dark geographies of Carl Schmitt and Walter Christaller', *Annals of the Association of American Geographers*, 103(3): 669–87.

Bar-On, T. (2011), 'Transnationalism and the French Nouvelle Droite', *Patterns of Prejudice*, 45(3): 199–223.

Bar-On, T. (2016), *Where Have All the Fascists Gone?* Abingdon: Routledge.

Barros, R. (2002), *Constitutionalism and Dictatorship: Pinochet, the Junta, and the 1980 Constitution*, Cambridge: Cambridge University Press.

Barry, E. (2010), 'In Russia, jury is something to work around', *New York Times*, 15 November, <https://www.nytimes.com/2010/11/16/world/europe/16jury.html?pagewanted=all> (last accessed 26 May 2019).

Bartosh, A. (2018), 'Strategiya i kontrstrategiya gibridnoi voiny', *Voennaya mysl'*, 10 October.

Bassin, M. (1987), 'Race contra space: the conflict between German geopolitik and national socialism', *Political Geography*, 6(2): 115–34.

Bassin, M. (2015), 'Lev Gumilev and the European New Right', *Nationalities Papers*, 43(6): 840–65.

Bassin, M. (2016), *The Gumilev Mystique: Biopolitics, Eurasianism, and the Construction of Community in Modern Russia*, Ithaca, NY: Cornell University Press.

Bassin, M. and K. E. Aksenov (2006), 'Mackinder and the heartland theory in post-Soviet geopolitical discourse', *Geopolitics*, 11(1): 99–118.

Bassin, M., S. Glebov and M. Laruelle (eds) (2015), *Between Europe and Asia: The Origins, Theories, and Legacies of Russian Eurasianism*, Pittsburgh: University of Pittsburgh Press.

Bauman, Z. (1991), 'Modernity and ambivalence', in M. Featherstone (ed.), *Global Culture: Nationalism, Modernization, and Modernity*, London: Sage, pp. 143–69.

Bauman, Z. (2004), 'Stalin', *Cultural Studies, Critical Methodologies*, 4(1): 3–11.

BBC (2014), 'Hillary Clinton's Putin–Hitler analogy', *BBC News*, 6 March, <http://www.bbc.com/news/blogs-echochambers-26476643> (last accessed 26 May 2019).

BBC (2018), 'Ukraine conflict: Russia completes Crimea security fence', *BBC News*, 28 December, <https://www.bbc.co.uk/news/world-europe-46699807> (last accessed 26 May 2019).

Bekbulatova, T. (2018), 'Russia's invisible, ubiquitous lobbyists', *Meduza*, 8 January, <https://meduza.io/en/feature/2018/01/08/russia-s-invisible-ubiquitous-lobbyists> (last accessed 26 May 2019).

Bendersky, J. W. (1983), *Carl Schmitt: Theorist for the Reich*, Princeton, NJ: Princeton University Press.

Bendersky, J. W. (1987), 'Carl Schmitt and the conservative revolution', *Telos*, 72: 27–42.

Bendersky, J. W. (2010), 'Carl Schmitt and the Jews: the "Jewish Question", the Holocaust, and German legal theory', *Central European History*, 43(2): 377–80.

Benn, D. W. (2011), 'Russian historians defend the Molotov–Ribbentrop Pact', *International Affairs*, 87(3): 709–15.

Berdyaev, N. (1947), *The Russian Idea*, New York: Macmillan.

Berman, H. J. (1963), *Justice in the USSR: An Interpretation of Soviet Law*, rev. edn, Cambridge, MA: Harvard University Press.

Bershidsky, L. (2015), 'One year later, Crimeans prefer Russia', Bloomberg, 6 February, <https://www.bloomberg.com/opinion/articles/2015-02-06/one-year-later-crimeans-prefer-russia> (last accessed 29 September 2019).

Bevir, M. and R. A. W. Rhodes (eds) (2015), *Routledge Handbook of Interpretive Political Science*, Abingdon: Routledge.

Bhuta, N. (2015), 'The mystery of the state: state concept, state theory and statemaking in Schmitt and Oakeshott', in D. Dyzenhaus and T. Poole (ed.), *Law, Liberty and State: Oakeshott, Hayek and Schmitt on the Rule of Law*, Cambridge: Cambridge University Press, pp. 10–37.

Bielefeldt, H. (1998), 'Carl Schmitt's critique of liberalism: systematic reconstruction and countercriticism', in D. Dyzenhaus (ed.), *Law as Politics: Carl Schmitt's Critique of Liberalism*, Durham, NC: Duke University Press, pp. 23–36.

Billington, J. H. (2004), *Russia in Search of Itself*, Washington, DC: Woodrow Wilson Center Press.

Biznes-online (2019), 'Narod i v 1917 godu padal na koleni pered tsarem-batyushkoi, a potom vzyal i rasstrelyal', *Biznes-online*, 16 February, <https://www.business-gazeta.ru/article/413672> (last accessed 9 June 2019).

Blackburn, S. (2008), *The Oxford Dictionary of Philosophy*, 2nd rev. edn, Oxford: Oxford University Press.

Blakkisrud, H. (2015), 'Governing the governors: legitimacy vs. control in the reform of the Russian regional executive', *East European Politics*, 31(1): 104–21.

Blühm, K. (2016), 'Modernization, geopolitics and the new Russian conservatives', Arbeitspapiere des Osteuropa-Instituts, Freie Universität Berlin.

Blühm, K. and M. Varga (2019), 'Introduction: towards a new illiberal conservatism in Russia and East Central Europe', in K. Blühm and M. Varga (eds), *New Conservatives in Russia and East Central Europe*, London: Routledge, pp. 1–22.

Blühm, K. and M. Varga (eds) (2019), *New Conservatives in Russia and East Central Europe*, Abingdon: Routledge.

Bodenheimer, E. (1952), 'Justice in the USSR: an interpretation of Soviet law, by Harold J. Berman' (Book Review), *Louisiana Law Review*, 13(1): 159–62.

Bordachev, T. (2014), 'A total but peaceful battle over Ukraine, for a new world order', *Russia in Global Affairs*, 14 March, <http://eng.globalaffairs.ru/book/A-Total-But-Peaceful-Battle-Over-Ukraine-For-a-New-World-Order-16477> (last accessed 26 May 2019).

Bowring, B. (2013), *Law, Rights and Ideology in Russia: Landmarks in the Destiny of a Great Power*, Abingdon: Routledge.

Bowring, B. (2019), 'Russia and the Council of Europe: an incompatible ideology, and a transplanted legal regime?', in P. S. Morris (ed.), *Russian Discourses on International Law: Sociological and Philosophical Phenomenon*, Abingdon: Routledge, pp. 133–57.

Brännström, L. (2016), 'Carl Schmitt's definition of sovereignty as authorized leadership', in M. Arvidsson, L. Brännström and P. Minkkinen (eds), *The Contemporary Relevance of Carl Schmitt: Law, Politics, Theology*, Abingdon: Routledge, pp. 19–33.

Braw, E. (2015), 'Russia's conscription conundrum: the obstacles to modernizing the country's armed forces', *Foreign Affairs*, 25 August, <https://www.foreignaffairs.com/articles/russia-fsu/2015-08-25/russias-conscription-conundrum> (last accessed 22 September 2019).

Brown, C. (2007), 'The twilight of international morality? Hans J. Morgenthau and Carl Schmitt on the end of the Jus Publicum Europaeum', in M. C. Williams (ed.), *Realism Reconsidered: The Legacy of Hans Morgenthau in International Relations*, Oxford: Oxford University Press, pp. 42–67.

Brownlee, J. (2007), *Durable Authoritarianism in an Age of Democratization*, Cambridge: Cambridge University Press.

Bryanski, G. (2011), 'Putin likens U.N. Libya resolution to crusades', *Reuters*, 21 March, <http://www.reuters.com/article/us-libya-russia-idUSTRE72K3JR20110321?> (last accessed 26 May 2019).

Buldakov, V. P. (2005), 'Sistemnye krizisy v Rossii: sravnitelnoe issledovanie massovoi psikhologii 1904–1921 i 1985–2002', *Acta Slavica Japonica*, 22: 95–119.

Buldakov, V. P., P. P. Marchenya and S. Yu. Razin (2010), '"Narod i vlast' v rossiiskoi smute", proshloe i nastoyashchee sistemnykh krizisov v Rossii', *Vestnik arkhivista*, 3: 288–302, <http://www.vestarchive.ru/issledovaniia/1083-l-n---n.html> (last accessed 26 May 2019).

Bull, H. (1977), *The Anarchical Society: A Study of Order in World Politics*, New York: Columbia University Press.

Burger, E. S. and M. Holland (2008), 'Law as politics: the Russian procuracy and its investigative committee', New York University Public Law and Legal Theory Working Papers, 108.

Burke-White, W. W. (2014), 'Crimea and the international legal order', *Survival*, 56(4): 65–80.

Burnell, P. and O. Schlumberger (2010), 'Promoting democracy – promoting autocracy? International politics and national political regimes', *Contemporary Politics*, 16(1): 1–15.

Business Insider (2014), '12 prominent people who compared Putin to Hitler', *Business Insider*, 22 May, <http://www.businessinsider.com/people-who-compared-putin-to-hitler-2014-5> (last accessed 26 May 2019).

Buttegieg, J. (2011), 'Antonio Gramsci: liberation begins with critical thinking', in C. H. Zuckert (ed.), *Political Philosophy in the Twentieth Century*, Cambridge: Cambridge University Press, pp. 44–57.

Byrnes, R. F. (1969), 'Russian conservative thought before the revolution', in T. G. Stavrou (ed.), *Russia under the Last Tsar*, Minneapolis: University of Minnesota Press, pp. 42–68.

Camus, J.-Y. and N. Lebourg (2017), *Far-Right Politics in Europe*, trans. by J. M. Todd, Cambridge, MA: Harvard University Press.

Carnaghan, E. (2010), *Out of Order: Russian Political Values in an Imperfect World*, Pennsylvania: Penn State Press.

Casula, P. (2013), 'Sovereign democracy, populism, and depoliticization in Russia', *Problems of Post-Communism*, 60(3): 3–15.

Chebankova, E. (2013a), 'Russian fundamental conservatism: in search of modernity', *Post-Soviet Affairs*, 29(4): 287–313.

Chebankova, E. (2013b), *Civil Society in Putin's Russia*, London: Routledge.

Chebankova, E. (2017), 'Ideas, ideology & intellectuals in search of Russia's political future', *Daedalus*, 146(2): 76–88.

Chen, A. (2015), 'The Agency', *New York Times Magazine*, 2 June, <http://www.nytimes.com/2015/06/07/magazine/the-agency.html> (last accessed 26 May 2019).

Cheskin, A. and L. March (2015), 'State–society relations in contemporary Russia: new forms of political and social contention', *East European Politics*, 31(3): 261–73.

Clark, C. and K. Spohr (2015), 'Moscow's account of Nato expansion is a case of false memory syndrome', *Guardian*, 24 May, <https://www.theguardian.com/commentisfree/2015/may/24/russia-nato-expansion-memory-grievances> (last accessed 1 October 2019).

Clover, C. (2011), 'Carte blanche for FSB's Directorate K', *Financial Times*, 13 September, <https://www.ft.com/content/94390c4c-de23-11e0-9fb7-00144feabdc0> (last accessed 21 June 2019).

Clover, C. (2016), *Black Wind, White Snow: The Rise of Russia's New Nationalism*, New Haven, CT: Yale University Press.

Clowes, E. (2011), *Russia on the Edge: Imagined Geographies and Post-Soviet Identity*, Ithaca, NY: Cornell University Press.

Coalson, R. (2015), 'Turning back time: putting Putin's Molotov–Ribbentrop defense into context', *RFE/RL*, 15 May, <https://www.rferl.org/a/putin-russia-Molotov-Ribbentrop-pact/27017723.html> (last accessed 26 May 2019).

Cooley, A. (2012), *Great Games, Local Rules: The New Power Contest in Central Asia*, Oxford: Oxford University Press.

Costa Buranelli, F. (2018), 'Spheres of influence as negotiated hegemony: the case of Central Asia', *Geopolitics*, 23(2): 378–403.

Crotty, J., S. M. Hall and S. Ljubownikow (2014), 'Post-Soviet civil society development in the Russian Federation: the impact of the NGO law', *Europe-Asia Studies*, 66(8): 1253–69.

CSR/RIAC (2017), *Theses on Russia's Foreign Policy and Global Positioning (2017–2024)*, Centre for Strategic Research (CSR) and Russian International Affairs Council (RIAC), Moscow, June.

Dahl, F. (2014), 'Crimea referendum illegal, no OSCE monitoring – Swiss', *Reuters*, 12 March, <http://in.reuters.com/article/ukraine-crisis-referendum-osce-idINDEEA2A0DS20140311> (last accessed 26 May 2019).

Dannreuther, R. (2015), 'Russia and the Arab Spring: supporting the counter-revolution', *Journal of European Integration*, 37(1): 77–94.

Davletbaev, M. and M. Issaeva (2014), 'Arkhaichny yazyk rossiiskoi diplomatii', *Vedemosti*, 13 August, <https://www.vedomosti.ru/opinion/articles/2014/08/13/arhaichnyj-yazyk-rossijskoj-diplomatii#_> (last accessed 26 May 2019).

Dawisha, K. (2015), *Putin's Kleptocracy: Who Owns Russia?*, New York: Simon & Schuster.

De Benoist, A. (2013), *Carl Schmitt Today: Terrorism, Just War, and the State of Emergency*, London: Arktos.

De Benoist, A. (2014), *Karl Shmitt segodnya: 'Spravedlivaya voina', terrorizm, chrezvychainoe polozenie, 'Nomos Zemli'*, Moscow: Institut Obshchegumanytarnykh Issledovanii.

Denisov, D. (2010), 'Business lobbying and government relations in Russia: the need for new principles', Reuters Institute for the Study of Journalism, Fellowship paper 27.

Deyermond, R. (2016), 'The uses of sovereignty in twenty-first century Russian foreign policy', *Europe-Asia Studies*, 68(6): 957–84.

Dobrolyubov, N. (2016), 'Slepoe proslushivanie: kak generaly SKR khoteli zakhvatit' SEB FSB', *Life.ru*, 10 October, <https://bit.ly/2rkiLme> (last accessed 21 June).

Drolet, J.-F. and M. C. Williams (2018), 'Radical conservatism and global order: international theory and the new right', *International Theory*, 10(3): 285–313.

Dugin, A. (1992), 'Velikaya voina kontinentov', *Den'*, 4(32), reprinted in A. Dugin (1992), *Konspiralogiya*, Moscow: Arktogeia, <http://arcto.ru/article/171> (last accessed 26 May 2018).

Dugin, A. (1994), *Konservativnaya revolutsiya*, Moscow: Arctogeia.

Dugin, A. (1996), *Metafizika blagoi vesti: pravoslavnyi ezoterizm*, Moscow: Arctogeia.

Dugin, A. (1997a), 'Katekhon i revolutsiya', in *Tampliery Proletariata*, Moscow: Arctogeia, <http://my.arcto.ru/public/templars/kateh.htm> (last accessed 26 May 2019).

Dugin, A. (1997b), *Osnovy geopolitiki: Geopoliticheskoe budushchee Rossii*, Moscow: Arctogeia.

Dugin, A. (2009), *Chetvertaya politicheskaya teoriya: Rossiya i politicheskiie idei XXI veka*, St Petersburg: Amfora.

Dugin, A. (2010), 'Konflikt zhivoi nauki s vyzhivshim iz uma dogmatizmom', *Maxpark*, 13 November, <http://maxpark.com/user/556697085/content/550099> (last accessed 26 May 2019).

Dugin, A. (2012), *The Fourth Political Theory*, London: Arktos.

Dugin, A. (2014a), *Voina kontinentov*, Moscow: Akademicheskii proekt.

Dugin, A. (2014b), *Putin vs Putin: Vladimir Putin Viewed from the Right*, London: Arktos.

Dugin, A. (2014c), 'Shestaya kolonna', *Vzglyad*, 29 April, <http://www.vz.ru/opinions/2014/4/29/684247.print.html> (last accessed 17 December 2018).

Dugin, A. (2014d), 'Aleksandr Dugin: Protiv Putina gotovitsya zagovor', 3 October, <http://novorossia.su/ru/news/aleksandr-dugin-protiv-putina-gotovitsya-zagovor> (last accessed 19 June 2019).

Dugin, A. (2015), *Ukraina: moya voina – Geopoliticheskii dnevnik*, Moscow: Tsentropoligraf.

Duncan, P. (2000), *Russian Messianism: Third Rome, Revolution, Communism and After*, London: Routledge.
Dunlop, J. B. (1995), *The Rise of Russia and the Fall of the Soviet Empire*, Princeton: Princeton University Press.
Dunlop, J. B. (2001), 'Aleksandr Dugin's "Neo-Eurasian" textbook and Dmitrii Trenin's ambivalent response', *Harvard Ukrainian Studies*, 25(1/2): 91–127.
Dunlop, J. B. (2019), *The February 2015 Assassination of Boris Nemtsov and the Flawed Trial of His Alleged Killers*, New York: Columbia University Press.
Dyukov, A. (2009), *Pakt Molotova–Ribbentropa' v voprosakh i otvetakh*, Moscow: Fond Istoricheskaya Pamyat'.
Dyzenhaus, D. (1998), 'Introduction', in D. Dyzenhaus (ed.), *Law as Politics: Carl Schmitt's Critique of Liberalism*, Durham, NC: Duke University Press, pp. 1–20.
Dyzenhaus, D. (2011), 'Review: emergency, liberalism, and the state', *Perspectives on Politics*, 9(1): 69–78.
Dyzenhaus, D. (2016), 'The concept of the rule-of-law state in Carl Schmitt's *Verfassungslehre*', in J. Meierhenrich and O. Simons (eds), *The Oxford Handbook of Carl Schmitt*, Oxford: Oxford University Press, pp. 490–509.
Economist (2016), 'A Russian orchestra plays Bach and Prokofiev in the ruins of Palmyra', *The Economist*, 6 May, <https://www.economist.com/europe/2016/05/06/a-russian-orchestra-plays-bach-and-prokofiev-in-the-ruins-of-palmyra> (last accessed 26 May 2019).
ECtHR (2016), 'Navalny and Ofitserov v Russia (Applications nos. 46632/13 and 28671/14)', European Court of Human Rights, 4 July.
Ek, R. (2006), 'Giorgio Agamben and the spatialities of the camp: an introduction', *Geografiska Annaler Series B Human Geography*, 88B(4): 363–86.
Elden, S. (2011), 'Reading Schmitt geopolitically', in S. Legg (ed.), *Spatiality, Sovereignty and Carl Schmitt: Geographies of the Nomos*, Abingdon: Routledge, pp. 91–105.
Engström, M. (2014), 'Contemporary Russian messianism and new Russian foreign policy', *Contemporary Security Policy*, 35(3): 356–79.
Engström, M. (2016), 'Apollo against Black Square: conservative futurism in contemporary Russia', in G. Berghaus (ed.), *International Yearbook of Futurism Studies*, vol. 6, Berlin: De Gruyter, pp. 328–53.
Esakov, G. (2012), 'The Russian criminal jury: recent developments, practice, and current problems', *American Journal of Comparative Law*, 60: 665–702.
Evangelista, M. (2004), *The Chechen Wars: Will Russia Go the Way of the Soviet Union?*, Washington, DC: Brookings Institution Press.
Fedor, J. (2011), 'Chekists look back on the Cold War: the polemical literature', *Intelligence and National Security*, 26(6): 842–63.
Fedor, J. and R. Fredheim (2017), '"We need more clips about Putin, and lots of them": Russia's state-commissioned online visual culture', *Nationalities Papers*, 45(2): 161–81.
Feifer, G. (1964), *Justice in Moscow*, New York: Dell Publishing.

Feklyunina, V. A. (2016), 'Soft power and identity: Russia, Ukraine and the Russian World(s)', *European Journal of International Relations*, 22(4): 773–96.
Felshtinsky, Y. and V. Pribylovsky (2008), *The Corporation: Russia and the KGB in the Age of President Putin*, New York: Encounter Books.
Filippov, A. F. (2000), 'Karl Shmitt: Rastsvet i katastrofa', in K. Shmitt, *Politicheskaya teologiya*, Moscow: Canon-Press, <http://textarchive.ru/c-1124955.html> (last accessed 13 June 2019).
Filippov, A. F. (2006), 'Suverenitet kak politicheskii vybor', in N. V. Garadzha (ed.), *Suverenitet*, Moscow: Evropa, pp. 173–200.
Filippov, A. F. (2007), 'Razgovor o vlasti i o dostupe k vlastiteliu', *Sotsiologicheskoe obozrenie*, 6(2): 27–38.
Filippov, A. F. (2008a), 'Ozhirevskii Leviafan: Chitaiut li v Kremle Karla Shmitta?', *Russkii zhurnal*, 1: 50–7.
Filippov, A. F. (2008b), 'Vlast' kak sredstvo i sreda: dva rassuzhdenniya na temu Karla Shmitta', *Sinii Divan*, 12, <http://www.polit.ru/research/2008/11/26/karlschmitt.html> (last accessed 2 October 2018).
Filippov, A. F. (2009a), 'Shag vperyod v diskussii', *Russkii zhurnal*, 9 June, <http://www.hse.ru/news/8353726.html> (last accessed 2 October 2018).
Filippov, A. F. (2009b), 'K politiko-pravovoi filosofii prostranstva Karla Shmitta', *Sotsiologicheskoe obozrenie*, 8(2): 41–52.
Filippov, A. F. (2009c), 'Ne nado zanimat'sya intellectual'nym moshenichestvom', *Russkii zhurnal*, 12 May, <www.russ.ru/Mirovaya-povestka/Ne-nado-zanimat-sya-intellektual-nym-moshennichestvom> (last accessed 23 June 2019).
Filippov, A. F. (2015), *Sociologia: Nablyudeniya, opyty, perspektivy*, vol. 2, ed. by S. P. Bankovskaya, St Petersburg: Vladimir Dal'.
Filippov, A. F. (2016a), 'K istorii ponyatiya politicheskogo: proshloe odnogo proekta', in K. Shmitt, *Ponyatie politicheskogo*, trans. by A. F. Filippov, St Petersburg: Nauka, pp. 433–52.
Filippov, A. F. (2016b), 'Ustroistvo vlasti v "Leviafane" Tomasa Gobbsa', in T. Gobbs, *Leviafan*, Moscow: Ripol Klassik, pp. 5–56.
Finn, P. (2005), 'Fear rules in Russia's courtrooms: judges who acquit forced off bench', *Washington Post*, 27 February, <www.washingtonpost.com/wp-dyn/articles/A56441-2005Feb26.html> (last accessed 21 June 2019).
Finnin, R. (2011), 'Forgetting nothing, forgetting no one: Boris Chichibabin, Viktor Nekipelov, and the deportation of the Crimean Tatars', *Modern Language Review*, 106(4): 1091–1124.
Firestone, T. (2009), 'Armed injustice: abuse of the law and complex crime in post-Soviet Russia', *Denver Journal of International Law and Policy*, 38: 555–80.
Fish, S. M. (1997), 'The pitfalls of Russian superpresidentialism', *Current History*, 96: 326–30.
Fish, S. M. (2005), *Democracy Derailed in Russia: The Failure of Open Politics*, Cambridge: Cambridge University Press.
Fish, S. M. (2017), 'The Kremlin emboldened: what is Putinism?', *Journal of Democracy*, 28(4): 61–75.

Foxall, A. (2017), 'From Evropa to Gayropa: a critical geopolitics of the European Union as seen from Russia', *Geopolitics*, 24(1): 174–93.
Foy, H. (2018), 'Oligarch Vladimir Potanin on money, power and Putin', *Financial Times*, 13 April.
Fraenkel, E. (2017 [1941]), *The Dual State: A Contribution to the Theory of Dictatorship*, trans. E. A. Shils, Oxford: Oxford University Press.
Frantz, E. and N. M. Ezrow (2011), *The Politics of Dictatorship: Institutions and Outcomes in Authoritarian Regimes*, Boulder, CO: Lynne Rienner Publishers.
Freeden, M. (1996), *Ideologies and Political Theory: A Conceptual Approach*, Oxford: Oxford University Press.
Friedrich, C. J. (1968), 'The dialectic of political order and freedom', in P. Kuntz (ed.), *The Concept of Order*, Seattle: University of Washington Press, pp. 339–54.
Frolov, V. (2017), 'Takoi khrupkii rezhim: Chto meshaet Putinu poiti na sblizhenie s Zapadom?', *Republic.ru*, 10 August, <https://republic.ru/posts/85752> (last accessed 27 May 2019).
Fukuyama, F. (1992), *The End of History and the Last Man*, New York: The Free Press.
Fukuyama, F. (2011), *The Origins of Political Order: From Prehuman Times to the French Revolution*, London: Profile Books.
Fukuyama, F. (2014), *Political Order and Political Decay: From the Industrial Revolution to the Globalization of Democracy*, London: Profile Books.
Gaaze, K. (2018a), 'Kak mozhet vygliadet' novyi kurs prezidenta Putina', Carnegie Moscow Center, 16 March, <https://carnegie.ru/commentary/75815> (last accessed 27 May 2019).
Gaaze, K. (2018b), 'Why Russia's Crimean consensus is over (and what comes next)', Carnegie Moscow Center, 21 September, <https://carnegie.ru/commentary/77310> (last accessed 27 May 2019).
Galeotti, M. (2016), 'Putin's hydra: inside Russia's intelligence services', European Council on Foreign Relations, 11 May, http://www.ecfr.eu/publications/summary/putins_hydra_inside_russias_intelligence_services (last accessed 27 May 2019).
Galeotti, M. (2018), 'A tale of two Putins', *Eurozine*, 14 March, <https://www.eurozine.com/tale-two-putins/> (last accessed 27 May 2018).
Galeotti, M. (2019), *We Need to Talk about Putin: Why the West Gets Him Wrong, and How to Get Him Right*, London: Penguin.
Galyamina, Yu. (2016), 'My - oni: kak v diskurse Vladimira Putina raznykh let konstatiruetsia identichnost', *Politicheskaya nauka*, 3: 152–68.
Galli, C. (2010), 'Carl Schmitt and the golden age', *The New Centennial Review*, 10(2): 1–26.
Gandhi, J. (2010), *Political Institutions under Dictatorship*, Cambridge: Cambridge University Press.
Ganev, V. I. (2001), 'The separation of party and state as a logistical problem: a glance at the causes of state weakness in postcommunism', *East European Politics and Societies*, 15(2): 389–420.

Gans-Morse, J. (2012), 'Threats to property rights in Russia: from private coercion to state aggression', *Post-Soviet Affairs*, 28: 263–95.
Gans-Morse, J. (2017), 'Demand for law and the security of property rights: the case of post-Soviet Russia', *American Political Science Review*, 111(2): 338–59.
Garadzha, N. V. (ed.) (2006), *Suverenitet*, Moscow: Evropa.
Gazeta.ru (2015), 'Ne mesto dlya raboty', *Gazeta.ru*, 7 August, <https://www.gazeta.ru/comments/2015/07/07_e_7597253.shtml> (last accessed 23 September 2019).
Gelman, V. (2015), *Authoritarian Russia: Analyzing Post-Soviet Regime Changes*, Pittsburgh: University of Pittsburgh Press.
Gessen, M. (2016), 'Alexey Navalny's very strange form of freedom', *The New Yorker*, 15 January, <http://www.newyorker.com/news/news-desk/alexey-navalnys-very-strange-form-of-freedom> (last accessed 27 May 2019).
Gill, G. (2015), *Building an Authoritarian Polity*, Cambridge: Cambridge University Press.
Gilligan, E. (2016), 'Propaganda and the question of criminal intent: the semantics of the zachistka', *Europe-Asia Studies*, 68(6): 1036–66.
Glazyev, S. (2015), 'Russia and the Eurasian Union', in P. Dutkiewicz and R. Sakwa (eds), *Eurasian Integration: The View from Within*, Abingdon: Routledge, pp. 84–96.
Glebov, S. (2015), 'N. S. Trubetskoi's *Europe and Mankind* and Eurasianist antievolutionism: one unknown source', in M. Bassin, S. Glebov and M. Laruelle (eds), *Between Europe and Asia: The Origins, Theories, and Legacies of Russian Eurasianism*, Pittsburgh: University of Pittsburgh Press, pp. 48–67.
Gould-Davies, N. (2016), *Russia's Sovereign Globalization: Rise, Fall and Future*, Chatham House Paper, London: Royal Institute of International Affairs.
Greenberg, J. D. (2009), 'The Kremlin's eye: the 21st century prokuratura in the Russian authoritarian tradition', *Stanford Journal of International Law*, 45: 1–50.
Greene, S. A. (2014), *Moscow in Movement: Power and Opposition in Putin's Russia*, Redwood City, CA: Stanford University Press.
Grier, P. T. (1994), 'The complex legacy of Ivan Il'in', in J. P. Scanlon (ed.), *Russian Thought after Communism: The Recovery of a Philosophical Heritage*, Armonk, NY: ME Sharpe, pp. 165–86.
Griffin, R. (2000), 'Between metapolitics and apoliteia: the Nouvelle Droite's strategy for conserving the fascist vision in the "interregnum"', *Modern & Contemporary France*, 8(1): 35–53.
Grigas, A. (2016), *Beyond Crimea: The New Russian Empire*, New Haven, CT: Yale University Press.
Grigoreva, E. (2005), 'Kak zakalyalsya vertikal', *Izvestiya*, 20 July, <https://iz.ru/news/304368> (last accessed 27 May 2019).
Gross, R. (2016), 'The "true enemy": antisemitism in Carl Schmitt's life and work', in J. Meierhenrich and O. Simons (eds), *The Oxford Handbook of Carl Schmitt*, Oxford: Oxford University Press, pp. 96–116.
Gryzlov, B. (2017), 'Putin ostaetsya liderom Rossii', *Rossiiskaya gazeta*, 17 October, <https://rg.ru/2007/10/17/grizlov.html> (last accessed 27 May 2019).

Gudkov, L. (2011), 'The nature of Putinism', *Russian Social Science Review*, 52(6): 7–33.
Guzikova, M. O. (2015), 'Reshenie ili pravo: suverenitet po Karlu Shmitta', *Sotsium i vlast'*, 3(53): 45–9.
Hale, H. E. (2010), 'Eurasian polities as hybrid regimes: the case of Putin's Russia', *Journal of Eurasian studies*, 1(1): 33–41.
Hale, H. E. (2015), *Patronal Politics: Eurasian Regime Dynamics in Comparative Perspective*, Cambridge: Cambridge University Press.
Hamburg, G. M. (2005), 'The revival of Russian conservatism', *Kritika: Explorations in Russian and Eurasian History*, 6(1): 107–27.
Hanson, P. (2014), *Reiderstvo: Asset-Grabbing in Russia*, London: Chatham House.
Hanson, S. E. and J. S. Kopstein (1997), 'The Weimar/Russia comparison', *Post-Soviet Affairs*, 13(3): 252–83.
Hell, J. (2009), 'Katechon: Carl Schmitt's imperial theology and the ruins of the future', *The Germanic Review: Literature, Culture, Theory*, 84(4): 283–326.
Hemment, J. (2012), 'Nashi, youth voluntarism, and Potemkin NGOs: making sense of civil society in post-Soviet Russia', *Slavic Review*, 71(2): 234–60.
Hemment, J. (2015), *Youth Politics in Putin's Russia: Producing Patriots and Entrepreneurs*, Bloomington: Indiana University Press.
Hendley, K. (2017), *Everyday Law in Russia*, Ithaca, NY: Cornell University Press.
Higgins, A. (2014), 'As his fortunes fell in Ukraine, a president clung to illusions', *New York Times*, 23 February, <https://www.nytimes.com/2014/02/24/world/europe/as-his-fortunes-fell-in-ukraine-a-president-clung-to-illusions.html> (last accessed 27 May 2019).
Hill, F. and C. G. Gaddy (2015), *Mr. Putin: Operative in the Kremlin*, Washington, DC: Brookings Institution Press.
Hilpold, P. (2015), 'Ukraine, Crimea and new international law: balancing international law with arguments drawn from history', *Chinese Journal of International Law*, 14(2): 237–70.
Hoffman, D. (1999), 'Yeltsin's absentee rule raises spector of a "failed state"', *Washington Post*, 26 February, <http://www.washingtonpost.com/wp-srv/inatl/longterm/russiagov/stories/absent022699.htm> (last accessed 27 May 2019).
Holmes, S. (1996), *The Anatomy of Antiliberalism*, Cambridge, MA: Harvard University Press.
Hooker, W. (2009), *Carl Schmitt's International Thought*, Cambridge: Cambridge University Press.
Horvath, R. (2011), 'Putin's "preventive counter-revolution": post-Soviet authoritarianism and the spectre of velvet revolution', *Europe-Asia Studies*, 63(1): 1–25.
Horvath, R. (2016), 'The reinvention of "traditional values": Nataliya Narochnitskaya and Russia's assault on universal human rights', *Europe-Asia Studies*, 68(5): 868–92.
Hosking, G. (1997), *Russia: People and Empire 1552–1917*, Cambridge, MA: Harvard University Press.

Howland, D. (2018), 'Carl Schmitt's turn to sovereignty in jurisprudence', *Beijing Law Review*, 9: 211–34.
HRW (2000), *'Welcome to Hell': Arbitrary Detention, Torture, and Extortion in Chechnya*, New York: Human Rights Watch, <https://www.hrw.org/reports/2000/russia_chechnya4/> (last accessed 22 September 2019).
HRW (2017), *Crimea: Persecution of Crimean Tatars Intensifies – Arbitrary Detentions; Separatism, Terrorism Charges*, New York: Human Rights Watch, 14 November, <https://www.hrw.org/news/2017/11/14/crimea-persecution-crimean-tatars-intensifies> (last accessed 27 May 2019).
HRW (2018), *Russia: Government vs. Rights Groups – The Battle Chronicle*, New York: Human Rights Watch, 18 June, <https://www.hrw.org/russia-government-against-rights-groups-battle-chronicle> (last accessed 27 May 2019).
Humphrey, C. (2002), *The Unmaking of Soviet Life: Everyday Economies after Socialism*, Ithaca, NY: Cornell University Press.
Huntington, S. P. (1969), *Political Order in Changing Societies*, New Haven, CT: Yale University Press.
ICG (2015), *Chechnya: The Inner Abroad*, Brussels: International Crisis Group, 30 June.
ICG (2016), *The Eurasian Economic Union: Power, Politics and Trade*, Brussels: International Crisis Group, 20 July.
Ikenberry, G. J. and C. A. Kupchan (1990), 'Socialization and hegemonic power', *International Organization*, 44(3): 283–315.
Ilyin, I. (1933), 'Natsional-sotsializm: novyi dukh I', *Vozrozhdenie* (Paris), 17 May, <http://iljinru.tsygankov.ru/works/vozr170533full.html> (last accessed 27 May 2019).
Ilyin, I. (1948a), 'O fashizme', <http://gosudarstvo.voskres.ru/ilin/nz/iljin-nz.htm>.
Ilyin, I. (1948b), 'O razchleniteliakh Rossii', <http://gosudarstvo.voskres.ru/ilin/nz/nz-68.htm>.
Ingram, A. (2001), 'Alexander Dugin: geopolitics and neo-Fascism in post-Soviet Russia', *Political Geography*, 20(8): 1029–51.
Inozemtsev, V. (2017), 'Putin's Russia: a moderate fascist state', *The American Interest*, 12(4), 23 January.
Institute of National Strategy (2014), 'Konservatizm kak faktor myagkoi sily Rossii', *Tetradi po konservatizmu*, 2(2): 93–125.
Interfax (2014), 'Russia-led security bloc turns away from NATO towards China, chief slams West', *Interfax*, 17 June, via JRL Russia List, <http://russialist.org/russia-led-security-bloc-turns-away-from-nato-towards-china-chief-slams-west/> (last accessed 29 May 2019).
Interfax (2015a), 'Putin nazval osnovnuiu zadachu rossiiskikh voennykh v Sirii', *Interfax*, 11 October, <www.interfax.ru/russia/472593> (last accessed 18 November 2018).
Interfax (2015b), 'Putin podpisal zakon o nezhelatel'nykh inostrannykh organizatsiiakh', *Interfax*, 23 May 2016, <https://www.interfax.ru/russia/443348 > (last accessed 17 December 2018).

Ioffe, J. (2010), 'Russia's nationalist summer camp', *The New Yorker*, 16 August, <https://www.newyorker.com/news/news-desk/russias-nationalist-summer-camp> (last accessed 30 May 2019).

Isaev, V. A. (2016), *Geopolitika: Uchebnik dlya vuzov – Standart tret'ego pokoleniya*, St Petersburg: Piter.

Issaeva, M. (2017), 'Quarter of a century on from the Soviet era: reflections on Russian doctrinal responses to the annexation of Crimea', *Russian Law Journal*, 5(3): 86–112.

Ivanov, I. (2015), 'Zakat Bol'shoi Yevropy', speech at the Twentieth Conference of the Baltic Forum, Yurmala, Latvia, 12 September, <http://russiancouncil.ru/analytics-and-comments/analytics/zakat-bolshoy-evropy/> (last accessed 30 May 2019).

Izborsky Club (2017), 'Pervaya studiya, Krym: Vozvrashchenie domoi', 12 March, <https://izborsk-club.ru/12775> (last accessed 22 June 2019).

Izborsky Club (2019), official website, <https://izborsk-club.ru/about> (last accessed 3 December 2019.

Jahn, B. (2012), 'Critique in a time of liberal world order', *Journal of International Relations and Development*, 15(2): 145–57.

Jameson, F. (2009), 'Zametki o "Nomose"', *Sotsiologicheskoe obozrenie*, 8(2): 17–20.

Jayasuriya, K. (2001), 'The exception becomes the norm: law and regimes of exception in East Asia', *Asian-Pacific Law & Policy Journal*, 2(1), 108–24.

Jenson, D. N. (1999), 'Is Russia another Somalia?', RFE/RL Newsline, 27 January, <http://www.russialist.org/archives/3035.html##4> (last accessed 30 May 2019).

Jokubaitis, L. (2013), 'Carl Schmitt and the conservative revolutionaries', blogpost, *Teloscope*, 3 December, <http://www.telospress.com/carl-schmitt-and-the-conservative-revolutionaries/> (last accessed 15 June 2019).

Judah, B. (2014), 'Behind the scenes in Putin's court: the private habits of a latter-day dictator', *Newsweek*, 23 July, <http://www.newsweek.com/2014/08/01/behind-scenes-putins-court-private-habits-latter-day-dictator-260640.html> (last accessed 20 May 2019).

Jurkevics, A. (2017), 'Hannah Arendt reads Carl Schmitt's *The Nomos of the Earth*: a dialogue on law and geopolitics from the margins', *European Journal of Political Theory*, 16(3): 345–66.

Kahn, J. (2006), 'The search for the rule of law in Russia', *Georgetown Journal of International Law*, 37(2): 353–410.

Kahn, J. (2008), 'Vladimir Putin and the rule of law in Russia', *Georgia Journal of International and Comparative Law*, 36(3): 511–58.

Kailitz, S. and A. Umland (2016), 'Why fascists took over the Reichstag but have not captured the Kremlin: a comparison of Weimar Germany and post-Soviet Russia', *Nationalities Papers*, 45(2): 1–16.

Kalashnikov, M. (2015), 'Iz kogo sostoit "pyataya kolonna"', in A. Prokhanov and S. Glaz"ev (eds), *Kholodnaya voina 2.0: Strategiya russkoi pobedy*, Moscow: Knizhnyi mir, pp. 319–28.

Kalikulov, D. (2014), 'V Kazakhstane ozadacheny slovami Putina o russkom mire', BBC, 2 September, <https://www.bbc.com/russian/international/2014/09/140901_kazakhstan_putin> (last accessed 30 May 2019).

Kamyshev, D. and E. Mukhametshina (2019), 'Putinskoe "Politbyuro 2.0" mozhet ne perezhit' novykh vyzovov', *Vedemosti*, 5 June, <https://www.vedomosti.ru/politics/articles/2019/06/04/803347-putinskoe-politbyuro> (last accessed 17 June 2019).

Kapustin, A. (2014), 'Circular letter to the Executive Council of the International Law Association', June 2014, <http://www.ilarb.ru/html/news/2014/5062014.pdf> (last accessed 22 June 2019).

Karaganov, S. (2013), 'Why do we need national identity?', *Russia in Global Affairs*, 2 October, <http://eng.globalaffairs.ru/pubcol/Why-do-we-need-national-identity-16140> (last accessed 30 May 2019).

Karaganov, S. (2014), 'The watershed year: interim results', *Russia in Global Affairs*, 18 December, <http://eng.globalaffairs.ru/number/The-Watershed-Year-Interim-Results-17210> (last accessed 30 May 2019).

Karaganov, S. (2015), 'Evroaziatskii vykhod iz evropeiskogo krizisa', *Rossiya v global'noi politike*, 24 August, <http://globalaffairs.ru/number/Evroaziatskii-vykhod-iz-evropeiskogo-krizisa-17641> (last accessed 30 May 2019).

Karaganov, S. (2016), 'New ideological struggle?', *Russia in Global Politics*, 26 April, <http://eng.globalaffairs.ru/pubcol/New-ideological-struggle-18124> (last accessed 30 May 2019).

Karaganov, S. (2017a), 'God pobed: chto dal'she?', *Rossiiskaya gazeta*, 15 January, <https://rg.ru/2017/01/15/sergej-karaganov-vozobnovlenie-dialoga-rossiia-nato-oshibka.html> (last accessed 30 May 2019).

Karaganov, S. (2017b), 'Pobeda konservativnogo realizma', *Rossiya v global'noi politike*, 31 October, <http://globalaffairs.ru/number/2016--pobeda-konservativnogo-realizma-18556> (last accessed 30 May 2019).

Karagiannis, E. (2014), 'The Russian interventions in South Ossetia and Crimea compared: military performance, legitimacy and goals', *Contemporary Security Policy*, 35(3): 400–20.

Kashin, O. (2017), 'Surkov i anneksiya Kryma: pravdu li govorit byvshii deputat Voronenkov', *Republic.ru*, 16 February, <https://republic.ru/posts/79742> (last accessed 30 September 2019).

Kashin, O. (2018), 'Zastoi protiv zastoya: vosemnadtsat' let bessmyslennoi bor'by protiv Putina', *Republic.ru*, 9 March, <https://republic.ru/posts/89900> (last accessed 9 June 2019).

Kazakova, V. I. (2012), 'Grossraum kak neveroiatnost' kommunikatsii: "vyzovy" Karla Shmitta v sotsial'nom prostranstve sovremennoi Rossii', Vestnik NGTU im R.E. Alekseeva, 1: 18–25, <http://www.vestnikngtu.ru/assets/2012_01_002.pdf> (last accessed 2 October 2018).

Keating, V. C. and K. Kaczmarska (2019), 'Conservative soft power: liberal soft power bias and the "hidden" attraction of Russia', *Journal of International Relations and Development*, 22(1): 1–27.

Kervégen, J.-F. (1999), 'Carl Schmitt and world unity', in C. Mouffe (ed.), *The Challenge of Carl Schmitt*, London: Verso, pp. 54–74.

Khachatryan, D. (2015), 'Kak stat' troll'hanterom', *Novaya gazeta*, 10 March, <https://www.novayagazeta.ru/articles/2015/03/10/63342-kak-stat-trollhanterom> (last accessed 31 May 2019).

Khairemdinov, L. (2017), 'Rossiya chustvuet sebya uverenno i komfortno', *Krasnaya Zvezda*, 6 March, <http://archive.redstar.ru/index.php/2011-07-25-15-57-8/item/32445-rossiya-chuvstvuet-sebya-uverenno-i-komfortno> (last accessed 31 May 2019).

Khlobustov, O. (2005), 'Yavliaetsya li "Plan Dallesa" fal'shivkoi?', *chekist.ru*, 4 November, <http://www.chekist.ru/article/886> (last accessed 31 May 2019).

Kholmogorov, Ye. (2005a), *Russkii proekt: restavratsiya budushchego*, Moscow: Algoritm/Eksmo.

Kholmogorov, Ye. (2005b), 'Proiskhozhdeniye smyslokratii', *Pravaya.ru*, <http://www.pravaya.ru/leftright/472/5481> (last accessed 31 May 2019).

Kholmogorov, Ye. (2006a), 'Smyslokratiya', *Zavtra*, 32(664), 8 August, <http://zavtra.ru/blogs/2006-08-0933> (last accessed 31 May 2019).

Kholmogorov, Ye. (2006b), 'Moral'noe bol'shinstvo protiv immoralizma men'shinstv', *Pravaya.ru*, <http://www.pravaya.ru/dailynews/7803> (last accessed 31 May 2019).

Khristoforov, I. (2009), 'Nineteenth-century Russian conservatism: problems and contradictions', *Russian Studies in History*, 48(2): 56–77.

Kildyushov, O. (2009), 'Karl Shmitt kak teoretik (post)putinskoi Rossii', *Politicheskii klass*, 1(49), <http://www.intelros.ru/intelros/reiting/reyting_09/material_sofiy/5890-karl-shmitt-kak-teoretik-postputinskoj-rossii.html> (last accessed on 31 May 2019).

Kildyushov, O. (2010), 'Chitaya Shmitta', in K. Shmitt, *Gosudarstvo i politicheskaya forma*, Moscow: Higher School of Economics, pp. 7–32.

Kobyakov, A. B. and V. V. Aver'yanov (eds) (2005), *Russkaya doktrina*, <http://www.rusdoctrina.ru/page95504.html> (last accessed 31 May 2019).

Kolesnikov, A. (2017), 'V ozhidanii chetvertogo sroka: Rossiiskii politicheskii rezhim za god do vyborov', Carnegie Moscow Center, <https://carnegie.ru/2017/04/04/ru-pub-68501> (last accessed 31 May 2019).

Kolesnikov, A. (2018), 'History is the future: Russia in search of the lost empire', Carnegie Moscow Center, 15 February, <https://carnegie.ru/commentary/75544> (last accessed 31 May 2019).

Kolstø, P. (2016a), 'Introduction: Russian nationalism is back – but precisely what does that mean?', in P. Kolstø and H. Blakkisrud (eds), *The New Russian Nationalism: Imperialism, Ethnicity and Authoritarianism*, Edinburgh: Edinburgh University Press, pp. 1–17.

Kolstø, P. (2016b), 'Crimea vs. Donbas: how Putin won Russian nationalist support – and lost it again', *Slavic Review*, 75(3): 702–25.

Kolstø, P. (2016c), 'The ethnification of Russian nationalism', in P. Kolstø and H. Blakkisrud (eds), *The New Russian Nationalism: Imperialism, Ethnicity and Authoritarianism*, Edinburgh: Edinburgh University Press, pp. 18–45.

Kolstø, P. and H. Blakkisrud (2018), *Russia Before and After Crimea: Nationalism and Identity 2010–17*, Edinburgh: Edinburgh University Press.

Kommersant (2013), 'Valerii Zor'kin sveryaet pozitsii Konstitutsionnogo suda s "dukhom zhizni"', *Kommersant*, 23 March, <https://www.kommersant.ru/doc/2153284> (last accessed 23 September 2019).

Kommersant (2016), 'Chem zakanchivalis' korruptsionniye skandaly v Sledstvennom komitete', *Kommersant*, 19 July, <http://www.kommersant.ru/doc/3042686> (last accessed 31 May 2019).

Kommersant (2018), 'Lavrov zayavil o planakh Ukrainy ustroit' provokatsiyu na granitse s Krymom v dekabre', *Kommersant*, 17 December, <https://www.kommersant.ru/doc/3833809> (last accessed 22 June 2019).

Kommersant (2019), 'Na smenu zakaznym delam prishli prikaznye dela', *Kommersant*, 31 January, <https://www.kommersant.ru/doc/3868834> (last accessed 21 June 2019).

Korotkov, D. (2016), 'Oni srazhalis' za Pal'miru', *Fontanka.ru*, 29 March, <https://www.fontanka.ru/2016/03/28/171/> (last accessed 31 May 2019).

Koskenniemi, M. (2004), 'International law as political theology: how to read *Nomos der Erde*?', *Constellations*, 11(4): 492–511.

Koskenniemi, M. (2013), 'Letter in response to Michael Salter's recent paper on Carl Schmitt's *Großraum*', *Chinese Journal of International Law*, 12(1): 201–2.

Koskenniemi, M. (2016), 'Carl Schmitt and international law', in J. Meierhenrich and O. Simons (eds), *The Oxford Handbook of Carl Schmitt*, Oxford: Oxford University Press, pp. 592–611.

Kotkina, I. (2017), 'Geopolitical imagination and popular geopolitics between the Eurasian Union and Russkii Mir', in M. Bassin and G. Pozo (eds), *The Politics of Eurasianism: Identity, Popular Culture and Russia's Foreign Policy*, London: Rowman & Littlefield, pp. 59–78.

Krasner, S. D. (1999), *Sovereignty: Organized Hypocrisy*, Princeton, NJ: Princeton University Press.

Krastev, I. (2011), 'Paradoxes of the new authoritarianism', *Journal of Democracy*, 22(2): 5–16.

Krastev, I. (2015), 'What we don't get about Russia', *International New York Times*, 14 August, p. 6.

Krastev, I. and S. Holmes (2012), 'An autopsy of managed democracy', *Journal of Democracy*, 23(3): 33–45.

Kropatcheva, E. (2015), 'The evolution of Russia's OSCE policy: from the promises of the Helsinki Final Act to the Ukrainian Crisis', *Journal of Contemporary European Studies*, 23(1): 6–24.

Kryshtanovskaya, O. (2007), 'Polozhenie chekistov segodnya fantasticheski ustoichivo', *Kommersant*, 19 March, <https://www.kommersant.ru/doc/750887> (last accessed 31 May 2019).

Kryshtanovskaya, O. and S. White (2003), 'Putin's militocracy', *Post-Soviet Affairs*, 19(4): 289–306.

Kryshtanovskaya, O. and S. White (2005), 'Inside the Putin court: a research note', *Europe–Asia Studies*, 57(7): 1065–75.
Kuchins, A. C. and I. A. Zevelev (2012), 'Russian foreign policy: continuity in change', *The Washington Quarterly*, 35(1): 147–61.
Kurennoi, V. (2007), 'Mertsayushchaya diktatura: dialektika politicheskoi sistemy sovremmenoi Rossii', *Levaya politika*, 1: 17–24.
Kurilla, I. (2010), 'Rethinking the revolutionary past: how color revolutions have led to new interpretations of Russian history', PONARS Eurasia Policy Memo 99, <http://www.ponarseurasia.org/memo/rethinking-revolutionary-past-how-color-revolutions-have-led-new-interpretations-russian> (last accessed 31 May 2019).
Kurowska, X. and A. Reshetnikov (2018), 'Neutrollization: industrialized trolling as a pro-Kremlin strategy of desecuritization', *Security Dialogue*, 49(5): 345–63.
Landa, M. (2015), *Maximilian Voloshin's Poetic Legacy and the Post-Soviet Russian Identity*, Basingstoke: Palgrave.
Lapshin, K. N. (2012), 'Mif gosudarstva K. Shmitta', *Obshchestvo i pravo*, 38(1): 43–4.
Laruelle, M. (2006), *Aleksandr Dugin: A Russian Version of the European Radical Right?*, Woodrow Wilson Center Occasional Papers, 294, Washington, DC: Kennan Institute for Advanced Russian Studies.
Laruelle, M. (2008), *Russian Eurasianism: An Ideology of Empire*, Washington, DC: Woodrow Wilson Center Press.
Laruelle, M. (2009), *Inside and Around the Kremlin's Black Box: The New Nationalist Think Tanks in Russia*, Stockholm: Institute for Security and Development Policy.
Laruelle, M. (2015a), 'Russia as a "divided nation," from compatriots to Crimea: a contribution to the discussion on nationalism and foreign policy', *Problems of Post-Communism*, 62(2): 88–97.
Laruelle, M. (2015b), 'The Iuzhinskii Circle: far-right metaphysics in the Soviet underground and its legacy today', *The Russian Review*, 74(5): 563–80.
Laruelle, M. (2015c), 'Scared of Putin's shadow: in sanctioning Dugin, Washington got the wrong man', *Foreign Affairs*, 25 March, <https://www.foreignaffairs.com/articles/russian-federation/2015-03-25/scared-putins-shadow>.
Laruelle, M. (2015d), 'Eurasia, Eurasianism, Eurasian Union: terminological gaps and overlaps', *PONARS Eurasia*, no. 366.
Laruelle, M. (2015e), 'Conceiving the territory: Eurasianism as a geographical ideology', in M. Bassin, S. Glebov and M. Laruelle (eds), *Between Europe and Asia: The Origins, Theories and Legacies of Russian Eurasianism*, Pittsburgh: University of Pittsburgh Press, pp. 68–96.
Laruelle, M. (2015f), *The 'Russian World': Russia's Soft Power and Geopolitical Imagination*, Washington, DC: Center on Global Interests.
Laruelle, M. (2016a), 'The three colors of Novorossiya, or the Russian nationalist mythmaking of the Ukrainian crisis', *Post-Soviet Affairs*, 32(1): 55–74.
Laruelle, M. (2016b), 'The Izborsky Club, or the new conservative avant-garde in Russia', *The Russian Review*, 75(4): 626–44.

Laruelle, M. (2017a), 'When Eurasia looks east: is Eurasianism Sinophile or Sinophobe?', in M. Bassin and G. Pozo (eds), *The Politics of Eurasianism: Identity, Popular Culture and Russia's Foreign Policy*, London: Rowman & Littlefield, pp. 145–59.

Laruelle, M. (2017b), 'In search of Putin's philosopher', *Intersection*, 3 March, <http://intersectionproject.eu/article/politics/search-putins-philosopher> (last accessed 9 June 2019).

Laruelle, M. (2017c), 'Is nationalism a force for change in Russia?', *Daedalus*, 146(2): 89–100.

Laruelle, M. (2019), 'Russia's militia groups and their use at home and abroad', *Russie.Nei.Visions*, No. 113, Ifri, April.

Latham, R. (2000), 'Social sovereignty', *Theory, Culture & Society*, 17(4): 1–18.

Lavrov, S. (2005), 'Democracy, international governance, and the future world order', *Russia in Global Affairs*, 9 February, <https://eng.globalaffairs.ru/number/n_4422> (last accessed 31 May 2019).

Lavrov, S. (2016), 'Russia's foreign policy in a historical perspective', *Russia in Global Affairs*, 30 March, <http://eng.globalaffairs.ru/number/Russias-Foreign-Policy-in-a-Historical-Perspective-18067> (last accessed 31 May 2019).

Lebow, R. N. (2018), *The Rise and Fall of Political Orders*, Cambridge: Cambridge University Press.

Ledeneva, A. V. (2008), 'Telephone justice in Russia', *Post-Soviet Affairs*, 24(4): 324–50.

Ledeneva, A. V. (2013), *Can Russia Modernise? Sistema, Power Networks and Informal Governance*, Cambridge: Cambridge University Press.

Legg, S. (ed.) (2011), *Spatiality, Sovereignty and Carl Schmitt: Geographies of the Nomos*, Abingdon: Routledge.

Leonov, N. (2003), 'Na kogo rabotayut "pravozashchitniki" v Rossii', *Radonezh*, No. 9, 3 November, <http://radonezh.ru/analytics/na-kogo-rabotayut-pravozaschitniki-v-rossii-gen-n-s-leonov-48055.html> (last accessed 31 May 2019).

Levada (2011a), 'Poryadok ili demokratiya?', *Levada*, 17 January, <https://www.levada.ru/2011/01/17/poryadok-ili-demokratiya/> (last accessed 10 June 2019).

Levada (2011b), 'Vtoroi sud nad M. Khodorkovskim i P. Lebedevym po delu "Yukosa"', *Levada*, 14 February, <https://www.levada.ru/2011/02/15/vtoroj-sud-nad-m-hodorkovskim-i-p-lebedevym-po-delu-yukosa/> (last accessed 31 May 2019).

Levada (2015), 'Bol'shinstvo rossiyan predpochitayut demokratii poryadok', *Levada*, 15 April, <https://www.levada.ru/2015/04/15/bolshinstvo-rossiyan-predpochitayut-demokratii-poryadok/> (last accessed 10 June 2019).

Levada (2016), 'Soyuzniki i "vragi" Rossii, evropeiskaya integratsiya', *Levada*, 2 June, <http://www.levada.ru/2016/06/02/13400/> (last accessed 31 May 2019).

Levada (2017), 'Pakt Molotova-Ribbentropa', *Levada*, 13 September, <https://www.levada.ru/2017/09/13/16612/> (last accessed 31 May 2019).

Levada (2018), 'Krym: chetyre goda spustya', *Levada*, 15 March, <https://www.levada.ru/2018/03/15/krym-chetyre-goda-spustya/> (last accessed 31 May 2019).

Levada (2019), 'Soyuzniki i vragi', Levada, 14 June, <https://www.levada.ru/2019/06/14/soyuzniki-i-vragi-sredi-stran/> (last accessed 19 June 2019).

Levitsky, S. and L. A. Way (2010), *Competitive Authoritarianism: Hybrid Regimes after the Cold War*, Cambridge: Cambridge University Press.

Lewis, D. (2008), *The Temptations of Tyranny in Central Asia*, London: Hurst.

Lewis, D. (2012), 'Who's socialising whom? Regional organisations and contested norms in Central Asia', *Europe-Asia Studies*, 64(7): 1219–37.

Lewis, D. (2013), 'Civil society and the authoritarian state: cooperation, contestation and discourse', *Journal of Civil Society*, 9(3): 325–40.

Lewis, D. (2015), 'Reasserting hegemony in Central Asia: Russian policy in post-2010 Kyrgyzstan', *Comillas Journal of International Relations*, 31(1): 58–80.

Lewis, D. (2016a), '"Blogging Zhanaozen": hegemonic discourse and authoritarian resilience in Kazakhstan', *Central Asian Survey*, 35(3): 421–38.

Lewis, D. (2016b), 'Carl Schmitt: Nazi-era philosopher who wrote blueprint for new authoritarianism', *The Conversation*, 25 May, < https://theconversation.com/carl-schmitt-nazi-era-philosopher-who-wrote-blueprint-for-new-authoritarianism-59835> (last accessed 24 November 2018).

Lewis, D. (2016c), 'The "Moscow Consensus": constructing autocracy in Post-Soviet Eurasia', in A. Hug (ed.), *Sharing Worst Practice: How Countries and Institutions in the Former Soviet Union Create Legal Tools of Repression*, London: Foreign Policy Centre.

Lewis, D. (2017a), 'The myopic Foucauldian gaze: discourse, knowledge and the authoritarian peace', *Journal of Intervention and Statebuilding*, 11(1): 21–41.

Lewis, D. G. (2017b), 'Carl Schmitt in Moscow: counter-revolutionary ideology and the Putinist state', *Russian Analytical Digest*, No. 211, 12 December, <http://www.css.ethz.ch/content/dam/ethz/special-interest/gess/cis/center-for-securities-studies/pdfs/RAD211.pdf>.

Lewis D. G. (2018a), 'Geopolitical imaginaries in Russian foreign policy: the evolution of "Greater Eurasia"', *Europe–Asia Studies*, 70(10): 1612–37.

Lewis, D. G. (2018b), 'Central Asia: fractured region, illiberal regionalism', in A. Ohanyan (ed.), *Fractured Regionalism in Europe and Eurasia*, Washington, DC: Georgetown University Press.

Lewis, D. G., J. Heathershaw and N. Megoran (2018), 'Illiberal peace? Authoritarian modes of conflict management', *Cooperation and Conflict*, 53(4): 486–506.

Lievens, M. (2016), 'Carl Schmitt's concept of history', in J. Meierhenrich and O. Simons (eds), *The Oxford Handbook of Carl Schmitt*, Oxford: Oxford University Press, pp. 401–25.

Light, M. (2015), 'Russian foreign policy themes in official documents and speeches: tracing continuity and change', in D. Cadier and M. Light (eds), *Russia's Foreign Policy: Ideas, Domestic Politics and External Relations*, Basingstoke: Palgrave, pp. 13–29.

Liik, K. (2014), 'Introduction: Russia's pivot to (Eur)asia', in K. Liik (ed.), *Russia's 'Pivot' to Eurasia*, London: European Council on Foreign Relations.

Linde, F. (2016), 'State civilisation: the statist core of Vladimir Putin's civilisational discourse and its implications for Russian foreign policy', *Politics in Central Europe*, 12(1): 21–35.

Lipman, M. (2015), 'The undesirables', *European Council on Foreign Relations*, 22 March, <http://www.ecfr.eu/article/commentary_the_undesirables3041> (last accessed 31 May 2019).

Lipman, M., A. Kachkaeva and M. Poyker (2018), 'Media in Russia', in D. Treisman (ed.), *The New Autocracy: Information, Politics and Policy in Putin's Russia*, Washington, DC: Brookings Institution Press, pp. 159–90.

Lo, B. (2002), *Russian Foreign Policy in the Post-Soviet Era: Reality, Illusion and Mythmaking*, Basingstoke: Palgrave Macmillan.

Lo, B. (2015), *Russia and the New World Disorder*, London: Royal Institute of International Affairs.

Luchterhandt, O. (2006), 'Legal nihilism in action: the YUKOS–Khodorkovsky trial in Moscow', *Eurozine*, 4 April, <https://www.eurozine.com/legal-nihilism-in-action/> (last accessed 31 May 2019).

Lukin, A. (2014), 'Eurasian integration and the clash of values', *Survival*, 56(3): 43–60.

Luks, L. (2008), 'Weimar Russia? Notes on a controversial concept', *Russian Social Science Review*, 49(6): 30–48.

Luks, L. (2009), 'A "Third Way" – or back to the Third Reich?', *Russian Politics & Law*, 47(1): 7–23.

Lukyanov, F. (2015), 'Zapros na poryadok', *Rossiiskaya gazeta*, 21 October, <https://rg.ru/2015/10/21/lukjanov.html> (last accessed 31 May 2019).

Lukyanov, F. (2016), 'Nebol'shaya Evropa', *Rossiiskaya gazeta*, 16 August, <https://rg.ru/2016/08/16/fedor-lukianov-evrosoiuz-vpal-v-konceptualnyj-stupor.html> (last accessed 31 May 2019).

Lutsevych, O. (2016), *Agents of the Russian World: Proxy Groups in the Contested Neighbourhood*, April, London: Chatham House.

Lynch, A. C. (2016), 'The influence of regime type on Russian foreign policy toward "the West", 1992–2015', *Communist and Post-Communist Studies*, 49(1): 101–11.

MacCormick, N. (2010), 'Sovereignty and after', in H. Kalmo and Q. Skinner (eds), *Sovereignty in Fragments: The Past, Present and Future of a Contested Concept*, Cambridge: Cambridge University Press, pp. 151–68.

McCormick, J. (1997), *Carl Schmitt's Critique of Liberalism: Against Politics as Technology*, Cambridge: Cambridge University Press.

McCormick, J. (1998), 'Review: political theory and political theology – the second wave of Carl Schmitt', *Political Theory*, 26(6): 830–54.

McDougal, T. (2015), 'A new imperialism? Evaluating Russia's acquisition of Crimea in the context of national and international law', *Brigham Young University Law Review*, 6: 1847–87.

Macfarlane, N. S. (2003), 'Russian perspectives on order and justice', in R. Foot, J. Gaddis and A. Hurrell (eds), *Order and Justice in International Relations*, Oxford: Oxford University Press, pp. 184–206.

MacFarquhar, N. (2016), 'A powerful Russian weapon: the spread of false stories', *New York Times*, 28 August, <https://www.nytimes.com/2016/08/29/world/europe/russia-sweden-disinformation.html> (last accessed 31 May 2019).

MacFarquhar, N. (2018), 'Yevgeny Prigozhin, Russian oligarch indicted by U.S., is known as "Putin's Cook"', *New York Times*, 16 February, <https://www.nytimes.com/2018/02/16/world/europe/prigozhin-russia-indictment-mueller.html> (last accessed 1 October 2019).

MacFarquhar, N. and D. E. Sanger (2018), 'Putin's "invincible" missile is aimed at U.S. vulnerabilities', *New York Times*, 1 March, <https://www.nytimes.com/2018/03/01/world/europe/russia-putin-speech.html> (last accessed 31 May 2019).

McFaul, M. and K. Stoner-Weiss (2008), 'The myth of the authoritarian model: how Putin's crackdown holds Russia back', *Foreign Affairs*, 87: 68–80, 82–4.

Makarychev, A. (2005), 'Depolitizirovannyi federalizm', *Russkii zhurnal*, 25 July, <http://old.russ.ru/culture/20050725makarichev.html#10> (last accessed 31 May 2019).

Makarychev, A. (2013), 'Inside Russia's foreign policy theorizing: a conceptual conundrum', *Debatte: Journal of Contemporary Central and Eastern Europe*, 21(2/3): 237–58.

Makarychev, A. (2016), 'The war in Chechnya in Russian cinematographic representations: biopolitical patriotism in "unsovereign" times', *Transcultural Studies: A Series in Interdisciplinary Research*, 12(1): 115–35.

Makarychev, A. and A. Yatsyk (2017), 'The sword and the violin: aesthetics of Russia's security policy', *The Journal of Slavic Military Studies*, 30(4): 543–60.

Mälksoo, L. (2017), *Russian Approaches to International Law*, Oxford: Oxford University Press.

Mälksoo, L. and W. Benedek (eds) (2017), *Russia and the European Court of Human Rights: The Strasbourg Effect*, Cambridge: Cambridge University Press.

Mann, M. (1984), 'The autonomous power of the state: its origins, mechanisms and results', *European Journal of Sociology/Archives européennes de sociologie*, 25(2): 185–213.

Manoilo, A. V. (2014), 'Rol' strategii upravlyaemogo khaosa v formirovanii novogo miroporyadka', *Pravo i politika*, 5: 638–51.

March, L. (2012), 'Nationalism for export? The domestic and foreign-policy implications of the new "Russian idea"', *Europe–Asia Studies*, 64(3): 401–25.

Marchal, K. and C. K. Y. Shaw (2017), *Carl Schmitt and Leo Strauss in the Chinese-Speaking World: Reorienting the Political*, New York: Lexington Books.

Marchenya, P. P. (2010), '"Smuta" kak problema otechestvennoi istorii: chemu uchat sistemnye krizisi Rossii?', *Istoriya v podrobnostyakh*, 5: 86–91, <http://users4496447.socionet.ru/files/smuta.pdf> (last accessed 31 May 2019).

Markov, S. (2012), 'Pochemu ikh nel'zya prostit'', *Vedomosti*, 17 March, <http://www.vedomosti.ru/opinion/articles/2012/08/17/pochemu_ih_nelzya_prostit#/cut> (last accessed 31 May 2019).

Marshall, K. (2013), *Corridor: Media Architectures in American Fiction*, Minneapolis: University of Minnesota Press.

Marten, K. (2019), 'Russia's use of semi-state security forces: the case of the Wagner Group', *Post-Soviet Affairs*, 35(3): 181–204.
Marxsen, C. (2014), 'The Crimea crisis: an international law perspective', *ZaöRV*, 74: 367–91.
Masyuk, Ye. (2015), 'Boris Nemtsov: "Oni ne smogut zastavit' menya zamolchat', prosto ne smogut"', *Novaya gazeta*, 27 February, <http://president-sovet.ru/members/blogs/post/1180/> (last accessed 1 June 2019).
Matlock, J. F. (1996), 'Dealing with a Russia in turmoil', *Foreign Affairs*, 75, <https://www.foreignaffairs.com/articles/russia-fsu/1996-05-01/dealing-russia-turmoil-future-partnership> (last accessed 31 May 2019).
Matveichev, O. A. (2014), 'Aktual'nost' ponyatiya "suverentiteta" v sovremennom mire', *Tetradi po konservatizmu*, 3: 157–8.
Medinsky, V. (2016), 'Zachem miru nuzhny russkiye pobedy: ministr kul'tury RF Medinskii o kontserte v Pal'mire', *TASS*, 6 May 2018, <https://tass.ru/kultura/3264955> (last accessed 1 June 2019).
Medvedev, D. (2008), 'Pol'nyi tekst vystupleniya Dmitriya Medvedeva na II grazhdanskom forume v Moskve 22 yanvarya 2008 goda', *Rossiiskaya gazeta*, 24 January, <http://rg.ru/printable/2008/01/24/tekst.html> (last accessed 6 October 2019).
Medvedev, D. (2011), 'Statement by Dmitry Medvedev on the situation in Libya', 21 March, <http://en.kremlin.ru/events/president/news/10701> (last accessed 1 June 2019).
Medvedev, S. (2014), 'Russkii resentiment', *Otechestvennye zapiski*, 6(63), <http://www.strana-oz.ru/2014/6/russkiy-resentiment> (last accessed 1 June 2019).
Meduza (2019), 'The top 1% controls a third of the wealth, and the poor are getting poorer. How Russia became one of the most unequal places on Earth', *Meduza*, 23 January, <https://meduza.io/en/feature/2019/01/23/the-top-1-controls-a-third-of-the-wealth-and-the-poor-are-getting-poorer-how-russia-became-one-of-the-most-unequal-places-on-earth> (last accessed 9 June 2019).
Mehring, R. (2014), *Carl Schmitt: A Biography*, trans. by D. Steuer, Cambridge: Polity.
Mehring, R. (2018), 'Rabota Karla Shmitta "Sostoyanie evropeiskoi iurisprudentsii"', *Sotsiologicheskoe obozreniye*, 17(1): 30–58.
Meier, H. (1998), *The Lesson of Carl Schmitt: Four Chapters on the Distinction between Political Theology and Political Philosophy*, Chicago: University of Chicago Press.
Meierhenrich, J. (2018), *The Remnants of the Rechtsstaat: An Ethnography of Nazi Law*, Oxford: Oxford University Press.
Meierhenrich, J. and O. Simons (2016), 'A fanatic of order in an epoch of confusing turmoil', in J. Meierhenrich and O. Simons (eds), *The Oxford Handbook of Carl Schmitt*, Oxford: Oxford University Press, pp. 3–70.
Memorial (1999), 'Report on the observer mission to the zone of the armed conflict, based on the inspection results in Ingushetia and Chechnya', Memorial, 18 October, <http://reliefweb.int/report/russian-federation/report-observer-mission-zone-armed-conflict-based-inspection-results> (last accessed 22 September 2019).

Memorial (2015), 'List of people recognised as political prisoners by the Memorial Human Rights Centre on June 1, 2015', Memorial, 11 June, <https://memohrc.org/ru/news/list-people-recognised-political-prisoners-memorial-human-rights-centre-june-1-2015> (last accessed 21 June 2019).

Mezhuev, B., A. Cherniaev and N. Kurkin (2010), 'Politicheskaya gegemoniya bol'shinstva', *Russkii zhurnal*, 21 January, <http://www.russ.ru/pole/Politicheskaya-gegemoniya-bol-shinstva> (last accessed 1 June 2019).

MFA RF (2014), 'Statement by the Russian Ministry of Foreign Affairs regarding accusations of Russia's violation of its obligations under the Budapest Memorandum of 5 December 1994', 1 April, <http://www.mid.ru/en/press_service/spokesman/official_statement/-/asset_publisher/t2GCdmD8RNIr/content/id/68078> (last accessed 22 June 2019).

MFA RF (2017), 'Briefing by Foreign Ministry spokesperson Maria Zakharova', Moscow, March, <http://www.mid.ru/en/web/guest/foreign_policy/news/-/asset_publisher/cKNonkJE02Bw/content/id/2687802> (last accessed 1 June 2019).

Michel, C. (2017), 'The rise of the "Traditionalist International": how the American Right learned to love Moscow in the era of Trump', Right Wing Watch, March, <http://www.rightwingwatch.org/report/the-rise-of-the-traditionalist-international-how-the-american-right-learned-to-love-moscow-in-the-era-of-trump/> (last accessed 22 June 2019).

Mikhailovsky, A. (2008a), 'Bor'ba za Karla Shmitta: o retseptsii i aktual'nosti ponyatiya politicheskogo', *Voprosy Philosophii*, 7: 158–71, <http://www.phil63.ru/borba-za-karla-shmitta> (last accessed on 1 June 2019) [also published in English as A. Mikhailovsky (2009), 'The struggle for Carl Schmitt: on the perception and relevance of the concept of the political', *Social Sciences: A Quarterly Journal of the Russian Academy of Sciences*, 40(4): 56–73].

Mikhailovsky, A. (2008b), 'Universal'naya filosofiya', 15 January, <https://www.hse.ru/news/science/3795936.html> (last accessed 14 June 2019).

Mikhailovsky, A. (2009), 'Biograficheskii pazl: Rainhard Mering o "Vzlete i padenii" Karla Shmitta', *Sotsiologicheskoe obozrenie*, 8(3), 71–5.

Mikhailovsky, A. V. (2015), 'Politicheskaya teologiya Karla Shmitta', in D. Shlenov (ed.), *Vzaimodeistvie dukhovnogo i svetskogo obrazovaniya v Rossii na primere Moskovskoi dukhovnoi akademii*, Sergiev Posad: Moskovskaya dukhovnaya akademiya, pp. 168–205.

Mikhailovsky, A. (2016), 'Konservativnye revolyutsionery v Germanii nedootsenili "dinamiku korichnevykh kolonn"', *Russkaya Idea*, <https://politconservatism.ru/thinking/konservativnye-revolyutsionery-v-germanii-nedootsenili-dinamiku-korichnevyh-kolonn> (last accessed 14 June 2019).

Millerman, M. (2014), 'Carl Schmitt in the twenty-first century', *Telos*, 12 August, <http://www.telospress.com/carl-schmitt-in-the-twenty-first-century/> (last accessed 23 June 2019).

Minakov, A. Yu. (2014), 'Rozhdenie russkogo konservatizma: uroki proshlogo', *Tetradi po konservatizmu*, 3: 12–31, <http://essaysonconservatism.ru/rozhdenie-russkogo-konservatizma-uroki-proshlogo/> (last accessed 1 June 2019).

Minca, C. and R. Rowan (2015a), 'The question of space in Carl Schmitt', *Progress in Human Geography*, 39(3): 268–89.
Minca, C. and R. Rowan (2015b), *On Schmitt and Space*, London: Routledge.
Minchenko (2016), *Politburo 2.0: demontazh ili perezagruzka?*, Minchenko Consulting, 7 November, <http://www.minchenko.ru/analitika/analitika_61.html> (last accessed 1 June 2019).
Minchenko (2017), *Politburo 2.0: Renovation Instead of Dismantling*, Minchenko Consulting, 12 October, <http://www.minchenko.ru/netcat_files/userfiles/2/Dokumenty/Politburo_2.0_October_2017_ENG.pdf> (last accessed 1 June 2019).
Mjør, K. J. (2016), 'A morphology of Russia? The Russian civilisational turn and its cyclical idea of history', in A. Mustajoki and K. Lehtisaari (eds), *Philosophical and Cultural Interpretations of Russian Modernisation*, Abingdon: Routledge, pp. 44–58.
MK (2015), 'V Moskve proshlo shestvie i miting storonnikov "Antimaidana"', *MK*, 21 February 2015, <http://www.mk.ru/politics/2015/02/21/v-moskve-proshlo-shestvie-i-miting-storonnikov-antimaydana.html> (last accessed 1 June 2019).
MK (2019), 'Politolog Valerii Solovei predskazal Rossii potryaseniya', *MK*, 4 April, <https://www.mk.ru/politics/2019/04/04/politolog-valeriy-solovey-predskazal-rossii-potryaseniya.html> (last accessed 19 June 2019).
Monaghan, A. (2012), 'The Vertikal: power and authority in Russia', *International Affairs*, 88(1): 1–16.
Monaghan, A. (2016), *The New Politics of Russia: Interpreting Change*, Manchester: Manchester University Press.
Morozov, V. (2005), 'Russia's changing attitude toward the OSCE: contradictions and continuity', *S+F: Sicherheit und Frieden*, 23(2): 69–73.
Morozov, V. (2008), 'Sovereignty and democracy in contemporary Russia: a modern subject faces the post-modern world', *Journal of International Relations and Development*, 11(2): 152–80.
Morris, P. S. (2019), '"Sovereign Democracy" and international law: legitimation and legal ideology', in P. S. Morris (ed.), *Russian Discourses on International Law: Sociological and Philosophical Phenomenon*, Abingdon: Routledge.
Moscow Times (2014), '"No Putin, No Russia" says Kremlin deputy chief of staff', *Moscow Times*, 23 October, <https://themoscowtimes.com/articles/no-putin-no-russia-says-kremlin-deputy-chief-of-staff-40702> (last accessed 27 October 2018).
Moscow Times (2018), 'Top Moscow investigator sentenced in major mafia bribe case', *Moscow Times*, 16 August, <https://themoscowtimes.com/news/top-moscow-investigator-sentenced-in-major-mafia-bribe-case-62544> (last accessed 1 June 2019).
Moshchelnikov, E. N. and O. Yu. Boitsovaya (eds) (2014), *Filosofiia politiki i prava: Ezhegodnik nauchnykh rabot*, vyp. 5. 'Politika i politicheskoe', Moscow: Tsentr strategichekoi konyunktury.
Motyl, A. J. (2010), 'Russia's systemic transformations since Perestroika: from totalitarianism to authoritarianism to democracy – to fascism?', *The Harriman Review*, 17(2): 1–14.

Motyl, A. J. (2016), 'Putin's Russia as a fascist political system', *Communist and Post-Communist Studies*, 49(1): 25–36.

Mouffe, C. (1993), *The Return of the Political*, London: Verso.

Mouffe, C. (1999), 'Carl Schmitt and the paradox of liberal democracy', in C. Mouffe (ed.), *The Challenge of Carl Schmitt*, London: Verso, pp. 38–53.

Mouffe, C. (2005a), *On the Political*, London: Routledge.

Mouffe, C. (2005b), 'Schmitt's vision of a multipolar world order', *South Atlantic Quarterly*, 104(2): 245–51.

Mukhin, V. (2015), 'Armiya i spetssluzhby obespechat Krymu bezopasnost', *Nezavisimaya gazeta*, 21 August, <http://www.ng.ru/armies/2015-08-21/1_crimea.html> (last accessed 1 June 2019).

Mueller, R. S. (2019), 'Report on the Investigation into Russian Interference in the 2016 Presidential Election', vol. 1, Washington, DC, March, pp. 14–35.

Müller, J.-W. (1997), 'Carl Schmitt: an occasional nationalist?', *History of European Ideas*, 23(1): 19–34.

Müller, J.-W. (2003), *A Dangerous Mind: Carl Schmitt in Post-War European Thought*, New Haven, CT: Yale University Press.

Müllerson, R. (2014), 'Ukraine: victim of geopolitics', *Chinese Journal of International Law*, 13(1): 133–45.

Myers, S. L. (2014), 'Russia's move into Ukraine said to be born in shadows', *New York Times*, 7 March, <http://www.nytimes.com/2014/03/08/world/europe/russias-move-into-ukraine-said-to-be-born-in-shadows.html?ref=ellenbarry&_r=2> (last accessed 1 June 2019).

Narochnitskaya, N. (2003), *Rossiya i russkie v mirovoi istorii*, Moscow: Mezhdunardonie otnosheniya.

Neumann, I. B. (2016), *Russia and the Idea of Europe: A Study in Identity and International Relations*, Abingdon: Routledge.

Newsru (2006), 'Yury Chaika priznal za prokuraturoi "zakaznye dela"', *Newsru*, 16 August, <https://www.newsru.com/russia/16aug2006/chayka.html> (last accessed 1 June 2016).

Newsru (2009), 'Volgogradskii sud"ya posle nespravedlivogo uvol'neniya raskryla mekhanizmy, kak v Rossii reshayut "zakaznye" dela', *Newsru*, 27 August, <https://www.newsru.com/russia/27aug2009/zakazcase.html> (last accessed 21 June 2019).

Nikiforov, V. (2015), 'Gubernator Sevastopolia ob"yavil opponentov agentami Gosdepa', *Kommersant*, 10 September, <http://www.kommersant.ru/doc/2806445>, last accessed 1 June 2019).

Nikolskii, A. (2019), 'FSB vpervye soobshchila o zaderzhanii svoego vysokopostavlennogo ofitsera', *Vedemosti*, 25 April, <https://www.vedomosti.ru/politics/articles/2019/04/25/800273-fsb-zaderzhanii-ofitsera> (last accessed 21 June 2019).

Noble, B. and E. Schulmann (2018), 'Not just a rubber stamp: parliament and law-making', in D. Treisman (ed.), *The New Autocracy: Information, Politics and Policy in Putin's Russia*, Washington, DC: Brookings Institution Press, pp. 49–82.

North, D., J. Willis and B. Weingast (2009), *Violence and Social Orders: A Conceptual Framework for Interpreting Recorded Human History*, New York: Cambridge University Press.

Nunan, T. (2011), 'Translator's introduction', in C. Schmitt, *Writings on War*, trans. and ed. by T. Nunan, Cambridge: Polity, pp. 1–26.

O'Donnell, G. (1998), 'Polyarchies and the (un)rule of law in Latin America', Paper presented at the Meeting of the Latin American Studies Association, Chicago.

O'Loughlin, J. and G. Toal (2019), 'The Crimea conundrum: legitimacy and public opinion after annexation', *Eurasian Geography and Economics*, 60(1): 6–27.

O'Loughlin, J., G. Toal and V. Kolosov (2017), 'Who identifies with the "Russian World?" Geopolitical attitudes in southeastern Ukraine, Crimea, Abkhazia, South Ossetia, and Transnistria', *Eurasian Geography and Economics*, 57(6): 745–78.

Orlov, D. (2008), 'The new Russian age and sovereign democracy', *Russian Politics and Law*, 46(5): 72–6.

Ortmann, S. (2018), 'Beyond spheres of influence: the myth of the state and Russia's seductive power in Kyrgyzstan', *Geopolitics*, 23(2): 404–35.

Østbø, J. (2016), *The New Third Rome: Readings of a Russian Nationalist Myth*, Stuttgart: ibidem-Verlag.

Ostromensky, M. P. (2016), 'K teorii partizana K. Shmitta: sotsial'no-politicheskaya eventual'nost' poyavleniya partizana', *Vestnik MGIMO Universiteta*, 5(50): 86–93.

Pain, E. (2016), 'The imperial syndrome and its influence on Russian nationalism', in P. Kolstø and H. Blakkisrud (eds), *The New Russian Nationalism: Imperialism, Ethnicity and Authoritarianism*, Edinburgh: Edinburgh University Press, pp. 46–74.

Paneyakh, E. (2016), 'The practical logic of judicial decision-making', *Russian Politics and Law*, 54(2/3): 138–63.

Paneyakh, E. and D. Rosenberg (2018), 'The courts, law enforcement, and politics', in D. Treisman (ed.), *The New Autocracy: Information, Politics and Policy in Putin's Russia*, Washington, DC: Brookings Institution Press, pp. 217–47.

Papchenko, M. and A. Prokopenko (2016), 'Kudrin predlozhil Putinu snizit' geopoliticheskuyu napryazhennost'', *Vedomosti*, 30 May, <https://www.vedomosti.ru/economics/articles/2016/05/30/642871-kudrin-putinu> (last accessed 1 June 2019).

Parland, T. (2005), *The Extreme Nationalist Threat in Russia: The Growing Influence of Western Rightist Ideas*, London: Routledge.

Pavlovsky, G. (2016), 'Russian politics under Putin', *Foreign Affairs*, May/June.

Pavlovsky, G. (2017), 'Osen' politika: Putin v epokhu kollektivnogo regentstva', Carnegie Moscow Center, 8 November, <http://carnegie.ru/commentary/74661> (last accessed 1 June 2019).

Pavlovsky, G. (2018), 'Putin khot' i iz KGB, no paren' svoi – absoliutno otmorozhennyi', *Republic*, 10 August, <https://republic.ru/posts/91732> (1 June 2019).

Payne, D. (2010), 'Spiritual security, the Russian Orthodox Church, and the Russian Foreign Ministry: collaboration or cooptation?', *Journal of Church and State*, 52(4): 712–27.

Pennycook, A. (1994), 'The politics of pronouns', *ELT Journal*, 48(2): 173–8.

Pepinsky, T. (2014), 'The institutional turn in comparative authoritarianism', *British Journal of Political Science*, 44: 631–53.
Petersson, B. (2013), 'The eternal great power meets the recurring times of troubles: twin political myths in contemporary Russian politics', *European Studies: A Journal of European Culture, History and Politics*, 30(1): 301–26.
Petkova, M. (2017), 'The death of the Russian far right', *Al Jazeera*, 16 December, <https://www.aljazeera.com/indepth/features/2017/11/death-russian-171123102640298.html> (last accessed 19 June 2019).
Petro, N. N. (2018), 'Russian Orthodox Church', in A. Tsygankov (ed.), *Routledge Handbook of Russian Foreign Policy*, Abingdon: Routledge, pp. 217–32.
Petrov, N., M. Lipman and H. E. Hale (2014), 'Three dilemmas of hybrid regime governance: Russia from Putin to Putin', *Post-Soviet Affairs*, 30(1): 1–26.
Petrov, N. and E. Nazrullaeva (2018), 'Regional elites and Moscow', in D. Treisman (ed.), *The New Autocracy: Information, Politics and Policy in Putin's Russia*, Washington, DC: Brookings Institution Press, pp. 109–35.
Peunova, M. (2008), 'An Eastern incarnation of the European New Right: Aleksandr Panarin and New Eurasianist discourse in contemporary Russia', *Journal of Contemporary European Studies*, 16(3): 407–19.
Pipes, R. (2004), 'Flight from freedom: what Russians think and want', *Foreign Affairs*, May–June.
Pipes, R. (2005), *Russian Conservatism and Its Critics: A Study in Political Culture*, New Haven, CT: Yale University Press.
Plotnikova, Ye. and R. Coalson (2016), 'Samara governor offers a stark choice: United Russia or the CIA', *RFE/RL*, 10 September, <https://www.rferl.org/a/russia-samara-governor-merkushkin-united-russia-cia/27978955.html> (last accessed 1 June 2019).
Podberezkin, K. P., O. Borishpolets and A. Podberezkina (2013), *Evraziya i Rossiya*, Moscow: MGIMO.
Poe, M. (2001), 'Moscow, the Third Rome: the origins and transformations of a "pivotal moment"', *Jahrbücher für Geschichte Osteuropas*, Neue Folge, 49(3): 412–29.
Pohl, M. (2007), 'Anna Politkovskaya and Ramzan Kadyrov: exposing the Kadyrov syndrome', *Problems of Post-Communism*, 54(5): 30–9.
Politonline.ru (2012), 'Bolotnaya schitaet narod bydlom, der'mom i rabami', *Politonline.ru*, 6 February, <http://www.politonline.ru/provocation/10448.html> (last accessed 19 June 2019).
Polyakov, L. (2000), 'Liberal'nyi konservator', *Nezavisimaya gazeta*, 2 February, <www.ng.ru/ideas/2000-02-02/8_conserve.html> (last accessed 2 June 2019).
Polyakov, L. V. (2007), '"Suverennaya demokratiya": politicheskii fakt kak teoreticheskaya predmetnost'', *Obshchestvennyye nauki i sovremennost'*, 2: 59–68.
Polyakov, L. V. (2014), 'Shans ob"edineniya vlasti i naroda na odnoi tsennostnoi osnove', *Tetradi po konservatizmu*, 1(1): 41–58.

Polyakov, L. (2015), '"Conservatism" in Russia: political tool or historical choice', IFRI, December, <https://www.ifri.org/sites/default/files/atoms/files/ifri_rnv_90_eng_poliakkov_protege.pdf> (last accessed 24 June 2019).
Polunin, A. (2016), 'Gref nameren nachat' Perestroiku 2.0. Pomozhet li reforma gosupravleniya podnyat' ekonomiku RF?', *Svobodnaya Pressa*, 16 March, <http://svpressa.ru/ economy/article/144471/> (last accessed 2 June 2019).
Popova, M. (2012), *Politicized Justice in Emerging Democracies: A Study of Courts in Russia and Ukraine*, Cambridge: Cambridge University Press.
Popova, M. (2017), 'Putin-style "rule of law" and the prospects for change', *Daedalus*, 146(2): 64–75.
Prozorov, S. (2004), 'Russian conservatism in the Putin presidency: the dispersion of a hegemonic discourse', Danish Institute for International Studies, Working Paper.
Prozorov, S. (2005), 'Russian conservatism in the Putin presidency: the dispersion of a hegemonic discourse', *Journal of Political Ideologies*, 10(2): 121–43.
Prozorov, S. (2009), 'In and out of Europe: identity politics in Russian–European relations', in E. Berg and P. Ehin (eds), *Identity and Foreign Policy: Baltic–Russian Relations and European Integration*, Abingdon: Routledge, pp. 133–60.
Prozorov, S. (2012), 'The katechon in the age of biopolitical nihilism', *Continental Philosophy Review*, 45(4): 483–503.
Pursiainen, C. and T. Forsberg (2018), 'The principle of territorial integrity in Russian international law doctrine: the case of Crimea', in P. S. Morris (ed.), *Russian Discourses on International Law: Sociological and Philosophical Phenomenon*, Abingdon: Routledge, pp. 232–54.
Putin, V. (1999), 'Vladimir Putin, "Rossiya na rubezhe tysyacheletii"', *Nezavisimaya gazeta*, 30 December, <http://www.ng.ru/politics/1999-12-30/4_millenium.html> (last accessed 1 June 2019).
Putin, V. (2000a), *First Person: An Astonishingly Frank Self-Portrait by Russia's President*, New York: Public Affairs.
Putin V. (2000b), 'Televizionnoe obrashchenie k grazhdanam Rossii', Moscow, 17 May, <http://kremlin.ru/events/president/transcripts/21440> (last accessed 2 June 2019).
Putin, V. (2000c), '"Otkrytoe pis'mo" izbiratelyam', 25 February, <http://kremlin.ru/events/president/transcripts/24144> (last accessed 2 June 2019).
Putin, V. (2000d), 'Poslanie Federal'nomu Sobraniyu Rossiiskoi Federatsii', Moscow, 8 July, <http://kremlin.ru/events/president/transcripts/21480> (last accessed 2 June 2019).
Putin, V. (2002), 'Poslanie Federal'nomu Sobraniyu Rossiiskoi Federatsii', Moscow, 18 April, <http://kremlin.ru/events/president/transcripts/21567> (last accessed 21 September 2019).
Putin, V. (2003), 'Poslanie Federal'nomu Sobraniyu Rossiiskoi Federatsii', Moscow, 16 May, <http://kremlin.ru/events/president/transcripts/21998> (last accessed 2 June 2019).

Putin, V. (2006), 'Vystuplenie na gosudarstvennom prieme, posviashchennom Dnyu narodnogo edinstva', Bol'shoi Kremlevskii dvorets, Moscow, 4 November, <http://kremlin.ru/events/president/transcripts/23882> (last accessed 2 June 2019).

Putin, V. (2007a), 'Vystuplenie i diskussiya na Myunkhenskoi konferentsii po voprosam politiki bezopasnosti', Munich, 10 February, <http://kremlin.ru/events/president/transcripts/24034> (last accessed 2 June 2019).

Putin, V. (2007b), 'Polveka evropeiskoi integratsii i Rossiya', 25 March, <http://en.kremlin.ru/events/president/transcripts/24094> (last accessed 2 June 2019).

Putin, V. (2007c), 'Interview with Arab satellite channel Al-Jazeera', 10 February, <http://en.kremlin.ru/events/president/transcripts/24035> (last accessed 22 June 2019).

Putin, V. (2012a), 'Poslanie Federal'nomu Sobraniyu Rossiiskoi Federatsii', Moscow, 12 December, <http://kremlin.ru/events/president/news/17118> (last accessed 2 June 2019).

Putin, V. (2012b), 'Rossiya i menyaiushchiisya mir', *Rossiisskaya gazeta*, 27 February, <https://rg.ru/2012/02/27/putin-politika.html> (last accessed 2 June 2019).

Putin, V. (2012c), 'Obrashchenie Vladimira Putina k rossiyanam: slovo – za vami', *Vesti.ru*, 2 March, <http://www.vesti.ru/doc.html?id=731562> (last accessed 2 June 2019).

Putin, V. (2013a), 'Zasedanie mezhdunarodnogo diskussionnogo kluba "Valdai"', 19 September, <http://kremlin.ru/events/president/news/19243> (last accessed 2 June 2019).

Putin, V. (2013b), 'Poslanie Federal'nomu Sobraniyu Rossiiskoi Federatsii', 12 December, <http://kremlin.ru/events/president/news/19825> (last accessed 2 June 2019).

Putin, V. (2013c), 'Joint news conference with President of France Francois Hollande', 28 February, <http://en.kremlin.ru/events/president/transcripts/17597> (last accessed 2 June 2019).

Putin, V. (2013d), 'Interv'yu Pervomu kanalu i agentstvu Assoshieted Press', 4 September, <http://kremlin.ru/events/president/news/19143> (last accessed 24 June 2019).

Putin, V. (2014a), 'Obrashchenie Prezidenta Rossiiskoi Federatsii', Moscow, 18 March, <http://kremlin.ru/events/president/news/20603> (last accessed 2 June 2019).

Putin, V. (2014b), 'Zasedanie Mezhdunarodnogo diskussionnogo kluba "Valdai"', 24 October 2014, http://www.kremlin.ru/events/president/news/46860 (last accessed 2 June 2019).

Putin, V. (2014c), 'Poslanie Prezidenta Federal'nomu Sobraniyu', Moscow, 4 December, <http://kremlin.ru/events/president/news/47173> (last accessed 2 June 2019).

Putin, V. (2014d), 'Vstrecha s molodymi uchenymi i prepodavateliami istorii', 5 November, <http://kremlin.ru/events/president/news/46951> (last accessed 2 June 2019).

Putin, V. (2014e), 'Bol'shaya press-konferentsiya Vladimira Putina', 18 December, Moscow, <http://en.kremlin.ru/events/president/news/47250> (last accessed 2 June 2019).
Putin, V. (2014f), 'Direct Line with Vladimir Putin, President of Russia', 17 April, <http://en.kremlin.ru/events/president/news/20796> (last accessed 22 June 2019).
Putin, V. (2015a), '70-ya sessiya General'noi Assamblei OON', 28 September, New York, <http://kremlin.ru/events/president/news/50385> (last accessed 2 June 2019).
Putin, V. (2015b), 'Zayavlenie dlya pressy i otvety na voprosy zhurnalistov po itogam vstrechi s Federal'nym kantslerom Germanii Angeloi Merkel', 10 May, <http://kremlin.ru/events/president/transcripts/49455> (last accessed on 2 June 2019).
Putin, V. (2015c), 'Poslanie Prezidenta Federal'nomu Sobraniyu', 3 December, <http://kremlin.ru/events/president/news/50864> (last accessed 2 June 2019).
Putin, V. (2015d), 'Sammit ODKB', Dushanbe, 15 September, <http://en.kremlin.ru/events/president/news/50291> (last accessed 2 June 2019).
Putin, V. (2016a), 'Zasedanie mezhdunarodnogo diskussionnogo kluba "Valdai"', Sochi, 27 October, <http://kremlin.ru/events/president/news/53151> (last accessed 4 June 2019).
Putin, V. (2016b), 'Telephone conversation with UNESCO Director-General Irina Bokova', 27 March, <http://en.kremlin.ru/events/president/news/51574> (last accessed 2 June 2019).
Putin, V. (2016c), 'Telemost s siriiskoi Pal'miroi', 5 May 2016, <http://kremlin.ru/events/president/news/51877> (last accessed 2 June 2019).
Putin, V. (2017a), 'Zasedanie mezhdunarodnogo diskussionnogo kluba "Valdai"', 19 October, <http://kremlin.ru/events/president/news/55882> (last accessed 2 June 2019).
Putin, V. (2017b), 'Putin: evraziiskoe partnerstvo dolzhno izmenit' politicheskii landshaft kontinenta', *RIA Novosti*, 14 May, <http://1prime.ru/News/20170514/827449765.html> (last accessed 2 June 2019).
Rabinbach, A. (2013), 'The aftermath: reflections on the culture and ideology of National Socialism', in P. E. Gordon and J. P. McCormick (eds), *Weimar Thought: A Contested Legacy*, Princeton, NJ: Princeton University Press, pp. 394–406.
Rasch, W. (2000), 'Conflict as a vocation: Carl Schmitt and the possibility of politics', *Theory, Culture, and Society*, 17(6): 1–32.
Rasch, W. (2005), 'Introduction: Carl Schmitt and the new world order', *South Atlantic Quarterly*, 104(2): 177–83.
Rasch, W. (2016), 'Carl Schmitt's defense of democracy', in J. Meierhenrich and O. Simons (eds), *The Oxford Handbook of Carl Schmitt*, Oxford: Oxford University Press, pp. 312–37.
RBK (2011), 'V. Putin rasskazal, kak ubivali M. Kaddafi', *RBK*, 15 December, <https://www.rbc.ru/society/15/12/2011/5703f09b9a79477633d3b26f> (last accessed 3 June 2019).

RBK (2017), 'K delu Serebrennikova podklyuchili Sluzhbu zashchity konstitutsionnogo stroya FSB', *RBK*, 29 August, <https://www.rbc.ru/society/29/08/2017/59a500a19a794793f11cf65b#ws> (last accessed 23 September 2019).

Remington, T. F. (2014), *Presidential Decrees in Russia: A Comparative Perspective*, Cambridge: Cambridge University Press.

Remizov, M. (2002), *Opyt' konservativnoi kritiki*, Moscow: Fond nauchnykh issledovanii 'Pragmatika kul'tury'.

Remizov, M. (2006), 'Konservatizm segodnya: analiticheskii obzor', *Agenstvo politicheskikh novostei*, 27 January, <https://www.apn.ru/publications/article1748.htm> (last accessed 3 June 2019).

Remizov, M. (2008), 'Potomu chto my konservatory', *Agenstvo politicheskikh novostei*, <http://www.apn.ru/blog/article21145.htm> (last accessed 3 June 2019).

Remizov, M. (2009), 'Shmitt forever: Revolutsiya sprava v predelakh tol'ko akademii', *Agenstvo politicheskikh novostei*, <http://www.russ.ru/Mirovaya-povestka/SHmitt-forever> (last accessed 3 June 2019).

Remizov, M. (2010), 'Eshche raz ob umnom bol'shintsve', *Agenstvo politicheskikh novostei*, 28 January, <https://www.apn.ru/publications/article22341.htm> (last accessed 3 June 2019).

Remizov, M. (2011), 'Demokratiya plyus gegemoniya bol'shinstva', *Agenstvo politicheskikh novostei*, 24 June, <https://www.apn.ru/index.php?newsid=24379> (last accessed 3 June 2019).

Reuters (2017), 'Allies of slain Putin critic Nemtsov allege cover-up after guilty verdict', *Reuters*, 29 June, <https://www.reuters.com/article/us-russia-nemtsov/allies-of-slain-putin-critic-nemtsov-allege-cover-up-after-guilty-verdict-idUSKBN19K1UI?> (last accessed 3 June 2019).

Reynolds, M. (2000), 'War has no rules for Russian forces fighting in Chechnya', *Los Angeles Times*, 17 September, <http://articles.latimes.com/2000/sep/17/news/mn-22524> (last accessed on 22 September 2019).

RFE/RL (2015), 'Western militaries exit Central Asia as Germany shuts Uzbek base', RFE/RL, 15 October, <https://www.rferl.org/a/uzbekistan-germany-to-shut-base-last-western-in-central-asia/27308248.html> (last accessed 3 June 2019).

RIA-Novosti (2011a), 'Putin: nevozmozhno bez otvrashcheniya smotret' na kadry ubiistva Kaddafi', RIA-Novosti, 26 October, <https://ria.ru/arab_ly/20111026/471693000.html> (last accessed 3 June 2019).

RIA-Novosti (2011b), 'Putin dal dobro: oppositsii na mitingi, politsii na peresechenie narushenii', RIA-Novosti, 8 December, <https://ria.ru/politics/20111208/510316708.html> (last accessed 3 June 2019).

RIA-Novosti (2015), '"Put' na rodinu": Putin raskryl podrobnosti vossoedineniya Kryma s RF', RIA-Novosti, 15 March, <https://ria.ru/politics/20150315/1052668652.html> (last accessed 3 June 2019).

Rigi, J. (2012), 'The corrupt state of exception', *Social Analysis*, 56(3): 69–88.

Robertson, G. B. (2010), *The Politics of Protest in Hybrid Regimes: Managing Dissent in Post-Communist Russia*, Cambridge: Cambridge University Press.

Robinson, N. (2017), 'Russian neo-patrimonialism and Putin's "cultural turn"', *Europe-Asia Studies*, 69(2): 348–66.

Robinson, P. (2012), 'Putin's philosophy: the Russian leader's paradoxical, strong-state "liberal-conservatism"', *The American Conservative*, 28 March, <https://www.theamericanconservative.com/articles/putins-philosophy/> (last accessed 3 June 2019).

Rochlitz, M. (2014), 'Corporate raiding and the role of the state in Russia', *Post-Soviet Affairs*, 30(2/3): 89–114.

Rodkiewicz, W. and J. Rogoża (2015), *Potemkin Conservatism: An Ideological Tool of the Kremlin*, Warsaw: OSW.

Rogov, K. (2019), *Krepost' vrastaet v zemlyu*, Moscow: Liberal'naya missiya, <http://www.liberal.ru/upload/files/krepost.pdf> (last accessed 6 October 2019).

Rogov, K. and N. Petrov (2016), 'Konsolidatsiya silovoi vertikali', *New Times*, 37, 14 November, <https://newtimes.ru/articles/detail/116585/> (last accessed 3 June 2019).

Romanova, O. (2019), 'Ivan Golunov is free. Other victims of Russia's police are not so lucky', Carnegie Moscow Center, 13 June, <https://carnegie.ru/commentary/79304> (last accessed 21 June 2019).

Ross, C. (2005), 'Federalism and electoral authoritarianism under Putin', *Demokratizatsiya*, 13(3): 347–71.

Rossiiskaya gazeta (2010), 'Sudyat ne po dolzhnosti', *Rossiiskaya gazeta*, 25 December, <https://rg.ru/2010/12/25/krasheninnikov.html> (last accessed 3 June 2019).

Roxburgh, A. (2013), *The Strongman: Vladimir Putin and the Struggle for Russia*, London: IB Tauris.

RT (2014), 'Putin likens part of independent opposition to Bolsheviks, branding them as traitors', *Russia Today*, 29 August, <https://www.rt.com/politics/183708-putin-opposition-bolsheviks-seliger/> (last accessed 3 June 2019).

RT (2019), 'Russia's reserves fully cover nation's internal & foreign debt for 1st time ever', *RT*, 20 February, <https://www.rt.com/business/451954-russia-reserves-cover-debt/> (last accessed 3 December 2019).

Rubin, M., M. Zholobova and R. Badanin (2019), 'Povelitel' kukol', *Proekt media*, 23 January, <https://www.proekt.media/portrait/alexey-gromov> (last accessed 3 June 2019).

Russell, J. (2005), 'Terrorists, bandits, spooks and thieves: Russian demonisation of the Chechens before and since 9/11', *Third World Quarterly*, 26(1): 101–16.

Russian Federation (2013), 'Concept of the foreign policy of the Russian Federation', 18 February, <http://www.mid.ru/en/foreign_policy/official_documents/-/asset_publisher/CptICkB6BZ29/content/id/122186> (last accessed 3 June 2019).

Russian Federation (2014a), 'Zasedanie Soveta Bezopasnosti', 22 July, <http://kremlin.ru/events/president/news/46305> (last accessed 3 June 2019).

Russian Federation (2014b), 'Voennaya doktrina Rossiiskoi Federatsii', *Rossiiskaya gazeta*, 30 December, <https://rg.ru/2014/12/30/doktrina-dok.html> (last accessed 3 June 2019).

Russian Federation (2015), 'Strategiya natsional'noi bezopasnosti Rossiiskoi Federatsii', 31 December, <www.scrf.gov.ru/security/docs/document133/> (last accessed 3 June 2019).

Russian Federation (2016), 'Doktrina informatsionnoi bezopasnosti Rossiiskoi Federatsii', 5 December, <http://www.scrf.gov.ru/security/information/document5/ (last accessed 22 September 2019).

Ruvinsky, V. (2011), 'Private business rises against the Goliaths of graft', RBTH, 21 April, <http://rbth.com/articles/2011/04/21/private_business_rises_against_the_goliaths_of_graft_12792.html> (last accessed 21 June 2019).

Ryzhkov, V. (2014), 'Controlling Russians through travel bans', *Moscow Times*, 26 May, <https://themoscowtimes.com/articles/controlling-russians-through-travel-bans-35830> (last accessed 3 June 2019).

Sakwa, R. (2010a), 'The dual state in Russia', *Post-Soviet Affairs*, 26(3): 185–206.

Sakwa, R. (2010b), *The Crisis of Russian Democracy: The Dual State, Factionalism and the Medvedev Succession*, Cambridge: Cambridge University Press.

Sakwa, R. (2011), 'Surkov: dark prince of the Kremlin', *Open Democracy*, 7 April, <https://www.opendemocracy.net/od-russia/richard-sakwa/surkov-dark-princeof-kremlin> (last accessed 3 June 2019).

Sakwa, R. (2013), 'Systemic stalemate: reiderstvo and the dual state', in N. Robinson (ed.), *The Political Economy of Russia*, Plymouth: Rowman & Littlefield, pp. 69–96.

Sakwa, R. (2014a), *Putin Redux: Power and Contradiction in Contemporary Russia*, Abingdon: Routledge.

Sakwa, R. (2014b), *Putin and the Oligarch: The Khodorkovsky–Yukos Affair*, London: IB Tauris.

Sakwa, R. (2015a), 'Is Russia really a kleptocracy?', *TLS*, 4 February.

Sakwa, R. (2015b), 'The death of Europe? Continental fates after Ukraine', *International Affairs*, 91(3): 553–79.

Sakwa, R. (2016), 'Russian neo-revisionism and dilemmas of Eurasian integration', in R. E. Kanet and M. Sussex (eds), *Power, Politics and Confrontation in Eurasia: Foreign Policy in a Contested Region*, London: Palgrave Macmillan, pp. 111–34.

Sakwa, R. (2017), *Russia against the Rest: The Post-Cold War Crisis of World Order*, Cambridge: Cambridge University Press.

Salenko, A. (2015), 'Legal aspects of the dissolution of the Soviet Union in 1991 and its implications for the reunification of Crimea with Russia in 2014', *Heidelberg Journal of International Law*, 75: 141–66.

Salter, M. (2012), 'Law, power and international politics with special reference to East Asia: Carl Schmitt's Grossraum analysis', *Chinese Journal of International Law*, 11(3): 393–427.

Salter, M. and Y. Yin (2014), 'Analysing regionalism within international law and relations: the Shanghai Cooperation Organisation as a Großraum?', *Chinese Journal of International Law*, 13(4): 819–77.

Sasse, G. (2017), *Terra Incognita: The Public Mood in Crimea*, ZOiS Report, 3, November, <https://www.zois-berlin.de/fileadmin/media/Dateien/ZOiS_Reports/ZOiS_Report_3_2017.pdf> (last accessed 3 June 2019).

Sborov, A. (2005), 'Uvolen za nesootvetstvie zanimaemoi territorii', *Kommersant*, 22 August, <https://www.kommersant.ru/doc/602759> (last accessed 3 June 2019).

Scanlon, J. P. (ed.) (1994), *Russian Thought after Communism: The Recovery of a Philosophical Heritage*, Armonk, NY: ME Sharpe.

Schedler, A. (ed.) (2006), *Electoral Authoritarianism: The Dynamics of Unfree Competition*, Boulder, CO: Lynne Rienner.

Schedler, A. (2009), 'The new institutionalism in the study of authoritarian regimes', *Totalitarismus und Demokratie*, 6(2): 323–40.

Scherrer, J. (2013), 'The "cultural/civilizational turn" in post-Soviet identity building', in J. Scherrer, P. Bodin, S. Hedlund and E. Namli (eds), *Power and Legitimacy: Challenges from Russia*, London: Routledge, pp. 152–68.

Scheuerman, W. E. (1999), *Carl Schmitt: The End of Law*, Lanham, MD: Rowman & Littlefield.

Scheuerman, W. E. (2007), 'Carl Schmitt and Hans Morgenthau: realism and beyond', in M. Williams (ed.), *Realism Reconsidered: The Legacy of Hans Morgenthau in International Relations*, Oxford: Oxford University Press, pp. 62–92.

Schmitt, C. (1985a [1934]), *Political Theology: Four Chapters on the Concept of Sovereignty*, trans. by G. Schwab, Cambridge, MA: MIT Press.

Schmitt, C. (1985b [1926]), *The Crisis of Parliamentary Democracy*, trans. by E. Kennedy, Cambridge, MA: MIT Press.

Schmitt, C. (1985c [1926]), 'Preface to the second edition: on the contradiction between parliamentarianism and democracy', in C. Schmitt, *The Crisis of Parliamentary Democracy*, trans. by E. Kennedy, Cambridge, MA: MIT Press, pp. 1–17.

Schmitt, C. (1990), 'The plight of European jurisprudence', *Telos*, 83: 35 70.

Schmitt, C. (1991), *Glossarium: Aufzeichnungen der Jahre 1947–1951*, ed. by E. Freiherr von Medem, Berlin: Duncker and Humblot.

Schmitt, C. (1995), *Staat, Großraum, Nomos: Arbeiten aus den Jahren 1916–1969*, Berlin: Duncker & Humblot.

Schmitt, C. (1996 [1923]), *Roman Catholicism and Political Form*, trans. by G. L. Ulmen, Westport, CT: Greenwood Press.

Schmitt, C. (1999), 'Ethic of state and pluralistic state', in C. Mouffe (ed.), *The Challenge of Carl Schmitt*, London: Verso, pp. 195–208.

Schmitt, C. (2001 [1933]), *State, Movement, People: The Triadic Structure of the Political Unity; The Question of Legality*, ed. and trans. S. Draghici, Corvallis, OR: Plutarch Press.

Schmitt, C. (2003 [1950]), *The Nomos of the Earth in the International Law of Jus Publicum Europeaum*, trans. by G. L. Ulmen, New York: Telos Press.

Schmitt, C. (2004a [1934]), *On the Three Types of Juristic Thought*, trans. by J. W. Bendersky, Westport, CT: Praeger Publishers.

Schmitt, C. (2004b [1932]), *Legality and Legitimacy*, Durham, NC: Duke University Press.

Schmitt, C. (2007a [1932]), *Concept of the Political*, Chicago: Chicago University Press.

Schmitt, C. (2007b [1929]), 'The age of neutralizations and depoliticizations', trans. by M. Konzett and J. P. McCormick, in C. Schmitt, *Concept of the Political*, Chicago: Chicago University Press, pp. 80–96.

Schmitt, C. (2007c), *Theory of the Partisan*, Candor, NY: Telos Press.

Schmitt, C. (2008a [1928]), *Constitutional Theory*, trans. and ed. by J. Seitzer, Durham, NC: Duke University Press.

Schmitt, C. (2008b [1938]), *The Leviathan in the State Theory of Thomas Hobbes*, trans. by G. Schwab and E. Hilfstein, Chicago: University of Chicago Press.

Schmitt, C. (2008c [1954]), *Gespräch über die Macht und den Zugang zum Machthaber*, Stuttgart: Klett-Cotta.

Schmitt, C. (2009), *Hamlet or Hecuba: The Intrusion of the Time into the Play*, New York: Telos.

Schmitt, C. (2011a [1941]), 'The Großraum order of international law with a ban on intervention for spatially foreign powers: a contribution to the concept of Reich in international law (1939–1941)', in C. Schmitt, *Writings on War*, trans. and ed. by T. Nunan, Cambridge: Polity, pp. 75–124.

Schmitt, C. (2011b [1933]), 'Forms of modern imperialism in international law', trans. by M. Hannah, in S. Legg (ed.), *Spatiality, Sovereignty and Carl Schmitt: Geographies of the Nomos*, Abingdon: Routledge, pp. 29–44.

Schmitt, C. (2011c [1939]), 'Großraum versus universalism: the international legal struggle over the Monroe Doctrine', trans. by M. Hannah, in S. Legg (ed.), *Spatiality, Sovereignty and Carl Schmitt: Geographies of the Nomos*, Abingdon: Routledge, pp. 46–54.

Schmitt, C. (2014a [1921]), *On Dictatorship. From the Origin of the Modern Concept of Sovereignty to Proletarian Class Struggle*, trans. by M. Hoelzl and G. Ward, Cambridge: Polity Press.

Schmitt, C. (2014b [1925]), 'Die Rheinlande als Objekt internationaler Politik', in C. Schmitt, *Positionen und Begriffe im Kampf mit Weimar-Genf-Versailles, 1923–1939*, Berlin: Duncker and Humblot, pp. 29–37.

Schmitt, C. (2015 [1942]), *Land and Sea: A World-Historical Meditation*, trans. by S. G. Zeitlin, Candor, NY: Telos.

Schmitt, C. (2018), *The Tyranny of Values*, New York: Telos.

Schwab, G. (2005), 'Introduction', in C. Schmitt, *Political Theology: Four Chapters on the Concept of Sovereignty*, trans. by G. Schwab, Cambridge, MA: MIT Press, pp. xxxvii–lii.

Senderov, V. A. (2007), 'Conservative revolution in post-Soviet Russia: overview of the main ideas', *Voprosy filosofii*: 63–81 [in English].

Senderov, V. A. (2014), 'Totalitarnoe myshlenie v Rossii i Karl Shmitt', *Voprosy filosofii*, 8: 167–75.

Sergeev, N. and S. Sergeev (2019), 'Na FSB nashlos' USB', *Kommersant*, 26 April, <https://www.kommersant.ru/doc/3955416> (last accessed 21 June 2019).

Sharafutdinova, G. (2014), 'The Pussy Riot affair and Putin's demarche from sovereign democracy to sovereign morality', *Nationalities Papers*, 42(4): 615–21.

Sharlet, R. S. (1977), 'Stalinism and Soviet legal culture', in R. C. Tucker (ed.), *Stalinism: Essays in Historical Interpretation*, New York: Norton, pp. 155–79.
Sheerin, C. (2017), 'Russia wages legal and cultural war on LGBTIs', IFEX, 27 March, <http://www.petertatchell.net/international/russia/russia-wages-legal-cultural-war-on-lgbtis/> (last accessed 7 June 2019).
Shekhovtsov, A. (2017), *Russia and the Western Far Right: Tango Noir*, Abingdon: Routledge.
Shekhovtsov, A. and A. Umland (2009), 'Is Aleksandr Dugin a traditionalist? "Neo-Eurasianism" and perennial philosophy', *The Russian Review*, 68(4): 662–78.
Shenfield, S. D. (1998), 'The Weimar/Russia comparison: reflections on Hanson and Kopstein', *Post-Soviet Affairs*, 14(4): 355–68.
Shenfield, S. (2001), *Russian Fascism: Traditions, Tendencies and Movements*, London: Routledge.
Shevel, O. (2011), 'Russian nation-building from Yel'tsin to Medvedev: ethnic, civic or purposefully ambiguous?', *Europe–Asia Studies*, 63(2): 179–202.
Shevtsova, L. (2003), *Putin's Russia*, Washington, DC: Carnegie Endowment.
Shevtsova, L. (2007), *Russia: Lost in Transition – the Yeltsin and Putin Legacies*, Washington, DC: Carnegie Endowment.
Shevtsova, L. (2014), 'How long Russians will believe in fairy tale?', Carnegie Center, 25 June, <http://carnegie.ru/commentary/?fa=56003> (last accessed 7 June 2019).
Shevtsova, L. (2015), 'Humiliation as a tool of blackmail', *The American Interest*, 2 June, <https://www.the-american-interest.com/2015/06/02/humiliation-as-a-tool-of-blackmail/> (last accessed 7 June 2019).
Shklyaruk, M. (2016), 'Zakaz ot sistemy', *Vedomosti*, 2 March, <https://www.vedomosti.ru/opinion/articles/2016/03/03/632300-zakaz-sistemi> (last accessed 7 June 2019).
Shklyaruk, M. and I. Chetverikova (2016), 'Predprinmatelskie grabli 2.0', *Vedomosti*, 28 April, <https://www.vedomosti.ru/opinion/articles/2016/04/28/639472-predprinimatelskie-grabli-20> (last accessed 7 June 2019).
Shlapentokh, D. (2007), 'Dugin Eurasianism: a window on the minds of the Russian elite or an intellectual ploy?' *Studies in East European Thought*, 59(3): 215–36.
Shlychkov, V. V., I. K. Kiyamov, S. M. Kulish, D. R. Nestulaeva and I. G. Alafuzov (2016), 'Ob otdelnykh aspektakh primeninyia "ruchnogo upravleniya" organami rossiiskoi gosudarstvenno-munitsipal'noi vlasti', *Aktual'nye problemy ekonomiki i prava*, 10(3): 39–54.
Shmitt, K. (1992), 'Ponyatie politicheskogo', trans. by A. F. Filippov, *Voprosy sotsiologii*, 1(1): 35–67.
Shmitt, K. (2007 [1963]), *Teoriya partizana: Promezhutochnoe zamechanie k ponyatiyu politicheskogo*, Moscow: Praxis.
Shmitt, K. (2008), *Nomos zemli v prave narodov jus publicum europaeum*, trans. by K. Loshchevskii and Yu. Korinets, St Petersburg: Vladimir Dal'.
Shmitt, K. (2016), *Ponyatie politicheskogo*, trans. and ed. by A. F. Filippov, St Petersburg: Nauka.

Shmitt, K., Yu. Korinets and A. Filippov (2012), 'Glossarii', *Sotsiologicheskoe obozrenie*, 10(3): 110–14.

Sidorov, D. (2006), 'Post-imperial Third Romes: resurrections of a Russian Orthodox geopolitical metaphor', *Geopolitics*, 11(2): 317–47.

Sim, Soek-Fang (2004), 'Dewesternising theories of authoritarianism: economics, ideology and the Asian Economic Crisis in Singapore', Working Paper No. 103, June 2004.

Sinitsyna, N. V. (1998), *Tretii Rim: Istoki i evolutsiya russkoi srednevekovoi kontseptsii (XV–XVI vv)*, Moscow: Indrik.

Sitze, A. (2010), 'A farewell to Schmitt: notes on the work of Carlo Galli', *CR: The New Centennial Review*, 10(2): 27–72.

Slater, D. (2010), *Ordering Power: Contentious Politics, State-Building, and Authoritarian Durability in Southeast Asia*, Cambridge: Cambridge University Press.

Slaughter, A. M. (2004), *A New World Order*, Princeton, NJ: Princeton University Press.

Smirnov, A. (2009), 'Ne nado zanimat'sya intellektual'nym moshennichestvom 2', *Russkii zhurnal*, 8 June, <http://www.russ.ru/pole/Ne-nado-zanimat-sya-intellektual-nym-moshennichestvom-2> (last accessed 7 June 2019).

Smirnov, G. N., I. A. Dmitrieva, V. E. Dmitriev and E. L. Bumagina (2016), *Geopolitika: teoriya i praktika – Voprosy i otvety*, Moscow: Prospekt.

Smith, H. (2016), 'Putin's third term and Russia as a great power', in M. Suslov and M. Bassin (eds), *Eurasia 2.0: Post-Soviet Geopolitics in the Age of New Media*, New York: Lexington Books, pp. 125–47.

Snow, D. A. and R. D. Benford (1992), 'Master frames and cycles of protest', in A. D. Morris and C. McClurg Mueller (eds), *Frontiers in Social Movement Theory*, New Haven, CT: Yale University Press, pp. 133–55.

Snyder, T. (2018), *The Road to Unfreedom: Russia, Europe, America*, London: Bodley Head.

Snyder, T. (2018b), 'Ivan Ilyin, Putin's philosopher of Russian fascism', *New York Review of Books*, 5 April, <https://www.nybooks.com/daily/2018/03/16/ivan-ilyin-putins-philosopher-of-russian-fascism/> (last accessed 7 June 2019).

Soldatov, A. and M. Rochlitz (2018), 'The siloviki in Russian politics', in D. Treisman (ed.), *The New Autocracy: Information, Politics and Policy in Putin's Russia*, Washington, DC: Brookings Institution Press, pp. 83–108.

Solomon, P. H. (1996), *Soviet Criminal Justice under Stalin*, Cambridge: Cambridge University Press.

Solomon, P. H. (2007), 'Courts and judges in authoritarian regimes', *World Politics*, 60(1): 122–45.

Solomon, P. H. (2008), 'Assessing the courts in Russia: parameters of progress under Putin', *International Journal for Court Administration*, 1(2): 26–32.

Solovei, V. (2004), 'Rossiya nakanune smuty', *Svobodnaya mysl'*, 21(12): 38–48, <www.intelros.org/lib/statyi/solovey1.htm> (last accessed 2 October 2019).

Solovyov, V. (2018), 'Moskva vygovorilas' v adres soyuznikov', *Kommersant*, 11 June, <https://www.kommersant.ru/doc/3656500> (last accessed 7 June 2019).

Solzhenitsyn, A. (1973), *The Gulag Archipelago, 1918–1956: An Experiment in Literary Investigation*, vols. 5–7, trans. by H. T. Willetts, London: Collins & Harvill Press.

Sonevytsky, M. (2019), 'Radio Meydan: "Eastern Music" and the liminal sovereign imaginaries of Crimea', *Public Culture*, 31(1): 93–116.

Souleimanov, E. and O. Ditrych (2008), 'The internationalisation of the Russian–Chechen conflict: myths and reality', *Europe–Asia Studies*, 60(7): 1199–1222.

Sova (2016), 'Russian March – 2016', 15 November, <https://www.sova-center.ru/en/xenophobia/news-releases/2016/11/d35822/> (last accessed 19 June 2019).

Spaiser, V., V. T. Chadefaux, K. Donnay, F. Russmann and D. Helbing (2017), 'Communication power struggles on social media: a case study of the 2011–12 Russian protests', *Journal of Information Technology & Politics*, 14(2): 132–53.

Stanovaya, T. (2015), '"Ne znayu" i "ne ponimayu": chto ne tak s Putinym?', Moscow Carnegie Center, 17 December, <carnegie.ru/commentary/?fa=62311> (last accessed 7 June 2019).

Stanovaya, T. (2017), 'Transformatsiya putinskikh elit: 2014–2024', Moscow Carnegie Center, 26 July, <http://carnegie.ru/2017/07/26/ru-pub-72625> (last accessed 7 June 2019).

Stanovaya, T. (2019), 'Every man for himself: the Russian regime turns on itself', Carnegie Moscow Centre, 22 May, <https://carnegie.ru/commentary/79158> (last accessed 24 June 2019).

Starikov, N. (2018), 'Kaspiiskoe more, gaz i "truba"', Izborsky club, 16 August, <https://izborsk-club.ru/15697> (last accessed 7 June 2019).

State Duma (2003), 'Stenogramma zasedaniya 29 December 2003', <http://transcript.duma.gov.ru/node/1386/> (last accessed 7 June 2019).

Stent, A. (2007), 'Reluctant Europeans: three centuries of Russian ambivalence toward the West', in R. Legvold (ed.), *Russian Foreign Policy in the Twenty-First Century and the Shadow of the Past*, New York: Columbia University Press.

Stephenson, S. (2011), 'The Kazan Leviathan: Russian street gangs as agents of social order', *The Sociological Review*, 59(2): 324–47.

Stiles, K. and W. Sandholtz (2009), *Cycles of International Norm Change*, Oxford: Oxford University Press.

Strauss, L. (1976), 'Comments on Carl Schmitt's "Der Begriff des Politischen"', in C. Schmitt, *The Concept of the Political*, trans. by G. Schwab, New Brunswick, NJ: Rutgers University Press.

Strauss, L. (2007), 'Notes on Carl Schmitt, *The Concept of the Political*', trans. by J. Harvey Lomax, in C. Schmitt, *The Concept of the Political*, Chicago: Chicago University Press, pp. 97–122.

Strong, T. B. (2007), 'Dimensions of the new debate around Carl Schmitt', in C. Schmitt, *The Concept of the Political*, trans. by G. Schwab, Chicago: University of Chicago Press, pp. ix–xxxi.

Strong, T. B. (2008), 'Foreword: Carl Schmitt and Thomas Hobbes – myth and politics', in C. Schmitt, *The Leviathan in the State Theory of Thomas Hobbes*, trans. by G. Schwab and E. Hilfstein, Chicago: University of Chicago Press, pp. vii–xxviii.

Strong, T. B. (2011), 'Carl Schmitt: political theology and the concept of the political', in C. H. Zuckert (ed.), *Political Philosophy in the Twentieth Century*, Cambridge: Cambridge University Press, pp. 32–43.
Sukhankin, S. (2017), 'Russia pours more military hardware into "Fortress Crimea"', *Eurasia Daily Monitor*, 14(147), 14 November, <https://jamestown.org/program/russia-pours-military-hardware-fortress-crimea/> (last accessed 7 June 2019).
Sunic, T. and A. de Benoist (2011), *Against Democracy and Equality: The European New Right*, London: Arktos.
Surkov, V. (2006a), 'Natsionalizatsiya budushchego: paragrafy pro suverennuyu demokratiyu', *Ekspert*, 43, <http://surkov.info/nacionalizaciya-budushhego-polnaya-versiya/> (last accessed 7 June 2019).
Surkov, V. (2006b), 'Suverenitet – eto politicheskii sinonim konkurentosposobnosti', in N. V. Garadzha (ed.), *Suverenitet*, Moscow: Evropa, pp. 43–79; also published by Rosbalt, 9 March, <http://www.rosbalt.ru/main/2006/03/09/246302.html> (last accessed 7 June 2019).
Surkov, V. (2008), 'Russian political culture: the view from utopia', *Russian Social Science Review*, 49(6): 81–97.
Surkov, V. (2018), 'The loneliness of the half-breed', *Russia in Global Affairs*, 28 May 2018, <https://eng.globalaffairs.ru/book/The-Loneliness-of-the-Half-Breed-19575> (last accessed 7 June 2019).
Surkov, V. (2019), 'Dolgoe gosudarstvo Putina', *Nezavisimaya gazeta*, 11 February, <http://www.ng.ru/ideas/2019-02-11/5_7503_surkov.html> (last accessed 7 June 2019).
Suslov, M. (2014), 'Mapping "Holy Russia": ideology and utopia in contemporary Russian Orthodoxy', *Russian Politics and Law*, 52(3): 67–86.
Suslov, M. (2018), 'Russian World concept: post-Soviet geopolitical ideology and the logic of "spheres of influence"', *Geopolitics*, 23(2): 330–53.
Svetlichnaja, J. and J. Heartfield (2010), 'Sovereign democracy: dictatorship over capitalism in contemporary Russia', *Radical Philosophy*, 159: 38–43.
Sytin, A. G. (2014), 'Smysl politiki po Karlu Shmittu i po Ivanu Il'inu: opyt sravnitel'nogo analiza', in E. N. Moshchelnikov and O. Yu. Boitsovaya (eds), *Filosofiya politiki i prava: Ezhegodnik nauchnykh rabot*, vyp. 5, Moscow: Tsentr strategicheskoi konyunktury, pp. 96–106.
Tang, W. (2016), *Populist Authoritarianism: Chinese Political Culture and Regime Sustainability*, New York: Oxford University Press.
Tansey, O. (2016), 'The problem with autocracy promotion', *Democratization*, 23(1): 141–63.
TASS (2014), 'Peskov: reshenie o vossoedinenii Kryma s Rossiei prinimal lichno Putin', *TASS*, 19 April, <http://tass.ru/politika/1133645> (last accessed 8 June 2019).
TASS (2017), 'Lavrov on IS destroying Palmyra monuments: barbarians are barbarians', *TASS*, 20 January, <http://tass.com/politics/926313> (last accessed 8 June 2019).

Taylor, B. (2011), *State Building in Putin's Russia: Policing and Coercion after Communism*, Cambridge: Cambridge University Press.

Teets, J. C. (2013), 'Let many civil societies bloom: the rise of consultative authoritarianism in China', *The China Quarterly*, 213: 19–38.

Teschke, B. G. (2011), 'Fatal attraction: a critique of Carl Schmitt's international political and legal theory', *International Theory*, 3(2): 179–227.

Teschke, B. (2016), 'Carl Schmitt's concepts of war', in J. Meierhenrich and O. Simons (eds), *The Oxford Handbook of Carl Schmitt*, Oxford: Oxford University Press, pp. 367–400.

Tilly, C. (1985), 'War making and state making as organized crime', in P. Evans, D. Rueschemeyer and T. Skocpol (eds), *Bringing the State Back*, Cambridge: Cambridge University Press.

Titaev, K. and I. Chetverikova (2017), 'Izbytochnaya kriminalizatsiya ekonomicheskoi deyatelnosti v Rossii: kak eto proiskhodit i chto s etim delat', Center for Strategic Research, Moscow, November, <https://www.csr.ru/news/izbytochnaya-kriminalizatsiya-ekonomicheskoj-deyatelnosti-v-rossii-kak-eto-proishodit-i-chto-s-etim-delat/ > (last accessed 21 June 2019).

Titayev, K. (2013), 'Rehabilitating the court system', *Moscow Times*, 5 June, <https://www.themoscowtimes.com/2013/06/05/rehabilitating-the-court-system-a24707> (last accessed 21 June 2019).

Toal, G. (2017), *Near Abroad: Putin, the West and the Contest over Ukraine and the Caucasus*, Oxford: Oxford University Press.

Tolstykh, V. (2014), 'Reunification of Crimea with Russia: a Russian perspective', *Chinese Journal of International Law*, 13(4): 879–86.

Tolstykh, V. (2015), 'Three ideas of self-determination in international law and the reunification of Crimea with Russia', *Heidelberg Journal of International Law (ZaöRV)*, 75: 119–39.

Tolstykh, V. L. (2019), 'The nature of Russian discourses on international law: a contemporary survey', in P. S. Morris (ed.), *Russian Discourses on International Law: Sociological and Philosophical Phenomenon*, Abingdon: Routledge, pp. 5–26.

Tolz, V. (2001), *Russia*, London: Arnold.

Treisman, D. (2011), 'Presidential popularity in a hybrid regime: Russia under Yeltsin and Putin', *American Journal of Political Science*, 55(3): 590–609.

Treisman, D. (2016), 'Crimea: anatomy of a decision', in D. Treisman (ed.), *The New Autocracy: Information, Politics, and Policy in Putin's Russia*, Washington, DC: Brookings, pp. 277–97.

Treisman, D. (ed.) (2018), *The New Autocracy: Information, Politics and Policy in Putin's Russia*, Washington, DC: Brookings Institution Press.

Trenin, D. (2011), *Post-Imperium: A Eurasian Story*, Washington, DC: Brookings Institution Press.

Trenin, D. (2015), 'Russian foreign policy as exercise in nation building', in D. Cadier and M. Light (eds), *Russia's Foreign Policy*, London: Palgrave Macmillan, pp. 30–41.

Trenin, D. (2016), 'The revival of the Russian military: how Moscow reloaded', *Foreign Affairs*, May–June, <https://www.foreignaffairs.com/articles/russia-fsu/2016-04-18/revival-russian-military> (last accessed 16 June 2019).

Trenin, D. (2019), 'Konturnaya karta rossiiskoi geopolitiki: vozmozhnaya strategiya Moskvy v Bol'shoi Yevrazii', Carnegie Center Moscow, 11 February, <https://carnegie.ru/commentary/78913> (last accessed 8 June 2019).

Trochev, A. (2017), 'The Russian Constitutional Court and the Strasbourg Court: judicial pragmatism in a dual state', in L. Mälksoo and W. Benedek (eds), *Russia and the European Court of Human Rights: The Strasbourg Effect*, Cambridge: Cambridge University Press, pp. 125–49.

Trochev, A. and P. H. Solomon, Jr (2018), 'Authoritarian constitutionalism in Putin's Russia: a pragmatic constitutional court in a dual state', *Communist and Post-Communist Studies*, 51(3): 201–14.

Tsygankov, A. P. (2006), *Russia's Foreign Policy: Change and Continuity in National Identity*, Lanham, MD: Rowman & Littlefield.

Tsygankov, A. P. (2007), 'Finding a civilisational idea: "West," Eurasia," and "Euro-East" in Russia's foreign policy', *Geopolitics*, 12(3): 375–99.

Tsygankov, A. P. (2016), 'Crafting the state-civilization: Vladimir Putin's turn to distinct values', *Problems of Post-Communism*, 63(3): 146–58.

Tsygankov, A. P. and P. A. Tsygankov (2010), 'National ideology and IR theory: three incarnations of the "Russian idea"', *European Journal of International Relations*, 16(4): 663–86.

Tsymbursky, V. (2007), *Ostrov Rossiya: Geopoliticheskie i khronopoliticheskie raboty*, Moscow: ROSSPEN.

Uehling, G. (2015), 'Genocide's aftermath: neostalinism in contemporary Crimea', *Genocide Studies and Prevention*, 9(1): 3–17.

Ulmen, G. L. (2003), 'Translator's introduction', in C. Schmitt, *The Nomos of the Earth in the International Law of Jus Publicum Europeaum*, trans. by G. L. Ulmen, New York: Telos Press, pp. 9–34.

Umland, A. (2007), *Post-Soviet 'Uncivil Society' and the Rise of Aleksandr Dugin: A Case Study of the Extraparliamentary Radical Right in Contemporary Russia*, Unpublished Phd Thesis, University of Cambridge.

Umland, A. (2009), 'Pathological tendencies in Russian "Neo-Eurasianism": the significance of the rise of Aleksandr Dugin for the interpretation of public life in contemporary Russia', *Russian Politics and Law*, 47(1): 76–89.

Umland, A. (2010), 'Aleksandr Dugin's transformation from a lunatic fringe figure into a mainstream political publicist, 1980–1998: a case study in the rise of late and post-Soviet Russian fascism', *Journal of Eurasian Studies*, 1(2): 144–52.

UN (2012a), 'Speech by Ambassador Churkin', UN Security Council meeting, New York, 4 February, S/PV.6711.

UN (2012b), 'Speech by Ambassador Churkin', UN Security Council meeting, New York, 19 July, S/PV.6810.

UN (2014), 'Speech by Ambassador Churkin', UN Security Council meeting, 22 May, S/PV.7180.

Vasiliev, A. (2017), 'Kakim budet novyi mir?', *Rossiiskaya gazeta*, 7 April, <https://rg.ru/2017/04/06/eksperty-rasskazali-o-griadushchem-fundamentalnom-sdvige-v-geopolitike.html> (last accessed 8 June 2019).

Vedemosti (2019), 'Bol'shinstvo rossiyan zametili protesty v Moskve i ne veryat vo vmeshatel'stvo Zapada', *Vedemosti*, 2 September, <https://www.vedomosti.ru/politics/articles/2019/09/02/810271-bolshinstvo-rossiyan-zametili> (last accessed 4 October 2019).

Verkhovskii, A. (2004), 'Serafimovskii klub: Romantika liberal'nogo konservatizma', *Neprikosnovennyi zapas*, 5(37), <http://magazines.russ.ru/nz/2004/37/ve4-pr.html> (last accessed 8 June 2019).

VestiFM (2017), 'Bunt majorov', Radio Vesti [transcript], <https://radiovesti.ru/brand/60948/episode/1511586/> (last accessed 19 June 2019).

Vinokurov, E. (2013), 'Pragmatic Eurasianism: prospects for Eurasian integration', *Russia in Global Affairs*, 2(2): 87–96.

Vinokurov, E. and A. Libman (2012), *Evraziiskaya kontinental'naya integratsiya*, St Petersburg: Eurasian Development Bank.

Virno, P. (2008), *Multitude: Between Innovation and Negation*, Los Angeles, CA: Semiotext(e).

Vladimirov, F. (2014), 'Tak chto zhe s Novorossiei? Ona utonula?', *Zavtra*, 10 August, <http://zavtra.ru/content/view/tak-chto-zhe-s-novorossiej-ona-utonula/> (last accessed 8 June 2019).

Vladykin, O. (2015), 'Dlya NATO tranzit zakryt', *Nezavisimaya gazeta*, 22 May, <http://nvo.ng.ru/nvo/2015-05-22/1_nato.html> (last accessed 8 June 2019).

Volkov, V. (2002), *Violent Entrepreneurs: The Use of Force in the Making of Russian Capitalism*, Ithaca, NY: Cornell University Press.

VTsIOM (2018), 'Conspiracy theory against Russia', Russian Public Opinion Research Center, 20 August, <https://wciom.com/index.php?id=61&uid=1570> (last accessed 24 June 2019).

Walker, S. (2017), *The Long Hangover: Putin's New Russia and the Ghosts of the Past*, Oxford: Oxford University Press.

Wall Street Journal (2014), 'Obama says Russia "on the wrong side of history"', *Wall Street Journal*, 3 March, <https://www.wsj.com/articles/obama-says-russia-on-the-wrong-side-of-history-1393879029> (last accessed 8 June 2019).

Weaver, C. (2014), 'The Russian billionaire linking Moscow to the rebels', *Financial Times*, 24 July, <https://www.ft.com/content/84481538-1103-11e4-94f3-00144feabdc0> (last accessed 8 June 2019).

Wegren, S. K. and A. Konitzer (2007), 'Prospects for managed democracy in Russia', *Europe–Asia Studies*, 59(6): 1025–47.

White House (2014), 'Press Release, the White House, statement by the Press Secretary on Ukraine', 16 March, <https://obamawhitehouse.archives.gov/the-press-office/2014/03/16/statement-press-secretary-ukraine> (last accessed 3 December 2019).

Whitmore, B. (2016), 'Russia's solitary man', RFE/RL, 15 August, <http://www.rferl.org/a/russias-solitary-man/27923437.html> (last accessed 8 June 2019).
Wiederkehr, S. (2010), '"Kontinent Evraziya": klassicheskoe evraziistvo i geopolitika v izlozhenii Aleksandra Dugina', *Forum noveishei vostochnoevropeiskoi istorii i kul'tury*, No. 1, <http://www1.ku-eichstaett.de/ZIMOS/forum/inhaltruss13.html> (last accessed 8 June 2019).
Wilkinson, C. (2014), 'Putting "traditional values" into practice: the rise and contestation of anti-homopropaganda laws in Russia', *Journal of Human Rights*, 13(3): 363–79.
Willerton, J. P., M. Beznosov and M. Carrier (2005), 'Addressing the challenges of Russia's failing state: the legacy of Gorbachev and the promise of Putin', *Demokratizatsiya*, 13(2): 219–39.
Wilson, A. L. (2017), 'The Crimean Tatar question after annexation: a prism for changing nationalisms and rival versions of Eurasianism', *Journal of Soviet and Post-Soviet Politics and Society*, 3(2): 1–45.
Wintour, P. (2018), 'Boris Johnson compares Russian World Cup to Hitler's 1936 Olympics', *Guardian*, 21 March, <https://www.theguardian.com/football/2018/mar/21/boris-johnson-compares-russian-world-cup-to-hitlers-1936-olympics> (last accessed 7 June 2019).
Yaffa, J. (2017), 'Oligarchy 2.0', *New Yorker*, 29 May, pp. 46–55.
Yampolsky, M. (2014), 'V strane pobedivshego resentimenta', *Colta.ru*, 6 October, <http://www.colta.ru/articles/specials/4887> (last accessed 8 June 2019).
Yanov, A. (1978), 'The drama of the Time of Troubles, 1725–30', *Canadian-American Slavic Studies*, 12(1): v–60.
Yanov, A. (1995), *Posle Yeltsina: 'Veymarskaya' Rossiya*, Moscow: Moskovskaya Gorodskaya Tipografiya A. S. Pushkina.
Yanov, A. (2016), 'Tak nachinalas' Rossiya', *Snob.ru*, 22 March, <https://snob.ru/profile/11778/blog/106122> (last accessed 8 June 2019).
Yefremenko, D. (2016), 'Rozhdenie Bol'shoi Evrazii', *Rossiya v globalnoi politike*, 28 November, <https://globalaffairs.ru/number/Rozhdenie-Bolshoi-Evrazii-18478> (last accessed 8 June 2019).
Yegorov, I. (2015), 'Patrushev: Tsel' SShA – oslabit' Rossiyu', *Rossiiskaya gazeta*, 10 February, <https://rg.ru/2015/02/10/patrushev-interviu-site.html> (last accessed 8 June 2019).
Yegorov, I. (2017), 'Patrushev rasskazal o vzaimodeistvii s SShA posle prikhoda Trampa', *Rossiiskaya gazeta*, 15 January, <https://rg.ru/2017/01/15/patrushev-rasskazal-o-vzaimodejstvii-s-ssha-posle-prihoda-trampa.html> (last accessed 8 June 2019).
Zevelev, I. (2014), 'The Russian World boundaries', *Russia in Global Affairs*, 2, <http://eng.globalaffairs.ru/number/The-Russian-World-Boundaries-16707> (last accessed 8 June 2019).
Zheng, Q. (2012), 'Carl Schmitt in China', *Telos*, 160: 29–52.
Zheng, Q. (2015), *Carl Schmitt, Mao Zedong and the Politics of Transition*, Basingstoke: Palgrave Macmillan.

Zhikharev, G. N., M. Mazzucchi, L. A. Ganeeva and V. N. Gavrilov (2015), '"Dialogi o vlasti": Vzglyadi Karla Schmitta na genezis vlasti i ee razvitie', *Uchenye zapiski Kazanskogo universiteta*, 157(6): 41–51.

Ziegler, C. E. (2012), 'Conceptualizing sovereignty in Russian foreign policy: realist and constructivist perspectives', *International Politics*, 49(4): 400–17.

Žižek, S. (1999), 'Carl Schmitt in the age of post-politics', in C. Mouffe (ed.), *The Challenge of Carl Schmitt*, London: Verso, pp. 18–37.

Zorkin, V. (2015), 'Pravo protiv khaosa', *Rossiiskaya gazeta*, 24 November, <https://rg.ru/2015/11/24/khaos.html> (last accessed 8 June 2019).

Zubarevich, N. (2011), 'Chetyre Rossii', *Vedomosti*, 30 December, <https://www.vedomosti.ru/opinion/articles/2011/12/30/chetyre_rossii#ixzz1i5AXIsIj> (last accessed 18 June 2019).

Zygar, M. (2015), *Vsya kremlevskaya rat': Kratkaya istoriya sovremennoi Rossii*, Moscow: Intellektual'naya literatura.

Zygar, M. (2016), *All the Kremlin's Men: Inside the Court of Vladimir Putin*, New York: Public Affairs.

INDEX

Agamben, Giorgio, 34, 63, 78, 196
Akhiezer, Aleksander, 8
Arab Spring
   destabilisation threat from, xi, 104, 165
   Russia's response to, 181, 189, 205
Arendt, Hannah, 153, 154, 158, 173, 218–19
Atlanticism, 37, 110, 168
authoritarianism
   assertion of sovereignty through exceptionality, 22
   comparative, 3
   democratic authoritarianism, 81, 85–6
   ideology and, 3–5
   and the *katechontic* order, 196
   legalism and political decisionism in, 118
   new institutionalist approach, 3
   norm/exception relationship within, 77–9
   politicisation of the rule of law, 127
   Russia as a hybrid regime, 81
   Russia's new form of, vii, viii, xiii, 1–3, 216–17
   threat construction discourses, 4–5

Balakrishnan, Gopal, ix
Benoist, Alain de, 28, 29, 34, 36
bureaucracy
   manual control system for governance, 75–6
   problems of implementation, 74–5

Bush, George W., 53
businesses
   illegal corporate raiding, 130
   use of the legal system, 121–2
   see also oligarchs

Central Asia, 188
Chaika, Yuri, 131, 132
chaos
   applied to Syria, 207
   conservatism as force against chaos, 203–4
   within historical cycles, 4, 8–9
   the *katechon* figure and, 195–6, 204, 217, 221
   links between international and domestic order, 16–17
   personal experiences of chaos, 10, 11–12
   post-Soviet understandings of order, 10–12
   prioritisation of democracy over, 6–7, 10, 11
   within Putinism, 7–8, 216–17
   Russia as a bulwark against, xii, 193, 196–7, 203, 204–5, 212, 217
   Russia's crisis of the 1990s, viii, 9–10
   within a state of exceptionalism, 62, 63
   see also international order (*nomos*); order; political order

Chechnya
  during the 1990s, 10
  human rights in, 135
  non-declaration of state of emergency in, 62
  separatism of, 10, 51
  as a space of exception, 62–3
China, ix, 187
civilisation thesis
  barbarism/civilisation discourse in Syria, 207–8, 210
  and international relations, 167–8
  Russia's messianic discourse and, 193, 197
Clinton, Hillary, 98
colour revolutions
  Russia's reaction to, 105–6, 188–9
  as threat against Russia, xi, 16, 49, 104, 106, 165, 184, 189
conservatism
  conservative values agenda, 96–7
  history of, 24–5
  human rights and, 183
  influence of the European New Right (ENR), 28–9
  Ivan Ilyin's thought on political totalitarianism, 27–8
  Izborsky Club, 45–6
  katechontic thinking and, 200–3
  liberal conservatism, 25, 45
  located conservatism, 42
  new conservatives, 41
  Orthodox political conservatism, 27, 181–2
  and the politics of the majority, 92–6
  radical conservatism, vii, 25–8, 46
  reframing of the liberalism discourse, 60–1
  in Russia's foreign policy, 182–5, 203–4
  Schmitt's influence on, 29–30, 31–5, 45–6, 53
  sovereign status of Vladimir Putin, 66–7
  and traditional values, 182–3
  understandings of sovereignty, 53
  see also Dugin, Alexander; Remizov, Mikhail

Convention on the Legal Status of the Caspian Sea, 188
corruption
  amongst political elites, 3
  illegal corporate raiding, 130
  in the legal domain, 126–7
  in the procuracy (*prokuratura*), 132–3
  of Russian democracy in the 1990s, 86
Crimea
  annexation of, 55, 111, 139–40, 144–9, 153, 155
  Crimean Tatars, 156–8
  the friend–enemy distinction and, 156
  the general will of the people, 149–51
  involvement of non-state actors/ Night Wolves, 76
  Putin's decision to annex, 140–3
  RCC's ruling on, 122
  redrawn geography of, 156
  Russian World concept and, 172
  Russia's defence of the annexation of, 144–9
  as a sacral land to Russia, 155, 157
  as sovereignty asserted through exceptionalism, 139–40
Crimean Consensus, 114–15, 150

decision-making
  autonomous sovereign decision-making, 70–1, 72–3, 141, 142–3
  decision-making process of Putinism, 68–71
  exceptionalist decision-making by the sovereign, 22, 23, 37, 43–5, 61–3
  incidences of poor sovereign decision-making, 73
  information sources for, 73–4
  institutional measures for the implementation of, 74–5
  and internal sovereignty, 51
  Putin's decision to annex Crimea, 140–3
  regional sovereign decision-making powers, 52, 64–6
  sovereignty as the freedom to choose, 52–3, 55
  weak Russian state in the 1990s, 64

democracy
  corruption of in the 1990s, 86
  democracy/dictatorship binary, 6–7, 84
  democratic authoritarianism, 81, 85–6
  homogeneity in, 83–4
  identitarian democracy, 83
  liberal democracy, 82, 83, 84
  managed democracy, x, 86–8
  mass popular opinion within democratic authoritarianism, 81, 85–6
  parliamentarianism as a sham, 82, 86–7
  prioritisation of over order, 6–7, 10, 11
  and Putinism, 81–6, 97
  representation within, 82–5
  Russia as a hybrid regime, 81
  Russia's democratic status, 2
  Russia's managed democracy, 86–8
  Schmitt's theory of, 82–6
  a strong state as a prerequisite for, 7–8
  Surkov's Sovereign Democracy concept, 33, 52, 58–9, 81–2, 172
  threat of political pluralism, 20–1
democratisation theory, 2, 6
dictatorships
  commissary dictatorships, 61
  democracy/dictatorship binary, 6–7, 84
  Ivan Ilyin's admiration for, 27–8
dual states
  dualist legal domains, 118, 122–3, 125–6, 129–30
  theory of, 77–9
Dugin, Alexander
  application of the *Großraum* theory to Russia, 168–9
  dissemination of Schmitt's thinking, 35, 36, 37
  as a Eurasianist, 39, 168, 174
  on the fifth column, 109–10
  the Fourth Political Theory of, 39–40
  influence on Russian conservatism, 36, 40–1
  interpretation of Schmitt's geopolitics, 38–9, 168
  as a political thinker, 35–6, 43
  on Russia as *katechon*, 200, 201–2
  on Russia's enemies, 102–3
  Schmitt's influence on, 36–40, 46
  sixth column notion, 110
  on Ukraine, 91
'Dulles Plan', 103–4

Economic Security Service (SEB), 133–4
economics
  dependence on external finance, 55–6
  prosecutions of economic cases, 133
  sovereign globalization strategy, 56–7
elections
  abolition of elections for regional governors, 64–6
  managed democracy, 86–8
  parliamentarianism as a sham, 82, 86–8
  representation of the people, 82–5
elites, political
  collective resentment discourses, 13–14
  conceptual maps of the political world, 4
  influence of conservatism on, 26–7
  perception of Russia's role in the world, xii–xiii
  Russia as a kleptocracy, 3
  utility maximisation theories, 2–3
enemies
  Crimean Consensus, 114–15
  discourse of the fifth column, 108–12
  Dulles Plan, 103–4
  existential meaning of, 101–2
  friend/enemy distinction and the political community, 22–3, 35, 37, 100–2, 115–16, 156, 219–20
  identification of by the state, 101
  internal enemies, 110–11
  legal identification of, 113

new discourses of the West as, 105-8
NGOs as foreign agents, 112-13
personal enemies, 100-1
and the possibility of war, 101
public enemies, 100-1
sixth column notion, 110
the US as an existential threat, 104, 108, 114
the West as Russia's enemy, historically, 102-5
Eurasianism
  Alexander Dugin as a Eurasianist, 39, 168, 174
  alternative versions of, 173-4
  Eurasia vs. Atlanticism, 36-7, 38
  Eurasian turn in Russia's foreign policy, 169-70, 173, 174
  as a Great Space, xii, 39
  'Greater Eurasia' idea, 174
  neo-Eurasianists, 25, 27, 39
  promotion of traditional values, 182-3
  Russian hegemony within, 174
  and Russian national identity, 12-13
  in Russian spatial thinking, 38
European Convention on Human Rights (ECHR), 120
European Court of Human Rights (ECtHR), 120-1, 122, 129
European New Right (ENR), 28-9, 36
exceptionalism
  assertion of sovereignty through exceptionality, xi, xiii, 22, 43-5, 50, 61-3, 139-40
  Chechnya as a space of exception, 62-3
  contradictions of the state of, 62-3, 219
  contrasted with the normative state, 77-9
  exceptionalist decision-making by the sovereign, 22, 23, 37, 43-5, 61-3
  in foreign policy, 139-40
  and the general will of the people, 150-1
  institutional measures for the implementation of, 74-5

  in the legal domain, xi, 118, 122-3, 125-6, 130-8
  manual control system for governance, 75-6
  Moscow as the 'Third Rome', 193, 198-9, 200, 202
  norm/exception distinction and the rule of law, 77-9, 122-3, 125-6, 129-30, 137-8
  order within, 62, 63
  and the Russian experience, 63-4
  in Schmitt's writing, 18, 37
  systemic duality of, 219
existentialism
  existential threat to the state, viii, 8-9, 16, 18, 22, 27, 30, 37
  friend/enemy distinction and the political community, 101-2
  politics as an existential moment, 44-5
  sovereignty as subjectivity in international relations, 55
  the US as Russia's existential threat, 104, 108, 114
  view of the world order, 170-1

fascism, 27-8, 40, 43, 153; see also Nazi regime
Federal Security Service (FSB)
  Economic Security Service (SEB), 133-4
  involvement in exceptional legal cases, 133
  Putin's intelligence briefings, 74
Filippov, Alexander, 30-3, 34, 35, 43, 46, 51, 70, 73
foreign policy
  exceptionalism in, 139-40
  Great Spaces theory in, 190-1
  sovereignty within US foreign policy, 53-4
  use of non-state actors, 76-7
  see also international relations
foreign policy, Russian
  alternative to liberal globalisation, xi-xii, xiii
  assertion of sovereignty through exceptionality, xi, 140-3

foreign policy, Russian (*cont.*)
  conservative turn in, 182–5, 203–4
  and defence of national sovereignty, 50–1
  differential understanding of sovereignty in, 176–7
  Eurasian turn in, 169–70, 173, 174
  exclusion of foreign powers, 186
  geopolitical turn in, 38–9, 143, 162, 165–8
  'Great Power thinking', 166, 170, 172
  Great Spaces theory and, 168, 169, 171
  Island Russia idea, 175–6
  messianic discourse, 193, 197, 198
  models of sovereignty within, 178
  Putin's decision to annex Crimea, 140–3
  Russia as a hegemonic power, 176–9
  Russia as 'the restrainer', 203–4
  Russian World concept, 172–3
  Russia's sense of exclusion under the Western order, xi
  spheres of influence, xii, xiii, 166, 167, 175, 178
Fourth Political Theory (Dugin), 39–40
Fraenkel, Ernst, 77–8, 123

al-Gaddafi, Muammar, 205–6
Gelman, Vladimir, 3, 4
Georgia
  colour revolutions, xi, 16, 49, 188
  in relation to Russian hegemony, 179
German Conservative Revolution, 43
Germany
  language and the interpretation of political concepts, 59
  Molotov–Ribbentrop Pact, 161–2, 168
  post-WW II allied liberal imperialism, 54
  Weimar Germany, 12, 13, 17, 30
Golunov, Ivan, 126
Great Spaces theory (*Großraum* order)
  adaptation of the Monroe Doctrine, 163–4, 185–6
  as an alternative to US hegemony, 164, 165
  applied to Russia, 168, 169, 171
  concept of, 151, 162, 163–5, 171
  in contemporary foreign policies, 190–1
  Dugin's reworking of, 168–9
  exclusion of foreign powers, 180–1, 185–9
  fundamental contradictions of, 220–1
  great powers within, 170, 176
  land/sea distinction, 164, 168
  Russia as hegemonic power, 171, 176–9
  Russia's great political idea and, 171, 179–85
  Russia's spatial projects, 171–6
  sovereignty of hegemons and ordinary states, 176–8
grievance narratives, 14–15
Gumilev, Lev, 26, 29
Gusinsky, Vladimir, 127, 133

history
  chaos/order within historical cycles, 4, 8–9
  Christian eschatology, 194
  Crimea as a sacral land, 155, 157
  the Molotov–Ribbentrop Pact, 161–2, 168
  the partisan figure in, 38, 154–5, 157
  role of *katechon* in, 195
  Russia as Europe's defender, 199, 208
  Russian messianic discourse, 197–200
  smuta (Time of Troubles), 8–9, 16
human rights
  activists as 'foreign agents', 109, 113
  in Chechnya, 62, 135
  European Convention on Human Rights (ECHR), 120
  European Court of Human Rights (ECtHR), 120–1, 122
  the 'humanitarian' intervention in Crimea, 144–5

LGBT rights, 94–5, 183
  and the majority view, 95
  political prisoners, 129
  and Russian conservatism, 183
  as a Western anti-Russia tool, xi, 27
Huntington, Samuel, 7, 42, 167

ideology
  of authoritarian regimes, 3–5
  defined, 5
  language and the interpretation of political concepts, 58–9
  of Putinism, 5–6, 82
illiberal politics
  Dugin's anti-liberalism (Fourth Political Theory), 39–40
  within global politics, vii–viii
  illiberal democracies, 18, 83–5
  managed democracies, x, 86–8
  renaissance of Carl Schmitt's thought, ix
Ilyin, Ivan, x, 25, 26, 27–8, 43
imperialism
  as distinct from land appropriation, 153
  katechon, and revival of empire, 212–13
Institute for Socio-Economic and Political Research (Foundation ISEPR), 45
institutions
  European legal institutions, 120–1, 122
  and the implementation of exceptional decision-making, 74–5
  informal institutions, 3
  manual control system for governance, 76–7
  new institutionalist approach, 3
  the procuracy (*prokuratura*), 131–3
  relations with the state, 65
  Soviet experiences of order/chaos, 10–11
international law
  alternative views of, 139
  annexation of Crimea as violation of, 144–6

civilisation thesis and, 167
concept of a *Großraum* and, 164
discourse of Western hypocrisy in, 146–8
European jurisprudence, 195
Russian scholarship on, 145–6
spatial aspects of, 150, 151
universalist conceptualisation of international law, 147–8
international order (*nomos*)
  nomos, term, 151, 152
  the political in, 151–2
  spatial division in, 151, 152, 164, 170–1
  through land appropriation, 140, 152–4, 158–9
international relations
  civilisationists, 167–8, 193
  conservative/realist debates on Russia's role, 166–7
  future geopolitical loneliness of Russia, 175
  geopolitical aims masked as minority protection, 180–1
  liberal imperialism, post-WW II, 54
  Molotov–Ribbentrop Pact, 161–2, 168
  revision of hegemony, 170–1
  Russia as hegemonic power, 176–9
  Russia's rejection of liberal world order, 15–16, 162–3, 175
  Schmittian thought on, 163
  sovereignty as Russian subjectivity, 52–5, 58, 175
  spatial theory of, 162
  spheres of influence, 166, 167, 175, 178
  statist positions, 167
  threat of US-led unipolar world, viii, xi–xii, 16, 52, 53–4, 104, 165
  Treaty of Friendship, Cooperation and Partnership, 144
  universalism-pluralism binary, 163, 180
  the West's hybrid war against Russia, 54–5
  see also foreign policy

Investigative Committee, 132–3
Izborsky Club, 45–6

Jünger, Ernst, 29, 30, 33, 35, 36, 43

Karaganov, Sergei, 14–15, 54, 60, 175, 184, 185, 210
katechon
  as the Antichrist, 196
  Biblical figure of, 194
  moral contradictions of *katechontic* thinking, 210–12, 221
  Orthodox conceptions of, 196, 200–2
  as the producer of order, 195–7
  and the revival of empire, 212–13
  Russia as, 200–6
  Russia as 'the restrainer', 194, 202, 203–4
  Russia in Syria, 206–10
  and Russia's messianic discourse, 197, 198–9, 202
  in Schmittian thought, xii, 194–7
  shield ideology and, 201, 204
Katehon.com, 202–3
Khodorkovsky, Mikhail, 56, 86, 117, 128, 133, 136
Kholmogorov, Yegor, 58, 94–5, 200, 201, 204
Kildyushov, Oleg, 29–30, 34–5
Kosovo, 146
Kyrgyzstan
  colour revolutions, xi, 49, 188
  in relation to Russian hegemony, 179
  temporary US military bases, 187

language
  anti-terrorist discourses, 204
  anti-Western discourses, 105–8, 146–8
  barbarism/civilisation discourse in Syria, 207–8, 210
  discourse of the fifth column, 108–12
  information warfare, 58–61
  and power in Schmittian thought, 59
  Russian reframing of the discourse of liberalism, 60–1
  Russia's discursive dilemma, 34–5
  threat construction discourses, 4–5
  see also messianic discourse
Lavrov, Sergei, 145, 181, 204–5, 207
the law
  acquittal rates, 134–5
  courts and judges in exceptional cases, xi, 134–6
  as a dualistic legalist and decisionist domain, 118, 122–3, 125–6, 129–30
  Federal Security Service (FSB), 133–4
  Fraenkel's conceptualisation of, 123
  high-profile political cases, 127–9
  illegal corporate raiding, 130
  impact of Council of Europe institutions, 120–1, 122
  institution of the procuracy (*prokuratura*), 131–3
  international perceptions of Russia's judicial system, 117–18
  the Investigative Committee, 132–3
  legal identification of enemies, 113
  legal reforms under Putin, 117, 120
  legality/legitimacy distinction, 119, 124–5, 144
  mechanisms of exception, 130–6
  and modern-day Russian business practices, 121–2
  norm/exception distinction, 77–9, 122–3, 125–6, 129–30, 137–8
  politicisation of, 126–31
  prosecutions-to-order cases, 126
  in Russia, 119–23
  Russian Constitutional Court (RCC), 122–3
  Schmitt's conceptualisation of, 118, 123–6, 147–8, 158
  Soviet legal system, 119–20
  spatial aspects of, 125, 150, 151
  subordination of the legal system to sovereign will, 131
  'telephone justice', 120, 131, 135
  in territorial possession, 140
  see also international law

LGBT rights, 94–5, 183
liberal conservatism, 25, 45
liberalism
   collapse of in Russia, 24
   critique of post-war liberal order, 15–16, 17, 18, 153, 154, 162–3, 175, 180
   as intrinsically dull, 221–2
   liberal democracy, 82, 83, 84
   rejection of, vii–viii
   in relation to political differences, 20
   Russian reframing of the discourse of liberalism, 60–1
   and universalism, 180
Libya, 205–6

manual control system for governance, 75–6
Markov, Sergei, 96
Medvedev, Dmitry, 45, 67, 98, 104, 205
Medvedev, Sergei, 13
Merkel, Angela, 161
messianic discourse
   historic narrative of, 197–8
   historical readings of, 199–200
   and the *katechontic* order, 197, 198–9, 202
   Moscow as the 'Third Rome', 193, 198–9, 200, 202
   Russia as Europe's defender, 199, 208
   in Russian foreign policy, 193, 197, 198
Mikhailovsky, Alexander, 31, 33–4, 35
military policy
   intervention in Syria, 57, 208, 210
   militarisation of the Crimean peninsula, 156
   'New Look' military reform policy, 57
   use of non-state actors, 76–7
   US-Russia relations, 104–5
Minin, Kuzma, 16–17, 91
Molotov–Ribbentrop Pact, 161–2
Monroe Doctrine, 163–4, 185–6
morality
   conservative values agenda, 96–7
   politics of the majority, 94–5
   silent moral majority, 96
   the sovereign position and, 68

Narochnitskaya, Natalya, 27, 200
Nashi movement, 106, 109, 112
national identity
   attainment of sovereignty as, 55
   charismatic leadership and, 13
   construction of political unity, 88–9
   Crimean Consensus, 114–15, 150
   loss of during the 1990s, 12–13, 23
   politics of the majority, 92–6
   power of collective resentment, 13–14
   in relation to Orthodoxy, 24, 91
   Soviet era, 89
   spatial visions of, 171–2
nationalism
   Crimean Consensus, 114–15
   Day of National Unity, 16, 91–2
   ethnic Russians outside the Federation, 92
   Nashi movement, 106, 109, 112
   'Novorossiya' project, 172–3
   Russian nationalism, 89–92
   statist vs. ethnic nationalist concepts of, 90–2
Navalny, Alexei, 98, 114, 117, 123, 129, 132, 136
Nazarov, Mikhail, 200
Nazi regime
   as a dual state, 77
   expansionism, 153, 162
   Ivan Ilyin's association with, 28
   Molotov–Ribbentrop Pact, 161–2, 168
   the political idea of, 180
   Schmitt's association with, ix, 17, 19
   soil imagery of, 154
Nemtsov, Boris, 107, 109, 111–12
new conservatives, 41
Night Wolves, 76, 92, 112
non-governmental organisations (NGOs), 112–13
norms
   norm/exception distinction and the rule of law, 77–9, 125–6
   norms and values in relations with NATO, 186–7

North Atlantic Treaty Organization
    (NATO)
  Central Asian resupply routes, 188
  and Crimea, 156
  expansion of, 55, 104, 145, 186
  hybrid warfare against Russia, 54
  spatial exclusion of from Russian
    space, 186–7
  threat to Russian security, 105, 145
Nouvelle Droite (ND), 28, 43

Obama, Barack, xii
oligarchs
  political powers of, 52, 64, 86, 110
  politicised justice cases against,
    127–9
  prosecutions of economic cases,
    133–4
  Putin's campaign against, x, 3, 15,
    49, 93, 117
order
  appropriation of land for order
    (*nomos*), 152–4, 158–9
  contrasted with utopia, 42
  the *katechon* as the producer of,
    195–7
  order/orientation emphasis, 42,
    151, 154
  reestablishment of in Putinism, 7–8,
    216–17
  reestablishment of through
    exceptional decision-making, 50
  within a state of exceptionalism,
    62, 63
  through spatial division, 151, 152
  see also chaos; international order
    (*nomos*); political order
Organisation for Security and
  Cooperation in Europe
  (OSCE), 181
Orthodoxy
  conservative tradition of, 27, 181–2
  and national identity, 24, 91
  Russia as *katechon*, 196, 200–2
  Russian messianic discourse,
    197–200
  Russian Orthodox Church (ROC),
    181–2

Patrushev, Nikolai, 105
Pavlovsky, Gleb, 14, 35, 69, 74, 75,
    105, 213
the people
  homogeneity amongst, 83–4
  mass popular opinion within
    democratic authoritarianism, 81,
    85–6
  within Putinism, 82
  representation of, 82–5
  and Schmitt's concept of the law,
    158
pluralism
  international pluralism, 61, 184
  as a threat to political order, 20–2,
    61, 64
  universalism-pluralism binary, 163,
    180, 184
the political
  and antagonism, 19–20, 44–5
  exceptionalist decision-making,
    43–5
  existential nature of, 102
  in the international order, 151–2
  politics-the political distinction,
    19–20, 44–5, 100
  in relation to political communities,
    219–20
political communities
  construction of political unity,
    88–9
  defined through the friend/enemy
    distinction, 22–3, 35, 37, 100–2,
    115–16, 156, 219–20
  homogeneity in, 83–4, 89
  the political and, 219–20
  politics of the majority, 92–6,
    149–51
  Russian nationalism, 89–92
political order
  conceptual maps of the political
    world, 4
  link between international and
    domestic order, 16–17
  political pluralism as threat to,
    20–2, 61
  prioritisation of democracy over
    order, 6–7, 10, 11

Schmittian managed democracy, x
Schmitt's conceptualisation of,
  19–20
through a strong state, 7–8, 9, 11
through opposition to the West,
  15–16
through strong leaders, 67–8
see also chaos; order
power
  dispersal of state power through
    pluralism, 20–2, 61, 64
  dispersal of to Putin's inner
    circle, 70
  hegemonic power, 179
  of information flows to the decision-
    maker, 73–4
  and language in Schmittian
    thought, 59
  of the oligarchs, 52, 64, 86, 110
  power of collective resentment,
    13–14
  recentralisation of within the state,
    52, 64–6
  Russia as hegemonic power, 171,
    176–9
  spatial aspects of, 71–3
  spheres of influence, 166, 167,
    175, 178
  unrestrained sovereign power
    problem, 73, 217–18
Pozharsky, Dmitry, 16–17, 91
Prigozhin, Yevgeny, 76
public holidays, Russian, 16, 45,
  91–2
Pussy Riot, 96
Putin, Vladimir
  as an autonomous sovereign
    decision-making agent, 70–1,
    72–3, 141, 142–3
  civilisationism during his third term,
    167, 193
  comparison with Nicholas I, 222
  criticism of non-governmental
    organisations (NGOs), 112
  decision to annex Crimea, 140–3
  decision-making processes and the
    inner circle of, 68–71
  early relations with the West, 15
  flexible ideology of, 5
  'Great Power thinking', 166
  'Greater Eurasia' idea, 174
  importance of state subjectivity,
    52–3, 55
  intelligence briefings, 73–4
  katechontic thinking, 203, 204
  liberal conservative position, 25
  on the Molotov–Ribbentrop
    Pact, 161
  outsider image of, 13–14, 93
  personal experiences of state
    chaos, 10
  on political order, 7
  politicised justice cases, 127–8
  on the politics of the majority, 95
  presidential decrees, 75
  regional policies of, 64–6
  relationship with ethnic
    nationalism, 90–1
  as representing the majority of the
    population, 92–3, 95, 96–7, 98,
    149–50
  response to the fall of Gaddafi,
    205–6
  on Russia's integration into Eurasia,
    169–70
  sovereign status of, 66–7
  sovereignty during the second term
    of, 49–51
  use of term 'fifth column', 111
  on the US-led unipolar world,
    53–4, 104
  US-Russian relations under Putin,
    104–5
  vision of democracy, 97
'Putinism'
  as backlash against liberalism, vii
  decision-making process of,
    68–71
  and democracy, 81–6
  within global politics, vii
  ideology of, 5–6, 82
  as a paradigm/ideational aspects
    of, 6
  political order through a strong
    state, 7–8, 9, 11
  rise of, vii–viii, 2

radical conservatism, vii, 25-8, 46
Remizov, Mikhail
  on the Conservative Revolution, 43
  exceptionalist decision-making, 43-5
  as a new conservative thinker, 41, 202
  on the rights of the majority, 93
  on the Russian experience, 63
  Schmitt's influence on, 41-5, 46
resentment
  collective resentment discourses, 13-14
  myth of the West's satisfaction at Russia's collapse, 13, 14-15, 27
Russia
  analogy with Weimar Germany, 12-13
  Bolotnaya protests, 98-9, 132
  conception of political order, viii-ix
  crisis of the 1990s, viii, 9, 12, 26
  demographics, 88-9
  historical mission of, xii-xiii
  membership of the OSCE, 181
  the State Duma under managed democracy, 86-8
Russian Constitutional Court (RCC), 122-3
Russian Orthodox Church (ROC), 181-2; *see also* Orthodoxy

Schmitt, Carl
  appropriation of land for order (*nomos*), 140, 152-4, 158-9
  assertion of sovereignty through exceptionality, 43-5, 139-40
  on the concept of humanity, 147
  conceptualisation of political order, 19-20
  construction of political unity, 88
  contemporary relevance of, ix, 215-16, 222
  convergence with the Nazi regime, 17, 19, 32-3, 40, 162
  critique of post-war liberal order, 17, 18, 153, 154
  critiques of the League of Nations, 54
  early writings in the context of Weimar, x, 12, 17-18, 20, 30
  friend/enemy distinction and the political community, 22-3, 35, 37, 100, 115-16
  global influence of, ix-x
  influence on Alexander Dugin, 36-40, 46
  influence on Mikhail Remizov, 41-5
  influence on Russian conservatism, 29-30, 31-5
  influence on the European New Right (ENR), 29
  on the internal enemy, 110
  the *katechon* figure, xii, 194-7
  language and the practice of sovereignty, 59
  legality/legitimacy distinction, 118, 119, 144
  on the Molotov-Ribbentrop Pact, 162, 168
  morality and sovereignty, 68
  norm/exception and the law, 118
  order/orientation emphasis, 42, 151, 154
  the partisan figure, 38, 154-5, 157
  politics/the political distinction, 19-20, 44-5, 100
  prerogative/normative state relationship, 77-8
  rejection of the mundane, 221-2
  in relation to civilisational thinking, 167, 168
  on representation of the people, 82-5
  the role of the people, 85-6
  Russian scholarship on, 30-5
  and Russia's new authoritarianism, 216-17
  on sovereignty, x, 18, 22, 32, 35, 50, 51, 61-2, 66
  spatial access to power, 72
  spatial aspects of the law, 125, 150, 151
  spatial theory of international relations, 140, 162
  on the supremacy of the state, 18
  theory of democracy, 82-6

theory of land appropriation, 140, 158–9
on the threat of political pluralism, 20–2
treatise on Thomas Hobbes's *Leviathan*, 218
understandings of the law, 118, 123–6, 147–8, 158
unrestrained sovereign power problem, 217–18
on utopia, 42
see also Great Spaces theory (*Großraum* order)
Senderov, Valery, 30, 41, 45–6
smuta (Time of Troubles), 8–9, 16
social media
anti-Western discourses on, 106–8
interaction with television programmes, 107
pro-Putin campaigns, 107
trolling factories, 76, 107
sovereignty
assertion of sovereign power, 63–8
assertion of sovereignty through exceptionality, xi, xiii, 22, 23, 37, 43–5, 50, 61–3, 139–40
autonomous sovereign decision-making agent, 70–1, 72–3, 141, 142–3
conceptualisations of political leadership, 67–8
debates over during Putin's second term, 49–51
disaggregated sovereignty, 51
discursive sovereignty, 58–61
in Great Spaces theory, 176–8
military capacity and, 57
moral position of, 68
overlap of internal and external meanings of, 51
Putin's decision to annex Crimea, 140–3
as Russian subjectivity, 52–5, 58, 175
during Russia's crisis of the 1990s, 10
within Russia's foreign policy, 178
Schmitt's understanding of, x, 18, 22, 32, 35, 50, 51, 61–2, 66

sovereign status of Vladimir Putin, 66–7
state's freedom to choose, x, 52–5, 58
subordination of the legal system to sovereign will, 131
Surkov's Sovereign Democracy concept, 33, 52, 58–9, 81–2, 172
and territorial integrity, 50–1
threat of political pluralism to, 20–2
unrestrained sovereign power problem, 73, 217–18
Soviet Union (USSR)
legal system, 119–20
national identity during, 89
understandings of order, 10–11
spatiality
access to power and, 71–3
ethnic Russians outside the Federation, 92
'Greater Russia' concept, 92
Island Russia idea, 175–6
land appropriation for spatial order, 140, 152–4, 158–9
land/sea distinction, 164, 168
the partisan figure in, 38, 154–5, 157
and the political idea, 179, 187
the rule of law and, 125, 150, 151
Russia as hegemonic power, 176–9
Russian World concept, 172–3
Russia's identity crisis and, 12–13, 23
spatial division in the international order, 151, 152, 164, 170–1
spheres of influence, xii, xiii, 166, 167, 175, 178
the state of exception, 62–3
theory of land appropriation, 140, 158–9
see also Eurasianism; Great Spaces theory (*Großraum* order)
the state
dual state theory, 77–9
existential threats to, viii, 8–9, 16, 18, 22, 27, 30, 37
identification of the enemy, 101
political order through a strong state, 7–8, 9, 11
recentralisation of decision-making power within, viii, 52, 64–6

the state (*cont.*)
  in relation to the political, 20
  relations with institutions, 65
  role in international relations, 163
  within Sovereign Democracy, 52
  supremacy of in Schmitt's writing, 18
  threat of political pluralism to, 20-2, 61, 64
  weak Russian state in the 1990s, 64
  Weberian definition of, 61
strong leaders, 67-8
Surkov, Vladislav
  challenge of Western hegemonic discourse, 60-1
  concern over colour revolution, 49
  on democracy, 81
  future geopolitical loneliness of Russia, 175
  'Great Power thinking', 170
  ideology of Putinism, xiii, 5-6, 82
  on internal/external sovereignty, 51-2
  Sovereign Democracy concept, 33, 52, 58-9, 81-2, 172
Syria
  barbarism/civilisation discourse, 207-8, 210
  chaos/order conceptual binary, 207
  Russia's intervention in, xii, 57, 208, 210
  Russia's use of UN veto, 209-10

terrorism, 204
traditional values, 182-3
Tsymbursky, Vadim, 175-6

Ukraine
  colour revolutions, xi, 16, 49, 188
  'Novorossiya' project, 172-3
  ousting of Yanukovich, 68, 141
  in relation to Russian hegemony, 178-9
  Russian World concept and, 13, 172
  Russia's incursion into, 90-1
  Treaty of Friendship, Cooperation and Partnership, 144
United States of America (USA)
  alt-right, ix, 29
  Central Asian resupply routes, 188
  Dulles Plan, 103-4
  hybrid war against Russia, 54-5
  Monroe Doctrine, 163-4, 185-6
  National Defense Strategy (2018), 165-6
  as Russia's existential threat, 104, 108, 114
  Russia's understanding of the foreign policy of, 15-16
  temporary US military bases, 187
  US-led unipolar world, xi-xii, 16, 52, 53-4, 104, 165
  US-Russian relations under Putin, 104-5
universalism
  universalism-pluralism binary, 163, 180, 184
  universalist conceptualisation of international law, 147-8
utopianism, 42
Uzbekistan, 187

Weber, Max, 61
the Westphalian state
  conceptions of sovereignty, 50, 163, 175, 178
  post-Westphalian international order, 164, 190
  Russia as post-Westphalian state, 175, 178, 193, 221

Yanukovich, Viktor Fedorovich, 67, 68, 141
Yeltsin, Boris, viii, 2, 26, 64, 108

EU representative:
Easy Access System Europe
Mustamäe tee 50, 10621 Tallinn, Estonia
Gpsr.requests@easproject.com

www.ingramcontent.com/pod-product-compliance
Lightning Source LLC
Chambersburg PA
CBHW071829230426
43672CB00013B/2796